Bernard Shaw

The

Ascent of the

Superman

Sally Peters

Yale University Press

New Haven and London

Frontispiece: Mephistophelean Shaw ca. 1887, age thirty-one.

Published with assistance from the foundation established in memory of
Philip Hamilton McMillan
of the Class of 1894, Yale College.

Designed by James J. Johnson and set in Ehrhardt Roman type by The Composing Room of Michigan, Inc.
Printed in the United States of America by Vail-Ballou Press, Binghamton, New York.

A catalogue record for this book is available from the British Library.

The paper in this book meets the guidelines for permanence and durability of the Committee on Production Guidelines for Book Longevity of the Council on Library Resources.

10 9 8 7 6 5 4 3 2 1

Library of Congress Cataloging-in-Publication Data

Peters, Sally.
    Bernard Shaw : the ascent of the superman / Sally Peters.
        p.   cm.
    Includes bibliographical references and index.
    ISBN 0-300-06097-1 (alk. paper)
    1. Shaw, Bernard, 1856–1950.
    2. Homosexuality and literature—Great Britain—History—19th century.
    3. Homosexuality and literature—Great Britain—History—20th century.
    4. Dramatists, Irish—20th century—Biography.   5. Man-woman relationships in literature.   I. Title.
    PR5366.P46   1995
    822'.912—DC20   95-37248

For my sons, Scott, Jeffrey, and Douglas, who have shown me the true joy in life.

The peculiar thing about Shaw is that we have the impression he has explained everything . . . though he always stops short in personal . . . matters.
—Eric Bentley

We can . . . look life straight in the face and see in it, not the fulfilment of a moral law or of the deductions of reason, but the satisfaction of a passion in us of which we can give no rational account whatever.

It is natural for man to shrink from the terrible responsibility thrown on him by this inexorable fact.
—Bernard Shaw

Contents

Preface

By the time of his death in 1950, Bernard Shaw had achieved a celebrity unprecedented for a living playwright, unsurpassed even by that of the great religious and political leaders of his day. A Nobel laureate for a quarter of a century, hailed by worshipping admirers as the second greatest playwright in the English language, the author of *Pygmalion* and *Saint Joan* had achieved virtual living sainthood. At the same time, his oddly flamboyant personality had given rise to a powerful personal legend. Seemingly a cultural exemplar of colossal wit married to bloodless asceticism, he exuberantly commented on everything from child care and diet to the art of boxing and the science of war. No wonder there were omnipresent detractors ready to charge him with charlatanism.

In spite of histrionics, Shaw preferred that his work be the focus of adoration, not his life: "Now I have had no heroic adventures. Things have not happened to me: on the contrary it is I who have happened to them; and all my happenings have taken the form of books and plays. Read them, or spectate them; and you have my whole story: the rest is only breakfast, lunch, dinner, sleeping, wakening, and washing, my routine being just the same as everybody's routine."[1]

In one way, he was right. It is not for biography to content itself with the formulaic and routine. Rather it is the peculiar spinning out of the life history, the forging of the personal life myth, that fascinates. But Shaw, intent on diverting attention from the whole story, was also wrong on purpose. It is precisely the realm of everyday life that offers a pathway into secret spheres, including the labyrinthian psyche of the great creative artist. Although Shaw's life and art are not to be equated, the two are intimately connected. That glorious drama of wit and vitality, of peculiar vision and driving purpose, of intellectual passion and evolutionary obsession, could only have been brought forth by Bernard Shaw living the life he lived. To grapple with his phantasmagoric personality and convoluted inner life is to glimpse the transcendent mysteries of the artistic process itself.

Few lives have been documented in such detail as Shaw's and by so many hands—providing reminiscences, memoirs, portraits. Thanks especially to the long and devoted labors of Dan H. Laurence and Stanley Weintraub, a wealth of information has been recorded. Additionally, Margot Peters has richly detailed Shaw's relationships with actresses. Meanwhile, psychoanalytic studies "explain" the man and his art, and certainly these analyses are interesting. Yet many bright Irish Protestant boys endured similar circumstances and exhibited exactly the cited tendencies, but no other playwright has exercised exactly Shaw's influence on society. Most recently, following the tradition established earlier in the century with Archibald Henderson's three huge volumes, Michael Holroyd, in highly readable fashion, has presented an encyclopedic synthesis. But why does the authorized biographer so confidently take his subject's statements at face value while relegating the drama of the life to a tripartite Freudian superstructure, neatly, one part per volume?

Despite the massive documentation and intense scrutiny, parts of Shaw's life remain veiled in secrecy, parts crucial to understanding both man and artist. The passions and the ambiguities revolve around the multitudinous ways in which Bernard Shaw—that unique, complex human being and no piece of deterministic debris—took the raw materials of an inauspicious youth and actively fashioned them into the life and art of a playwright of enduring worth. What did it mean *to Shaw* to have lived his life?

To probe the mystery of man and artist, I have forged my own method, using everything from existential phenomenology to popular culture to track down clues. I have isolated the themes of Shaw's life—his recurring patterns and passions—piecing them together to disclose the kaleidoscopic mosaic of his "world design," the pattern formed by his life choices.[2] To sweep away the obscuring clutter, I have included only those facts and events, whether known or just unearthed, that are significant in telling his story.

In his own psyche, that darkly guarded cache of conflicting desires and motives, Shaw played out the raucous nineteenth-century battle that pitted genetic inheritance against the power of individual will. Championing will even as he insisted that he was a born artist and genius, he transformed both the mundane and the momentous materials of his life into a wondrous stage drama whose unsurpassable pyrotechnics are also beacons of the human spirit. Striving unceasingly to ascend, possessed of monumental energy, he was in many ways a dazzling intimation of his wished-for superman. Indeed, Eric Bentley, who blazed a trail for Shaw critics a half century ago, has called him the "first civilized man."[3] But the soaring trajectory of the civilized superman was marked by tortuous paths studded with erotic secrets. If he had been born in 1956 instead of 1856, I believe he would not have chosen the sanctuary of secrecy. This is his story.

Shaw wanted to establish a phonetically based alphabet, and he often used unorthodox spelling. He also usually refused to use apostrophes and quotation marks, believing they spoiled the appearance of the page. In quotation, I retain his usage.

Acknowledgments

This book, the fruit of more than two decades' engagement with Shaw, has been a personal journey for me. I began by writing about the drama but became increasingly intrigued by the man who had spoken so forcefully on behalf of women. Throughout, I was inspired by Eric Bentley's groundbreaking analyses of Shaw and modern playwrights. Dan H. Laurence's meticulous editions, especially the *Collected Letters*, were an invaluable marvel, and I offer my sincere gratitude for his gracious and abundant generosity. In publishing and editing Shaw's diaries, the indefatigable Stanley Weintraub provided an enormous service for all scholars and a special boon to me, and I cordially thank him for his personal kindness as well.

I extend deep appreciation to Alfred Turco, Jr., for many years of shared enthusiasm on Shaw and for our unending dialogue on the intangible but rich rewards to be found in the search for truth. I warmly thank R. F. Dietrich for introducing me to the special pleasures of Shaw long ago in Florida. For their varied kindnesses, I am happy to thank Sidney P. Albert, Fred D. Crawford, Bernard F. Dukore, and Richard Nickson. Rodelle Weintraub urged me to write on Shaw and women for her *Fabian Feminist*, a volume now acclaimed as a landmark in Shaw feminist studies. Many generous correspondents responded to queries, and I am indebted to them. I also feel indebted to all Shaw scholars, and indeed to the legions of writers and thinkers, past and present, for their work, which undoubtedly has influenced me in ways I do not recognize.

For the example of his scholarship and humanity during my years in the Yale English department and after, I thank A. Dwight Culler. I am grateful to Harold Bloom, that visionary man of letters, for making it possible for my essay on *Man and Superman* to reach a wide audience.

For permission to quote from Shaw's published and unpublished writings, I am grateful to Roma Woodnutt and the Society of Authors. For permission to quote from unpublished material in its collection, I thank the Beinecke Rare Book and Manuscript Library, Yale University.

Parts of several chapters have appeared in print. A version of Chapter 11 appeared in *Rajah: The Rackham Journal of the Arts and Humanities,* 1991–92, 2–14. Portions of Chapters 12 and 18 appeared in *The Independent Shavian* 28, nos. 1–2 (1990): 3–16, and vol. 30, nos. 1–2 (1992): 16–25, respectively. Parts of Chapter 18 appeared in *Annals of Scholarship* 9, no. 3 (1992): 327–340. A portion of Chapter 23 appeared in *SHAW: The Annual of Bernard Shaw Studies* 7 (1987): 301–316.

I thank the research staffs at the Dan H. Laurence Collection, University of Guelph; the Library of Congress; the New York Public Library; the DeCoursey Fales Collection, New York University Library; the T. E. Hanley Collection, Humanities Research Center, University of Texas at Austin. Heartfelt thanks to the entire staff at Olin Library, Wesleyan University. The late Steven D. Lebergott, former head of Olin's interlibrary loan department, helped immeasurably. For their generosity, I thank Leith G. Johnson, Wesleyan Cinema Archives, and Isabella Rossellini.

At the Graduate Liberal Studies Program at Wesleyan University, I thank Barbara MacEachern for making it possible for me to teach what I love and only what I love, and I thank a decade of students for so good-naturedly enduring endless tales of Shaw.

At Yale University Press, I offer sincere appreciation to everyone who has been a part of this project. Heidi Downey was diligent in preparing the manuscript for press and cheerful in incorporating my interminable changes. I most warmly and wholeheartedly thank my editor, Jonathan Brent, for his truly saintly patience and for his firm belief that Shaw's story needed to be told.

My sister Rosalind Schnyder and my brother-in-law Mayer Schnyder were with me when I retraced Shaw's steps in Dublin and Dalkey, and I thank them for making that unforgettable time even more memorable. Most of all, I am profoundly grateful for the boundless love, faith, and support of my splendidly stouthearted sons—Scott, Jeffrey, and Douglas—through whom the Life Force courses joyously and to whom this book is dedicated.

Shaw Chronology

1852	George Carr Shaw and Lucinda Elizabeth Gurly marry.
1853	Lucinda Frances Shaw born.
1855	Elinor Agnes Shaw born.
1856	George Bernard Shaw born, 26 July.
1866	Shaw's parents form ménage à trois at Torca Cottage with George Vandeleur Lee.
1867	Lee moves into Hatch Street residence.
1871	Leaves school, becomes a clerk.
1872	Juvenile literary collaboration with Matthew Edward McNulty.
1873	Mother emigrates to London.
1876	Sister Elinor Agnes dies on the Isle of Wight, 27 March. Shaw emigrates to London, 31 March.
1877	Does ghostwriting for Lee (begun November 1876).
1878	*My Dear Dorothea* and *Passion Play* (latter was unfinished).
1879	Completes *Immaturity*, first novel, and tries work at the Edison Telephone Company.
1880	Begins addressing audiences at Zetetical Society. Writes second novel, *The Irrational Knot*. Meets Sidney Webb.
1881	Becomes a vegetarian. Begins third novel. Contracts smallpox.
1882	Completes third novel, *Love Among the Artists*. Meets Alice Lockett. Hears Henry George speak.
1883	Completes fourth novel, *Cashel Byron's Profession*. Competes in amateur boxing championships. Reads Karl Marx. Writes fifth novel, *An Unsocial Socialist*.
1884	Joins Fabian Society. Abortive dramatic collaboration with William Archer. A serialized *Unsocial Socialist* attracts the attention of William Morris.
1885	Father dies. Begins wearing Jaeger wool. Begins affair with Jenny Patterson. "Mystic Betrothal" to May Morris. Frequent visits to

	cottage of Henry and Kate Salt; Edward Carpenter also frequent visitor. Book reviews for the *Pall Mall Gazette* (to December 1888).
1886	George Vandeleur Lee dies. Writes art criticism for *The World* (through November 1890).
1887	Intimate friendship with Annie Besant. Speaks and marches in socialist demonstration on Bloody Sunday, in Trafalgar Square.
1888	Havelock Ellis invites a contribution to his Contemporary Science series. Involved with numerous women. Busy journalist, Fabian speaker.
1889	Writes music criticism as "Corno di Bassetto" in *The Star* (through May 1890). Edits *Fabian Essays*, writes two. Protests Labouchere Amendment.
1890	Meets Florence Farr. Music critic "G. B. S." in *The World* (through August 1894).
1891	*The Quintessence of Ibsenism.*
1892	Ménage à trois with May Morris and H. H. Sparling begins in December. Completes *Widowers' Houses* (begun 1884).
1893	Ends affair with Jenny Patterson. Writes *The Philanderer, Mrs Warren's Profession* (banned by censor).
1894	Completes *Arms and the Man*, writes *Candida*. Edward Carpenter's *Homogenic Love* published (appears January 1895).
1895	Writes *The Man of Destiny. A Degenerate's View of Nordau* (revised as *The Sanity of Art*, 1908). Oscar Wilde imprisoned.
1895–1898	Writes theater criticism for *The Saturday Review.*
1895–1900	Maintains "paper courtship" with Ellen Terry.
1896	Meets Charlotte Payne-Townshend. Completes *You Never Can Tell*, writes *The Devil's Disciple.*
1897	Elected vestryman, St. Pancras ward. Havelock Ellis publishes *Sexual Inversion.*
1898	Health breaks down. Marries Charlotte Payne-Townshend. Defends George Bedborough, who was arrested for selling *Sexual Inversion.* Writes *The Perfect Wagnerite, Caesar and Cleopatra.*
1899	Convalesces, writes *Captain Brassbound's Conversion.*
1900	Casts Harley Granville Barker as Eugene Marchbanks in *Candida.*
1901	Writes *The Admirable Bashville.*
1902	Completes *Man and Superman* (published 1903).
1903	Works with Harley Granville Barker in staging *The Admirable Bashville* at the Imperial Theatre.
1904	Writes *John Bull's Other Island, How He Lied to Her Husband.*
1904–1907	Provides most of the financial backing for the Royal Court Theatre venture of John Eugene Vedrenne and Harley Granville Barker.

1905	Writes *Major Barbara*.
1906	Harley Granville Barker marries Lillah McCarthy. Writes *The Doctor's Dilemma*.
1908	Completes *Getting Married*.
1909	Writes *The Shewing-Up of Blanco Posnet* (banned by censor), *Press Cuttings* (banned by censor), *The Fascinating Foundling, Misalliance*.
1910	Writes *The Dark Lady of the Sonnets*.
1911	Completes *Fanny's First Play*.
1912	Writes *Androcles and the Lion;* writes *Pygmalion;* infatuated with his Eliza, Mrs. Patrick Campbell; writes *Overruled*.
1913	Mother dies. Writes *Great Catherine*.
1914	*Common Sense about the War* appears.
1915	Writes playlets *The Inca of Perusalem, O'Flaherty, V. C.*
1916	Fails to persuade Barker not to leave Lillah McCarthy for Helen Huntington. Begins *Heartbreak House*.
1917	Completes *Heartbreak House* (published 1919), writes *Augustus Does His Bit, Annajanska*.
1918–1920	*Back to Methuselah* (published 1921).
1920	Sister Lucinda Frances dies.
1921	Completes translation and adaptation of *Jitta's Atonement*, drama by Siegfried Trebitsch, his German translator.
1922	Meets T. E. Lawrence (Lawrence of Arabia).
1923	Writes *Saint Joan*. T. E. Lawrence calls himself T. E. Shaw.
1924	William Archer dies. Edits *Seven Pillars of Wisdom* by T. E. Lawrence, published 1926.
1925	Shaw publicly embarrasses Barker.
1926	Awarded the Nobel Prize for Literature (for 1925).
1927	Completes *The Intelligent Woman's Guide to Socialism and Capitalism*.
1928	Writes *The Apple Cart*. Protests censorship of Radclyffe Hall's lesbian novel *The Well of Loneliness*. Meets Gene Tunney.
1929	Vacations with Gene Tunney on Italian isle of Brioni. Writes a preface to the Ellen Terry correspondence (published 1931). Addresses the International Congress of the World League for Sexual Reform.
1930–1938	Collected edition of works appears.
1931	Visits Russia, meets Josef Stalin, Maxim Gorki, Konstantin Stanislavsky. Meets Mahatma Gandhi. Writes *Too True to Be Good*.
1932	Writes and publishes *The Adventures of the Black Girl in Her Search for God*, a fable.
1933	First visit to America. Writes *Village Wooing, On the Rocks*.

1934   Writes *The Simpleton of the Unexpected Isles, The Millionairess, The Six of Calais.*

1936   Writes *Geneva* (final revision 1947), *Cymbeline Refinished.*

1938   Edits *Oscar Wilde,* by Frank Harris.

1939   Wins Academy Award for the screenplay of *Pygmalion* (for 1938). Completes *In Good King Charles's Golden Days.*

1943   Charlotte Shaw dies.

1944   Publishes *Everybody's Political What's What?* a labor of several years.

1946   Harley Granville Barker dies. Writes a tribute to him.

1947   Completes *Buoyant Billions.*

1948   Writes *Farfetched Fables.*

1949   Writes *Shakes Versus Shav.* Publishes *Sixteen Self Sketches.* Revises "Harley Granville-Barker," by Hesketh Pearson.

1950   Writes *Why She Would Not* to celebrate his ninety-fourth birthday. Works on *Bernard Shaw's Rhyming Picture Guide to Ayot Saint Lawrence.* George Bernard Shaw dies 2 November.

PART I
Dublin Foreshadowings

People come into the world ready-made.
—Mrs Byron, *Cashel Byron's Profession*

1

Casting a Downstart

> Even my personal recollections . . . are
> becoming vague and overlaid with those most
> misleading of all traditions, the traditions
> founded on the lies a man tells, and at last
> comes to believe, about himself *to* himself.
> —Preface to *The Irrational Knot,* 1905

Settled as Baile Atha Cliath—the town of the hurdle-ford—Dublin was a city of contrasts in the middle of the nineteenth century. As smoldering peat perfumed the air, the city's natural beauty inspired native sons to rhapsodies. To the west and south, violet hills vanished into hovering mists, silvery and luminous. On the perimeter old canals circled lazily. The city proper was quietly bisected by the River Liffey, whose bog-stained waters emptied into Dublin Bay to form the *Dubh Linn,* or black pool, that gave the city its name. The great statue-dotted garden squares, the steepled skyline, and the brick townhouses recalled the splendor and vitality of the eighteenth century. But this Dublin of grace and charm was also a provincial city where the Protestant minority coexisted uneasily with the Catholic majority, where the desperately poor crowded into the decaying shells of once fashionable homes, making the Dublin slums notorious in western Europe.

This juxtaposition of grandeur and squalor was observed daily by a young boy of genteel birth as he walked with his father, who told stories as they walked, or with the family servants, who stole an hour to visit their homes in the city's poorest parts. The young George Bernard Shaw—Sonny, as his family called him—was a sensitive boy who shrank from the filth and misery. One day wielding the ameliorative powers of art, he would seek to fulfill his self-appointed mission as prophet and deliverer of mankind.

Sonny's early social sensitivity did not need the stimulus of greater Dublin. He had only to become aware of the value his family placed on social position. The Shaw family's self-image depended on belief in a hierarchical society that placed them relatively high on the ladder of prestige. Shaw's earliest Irish ancestor, who was of Scottish descent, arrived in Ireland by way of Hampshire, England, in 1689, making the Shaws part of the resented Protestant minority.

Members of the ascendancy generally were more prosperous than their Catholic

3

countrymen, many of whom tilled land owned by English landlords. These less favored Irishmen were punished unrelentingly by the Great Famine of 1845 to 1849, and the specters of starvation and contagion still hovered over sod huts and city warrens during Sonny's early boyhood. Yet Shaw came to define his lot as far worse than that of the genuinely poor. The hardships that plagued Sonny were not those of physical survival but of emotional and psychological survival, as the Shaw family adhered to a constrictive worldview. So few vocations were considered suitable for sons of the ascendancy that ill-paying, mind-deadening clerkships were prized while the lucrative retail trade was contemptuously dismissed. Whatever the financial facts, social status demanded the appearance of money.

Monied or not, the Shaw family lineage appeared respectable enough. Lucinda Elizabeth Gurly Shaw (Bessie), Sonny's mother, was the daughter of a country gentle-man, Walter Bagnall Gurly. Left motherless at age nine, she was carefully raised by her maternal aunt, the humpbacked and fiercely genteel Ellen Whitcroft. Aunt Ellen's gen-tility quietly diverted attention from certain unmentionable topics, such as her father's ancestry, for the mysterious John Whitcroft seems himself to have had no legitimate father. Indeed, the rich and commanding squire of Whitechurch was also the pawnbroker of Bride Street, and he insisted on keeping the Dublin pawnshop open under the name of his employee.

Shaw believed that Aunt Ellen had intended that Bessie polish the family es-cutcheon. Instead, Bessie incurred her father's wrath by letting out the secret that he planned to marry the daughter of a friend whose bills he had paid with money borrowed from Aunt Ellen. The incensed Whitcrofts had the bridegroom arrested for debt on his wedding day. A few weeks later, in June 1852, Bessie escaped the commotion by marrying a matrimonial adventurer nearly twice her age. But just before her wedding, at her father's insistence, she transferred her current assets and her future income (Whitcroft money coming to her from her grandfather and from the marriage settlement of her parents) to a trust that would be safe from the bridegroom. Aunt Ellen, unamused by the marriage, disinherited her willful niece. Undaunted, Bessie gave birth within four years to Lucinda Frances (Lucy) in 1853, Elinor Agnes (Yuppy) in 1854, and, on 26 July 1856, to George Bernard. Yet not even the charms of the infant genius could placate the iron-willed Aunt Ellen. Shaw's failure was his first, but by no means his last, with women.[1]

George Carr Shaw, Sonny's father, possessed a squint, a sense of humor, sixty pounds a year, and kinship to a baronet. This kinship to Robert Shaw of Bushy Park was a matter of considerable family pride—a pride the son reflected late in his life by referring interested parties to *Burke's Landed Gentry*. But being related to a baronet did little to further the business acuity of the civil clerk turned wholesale corn merchant. Shaw was unwilling to give his father the benefit of the doubt and refused to call him an honest merchant. "I don't know whether he was or not; I do know that he was an entirely unsuccessful one."[2]

Although there was never enough money to allow the Shaws to live up to class expectations, the family was rich in pretensions, the soil of satire. Sonny was taught to despise the worker but to respect the gentleman, even when gentility had been lost to poverty. Remembering, the man lamented his status as a poor relation, which was the "very devil." He blamed the feudal system of primogeniture, in which the eldest inherits all, for from the beginning, the Shaws were younger sons. "I was a downstart and the son of a downstart. . . . I sing my own class: the Shabby Genteel, the Poor Relations, the Gentlemen who are no Gentlemen."[3] Angrily, incessantly, Shaw chanted his Whitmanesque ballad of the dispossessed and disregarded, the out of favor and out of luck.

But the Shaw family clung to its class, buoyed by a sense of superiority and, in Shaw's early childhood, by the attentions of second cousin Sir Robert Shaw. Cherishing their respectability, the family talked of themselves as *the Shaws* as one might speak of the great ruling families of Europe. It was the natural order of things for the boy, while the mature man became, he claimed, "completely reconciled to it" on learning, via the unverified research of Alexander Macintosh Shaw, that the Shaws were descended from Macduff, slayer of Macbeth: "It was as good as being descended from Shakespear, whom I had unconsciously resolved to reincarnate from my cradle." The appeal of reincarnation was not shared by the uncles. It was enough for them that they were Shaws.[4]

Satirically, Shaw suggests that "some devil, probably commissioned by the Life Force" to bring him into the world, prompted his father to propose marriage. A diabolical commission or not, the infant was named after an uncle who would become, in turn, a drunk, a voyeur, and an ingenious suicide. Even his christening had peculiar paternal resonances as Shaw records it. Because his godfather was drunk and did not show up for the event, the sexton promised and vowed "in his place."[5]

Nor did Sonny's christening provide the only singular omen surrounding his birth. While Lucy and Yuppy had been delivered without incident, Bessie's condition so worried the family physician that the eminent obstetrician and gynecologist Dr. John Ringland was called to the modest brick rowhouse at 3 Upper Synge Street (renumbered 33 Synge Street). Ringland attended Bessie through a successful delivery, recording the "vaginal breech birth" of an infant son. There is no evidence that Bessie was rendered sterile by her third delivery, but perhaps pain and trauma figured into the fact that she would bear no more children. "My mother began with two girls and finished with me," wrote Shaw, completely ignoring the paternal role. Behind the satire, behind the so-called unconscious resolve to reincarnate Shakespeare, another wish lay concealed by the man hurled backward into the world by his mother. For Macduff was not of woman born. He was "Macduff the Unborn," whose peculiar history climaxed in prophetic destiny.[6]

Throughout the autobiographical writing Shaw repeats the obsession with keeping up appearances. His "devouring malady" of "worldbettermentcraze" can be attributed in part to his wish to close the gap between appearance and reality.[7]

Wrenched from Innocence

From the first, the world was an uncertain place for Sonny. At eleven months, the "young beggar" amused his father by "roaring and heaving like a bull." Left to the charge of a nurse while his mother spent a month with her father, the infant suffered teething pain, stomach upset, and two falls on his head. Writing his wife, Shaw *père* joked that "Bob's" fall through a window did not appear "to have given him even a *pane* in his head."[8]

As a toddler Sonny was fond of nursery rhymes. In the last months of his life he recalled his "Opus 1," a rhyme he sang while he petted his dog Rover.

> Dumpitydoodledum big bowwow
> Dumpitydoodledum dandy[9]

Meanwhile, his sisters teased him with the old rhyme:

> Georgie Porgie, pudding and pie,
> Kissed the girls and made them cry;
> When the boys came out to play
> Georgie Porgie ran away.
> The life history had begun its fateful course.

By reconstructing a crucial life incident, we can see how the young boy responded to the dismantling of appearances he had taken for granted. One day George Carr Shaw, a man in the prime of life, and his young son walked together along pretty village streets into the Dublin countryside. Sonny was less than five years of age, about as tall as his father's boots.[10] They likely made a pleasant sight: the tall, frock-coated man and the small, fair boy dressed in the feminine shift and white petticoats worn by young children of both sexes. Sonny found his father a jolly companion with a wonderful bounty of stories he loved to tell. The elder Shaw delighted in ending his tales abruptly and anticlimactically, bursting into exuberant peals of laughter. That day exuberance took on a tragic cast.

On the "country side" of the canal bordering Dolphin's Barn, at the end of a village avenue, lay the grain mill that George Carr Shaw operated with George Clibborn. A large house flanked by gateposts bearing stone eagles guarded the way to a field and millpond. Father and son approached along familiar avenues; it was an outing they sometimes took before breakfast, though it was a "long walk for a child." Suddenly, George Carr Shaw was seized by a peculiar playfulness. He grabbed his son and tried to throw him into the canal. The terrified Sonny clung to solid ground, just above the dark boggy waters that threatened to swallow him, until the danger passed. He was old enough to guess the reason behind his father's frightening behavior. Once home, he reported "in an awestruck whisper . . . 'Mamma: I think Papa's drunk.'" He hoped that he was wrong, for it was an "awful and hardly credible discovery." But Bessie muttered, "When is he ever anything else?"[11] Her words had such shattering impact that Shaw claimed never to recover.

In middle age he revealed the meaning of the incident to the actress Ellen Terry: "I have never believed in anything since: then the scoffer began." Years later, he gave the familiar story a slightly different twist: "It is a rhetorical exaggeration to say I have never since believed in anything or anybody; but the wrench from my childish faith in my father as perfect and omniscient to the discovery that he was a hypocrite and a dipsomaniac was so sudden and violent that it must have left its mark on me." As he remembered and accused, Shaw elevated his father's action into a moment of mythic proportions for his own life history.

Shaw held to his account for half a century, with his biographers dutifully echoing him. But can the elder Shaw really be blamed for having "sown the seed which so annoys," as his son accused? For he seemed not to dwell on being marked as he remembered the "hell" into which his mother descended by living with an alcoholic husband. And what role did Bessie play? To the important Ellen Terry, Shaw offered the childhood experience as his first moral lesson, a preface to an appeal for her love. From this "devil of a childhood," drunkenness, lovelessness, and irretrievable loss intertwined on the subjects of women and morality.[12]

Despite his seeming sincerity, Shaw had told only part of the story. The apparent villain of the piece was George Carr Shaw. Allegedly a teetotaler, he would slip out, buy his liquor, and secretly drink, so that he was never completely sober and rarely completely drunk. At the canal he exposed his weakness to the world, forcing his son to be both witness and participant in the brief drama. The sudden shove confronted the boy with a transmuted world aptly reflected in the black waters below. Sonny was wrenched from childish innocence into shameful knowledge—a perverse baptism. Because the security of a loving parent represents an orderly world to a child, George Carr Shaw's actions meant more than a momentary loss of self-control. As Sonny's faith in his father vanished, so did his faith in an underlying world order.

World collapse threatened as Sonny rushed home, seeking comfort from his mother. It was a separate event yet yoked to the first. But her husband's behavior was "too much" for Bessie. Her contempt "suddenly opened" the boy's eyes, delivering his soul to a "derisive incredulity." "I shall carry traces of that disillusion to the grave," confessed Shaw in yet another version of the story he needed to retell.[13] Instead of "Don't worry,

Sonny; everything is all right," Bessie revealed that not only was her husband drunk now, he was always drunk. Emotional violence followed physical violence. Abruptly, the familiar garment of the world was ripped off. The force of this revelation indicates how essential it was to Sonny to dwell in an unaltered world. Unable to adjust to the rapid flow of events, he was knocked precipitously off course.

Before Freud, it would have appeared that the episode caused Sonny's trauma and resulting disillusion. But Freud demonstrated that seemingly harmless events can result in trauma or pathology. This is because prior fantasies—dreams and daydreams bearing conscious and unconscious content—are associated with these events. Yet neither of these explanations, Freudian or pre-Freudian, accounts for the fact that what is traumatic and lasting for some has little effect on others.

Although what Sonny learned might have disturbed any young child, gradual awareness would have been far less traumatic. For it was neither his father's tipsy antics nor the discovery that a teetotaler was really a drunkard that shaped his response. It was the form in which that knowledge came to him—via a sudden disruption in the flow of time. Overpowered by the sudden and urgent, the boy was thrown into isolation and uncanniness. He could not cope with change because of his overwhelming need for permanence.[14]

This crucial scenario of disruption would resonate. Beginning in the personal sphere and extending outward, Shaw's defiant worldview would have a peculiar relation to immutability and connectedness. He would mask with the incongruities of wit exactly what he imitated: the form and content of his first terrible encounter with a disjunctive and precarious world. More terrible still, this scenario—with its threat of womblike engulfment by water and the reality of maternal treachery—gave rise to feelings of longing and betrayal that would haunt him. Those feelings assumed a human face, and that face, veiled and transformed, was Bessie's.

Making That Skeleton Dance

"My first memory of George is a little boy in a Holland overall sitting at a table constructing a toy theatre," recalled Ada Tyrrell, a Dublin neighbor. He was always "rather apart from the others" and might be seen at the piano, "picking out airs with one finger." Sonny sought out the piano, the necessary musical instrument for girls being readied for the marriage market, and he played with his miniature theater, just as girls played with dollhouses. As he filled his cardboard theater with imaginary actors, male and female, he fashioned and refashioned his gender according to whim. Already the pleasures of fantasy were irresistible: "Ever since I can remember, I have only had to shut my eyes to be and do whatever I pleased." His imagination would never fail him. On the eve of his ninety-third birthday he assured the equally long-lived Ada Tyrrell that he was not steeped in grief: "I like being alone because I can always tell myself stories, and so am never lonely." In this he was his mother's son—a descriptive label neither he nor his fictional characters ever used—for Bessie had "plenty of imagination, and really lived in it and on it."[15]

Another memory of the drunken father charts the growth of the boy's protective devices. Again the episode is scantily treated. There was a trio—Sonny, now a little older, his father, an uncle. With a goose under one arm and a ham under the other, George Carr Shaw butted the garden wall thinking that he was pushing open the gate. He crushed his tall hat like an accordion. Looking back across sixty years, Shaw insisted that instead of feeling shame and anxiety at the spectacle, he was "so disabled by merriment (uproariously shared by the maternal uncle)" that he was hardly able to "rush to the rescue of the hat and pilot its wearer to safety."

Of the biographers, only Erik Erikson considers the incident important, believing that it marked the point at which the boy recognized his father's impotence. But there are other resonances. The disabling merriment disguised intense feelings as Sonny fell back on the "family weapon," for the drunkenness was "so humiliating that it would have been unendurable if we had not taken refuge in laughter."[16] Of course, there is the burlesque comedy of the finely dressed gentleman smashing his tall hat, the symbol of station and male authority. But only as long as Sonny maintained distance from his father could he laugh.

Through laughter, Sonny entered into an offensive alliance with his uncle, transforming George Carr Shaw into an object: he was merely the wearer of the hat. As for the drunkenness, "it had to be either a family tragedy or a family joke." Sonny either was part of the shameful tragedy or part of the mocking audience. There was no middle ground of love and support, and Bessie is noticeably absent from the story, even though it takes place in her garden. From this time on, Sonny distanced himself from the humiliations of his father and was always ready to attack him at his weakest point. The scrutinizing sensibility that would present the "criticism of morals and manners *viva voce*" is seen in embryo as Sonny sought refuge from the family tragedy.[17]

Shaw concluded that it was a "healthy instinct that decided us to get what ribald fun was possible out of it," but still the fun was "very little indeed." By labeling family behavior instinctual and by using the passive, Shaw implied that not only was it natural, but it was also inevitable, putting his boyish behavior in a more forgiving light in his own eyes. The element of self-deception, coupled with a willful lack of feeling, helps explain the rhetoric—replete with the classical devices of balance, parallelism, and alliteration—

that Shaw used as as he reconstructed the past out of memory. A boy who has seen his father behave ridiculously will not "make tragedies of trifles instead of making trifles of tragedies. If you cannot get rid of the family skeleton, you may as well make it dance."[18]

The dancing skeleton gives the lie to the cavalier treatment of fatedness, wittily asserting Sonny's decision to seize control in a hostile universe. Shaw learned early that real life was only a "squalid interruption to an imaginary paradise."[19] Accordingly, he set himself to bridging the gap between the discontinuities of the squalid and the unchanging delights of the paradise of imagination by refashioning the raw materials of his life.

In a sense, such refashioning was an aesthetic version of the family hypocrisy. That hypocrisy was not confined to George Carr Shaw's alleged teetotalism, and it encompassed—far more devastatingly for Sonny—an insistence on social superiority at the very moment the family was being ostracized by its own clan. After early childhood, Shaw remembered making no visits to the homes of relatives, nor did his parents ever go out for a social evening. In a society where appearances lubricated the social machinery, the vaunted Shaws appeared declassed, not even trying to teach their son the manners dictated by class.

"Sociology is not biography," cried Shaw, attempting to persuade St. John Ervine, his biographer, to turn the spotlight away from Protestant Dublin.[20] Yet as much as he wished it otherwise, Shaw's history was irrevocably tied to the history of the Irish Protestant ascendancy in mid-nineteenth-century Ireland. His vulnerability arose out of his birth into a class that defined itself as privileged, his identification with that class and his hatred of it, and his overwhelming feelings of deprivation, hypocrisy, and rage. Shaw was cheated of his birthright, and his fury remained unabated.

The Fight Against Fate: A Secret Kept for Eighty Years

Though in private Shaw bewailed his ignorance of social routine, publicly he took a position akin to that of John Tanner, his autobiographical hero in *Man and Superman* (1902): "When a man teaches something he does not know to somebody else who has no aptitude for it, and gives him a certificate of proficiency, the latter has completed the education of a gentleman," and more briefly: "He who can, does. He who cannot, teaches." Shaw, who was himself a teacher to the quick, despised formal education. Its real purpose, he said, was to prevent his being a nuisance to his mother by incarcerating him daily in "that damnable boy prison."[21]

Shaw's condescending attitude also was directed toward his governess, Miss Caroline Hill, who chiefly taught him to feel jubilant over good conduct and disgraced over bad. Yet surely Miss Hill had a most unusual pupil in Sonny, who later boasted that he could not remember ever finding a page of print unintelligible—a born reader, no less. As a small boy in his father's arms he he had once caused a sensation by reading advertisements plastered on the wall of a portico, where passersby had taken shelter from a sudden shower. This vivid memory of paternal approval contrasted with his disparagement of Miss Hill, a mother surrogate who, he conceded very late in life, "taught very well."[22]

Studying at home with sisters Lucy and Yuppy suited Sonny. He felt comfortable in the entirely female environment, where his love of books let him shine. Out on the streets the unkempt but "very dignified" boy flattered and impressed older girls with his quick wit. Despite his air of superiority, the girls noticed that he preferred their company to that of boys his own age. He might play three-hole marbles or daringly raid an orchard with another boy, but he was clumsy at the usual games of skill by which boys prove their manhood. His aesthetic temperament led him to prefer watercolors to contact sports, the artistic and the traditionally feminine over the vulgar and the traditionally masculine.[23] He set himself farther and farther apart from his rowdy, jeering peers.

After Sonny progressed beyond what Miss Hill could teach, he became a pupil of Uncle William George Carroll, the rector of St. Bride's, from whom he learned Latin with two male cousins. At age eleven he entered the Wesleyan Connexional School, but not for the first time. He had been enrolled previously for a single early summer quarter in 1865, when he was eight. Two years later he attended for a quarter and was absent for a quarter. Then he returned for a nine-month period. In the next three years he became an academic picaro. He attended a private school on Sandy Cove Road, a mile north of Dalkey near Glasthule and a short walk from the bathing spot and Martello Tower later celebrated by James Joyce in *Ulysses*. Back in Dublin he attended the Dublin English Scientific and Commercial Day School on Aungier Street, a handsome building boasting oak mantelpieces and ornamented ceilings. It was his "last school prison." He completed his formal education at age fifteen, having been taught "lying, dishonourable submission to tyranny, dirty stories, a blasphemous habit of treating love and maternity as obscene jokes, hopelessness, evasion, derision, cowardice, and all the blackguard's shifts by which the coward intimidates other cowards."[24]

This curriculum aside, the rapid succession of schools was bound to be unsettling to a shy and fearful youth who thought himself a coward and was "bitterly ashamed of it." For Sonny, every day was a trial. In his tenth decade Shaw disclosed an "abhorred secret": in his thirteenth year he had attended the Central Model Boys' School.[25]

He remembered the school as enormous, with "huge unscaleable railings and gates," which might as well have been inscribed "'All hope abandon, ye who enter here.'" He was confused and humiliated at discovering that his classmates were not the sons of Protestant gentlemen but of Catholic tradesmen. Then, Shaw recalled, he "lost caste" and became a boy other young Protestants avoided. In fact, his classmates were sons of retail merchants and craftsmen, and half of them were Protestant, as Sonny likely knew.

Yet, Shaw said, for eighty years he was afflicted with a shame that was "more or less a psychosis."[26] Given his animus against psychiatry—unless he acted the role of analyst himself—this bit of self-analysis seems revealing.

Shaw appears to link his shame to consorting with Catholics at school—the proof of fallen status. He does not mention that his mother's music teacher, George Vandeleur Lee, a Catholic, had arranged for him to attend the Model School. More than that, Lee had filled the Shaw home with Catholic musicians, outraging the Shaw relations. Shaw admitted to St. John Ervine that he grew up in a Roman Catholic atmosphere, but he never conceded that Lee was Catholic. "Lee had no creed," he insisted. Yet, according to biographer John O'Donovan, Lee made no secret of his Catholicism, remaining on good terms with Catholic clergy and burying both his mother and brother in a Catholic cemetery during Shaw's early childhood.[27] Since Shaw surely knew Lee's beliefs, it seems that he intended to keep them hidden, fearful at what prying eyes might discover. But the shame Sonny endured at the Model School cannot all be laid at Lee's doorstep, as his biographers would have it.

Exactly *what* did Shaw hide? Why the announcement that after the "ashamed silence" of eighty years, the torment of the "guilty secret," he was now "completely cured" of his "boyish shame"? *Was* he cured? Or did he compulsively seek to divert attention from a more painful secret? He attributed his "psychosis" to his "artist nature," which would not allow him to accept the poor as fellow creatures. But it appears even more likely that the reverse was true: that at puberty Sonny was rejected by his ruffian classmates, Catholic and Protestant alike, precisely because he wore his artist nature so conspicuously—so effeminately. To counter the shame of this deeply intimate rejection, the otherwise recalcitrant student paraded with his teachers during playtime, pretending to be a "superior being."[28]

Craving attention, he posed as a Fenian, a member of the secret society pledged to overthrow British rule by force. He daringly substituted Ireland for England when reading aloud in class, awing his classmates. His boldness in flouting authority that not only was despised but also absent satisfied the rebellious feelings he harbored against his parents. Mostly his boldness was used to divert attention from his self-incriminating blush, for it is the peculiar nature of shame that it reveals to others exactly what it seeks to conceal. Sonny learned that aggression veiled vulnerabilities.

The shame Sonny experienced, with its rage and self-hate, resembled the suspense that hovered over the family. Would George Carr Shaw come home drunk? At school and at home, a sudden awful knowing threatened assumptions about self and family. The future loomed full of fateful content. Anchored in expectancy, Sonny's perceptions of experience were essentially dramatic—the familiar merged with the unexpected. And the unexpected is the soul of wit.

Sonny moved anxiously amid disjunctive worlds: school threatened ostracism and canings, the streets taunts and fistfights. Home offered protection from such onslaughts, but it was an unsettling haven, a chaotic and cold cave harboring rumors. For refuge, he retreated to the world of his imagination. But there was no healthy interpenetration of his worlds, and he was torn in three directions. Then, having endured school from February to September 1869, he asserted his will: "I for the first time set myself against my fate, and flatly refused to go back to the Model School on any terms." At age thirteen, Sonny defiantly began the task of liberating himself: "My scruples began in the Model School." Offsetting this assertion of self was the choice of shamed silence, which he concealed with noisy posturings. He carried the acrid insult of a "pariah dog in Eire" into his ninety-fourth year, along with the still-buried secret of the Model School.[29]

Ménage à trois and Ecstasy

I always look at the sky.
—*Nine Answers*

Believing that his parents did not care about his education, Sonny focused on the one person who did: George Vandeleur Lee, first known as George John Lee. The Shaws' relationship to Lee is one of the most intriguing parts of Sonny's childhood. Meticulous sleuthing has yielded few facts about Lee, whose dark good looks and name seemed to Shaw to hint at gypsy origins. Nor was Shaw ever satisfied with the little he knew of Lee. Even in his nineties Shaw wondered about this elusive figure and "energetic genius," who carried the absence of all relatives and family "as if it were a quality instead of a defect." Lee intimated that he was the illegitimate son of the eminent Colonel Crofton Moore Vandeleur and was adopted at birth by the coal merchant Robert Lee and his wife, Eliza. The pertinent pages of registers that could prove this information disappeared long ago in Dublin.[1]

Whatever Lee's lineage, his striking appearance and mesmeric personality set him apart from prosaic humanity. Moreover, he had acquired a singular reputation based on his highly touted "Method," a yogalike approach to voice instruction that allowed its practitioners to retain purity of sound into advanced age. The Method incorporated knowledge that Lee gleaned in a very un-yogalike fashion, from clinically dissecting not only birds but also human cadavers. Bessie embraced the Method so devotedly that changes were wrought in the family structure as well as in her voice. In a stunningly defiant act she asserted an absolute female power that awed and shamed her son. For Shaw, memories of Lee, Bessie, and the Method seethed and boiled in a volatile concoction of gender roles, female energy, artistic freedom, and vivisection.

That Bessie succumbed emotionally—and publicly—to Lee and his artistic vision is a testimony to the man's persuasiveness and vitality. Another is his resourcefulness in forming an orchestra. According to Shaw, Lee simply walked about the city listening for the sounds of a stray instrument, whereupon he would knock on the door and insist that the bewildered amateur join his orchestra. His determination brought him considerable success in Dublin, and in 1870 he published his ghost-written tract *The Voice: Its Artistic Production, Development, and Preservation.*

14

Yet none of Lee's qualified contemporaries saw the genius Shaw claimed for him, a discrepancy that says something about the intensity of Sonny's adoration and suggests a later need to justify Lee. Certainly Lee, who displayed ingenuity and persistence in establishing himself and his orchestra, contrasted sharply with the unassertive, weak-willed George Carr Shaw. In Lee, Bessie found a spirit more like her own indomitable one. For his charm and enthusiasm were yoked to an unflagging will that diverted attention from the legacy of a childhood fall—a noticeably shortened leg. To what degree this deformity affected Lee's quest for power and his later venture in London, which Shaw denounced as charlatanism, can only be supposed. Shaw, however, claimed to come to the altogether strange conclusion that even though Lee "limped with peculiar elegance, still marriage and gallantry" were ruled out.[2] In fact, Lee's female pupils, including Lucy and Yuppy, idolized him.

Though Shaw, growing in critical acumen, may have judged Lee by more stringent London standards, it is likely that the charge of charlatanism conceals fears that Lee's relation to Bessie was more than musical. Shaw certainly harbored ambivalent feelings toward Lee. As a boy, Sonny enhanced his self-esteem by associating with alleged genius, even though he was acutely aware that Lee's presence stained the fabric of family life. Bessie's unforgivable exposure as daring artiste and George Carr Shaw's silent complicity figured into Sonny's need to conceal and the opposing pressure to reveal. The incubation of the "pantomime ostrich" had begun.[3]

Exactly when Bessie decided that Lee and his Method were indispensable is not known, but Sonny was quite young. Nor is it known when Bessie and Lee met, though Lee and the Shaws lived a few houses apart as early as 1853, three years before Sonny's birth—a bit of information Shaw never offers, possibly showing how deep his suspicions go. For whether he was told as a boy, surely he knew later. When Sonny was ten years old Lee gave up the bachelor quarters he had occupied since the death of his brother Harcourt four years before and made a move momentous to Shaw's history—in with the Shaws. The family then left Synge Street, the only home Sonny had known, to share Torca Cottage with Lee in Dalkey, about nine miles from Dublin. News of the impending move gave Sonny the single moment of "ecstatic happiness" in his childhood, a response revealing his feelings toward Synge Street as well as toward Dalkey.[4]

While living on Synge Street the Shaws condescended to speak only to people on their end—the upper, more fashionable one—politely ignoring the field cluttered with billboards across from their house. But Sonny noticed. The small back room that served both as his bedroom and as George Carr Shaw's dressing room jutted out from the house proper. From there he looked out on the high walled yard containing an ashpit and a privy for the males.

Sonny's tiny room framed his dreams and daydreams, the essence of the imaginative world of his childhood. Shadowy and inchoate, this room would remain encrypted in his dread world. The kitchen, where Sonny took his meals, was in the basement with the servants' quarters. Sonny ate in a gloomy subterranean world where the odors of diseased potatoes and boiling meat blended with the rank smell of perspiration and where the shrill voices of crude and ignorant women were in cacophonous counterpoint with the music upstairs. The cramped Synge Street house, without privacy or order, was emblematic of constriction and squalor. In the house of his birth, forever the embodiment of home for him, he felt uneasily lodged. Where he should have been most secure he felt abandoned, threatened, insidiously ousted. Homeless even at home, to the end of his life Shaw revisited his birthplace in dreams, "but always as an old stranger, not as a boy," so existentially aging and inhospitable had been his boyhood.[5]

Shaw's odd insistence that he was a sojourner on this planet and not a native of it arose from his Synge Street home and its indelible presence in him. The year before his death Shaw wrote his cousin Grace Goodliffe that the house of his unhappy childhood had just been decorated with a tablet commemorating his birth there: "I would see it blown to smithereens without the faintest regret, in fact, with exultation." Countering this destructive rage, he revealed in his last months of life that writing a book or play is "my way of building a house."[6] He built those books and plays, however, without conventional happy endings, just as he never achieved satisfying closure to the troubling early portion of his life. In *Heartbreak House* (1917), the house, built to resemble a ship, symbolizes decadent Western culture and is headed straight for the rocks. In his play, Shaw incarnated the disorder and underlying wickedness he associated with his boyhood home, transforming his feelings of transience and his longing for solid ground beneath his feet into his allegorical masterpiece.

The move to Dalkey in 1866 unveiled the beauty of nature to him. He could not believe such skies existed anywhere else until he read Shakespeare's " 'this majestical roof fretted with golden fire' and wondered where he could have seen it if not from Torca Cottage." Still in awe, in his last years of life, he praised the "joy of it," which had remained with him. His joy at scanning the skies from Torca Cottage marked more than the boy's sensitivity to nature. Dalkey had the distinct advantage of removing the family from the public eye. Whatever the ecstasy of the moment, it faded into the far from inspirational reality of everyday living. Lee was now a virtual member of the family— indeed its nominal head, having leased the cottage in his name.[7] In this sequestered space (four rooms, with a tiny back room for Sonny, and a kitchen and a pantry) was established what Shaw always called a ménage à trois, though he insisted that it was devoid of the usual connotation of the term. Innocent or not, the effect on the ten-year-old was considerable.

In that cottage on Torca Hill, Sonny gazed from the wings on the domestic drama being enacted. Condemned to the silence of a spectator, stirred by the intuition that his life story ran through the unfolding plot, he watched guardedly. He had plenty of opportunity to watch, for he was not sent to school during that year at Dalkey. Significantly, the Shaws had discontinued their Sunday churchgoing, never to resume it. Sonny, the childhood charge of a motherly Catholic nurse who had taken her job seriously enough to sprinkle him with holy water, was long accustomed to exercising his "literary genius" by composing his own prayers "in three movements, like a sonata," and he continued to entertain and propitiate the Almighty for a while. Then, in the interest of "intellectual integrity," he refrained from such "superstitious practices." The Shaw religion was the "religion of singing the right way."[8]

Symbolically banished to a back room just as he was gaining sexual understanding, Sonny defiantly painted watercolor frescoes of Mephistopheles on his whitewashed bedroom wall. So startling a reality did Mephistopheles assume that Sonny's boyhood friend Matthew Edward McNulty reported that cynical jests were often prefaced with "as Meffie would say." While Sonny openly idolized stage demons and villains, he secretly and silently identified himself with Faust. Even when he was a good boy, it was "only theatrically," as a part to be played. Later, as life imitated art, he thought that nature had equipped him with the visage of the operatic fiend he had idolized as a boy, complete with the upgrowing moustache and eyebrows and the flaring nostrils. But just as intense as his fiendish adventures were Sonny's imagined daring rescues of fair and helpless maidens. In that secluded cottage high upon Torca Hill, Sonny drowned in romantic literature and became a votary of the Uranian Venus. So enamored would he be of his fantasies of "amours on the plains of heavens," so apprehensive over dark visions of his mother that no flesh-and-blood woman could ever be adequate or properly console him.[9]

The airy heights of the hill itself provided sanctuary. There he was sheltered by those "canopied skies" and the "two great bays between Howth and Bray Head," maternal and enclosing, that would be inscribed in his memory. Unlike those dreamers who learn intimacy with their world through the welcoming embrace of home, Sonny fled home, racing wildly up the furze-covered hill. There, lying face up to the sky, he escaped into daydreams biblical in their splendor and power. He was a prince in the world of his own imagination, commanding "all the kingdoms of the earth, all the regions of the sky, and all the ages of history."[10]

Atop the hill was a tiny stone castle. Multi-chambered and soaring upward, it was the obverse of the constrictive cottage and perfectly symbolized Sonny's youthful ethereal longings. No longer did the "boy buccaneer" set fire to gorse bushes and watch as Torca Hill erupted in flame. His incendiary defiance took the young unfettered Prometheus on an ascending trajectory, impelling him toward those empyreal regions charted by Shelley and Blake. In a shower of "newly lit flames" was born the moral passion—the "mightiest of the passions," according to John Tanner. Its radiance transformed Sonny into a creature with a conscience.[11]

Yet more and more this world without shadow or limitation would insinuate itself into his wish world. Ominously, it would make all the more threatening his return to the dark, constrictive existence of everyday life swarming with shameful secrets. But it would also impel him to set himself against his fate. Later he would write, "You see things; and you say 'Why?' But I dream things that never were; and I say 'Why not?'"[12]

The opposing worlds of spaciousness and constriction, brightness and darkness, height and depth, airy dreams and subterranean secrets that had become so apparent in Dalkey would accrue ever more meaning as his life progressed. Always there was dialectic, confinement giving way to retreat. And so, on the grounds of his final home in the tiny village of Ayot St. Lawrence, the aged playwright would erect a little hut, a single room that revolved to catch the sun. In this primitive refuge, like an anchorite alone before God, one of the world's most famous men, self-exiled from the land of his birth, self-banished from the world, would work in concentrated solitude, seeking still the fiery skies of fantasy.

Mephistopheles and Catastrophe

By 1867 the family had left Torca Cottage for 1 Hatch Street, beginning a period of alternating between the two residences. In the span of a single year the family had moved from the modest Synge Street house to the relative luxury of both cottage and substantial home. The house on Hatch Street was a corner house, with no room for a garden, and it had this anomaly: the front entrance was on one side and the windows on another, with one exception. A window near the roof opened from Sonny's tiny bedroom. Hatch Street, near St. Stephen's Green, was a fashionable address, but for Sonny it meant a move into a radically different and therefore threatening sphere of experience.

Publicly, Shaw called the household arrangement with Lee economical, since the family could not afford a fashionable house and Lee "could not afford to give lessons in an unfashionable one." To Frank Harris, Shaw noted that the rent was much higher than on Synge Street. "Without Lee's contribution it was beyond my father's dwindling means." Earlier, to would-be biographer Thomas Demetrius O'Bolger, Shaw had been even more explicit: "Lee paid the rent."[13]

Bessie now pursued music more fully than remote Torca Cottage had allowed. With Lee conducting the orchestra, Bessie led the chorus, sang, copied music, and borrowed from piano arrangements "in complete innocence," according to her son, of the "forgery she was perpetrating." The Shaw household vibrated with musical exertions.[14] Although a trombonist, George Carr Shaw took no part in these proceedings. Instead, he observed irately but meekly as the children fended for themselves.

The impropriety of the nonmusical arrangement is obvious, though not conclusive, and Shaw, forever the faithful son, forever assured the world—and himself—of his mother's virtue. It was a "blameless *ménage à trois,*" he wrote biographer Archibald Henderson, and Bessie was the sort of woman who could have had a dozen men in her house "without any more scandal than a hotel keeper." Even more pointedly, he wrote O'Bolger that his mother could have been the matron of a cavalry barracks "without a stain on her character." Countering suspicion that he might be Lee's son, he added that he was so like his father that he gave a severe shock to a friend shortly after his father's death by walking into the Bank of Ireland. The friend "supposed I was my father's ghost." Whether or not the ghost-walking episode occurred, it was not shortly after his father's death, since Shaw did not return to Ireland for some thirty years.[15]

As if the scandalous look of the household arrangement were not enough, there was also a daring affront to the Shaw credo. Not only did Bessie welcome Catholic musicians into her home, eager to advance her career, she also sang mass at "that house of Belial," the Roman Catholic chapel. Meanwhile, presiding magisterially over Hatch Street— admired, petted, almost worshipped by Bessie—was the religiously suspect Lee. This "invasion by Lee" ended the period of "conventional respectability" and resulted in the Shaw family being dropped by their cousins, "Irish snob-Protestants," whom Sonny mocked by his loudly proclaimed atheism. In siding with his father, Shaw blamed his mother for costing him the company of the well-to-do Shaws, including Sir Robert. Very late in life he remembered the charm of the Bushy Park estate: "I loved the eagle on the parapet and cherish a photograph of the house."[16] Sonny's single visit to Bushy Park had been to Sir Robert's funeral in February 1869. That very month Sonny had begun attending the Model School. It was the end of the era of innocence and respectability.

An intruder with alien values, Lee threatened the family structure. Supplanting George Carr Shaw as the "dominant factor in the household," he foisted seemingly astonishing personal quirks on the family, such as eating brown bread and sleeping with the window open. Lee also foisted himself physically on Sonny. The "encounter was not a success," Shaw wrote laconically of his introduction to Lee at about age six. Lee had grabbed the struggling Sonny and drawn, with burnt cork, whiskers and a moustache on his face, despite the boy's "most furious resistance." This incident has been cited only in passing by Shaw's biographers. Yet through this odd action, Lee, who would never have a child, created a grotesque self-caricature and visibly marked his supremacy in the house-hold. Elsewhere Shaw notes that experiences between age six and thirteen influenced his freethinking, and he specifically mentions Lee.[17]

There appears to be more to the burnt cork incident. As a result of Lee's "notion of play," Shaw admitted that he developed a "defensive attitude" toward Lee that lasted "until the decay of his energies and the growth of mine put us on more than equal terms." Plainly, Sonny feared further physical attack from Lee. *Were* further attacks perpetrated by the man Shaw described as "too excessively unlike us, too completely a phenomenon, to rouse any primitive human feeling"?[18] If so, might Shaw's silence mean that something about those attacks provoked him into hiding a guilty secret, a secret all the more shameful and disturbing because of Lee's closeness to Bessie? Whatever the nature of the lameness that made a married Lee unthinkable, he exercised a compelling and lifelong hold on Shaw.

The single extant photograph of Lee shows him sharply and arrestingly be-whiskered, sitting with arms folded. Supremely confident and dressed entirely in black, he is surrounded by a standing court that includes Bessie and George Carr Shaw, the latter situated just outside the admiring circle and at the greatest distance from his own wife. And there it is—there in Lee's haughty demeanor is captured the portrait of the gloating Mephistopheles himself. Absent is the powerless Sonny.

In empowering himself Lee demolished Sonny's precariously balanced sense of family. Instead, the realigned family revolved around the "whirlpool of energy of which Lee was the centre." Envying him, Shaw would strive to achieve that explosive energy himself, seeking at the last to be absorbed into the "whirlpool in pure force." Com-pulsively emulating Lee, surpassing him as a music critic if not as a musician, Shaw refused to recognize in himself any resemblance to the charismatic genius. He would, however, remain excessively interested in the relation of genius to heredity, reading Francis Galton's *Hereditary Genius* (1869) and following Galton's research with consum-ing interest. Galton believed that "in the case of Poets and Artists, the influence of the female line is enormously less than the male." Galton further believed that the "inheri-tance of musical taste is notorious and undeniable," and that energy is the most important attribute of superior men, one "eminently transmissible by descent"—all ideas that might reinforce Shaw's uneasiness about Lee.[19]

In Lee, Sonny found the most extreme contrast with his father. Though George Carr Shaw was "gentle and amiable," any "brightness or youth" had been extinguished by Lee's whirlpool of energy, so that he took a schizoid approach to life. He was "full of self-reproaches and humiliations when he was not full of secret jokes, and was either biting his moustache and whispering deepdrawn Damns, or else shaking with paroxysms of laughter." In sketching his father's family history in his diary, Shaw would label him "eccentric," "very unstable," and "defiant in will," noting only the symptoms of declin-ing life.[20] Witness to an alcohol addiction that afflicted at least three Shaw brothers and a sister, and a strain of mental instability that saw both Uncle Barney (William Bernard) and Uncle Frederick (Richard Frederick) die in an asylum, Shaw could hardly fail to wonder whether the gifted and ascetic Lee might not more properly be his father.

To protect himself against that possibility, Sonny cultivated the Shavian derision to an "abnormal degree," thereby aligning himself with the Shaws: "all my comedy is a Shavian inheritance." Certainly it was less painful to laugh at poor Uncle Barney, his ophicleide-playing namesake who hung his room with white fabric in the belief he was the Holy Ghost, than it was to weep for this gentle man. Summoning up the "Shavian originality," Uncle Barney managed to commit suicide by putting his head into a carpet-bag. Later Shaw would admit that the Shaws were a "more amusing family on paper than in real life."[21]

Sonny was assisted in his irreverence by another significant male figure. Dr. Walter John Gurly, Bessie's brother, was Lee's opposite in many ways. A ship's surgeon and Rabelaisian raconteur, he lived with the Shaws between voyages. Dissipated, high-spirited, and uproariously blasphemous as he reduced religion to absurdity, he impressed Sonny as a "most exhilarating person." Although Uncle Walter was intermittently infirm by drink, Shaw remembered him with affection and admiration, for otherwise Uncle Walter was an "upstanding, healthy man." What Sonny found appealing in his uncle was a robust vitality that countered the assaults of liquor and differed so greatly from the piteous self-disgust that George Carr Shaw swallowed with his suds. Unencumbered by his sister's dignity, Uncle Walter spun out elaborate and indecent anecdotes, fantastic and irreverent tales. An inveterate rake, he advocated easy access to women to prevent homosexuality among schoolboys, Shaw recalled. Uncle Walter's marriage to an English widow whom he brought back from America did little to produce more sedate habits, but despite his profanity and blasphemy, county society accepted him because he was amusing and "perceptibly a gentleman and drove his own horse." In Uncle Walter's boisterous humor, the melancholy Sonny found a vicarious outlet for his own hostility. Sonny learned how society indulges its scoffers when they are entertaining. Although the vulgar sexuality of his mother's brother was a bit too close to her for comfort, Sonny found Uncle Walter to be a "liberating influence."[22] Certainly he taught the boy how differently society views male and female behavior in matters of sex.

Daily, then, Sonny came into contact with three men of markedly different temperaments and varying success in life. Just as in his play *Misalliance* (1909), in which the lover has three fathers, he also had "a natural father and two supplementaries," giving him "three varieties" to study. In the Frank Harris biography, which was at least 50 percent ghost-written by Shaw, a curious passage stands out in relief against his claim of three fathers. From his earliest childhood, he had lived a "secret life," imagining himself "eminent, fearless, powerful, victorious, a great fighter, a great lover." His secret life had one oddity: the fictitious Shaw was a foundling.[23]

The mature man did not wonder that "some people" thought ties of blood should be kept secret from those related and that the foundling's condition was "the happiest" because he could pass his relatives on the street without knowing them.[24] To the boy, the three fathers were an unholy trinity, veiling and obscuring. If this was a mystery with too many suspects, the foundling had none at all. The three fathers crowded the son in the home they shared, while the ménage à trois barricaded him outside its forbidden space. But the secret foundling, without father, mother, or home, could roam from kingdom to kingdom, in triumphant victory from battlefield to boudoir. Against this landscape of ambiguous blood ties and allegiances, Sonny longed for a single figure of authority, dispensing justice and affection, a parental superman unflawed by moral, spiritual, or physical infirmities. In the absence of such superhuman traits, he turned to fantasy, the realm of strength and energy, endowing himself. There he dreamed of Shakespeare, envisioned himself a savior, and became Don Juan incarnate as his secret life overspread his world.

In Shaw's fathers were three distinct categories of humor as well—the brimming exuberance of Uncle Walter, the sadistically tinged practical jokes of Lee, and the disrespectful anticlimaxes of his father. Shaw's own humor seems to owe something to all three: to his uncle's high spirits, to Lee's aggressiveness, and to his father's irreverence. All three men scoffed at authority and challenged class notions of male behavior, whether actively like Uncle Walter, insidiously like Lee, or passively like George Carr Shaw.

Despite surface differences, the psychology of the three was similar. The recklessness and sensuality of Uncle Walter and the emotion and energy of Lee were the obverse of the sexual repression and inhibited anger of George Carr Shaw. They were all versions of a personality easily frustrated and craving a passionate outlet. Elements of all three personality versions would fire Shaw: Lee's drive for adulation, George Carr Shaw's retreat from manhood, and Uncle Walter's vibrant wooing. Through his desire to transform physical energy into moral and intellectual passion Shaw would attempt to circumvent the disease plaguing the three men nearest him. Though there is no earthly cure for the human condition, the artist-biologist would labor valiantly to alleviate the symptoms.

The Worst Mother Conceivable

> She did not hate anybody, nor love anybody.
> —*Sixteen Self Sketches*

There is little agreement about the personality of Lucinda Elizabeth Gurly Shaw. To Aunt Emily, George Carr Shaw's sister and the wife of clergyman Uncle William, she was "that bitch!" To Georgina Musters, daughter of Arabella Gillmore, a younger half-sister of Bessie, she was the "favorite aunt." To Matthew Edward McNulty, she was a woman of "forcible character" and "placid and pleasant temperament" who shocked him once at tea by crying tearfully, "My children do not love me." But crucially, to Shaw, she was a "shocking bad mother."[1]

In a society where marriage and motherhood were considered woman's most exalted functions, Bessie's son accused her of being "neither a mother nor a wife." Absent on that poorly timed visit to her father, she managed to miss her son's first birthday and his first steps. Although she kept a photograph album of opera stars, she admitted that she did not have a photograph of her son until he was about seventeen. She was to remain unimpressed by her son's later fame, warning the idolizing Archibald Henderson that G. B. S. was a "dreadful procrastinator."[2]

Bessie's inadequacies would have been less devastating had George Carr Shaw been other than a "nullity" in the house, though he did make an "effort or two" at assuming moral responsibility. Shaw blamed him as he tried to exonerate his mother. Everyone had "disappointed her or betrayed her or tyrannized over her." The fact that she did not hate her own children was a testament to her humanity, her son said. His defense reveals both his own humanity and his ambivalence toward his "long-suffering" mother. Bessie was neither weak nor submissive, but "as she never revenged, so also she never forgave."[3] Strong, dominant, and unforgiving, the career-minded Bessie in no way fit the societal ideal of the domestic angel sacrificing herself for hearth and home.

Instead, Bessie "abandoned" her children to servants—"And *such* servants, Good God!" Except for Nurse Williams, they were "utterly unfit to be trusted with the charge of three cats, much less three children." They thumped him on the head when he annoyed them and they served loathsome meals of stewed beef washed down with tea turned to tannin. Poignantly, Shaw remembers: "I hated the servants and liked my mother because, on the one or two rare and delightful occasions when she buttered my bread for me, she buttered it thickly instead of merely wiping a knife on it."[4] Starved for maternal love, Sonny was slapped by his nurse for stealing sugar and developed a craving for sweets that never subsided.

Bessie's children were unhealthy, and Dr. Newland, the apothecary, was kept busy administering cathartics, surely a factor in her son's developing fastidiousness and hypochondria. Another factor was Bessie herself, who knew nothing about housekeeping or hygiene. Her household was one of "domestic anarchy," the lack of daily routine constantly reinforcing Sonny's dread of disruption. Her rebellion against assigned roles in a constrictive patriarchal society would be continued far more noisily and self-consciously by her son, who called her a "Bohemian anarchist with ladylike habits."[5]

For Bessie, living was "something that happened" and "not an art," but for her son, art and artifice would war with life's chaos. Cowardly by day, the boy was a conquering hero by night. From the irony of such contrast issues comedy, which thrives on the disorderly, the improbable, and the incongruous. But the man felt that "all the fun that is to be got out of me I have already extracted myself." As a boy he was deprived of a mother's love, and as a man he would envision a world where the nurture of the young no longer occurred. He would seek not the embrace of love but the airy grasp of intellect. For Shaw, Bessie really was the "worst mother conceivable."[6] And who but Shaw would conceive of such a pun?

There was one advantage to Bessie's neglect. Sonny could idolize her "to the utmost pitch" of his imagination without having any "sordid or disillusioning contacts with her."[7] Shaw's stage creations demonstrate a transforming if not idolizing capacity. His mothers are efficient, no-nonsense women, like the high-born Lady Britomart in *Major Barbara* (1905), who takes in stride being wife to a munitions dealer and mother to a Salvation Army major. Though born into poverty, Mrs Warren in *Mrs Warren's Profession* (1893) uses business acumen to make her brothels more humane workplaces than the matchstick factory and to raise her daughter as a member of the privileged class. In the spirited comedy of manners *You Never Can Tell* (1896), Mrs Clandon is a cultivated woman who imposes respect as she rules out passionate personal affection. She has never been in love, never had a love affair, nor ever regretted that lacuna in her experience. Here in the civilized and intellectual Mrs Clandon is an imagined Bessie, who in reality cared not at all for ideas, quite unlike her own son.

Without guidance or open affection, Sonny ran wild, his aggressiveness meant to force Bessie to notice him. Family, church, and school were all ridiculed by the boy atheist. He delighted in practical jokes, and McNulty recalled being tricked into hitting a ball through a church window, Sonny rolling on the grass in laughter at the commotion.

So restless was he that he had no memory of ever being physically tired, as he drew on his brimming energy to fill time. Even so, the adolescent was painfully shy and insecure. Instead of seeing the world from beneath a benevolent canopy of love, he armed himself with the family weapon: "the power of derisive dramatization."[8] Mockery, trickery, and fantasy began to interweave ingeniously and to empower him. At the same time, he developed an intolerance for gentle feeling, defending himself against an unloving world through a noisy contempt for tenderness.

Bessie rebelled against her tyrannical upbringing by crooked-back Aunt Ellen, which had forced on her so determinedly a ladylike mien that she carried its "straight-backed stamp" to her grave. Having betrayed her father on his wedding day, Bessie, by her own marriage, betrayed Aunt Ellen. She then betrayed the husband whose drinking betrayed her, and, finally, her children by her "almost complete neglect."[9] She withheld love as love was withheld from her.

Her impulsiveness in running off with the considerably older George Carr Shaw lay the foundation for her guilt and coldness. Ashamed of her earlier regard for her husband, a man fallen beneath his class, she made herself emotionally independent of him. Aunt Ellen's wayward pupil now saw herself reaping the bitter fruit of her fall from grace. Psychologically, she relegated George Carr Shaw to a bit part in the drama of her life. Her disdain for him was reinforced by her admiration of the suave Lee, the adored Dublin leading man and the guru of her religion of music. The bohemian mother might talk of respectability, but to her son she conveyed disturbing signals. The heightened sexual atmosphere of the house, the stringent proscriptions of respectable society against extra-marital sex, and Bessie's contempt for her lawful partner fatefully combined for Sonny. As the clandestine took on a special meaning for him, he became an adolescent highly sensitive to sexual innuendo and inordinately aware of societal customs, taboos, and hypocrisies, especially those assigned by gender.

Shaw explained his mother's behavior as resulting from her Spartan upbringing: "Misfortunes that would have crushed ten untrained women broke on her like waves on granite." Since the major misfortune Bessie suffered was her marriage, implicitly the issue of that marriage—her unloved son—was also a misfortune. Like the waves, he made no impression on her. Sonny and his sisters were "simply disappointing and inferior little animals" forced to meet life's difficulties by breaking their shins over them.[10] It was Bessie's sheer granite face that proved the most daunting to her son.

Shaw's view of his mother was tempered by an amazing discovery after her death: she had carefully preserved his baby cap. To the actress Mrs. Patrick Campbell he confessed that had "anyone suggested such a possibility I should have laughed at him (or her) to scorn. We never know anything about our parents." Beneath the tone of regret, designed to evoke from Stella Campbell the pity he never evoked from Bessie, lay his characteristic ambivalence toward his mother. He detailed her domestic failings because he could not detail his deepest fears about her. His apparent acceptance of her ladylike bohemianism concealed an inability or unwillingness to see her in any light but the flickering one of emotionalism, resentment, and defensiveness. Yet Joey Percival, the man in *Misalliance* with three fathers, is reported to have said that "if he could only have had three mothers as well, he'd have backed himself against Napoleon."[11]

In describing the three most important people in his life, Shaw used imagery that reflected his psychological orientation. At the age of four, Sonny was taught that the four elements—earth, air, fire, and water—were the basic elements of the inorganic world. They are not the elements of nature, but they are the elements of imaginative experience.

Granite, known for its hardness, is the essence of materialization. Because it is not subject to decay, it is commonly used in tombstones and therefore is a reminder of mortality. Formed by the cooling of molten rock, granite represents earth, Bessie's element, in its least fecund and inviting guise. It was Lee who was the "volcano," the one with "meteoric impact."[12] Both the meteor and the volcano are composed of flaming rock, characterized by brilliant displays, and may appear suddenly and threateningly.

If Lee was identified with rocks that flamed, George Carr Shaw was identified with water that burned—firewater. Alcohol can either inflame or submerge, with fire considered a masculine sign and water a feminine sign. A melancholy alcoholic, George Carr Shaw was dominated by the passive/feminine side of his nature. Where Lee was volatile and commanding, Shaw *père* was ineffectual and pathetic.

Though he shared his father's passive and feminine inclinations, Shaw battled them. His primary element, the one he unceasingly sought, was air, the realm of light and freedom, dematerialization and the Word. A "sprite" and "not a real person," he would rise "by sheer gravitation." He was always gazing at the skies, trying to take wing. But those skies that drew him were incandescent and flaming, for fire was his element as well. The blazes that the uncontrolled Sonny set on Torca Hill were mere portents. Whether exuding the "unmistakeable flavor of brimstone," or watching ribbons of flame "miraculously" cremate his mother, or imagining the funeral pyre of his martyred Saint Joan, whose heart would not burn, Shaw's climb toward the ethereal intersected with fire, the very image of energy and purification. Using the term *phenomenon* to describe both Lee and himself, Shaw alluded again to the meteor, literally a luminescent phenomenon.[13]

But while fire and earth are linked with eroticism, fire and air are linked with spiritual energy. Those elements linked him, man and boy, to the eagle, a creature whose daring flight toward the sun makes it the emblem of the spiritual principle. It is the eagle that announces the imperial power of Shaw's Caesar, the eagle that he loved at Bushy Park, the stone eagles that he remembered at Dolphin's Barn. Shaw's self-created destiny, like the eagle's, was to soar, but only through supreme ordeal could that destiny be fulfilled. For the ethereal realm had an ever-tightening hold on his psyche, creating an increasingly convoluted and extravagant interior life.

In 1910, as he celebrated his fifty-fourth birthday, Shaw would visit his homeland and be besieged by a strong sense of his own mortality. He decided to journey to the Skellig Islands off the Kerry coast, a two-hour trip in an open boat across perilous seas. Like partially submerged gothic cathedrals, "pinnacled, crocketed, spired, arched, caverned, minaretted," the Skelligs rose before him.

> Great Skellig rushes up 700 feet so suddenly that you have to go straight upstairs to the top—over 600 steps. And at the top amazing beehives of flat rubble stones, each overlapping the one below until the circles meet in a dome—cells, oratories, churches, and outside them cemeteries, wells, crosses, all clustering like shells on a prodigious rock pinnacle, with precipices sheer down on every hand, and, lodged on the projecting stones overhanging the deep, huge stone coffins made apparently by giants, and dropped there, God knows how. An incredible, impossible, mad place, which still tempts devotees to make "stations" of every stair landing, and to creep through "needle's eyes" at impossible altitudes, and kiss "stones of pain" jutting out 700 feet above the Atlantic.

Grotesque and remote, the rock reminded him of the legend of the Flying Dutchman and belonged to his "dream world."[14]

The hold of this fantastic rock on Shaw's imagination can be glimpsed in the strange outcroppings that surface in the settings for *Too True to Be Good* (1931) and *The Simpleton of the Unexpected Isles* (1934). With its supernatural landscape, Great Skellig was a primordial Torca Hill with a desolate lighthouse instead of a castle. Here was rock that sheltered, rock that inspired, rock that soared toward the heavens. It was reached only by a dangerous journey across the sea, the transitional medium between earth and air, and by traveling past a little Skellig obscenely white with screaming gannets and their guano. Pursued by "terrors" and "ghosts," he traveled back without compass under a mist-clouded moon with two silent women "like spirit rappers," a captain "possessed by ten devils," and ten rowers "superhuman in energy and endurance" who struck sparks of "white fire" from the Atlantic. At intervals the darkness exploded with cries of " 'Up-up-up-keep her up!' 'Up Kerry!' "[15] Soaked and aglow with spray, waves crashing over him, the taste of salt on his lips, Shaw crouched in the boat that cradled him like a womb.

Filled with wonder and awe, the next day he confessed, "I hardly feel real again yet." The pilgrimage to the great rock recalled the Celt and Saxon to him, stirring those ancient bloodlines. In the wildest, most isolated region of the land of his birth, he had discovered his source. Like the universal hero of ancient and modern myth, he had touched the umbilical point of his universe, the navel that nourished him with streams of spiritual energy. Late in life he would consciously associate Great Skellig with the motherland that filled him with ambivalence, making him a foreigner in every other country: "Whoever has not stood in the graveyards at the summit of that cliff, among those beehive dwellings and their beehive oratory, does not know Ireland through and through."[16]

The essence of Shaw's dream world, the stark landscape of his soul, was distilled in the graves and womblike dwellings at the summit of a cliff whose mysterious chambers lay unseen beneath the sea. In his unconscious, motherland and mother merged. Bessie, the woman of granite, against whom the fiery waves of her son broke and vanished like airy foam, had at last succumbed to the endless rhythms of sea and air, becoming a sheltering and transcendental haven.

4 Stopgap and Impostor

> "I wonder," said Smith to himself, as he
> walked home, "is there any profession in the
> world so contemptible as that of a clerk!"
> —Robert Smith, *Immaturity*

Just as Shaw laid claim to an unorthodox trio of fathers, he claimed three untraditional colleges: Dalkey, the National Gallery, and Lee's musical society. At Dalkey, the splendor of nature had fired his "real education," which was aesthetic. Back in Dublin, the world of art nurtured him. He roamed the nearby National Gallery as he had roamed the hillside. In that "cherished asylum" of his boyhood, he returned again and again to Raphael's Madonna and to Michelangelo's powerfully masculine figures, superhuman visions of motherhood and manhood. Seeking a focus for his restless nature, he tried drawing, hoping to become a great painter. Yet he claimed not to have had dreams of becoming a great writer "any more than a duck has of swimming." He fed his imagination on works of high poetry, romance, and fatedness, swallowing up *The Pilgrim's Progress*, *The Iliad*, *Gulliver's Travels*, La Rouchefoucauld's *Maxims*, Scripture, history, and the works of Sir Walter Scott, Charles Dickens, and Shakespeare. As a son of Ireland he was heir to a tradition that granted magical powers to the satirist. As an autodidact he felt drawn to *The Arabian Nights*, identifying with its exotic female storyteller—later he called himself a male Scheherazade.[1] Actual or imagined adventures filled his days and nights.

Increasingly, music moved him as his home was transformed into an opera hall. There were occasional visits to the opera itself, for opera was in vogue in Dublin. The gilded balcony and glittering audience set the scene for enchantment. At a performance of Mozart's *Zauberflöte*, Sonny "first breathed the air of the transcendental regions." The Theatre Royal housed both opera and theater, and Lee sometimes used it for his amateur opera evenings. Opera and drama fused gloriously in Sonny's imagination. Mozart's "perfect technique" became his model: "Mozart was a *master to masters*."[2]

Finally, his mother and her music meant glory instead of shame to Sonny. Here too, at the Theatre Royal, he first felt that the theater was a "secret paradise" where "talent is everything and pedigree nothing."[3] The theater that Sonny saw—farce, pantomime, melodrama, and Shakespeare—was grounded in suspense pleasurably garbed, even raised to rapture, in opera. It was a realm where suspense could be manipulated, neutralizing the accretions of shame and dread. So powerfully did suspense hold him throughout his life that without the semblance of suspense born of ceaseless activity there was nothing but emptiness.

With its combination of expectation and surprise, music thrilled and elevated him. Both sensuous and ethereal, music countered the pull of the sordid and stultifying, the menacing, dark world that, paradoxically, was associated with Bessie and Lee, the music-makers. Lingering in the background while Lee conducted rehearsals, Sonny proudly learned the works of more than a dozen composers. But it was the "noble charm" of Mozart's Don Giovanni and the "sardonic accents" of Gounod's Mephistopheles that fascinated him. Significantly, Bessie sang the roles of the corresponding operatic heroines, Donna Anna and Margaret.[4]

Yet Sonny's musical education was ignored in this highly musical home, except for a few lessons on an ancient cornet.[5] He could not play or read a note of music. Drowned in music's sensuality, however, he whistled scores to himself and forced his untrained voice into both male and female parts. With boyish naïveté he hoped to become a dashing opera singer. Perhaps then Bessie, the shadowy woman of his dreams, would pay attention. His influence on the London music scene and the world of grand opera, if not on Bessie, would far exceed his seemingly inflated aspirations.

In spite of Sonny's wishes and inclinations, the family saw his future in a far more practical light. At age thirteen he was sent job-hunting to a firm of cloth merchants who rejected him as too young. But the die was cast. He was then enrolled in the Dublin English Scientific and Commercial Day School. Such vocational preparation made college impossible even if George Carr Shaw had relented and offered to pay tuition. Since there was always money for liquor, Shaw never forgave his father for preferring the solace of a bottle over his son's future.

It was during his two years at the commercial school that Sonny met Matthew Edward McNulty, who would become a friend for life. McNulty became a banker and a writer (dropping his first name like his friend) and would propose to Lucy. McNulty's first impression of Shaw, recorded in middle age, was of a "tallish, slender" boy with "straw-colored hair, light greyish-blue eyes, a skin like that of a baby and lips like those of a beautiful girl." McNulty recalled that Sonny was cast as Ophelia for a production of *Hamlet* because he was the "most effeminate-looking member" of the dramatic society. He delivered his lines in a "shrill falsetto" while prancing about on his toes, an act of exhibitionism that transformed the tragedy into a farce.[6]

Matt shared Sonny's interest in literature and art. Together they eagerly awaited and read *The Boys of England*, a weekly filled with the adventures of daring heroes in an exciting, masculine world of action. The two enrolled in a late-afternoon class at the Royal Dublin Society's School of Art. There the admirer of Dalkey's vistas showed no interest in landscape art, even as his drama would largely be set in man-made interiors.

Instead, Sonny concentrated on drawing the human figure with "painfully precise" lines. Often the two secluded themselves to look at prints or read each other's literary attempts, Sonny writing a sardonic demon into his first serious effort. Then Sonny began to "hint darkly at a scheme" for studying the human form. Suddenly one afternoon in his tiny attic bedroom he vigorously pressed his friend to take off his clothes and be his naked model, arguing that he would return the favor. From his perch on the windowsill Matt refused, claiming to be afraid of catching cold. "We argued the point for some time. . . . I was very sorry for him."[7]

When Matt went to work for the Newry branch of the Bank of Ireland, north of Dublin, the friends poured their "unreserved soul histories" into long letters meant to be destroyed on receipt lest they fall into strange hands. Matt welcomed a visit from his friend, and the two spent summer evenings concocting a literary collection, "The Newry Nights' Entertainment." Their real pleasure lay in "reading and forcibly criticising one another's work," he remembered. In a secret ceremony, the friends signed a "declaration of Eternal Friendship" in their own blood, recalling age-old initiation rites of manhood. A photograph of the two bothered the adolescent Shaw, who complained several times: "You look like a man and I look like a nonentity!"[8]

After reading a typescript copy of the account McNulty published in 1901, Shaw did not contest McNulty's assertion that he had urged him to pose naked. He did contest McNulty's account of himself as Ophelia, observing in the margin that the "duel scene in *Romeo & Juliet* was our only achievement." He thereby viewed himself as practicing a manly art instead of effeminate cross-dressing. Certainly McNulty believed that his version was accurate. In 1941 he recalled both the Ophelia incident and the naked modeling incident in a letter to Shaw.[9]

Whether by coincidence or to counter his disappointment with Matt, Sonny grandiosely gave up art, with its fleshly emphasis on the human body, in favor of founding a new religion. Until the end of his life he would consider himself a missionary, preaching the gospel according to St. Bernard as he tracked the transcendental regions of the universe. Having relinquished the artist's pencil, Shaw would brandish his preferred, and more dangerous, precision instrument—the satirist's pen.

Sonny's schoolboy deeds and misdeeds came to a close when he was fifteen. Uncle Frederick, chief of the Land Valuation Office and apparently still in command of his senses, obtained a position for his nephew without paying the customary premium, making him in effect a poor relation in his first job. As part of his rite of passage he was known now by his detested first name—"Jorj . . . so horribly ugly." It was a name not improved by its rising popularity as Georgie, for girls, and at home there already was one George too many, George Lee. In working for ultra-respectable Charles Uniacke Townshend, a pillar of everything "pillarable," George found he had an aptitude for a job he hated. Surely the most onerous of his tasks was collecting rent from poor tenants. His contempt for the job would surface in his first play, *Widowers' Houses* (1892), which attacks slum landlordism, and in which the job of rent collecting falls to the miserably servile Lickcheese. Similarly, in his 1880 novel *The Irrational Knot,* landowners are denounced as "little better than thieves."[10]

"Chronically ashamed and even miserable," George, seeking approval, set himself up as a musical expert, teaching operatic fragments to fellow apprentices and astonishing Townshend. When George also vented his religious skepticism, the dismayed Townshend branded him an infidel and ordered him never to discuss religion in the office. George agreed but was so ashamed of the promise that it put office life "out of the question" as a career.[11] Not simply conscience-stricken, as he claimed later in life, George was mortified by being publicly forced to submit to a male he had hoped to impress.

George found the job of office boy so humiliating that he called himself a junior clerk instead. Sudden confusion reigned when the cashier absconded with office funds and an older clerk failed to make the cash balance. Cast into the job as a "stopgap," the former wayward schoolboy was so diligent that plans to hire an adult were dropped. The exultant sixteen-year-old became "chief cashier, head cashier, sole cashier," responsible for a "miniature banking business," as he would later proudly recall. Though George was now equal in status to anyone at the office and bought a tailed coat to prove it, he remained convinced that he was a "worthless impostor." Like Robert Smith, the clerk hero of his first novel, *Immaturity* (1879), he played a part "he did not believe to be a true representation of himself." It was all "socially pretentious," and he felt resentful and seditious even as he laid claim to privilege.[12]

Yet George tallied his accounts and sat submissively on his office stool at 15 Molesworth Street until C. J. Smyth, a fellow clerk remarked that every young man assumes that he will become great. This commonplace gave George such a "shock" and a "jar" that he suddenly realized that his "subconscious intention" all along had been to take greatness for granted. Roused by a casual comment, he vowed to seek the destiny he grandiosely thought he shared with Shakespeare, Mozart, and Michelangelo. A half-century later, full of vengeful glee, Shaw recalled the otherwise forgotten Smyth: "Well, you fool, *I was right.*"[13]

Though shocked and jarred, George bided his time. Then Townshend's nephew was welcomed into the office and given the coveted job of cashier, even though he lacked clerical experience. Transferred and incensed, George resigned. He was offered a raise but refused it. Ambivalently, he insisted on giving value—meaning having value—and shrank from being judged in the very economic terms he himself constantly used. Having already decided to leave, he now felt justified in his righteous anger. Much later, Shaw directly addressed the tenuous connection between compensation and ability: "Mozart could have made much more money as a valet than he did as the greatest composer of his time, and indeed one of the greatest composers of all time; nevertheless he chose to be a composer and not a valet." Those with exceptional ability need no inducement to exercise that ability.[14]

Leaving the office resembled Sonny's defiance in leaving the Model School. George did not need the impetus of Townshend's nephew to be convinced that he was driven by "unconscious ambition" to leave Dublin, but his unconscious motivations were more complex than he realized. They can be inferred from a curious dream recurring now and then to the mature man. In his dream he has neglected his duties over a long period of time: "Whole estates must have been sold up, widows and orphans left to starve, mortgages foreclosed, and the landed gentry of Ireland abandoned to general ruin, confusion, and anarchy," all through his "unaccountable omission" of his daily duties "for years and years." He would awake asking why "so disgracefully untrustworthy a person as myself" was given such responsibility.[15]

Significantly, Shaw offers his dream without comment. The break with the office was outwardly decisive, but psychologically he has not moved an inch from his feelings of imposture and rage; he has not aged "by a single day." Duties important in waking life are so magnified that Shaw's neglect pulls down the entire social structure of Ireland. As he rebels covertly through unaccountable omission, the landed gentry, the very class that plagued him, is consigned to ruin and anarchy. In his dream he possesses the power he wished for in his office days, especially as concerns Townshend and the authority he represents. In this sense it is a classic revenge dream. The waking parallel to the recurring dream, with its wish to demolish the existing social structure, would find artistic and political outlets. But in neither his waking nor his sleeping life could Shaw feel at ease with the violent implications of his wish.

It is unknown how often Shaw's sleeping brain set in motion the same dream. But by admitting that the dream recurred, Shaw unwittingly revealed his enslavement to his past in his nonwaking life. In his waking life his constriction would be dramatically evidenced in his nearly thirty-year self-imposed exile from his homeland, an exile ended in 1905 to please his wife. Even then he did not return to his native city. When he did at last return, in 1908, a fancy propelled him into the very office he had escaped so long before. There he was received by a frockcoated clerk of great dignity. When Shaw announced that he had once worked in that office, the clerk, full of contempt, said, "'I dont remember you.'" Shaw gasped. He had changed from "a nobody on an office stool to a celebrity with half a dozen reputations." Yet the clerk "left me nowhere in point of self-esteem!"[16] The exclamation mark deftly deflates any charge that Shaw takes himself too seriously. Yet it is on this note of shock and surprise that the account ends. What bearing can this seemingly trivial event have on Shaw's life history?

Repeatedly urged to return to Dublin, Shaw acquiesced only after becoming a celebrity, seeking then the affirmation that eluded him so long before. Although he did not recognize his motives, he set out to conquer Dublin. A "curious reluctance" to retrace his steps made him arrive "through the back door from Meath" rather than through the "front door on the sea." Coming in by the back door, with its hint of class differences, suggests both unworthiness and furtiveness. Yet the ambivalent Shaw arrived rather sensationally by automobile, emphasizing his station in life and attracting attention. In the end, his decades-long circuitous route to Dublin led straight to 15 Molesworth Street.[17] Here then is the classic wish to return to a scene of humiliation to find vindication. But Shaw's wish backfired. Both the actual return and the recording of the return, apparently so insignificant, mark the compulsion. There is irony as well. After all, Shaw thought he was depicting the unknown clerk's provincialism and his own miraculously thwarted fate. Instead, the encounter shows the lingering importance of his office life, exactly what lies behind the recurring dream.

Shaw seemed unaware of the psychological connection between dream and encounter, even though he recalled both in a brief essay. Moreover, by focusing on his humiliation at the office, Shaw avoided focusing on the more painful humiliation he had suffered at home. The vengeful wish to destroy the social system sanctioning Townshend concealed a parallel wish to obliterate all traces of the shameful ménage à trois. No wonder his psyche protected him from his own wrath, allowing him to operate by "unaccountable omission." His wrath was in no way dissipated on a return trip five years later: "I drove into Dublin today and cursed every separate house as I passed."[18]

Nor is it any wonder that Smith, the clerk in *Immaturity*, dreams resentfully of the office where he spent "nearly two-thirds of his waking existence." He entertains himself by imagining "that abominable office and every book, carpet, clerk, and partner" being "consumed to ashes." Although the narrator confides that Smith's "painful yearning" will not affect him "in maturer years," Shaw's own feelings resisted purgation.[19]

5

Unmaskings and Dublin Curtain

> The relation between parent and child has
> cruel moments.
> —Preface to *Misalliance*

In his ambitious rise in Dublin's musical society, Lee cast his net ever wider. Though he began with strictly amateur performances, he reached his Dublin eminence with a festival featuring leading singers from the Italian opera in London. George John Lee emerged variously as Mr. Geo. Lee, Mr. Geo. J. Lee, J. Vandeleur Lee, and, finally, Vandeleur Lee. Along with the new names came a barrage of self-advertisement, enough to incur the animus of the important musician Sir Robert Prescott Stewart, who looked askance at Lee and his aliases. Targeting Lee, Stewart boasted of doing "one good work in Dublin. I unmasked one arrant impostor and drove him away." The unmasked impostor conducted a concert on 26 May 1873, then canceled a series of concerts and his Tonic–Solfa music class to leave abruptly and permanently for London by 4 June.[1]

On 17 June the unsentimental Bessie celebrated her twenty-first wedding anniversary by following Lee to London. Gathering up pale-faced Agnes and sending for the talented Lucy, she abandoned both husband and son. Writing years later of the *"débâcle,"* Shaw insisted that it was not an "elopement." His "now elderly mother"—referring to Bessie at age forty-two—had been forced to leave because of "pecuniary necessity." He also insisted that the "elderly wife" took the time to sell their Hatch Street furniture and to relocate husband and son into comfortable lodgings before departing for London to wait for her plans to "materialize." In reality, the time sequence portrays a woman deserting her family, not pausing long enough to take both daughters, let alone settle her husband and son. True, Bessie did perform this service, but it was nearly a year later. It would be March 1874 before she returned to Dublin and helped in the move to 61 Harcourt Street. That was her sole visit to Dublin, the single time her son saw her in the three years between her initial departure and his emigration to London in 1876. George was a month shy of his seventeenth birthday when his mother first left. Remembering, he put his age at fifteen, suggesting how young and vulnerable the motherless adolescent felt.[2]

Evidence that more than faulty memory is at work here can be gleaned from Shaw's insistence that his father's drunkenness wrecked the marriage so that "we all deserted him." Although the last to desert, Shaw felt the most guilt. Glossed over in his account is a noteworthy fact: in about 1871, George Carr Shaw, frightened by a convulsive fall on his doorstep, had stopped drinking. This feat failed to impress either his wife or his son. The father remained a drunkard in his son's eyes. For Shaw to dwell on his father's resolve would suggest that Bessie should also have been gratified that her husband's chief fault had been eliminated. Instead, she followed Lee to London. To praise his father would be to condemn his mother. Although Shaw admitted that "nobody—not even my mother" could hate his father, he viewed him as a warning, "not a model," until very late in life.[3]

So Lee's unmasking cost the adolescent Shaw his mother, a pseudo-father, his sisters, and even the proud Hatch Street home and its music. Shaw glosses over Lee's departure, alleging that the musician became a charlatan after he arrived in London. Yet the only extant letters from that period suggest that Lee's London behavior was largely consistent with his Dublin persona. Writing to Lucy in February 1875, George advised her not to listen to Lee, who was badgering her to appear in his amateur opera series: "We all know what his tirades are worth, and I think his coming to Victoria Grove and launching out at you as he did, simply outrageous." The brotherly view of Lee was that "he is simply hopeless and incorrigible. Don't mind him at all. On the conducting stool, he is a talented man, anywhere else, he is to be avoided."[4]

George wrote Bessie that same day, defending Lucy against Lee's "vituperation." Lee should confine himself to music, where he is "unsurpassed." The successful clerk emphasized that Lee courted ruin every day and needed a man to handle his business affairs. On the subject of Lee, George thought his mother needed advice "a great deal worse" than Lucy. His letter is filled with exaggerations and mockery—of respect, of betrayal, of love: "I feel that even now you are wishing you could kiss me." It is a performance that shows George acting on own advice to Lucy: to laugh Bessie out of her ideas.[5]

Shaw would take pains to separate himself from Lee, not acknowledging the influence of Lee's resourcefulness and persistence. He disparaged Lee's ambitions as leading to his downfall while depicting himself as without ambition.[6] Yet Shaw, defensive about his lack of a university education and his status in society, inflated himself, like Lee, through endless self-advertisement.

Meanwhile, George wore his tailed coat, drew money at the bank, balanced his cash books, and internalized the impostor and charlatan. His sense of masquerade was in part a Shaw legacy, in part negative identification with Lee, whose downfall was in some ways his own. Troubled by nebulous fears of being unmasked himself, and by anger at his abandonment by Lee as well as by Bessie, he still felt the strange, unsettling power of the man. For him, Lee was literally a "magnetic conductor."[7] The mysteries of the ménage à trois, Lee's pose as mesmeric genius, his unmasking and flight, Bessie's humiliating pursuit—all would be obsessively reenacted in Shaw's own life history but with peculiarly Shavian twists and reversals.

The consequences of Bessie's abandonment were irremediable, as the family "broke up," fracturing the uneasy accommodation that had passed for security in George's world. Never to be properly reconstructed, the fragmented family would reappear as bits and pieces of the playwright's world design, splintered debris reassembled into plot and character, wit and didacticism. Manipulating disruption dramatically, he would transform the personally threatening into the artistically malleable. He would bludgeon his ghosts into compliance: "Except in my secret self I was not happy in Dublin; and when ghosts rise up from that period I want to lay them again with the poker."[8]

One ghost was his father. Together they lived in shared humiliation, first at Synge Steet, then reclusively in a boardinghouse. The older Shaw was so disillusioned and unsociable that George and Matt referred to him as the Hermit. Distancing himself from his father, George became friendly with Chichester Bell, a fellow lodger at the boardinghouse, and studied Italian with him. Bell was a cousin of Alexander Graham Bell, the inventor of the telephone, and nephew of Melville Bell, inventor of phonetic script. It was the remarkable Bell—chemist, physician, pugilist, and pianist—who encouraged George's love of music, converting him to Wagner.[9]

After the household broke up, George, suddenly without music, looked longingly at his mother's piano and bought a keyboard diagram. To teach himself how to play, he struggled with Bessie's music, starting with the overture to *Don Giovanni*. He got what he wanted: the power to learn a vocal score as if he had heard it "rehearsed by my mother and her colleagues"—as if he had been Lee.[10] So accomplished would the abandoned son become that later, in London, the piano duet would become ubiquitous as an instrument of seduction, and quite as effective as Lee's flashier baton. And when McNulty visited the Shaws in London, the two would play duets after breakfast.

Meanwhile, in Dublin, the theater beckoned. George usually avoided the Queen's Theatre, because it disturbed him to see the strutting prostitutes who congregated there. Instead, he paid two shillings to be admitted to the pit of the Theatre Royal. Little matter that he came out of the crush "with all my front buttons down the middle of my back." In that noble theater his spirit had space to soar. In contrast, the new Gaiety Theatre, built in 1871, crammed every inch of its space with rows of cushioned seats. In spite of the close quarters, his inner space was unfettered. It was at the Gaiety that he became acquainted with Gilbert and Sullivan and the "astonishingly 'churchy'" music of *Trial by Jury*.[11] Spiritually released, George could forget the office, the Hermit, and Dublin dreariness.

The Dublin theater offered him the chance to attend productions that featured touring stars from the London and international circuit, as well as Dublin stock company actors. He was caught up in the excitement surrounding the performances of the greatest actor of them all, Barry Sullivan, "the last of the race" of heroic stage figures. He felt the power exuded by the egotistical, intense, "sinister and yet dignified" Henry Irving, who was so peculiar that "caricature alone could give a truthful impression." He identified with Charles Mathews's portrayal of a shy young man who became a monster of impudence in the farce *Cool as a Cucumber*. He saw playwright Tom Taylor's *Joan of Arc*, with its historical heroine in male clothes. He watched as cross-dressed women took the "breeches part" in Shakespearean productions—as well as in pantomime, extravaganza, and burlesque—and cross-dressed men played the unappealing Dame.[12]

But he also saw Miss Marriott play the title role in *Hamlet,* a performance that hinged on the impenetrability of her male disguise. Seeing Miss Ada Cavendish, he instantly "fell wildly, madly, suicidally in love with the New Magdalen," referring to the Wilkie Collins play of that title. Yet he expressed his love in a somewhat odd manner. He polished "the most exquisite imitation of her in the part," perhaps in the shrill falsetto McNulty attributed to him in playing Ophelia and that he seemed unable to recall. But he boasted to Lucy of his ability to play the reformed prostitute who assumes the identity of a respectable young woman. Reviewing a revival of the play later in London, Shaw declared Mercy Merrick to be neither a real Magdalen nor a real woman: "Mercy is the oldfashioned manmade angel-woman."[13]

As a critic, Shaw insisted on the analogy between the theater and the church. Undoubtedly, part of its allure for him was the elusive nature of the communicants, who could ritualistically and effortlessly cloak themselves in another gender. In the Dublin theater, drenched in its seductive mystery, he first felt the compelling power of role reversal.

Breaking Loose

On 29 February 1876, George gave a month's notice, leaving Townshend's employ on Friday, 31 March.[14] Four days earlier his sister Agnes had died in Ventnor, on the Isle of Wight, where she had gone in vain for a cure for consumption. Agnes's death may have sped George's departure, but thoughts of a reunion with Bessie surely played a role. By overriding his ambivalent feelings he could demonstrate the devotion of a trusting son. Reestablishing continuity in his relationship with his mother would counter the rupture from Dublin and his father.

Another factor in his departure was his outrage at Townshend's nepotism, an injustice all too similar to those perpetrated by the system of primogeniture. In brief notes detailing the office, Shaw lists some nineteen apprentices and clerks, with dates of their employment by year. Only for Robert Cuthbert Heighington does Shaw note day, date, and year of employment commencement and termination—April 1873 to 31 March 1876. The coincidence of the apprentice leaving on exactly the same day as Shaw, and Shaw's keen recall of the date and the absence of similar detail in the other entries, suggest collusion between the two. The annoyed and resentful George may have goaded Heighington into resigning with him, thus fortifying his own resolve. Moreover, only one of the entries includes salary information, that of Townshend's nephew, a junior clerk and cashier who later earned two hundred pounds a year at Herries. George's Dublin salary was never more than eighty-four pounds.[15]

Exactly when George decided to leave Dublin is not known, but two of his novels written not long after in London contain clues that point to 21 December as the fateful day. Just as *Immaturity* opens on the shortest day of the year, so the author may have closed a chapter of his life on the shortest day. No longer "immature, and apparently an arrant prig," as in his Dublin years, Shaw may have delighted in secretly resurrecting the date of his decision. Shaw emphasizes the date by having the very practical Smith read a newspaper article on pagan festivals. It is plausible that the freethinking George would take the winter solstice as a time of symbolic renewal. Additionally, it likely would please him to resign precisely on the intercalary day of Leap Year, an exceptional and memorable point on the calendar. That the Dublin Shaw would have been aware of the pagan significance of the winter solstice as a sacred New Year's Day seems assured. In fact, *The Times* of London on 24 December 1875 carried a letter, which George may have read at the office, entitled "The Shortest Day." Having paid for bonding through 31 March may have been reason enough for the frugal George to put off his departure for three months.[16]

There is an even more revealing clue. Shaw's office dream resembles his conception of *An Unsocial Socialist,* written in 1883 during a flirtation with Marxism. Shaw envisioned the novel as "only the first chapter of a vast work depicting capitalist society in dissolution, with its downfall as the final grand catastrophe."[17] But having finished this chapter, he found that he had nothing more to say for the moment. In the novel, Sidney Trefusis is a moneyed Marxist who masquerades as Jeff Smilash, a common man. When Trefusis's wife, Henrietta, dies, her birthdate is revealed as Shaw's own—26 July 1856— and her date of death as 21 December 1875. Trefusis's prolonged tombstone arrangements call exaggerated attention to the dates.

In his red-bearded, ascetic mountebank, Shaw sketched a refracted version of himself. Less obvious is his self-connection to Henrietta, a "luxurious creature" of "serpent-like grace" who is nevertheless a conventional woman.[18] The daughter of a Jewish banker, Henrietta has been raised as a Christian. Her maiden name, Jansenius, ironically recalls the Jansenists, discontented Roman Catholics of the seventeenth and eighteenth centuries who believed in reforming rather than leaving the church. In contrast, the London Shaw, smarting under the sting of his Dublin compromises, considered mere reform of the established sociopolitical structure unacceptable. Indeed, aural puns concealed in his hero's name emphasize this posture of denial (Sid*nay* T*re-fuses*), and his alias suggests another pun: *I lash*. In Henrietta's dates, Shaw playfully entombed a troubling portion of his own life, even as he sought to escape the serpentlike coils of convention. As it turned out for Shaw, burying the past would prove far more laborious than Trefusis's bungled tombstone negotiations.

In accounting for his self-exile, the former cashier and erstwhile coward used the metaphors of economics and war. Feeling himself a slave, believing that his "business in life could not be transacted in Dublin," a place "of failure, of poverty, of obscurity" and of "ostracism and contempt," George "broke loose" and headed for London: "For London as London, or England as England, I cared nothing. If my subject had been science or music I should have made for Berlin or Leipsic. If painting, I should have made for Paris. . . . But as the English language was my weapon, there was nothing for it but London."[19]

After the score-long sojourn by the banks of the River Liffey, after the thousands of hours perched on an office stool, after the piano playing, the opera tutoring, the gallery trekking, the daily walks, the schools, the houses, the talk, the pain, Shaw set himself against the fate that gripped him. The promise of spring beckoned as he sailed for London, following his earlier Anglo-Irish countrymen Sheridan, Swift, and Goldsmith. His only baggage of note was indignant shame, a rapier wit, and the English language. It was the arsenal of a superman.

PART II

The Great Stage of London

Men certainly develop during their whole life
on certain lines. Listen to Beethoven's Septet
for wind instruments and then to his Ninth
Symphony, and all discussion on the point becomes absurd.
—Shaw to St. John Ervine, 1921

The Complete Outsider

> I daily pulled the threads of the puppet who
> represented me. . . . My natural character
> was impossible on the great stage of London.
> —Preface to *Immaturity*

Like the literary and mythological heroes of Sonny's boyhood, all of them ready to risk everything as they heeded the call of adventure, Shaw crossed the Irish Sea, seeking his destiny as world redeemer and Shakespearean heir. Passage across that narrow but treacherous body of water marked his movement into a radically different sphere of experience. To survive what he, like John Bunyan's hero Christian, called his nonage would require resilience, steadfastness, and adaptability. He moved from a country caught in the eighteenth century into the incongruity of late nineteenth-century London, that culturally splendid imperial throne atop a cesspool of squalor and misery. The extremes of privilege and poverty, freedom and entrapment, reinforced his impulse to polarize possibility. While Victorian London proved a far more inhospitable landscape than he had imagined, his journey inward presented an even more arduous challenge.

Ominously, Shaw's long-awaited reunion with his mother was effected in the wake of family tragedy. George Carr Shaw had been left resolutely behind—the son's literal flight from his father mirroring his psychological flight. Though he missed his sister's funeral, Shaw made his way to Ventnor.[1] In that seaside resort in the midst of the English Channel he found a grieving Bessie. For the first and last time her son witnessed in her the stirrings of maternal instinct, which aroused his own longings and fears. After a month's stay in Ventnor, Shaw took up residence in London with Bessie and Lucy, both of whom were trying to further their musical careers, his mother by teaching, his sister by singing in opéra bouffe.

Number 13 Victoria Grove was a semi-detached villa in a cul de sac off Brompton Road. It was countrified enough to boast garden and orchard space and pleasant enough for Arnold Bennett to set one of his novels there. Otherwise, life for the new emigrant was not auspicious. Living with two determined women, Shaw soon took on his father's role of disillusioned, ineffectual male. The reality of the strictures and anonymity he faced in England clashed radically with his hopes and aspirations in emigrating. In Dublin at least, he had the status of Townshend's respected firm to bolster him. Now he was one of the faceless unemployed. Though he was at last reunited with his mother, he found her unmoved by his presence. Writing to McNulty, fancy and bravado gilded a sense of fatefulness as he swore that his Dublin prospects had been "stupendous," his employer's daughter his for the asking, assuring him a partnership in the firm. "Strangely enough I am not in the least depressed, but elated, if anything, because it had to be."[2]

Whether her son's "notion hazy that mother thinks me crazy" was accurate, Bessie let him stay. Like a tolerated spinster aunt, he would contribute virtually nothing to the family coffers during the next nine years. Instead, the three lived on the proceeds of the Whitcroft legacy, the pound a week George Carr Shaw conscientiously sent from his scant resources, and the slender musical earnings of mother and daughter, Lucy even eking out a little by her pen as well. While Lucy haughtily defied traditional female roles, her brother's role reversal at her expense enraged her. She accused him of being a parasite, and later Shaw admitted that it was "monstrous" that he, "ablebodied and ableminded," had stayed home and let his family support him. In a culture that equated manliness with money, Shaw was unmanly from the day he arrived on England's shores.[3]

Prodded by introductions from Aunt Georgina Shaw (Uncle Frederick's wife) and from Lee, who was living nearby, Shaw made some desultory attempts to job hunt during his first spring in London, all "without result." "Unoccupied," he fought anxiety by visiting the National Gallery and roaming the city, spending his time much as he might have in Dublin.[4] But here he was trying to map out his territory, to establish a sense of place in a city that struck him as alien. Arriving in London, carpetbag in hand, he had been jarred by the cacophony that greeted him and was scarcely able to hail a cab amid the shower of Cockney. He was a stranger in a strange land and, most terrifying of all, rendered incommunicado.

London in the 1870s was daunting to newcomers, with its badly marked streets bearing unmarked buses. The underground railway, opened in 1863, discouraged intimate knowledge of the city, for the traveler navigated by place names, not by recognizing buildings, parks, or other landmarks. Because the language of the city had to be mastered before the city itself could be deciphered, Shaw felt distanced from it. Outside society, politics, sport, and the church, he was the "Complete Outsider."[5]

By September, desperate and disillusioned, he began studying to become a clerk of the Excise. But he soon dropped out of the course, forfeiting tuition he could ill afford to lose. This spared him the ignominy of starting over in a despised profession alongside younger men. Then there was the examination itself. Like the fictional Smith, who feared "idiotic questions," he objected on moral grounds to submitting his "merits to a false test." Shaw's salvation from clerkdom came in a peculiar form and from a peculiar quarter, allowing him to forget about mundane employment for a while. He was offered the chance to write musical criticism for a satirical paper as a "ghost for a musician."[6]

However shakily or ingloriously, the writing career of the Complete Outsider was launched.

A Ghost's Revenge

The musician whose pen-identity Shaw secretly assumed was the man who had wielded continuing power over him, first by his presence, then by his absence: none other than Lee. Just as Shaw emigrated because there was "nothing for it but London," for Lee there was no success "except a London success." Keenly conscious of the importance of the proper address, Lee was living in a narrow but fashionable house on swanky Park Lane. He used only the bedroom and the large music room, renting the rest of the rooms to lodgers who could afford the high rent he needed. Although this requirement excluded Bessie and Lucy, Lee came and went at 13 Victoria Grove "very much in his old fashion, except that he did not sleep there." Shaw claimed that he was "as much a matter of course to us as the hatstand."[7]

But Lee was no hatstand. By the time of Shaw's arrival, Lee had insisted that Lucy be the principal singer in his musical society, the Troubadours, the role Bessie had filled for him in Dublin. He had also tried to force his attentions on Lucy. "Lee and I are bitter enemies now; we are frostily civil to each other's faces, and horribly abusive behind backs," Lucy had written her brother in Dublin.[8] Even so, the old charisma of the man and his music was still compelling in the Shaw household, and Bessie went back and forth to 13 Park Lane, helping to host musical performances there. Now Shaw, forced to witness Lee's self-aggrandizement, found himself as superfluous as his father had been.

Why then would Shaw consent to becoming Lee's ghost, not to mention his publicist? Although Shaw needed a job, this one was hardly ideal: ghosts remain invisible. He complained that his reviews appeared with misprints and mutilations—a trumped-up complaint, according to Dan H. Laurence, who examined those reviews. After half a century of hiding yet another "guilty secret," Shaw revealed that the newspaper he had written for was *The Hornet*. What he did not reveal was the real source of the guilty secret. It was not that he was a ghost for *The Hornet* but that he had assumed the guise of Lee.[9]

Undercover as himself—the invisible outsider—Shaw became a "pseudo-Lee."[10] Seated anonymously beside Lee in the London concert halls, Shaw seemed to have resumed his old obeisance. But now the two men were bonded in conspiratorial impersonation. All the glamour and sensation surrounding those London premieres struck a chord, because it was with Lee that Sonny had attended those first thrilling operas. Also recalled were Lee's feats in Dublin's Antient Concert Rooms where, taking centerstage, the masterful conductor drew forth exquisitely pure melody from Sonny's harsh, withholding mother.

Ironically, as he began the coveted task of forging his identity through his pen, Shaw submerged himself in Lee's world. A devotee of the Method, Shaw knew that he could never vanquish Lee the consummate musician unless he could redefine the terms of combat. "I could make deaf stockbrokers read my two pages on music," he would claim of his later stint writing musical criticism for *The World*, "the alleged joke being that I knew nothing about it. The real joke was that I knew all about it." Of his experience with *The Hornet*, the alleged joke was that Lee was perpetrating the hoax. The real joke was that Shaw was the perpetrator. Even though the reviews were unsigned, he claimed to make Lee into "one of the most unpopular men in London," implying that he had reversed his role in the relationship from passive to active.[11]

Rebelling against the status quo as well, the neophyte determined to reform the music profession, assuming the stance with astonishing speed. In his first buzzing as a ghost apprentice in November 1876, he declared that Sir Frederic Cowen's new opera *Pauline* betrayed "weakness, which sometimes verges on absurdity." The following week, reviewing a performance of *Faust*, he deplored M. Ludwig's affectation of "delivering the words with a strong foreign inflexion." This was followed by a stinging review of Franz Liszt's *Mazeppa*, which the charlatan music critic—masquerading as *another* charlatan—exposed as "false art, due to the conception, not of a true musician, but of a charlatan." In May, somewhat grudgingly, the reviewer found Lee's Troubadours to have "satisfactorily executed" their program of Italian opera. As Shaw refashioned the passive and invisible role of ghost, he asserted himself so strongly that Lee bore the brunt of Shaw's aggressiveness. *The Hornet* critic regretfully reported that the paper had gotten "some grievous knocks" because of its unreasonable honesty in musical criticism.[12]

Almost two decades later Shaw would paint his ghostwriting experience in lurid colors, claiming he did not understand that what was "torturing" him at the time was the "guilt and shame" of "ignorance and incompetence": "The paper, with my assistance, died, and my sins are buried with it; but I still keep, in a safe hiding place, a set of the critical crimes I contributed to it, much as a murderer keeps the bloodstained knife under which his victim fell."[13] The purple prose of staged confession deflects from the truth. He saved the old reviews because they documented his assumption of Lee's role—the old Lee, who reigned supreme in Dublin and who was Shaw's targeted victim. The pseudo-son who preferred to imagine himself a foundling plunged the dagger into the pseudo-father whose place he had come to claim. It was but the first in a series of symbolic castrations that Shaw would manage with the pen, a phallic enough instrument.

As far as *The Hornet* went, Shaw's prose was not nearly that deadly. *The Hornet* kept stinging until February 1880, well beyond Shaw's final contribution, on 26 September

1877—advice on how a vocalist, especially a female, could achieve popularity "without taste, culture, or voice." Apparently the editor, one Captain Donald Shaw (unrelated to the ghost), had discovered how a music critic could achieve popularity without writing. Believing, oddly enough, that he had detected the "composition, idea and writing of a Lady," Captain Shaw put an end to the masquerade.[14]

To court the gushing London ladies who wanted to sing like prima donnas after only a few lessons, Lee had to betray the Method and change his name, wrote Shaw, who conveniently forgot the Dublin name changes. Now, sporting a waxed and pointed moustache and exuding an "obsequious attitude," Lee was "no longer the same man."[15] Shaw would drop his first name, as Lee had, and would grow a pointed moustache. But Shaw would add the whiskers and cultivate arrogance, signifiers of the old Lee, who had marked Sonny's psyche as surely as he had marked his face with cork. And Shaw knew all too well that his deaf stockbrokers were all too similar to Lee's gushing London ladies. He would apply almost the identical terms he directed at Lee—charlatan and humbug—to the fabricated GBS image.

Adding to the discomfort Shaw felt over Lee's degenerative use of the Method was his own complicity in his fallen idol's charade. Shaw was Lee's accompanist at rehearsals of the Troubadours, and he came to be regarded "as in some sense responsible for Lee's proceedings." By the end, Shaw had assumed the role of maestro, for Lee had lost his musicians' respect after he became enmeshed with his young housemaid, who, badly made-up, scandalously intruded on the musical evenings. Shaw insisted, however, that Lee's fall into "sexual sentimentality" was a "new thing."[16]

Blaming Lee for unethically using the Method also deflected attention from Shaw's personal relationship with Lee. According to her son, Bessie never forgave Lee for his musical charlatanism, and the only thing about him that ever provoked her was a misuse of musical technique. With "great difficulty," Shaw had coerced her into giving him a few lessons in the Method.[17] When Lee then assigned Shaw to sing tenor rather than his natural baritone, she allegedly became enraged. But perhaps it was Shaw himself, the sometime soprano, who became enraged at having his voice forced by Lee into an unnaturally high range.

Finished with Lee, Bessie, who thought nothing of putting her name to someone else's musical composition, now appropriated the Method and established herself as an independent voice teacher. Though life will go on as before for the fictional Henry Higgins, another voice teacher forsaken by another Elizabeth, Lee's fortunes, headed downward since their Dublin apex, continued to fall. The elegant music room once dedicated to Mozart and Verdi became a private nightclub of suspect character. But Shaw continued his allegiance to Lee, even writing a circular claiming that Lee could cure clergyman's sore throat.

Ironically, Shaw, still the pseudo-Lee, began ghostwriting a new version of *The Voice*, the document that represented the quintessence of Lee, the title itself representing Shaw's function to Lee. At age 91, Shaw would insist that "I dramatized myself as Lee, not very successfully, as the impersonation was false and foreign to my nature." Certainly, even a brief comparison of the original with the second version shows the revision to be unmistakably Shavian. It was not dramatization but self-dramatization. While Lee's 1870 ghost, the "scamp of a derelict doctor," punctuated his treatise with the rhapsodizing "Wonderful power! beautiful and strong! How unfathomable are thy ways!" Shaw compared Mozart with Molière and Dickens, calling Mozart "not only a born musician, but a born dramatist."[18]

Apart from the perceptive criticism, the comments of the struggling writer suggest a wishful identity with Mozart. For Mozart proved himself despite being fettered by his fastidious taste. Shaw concluded that "not one abnormally developed faculty, but an extraordinary assemblage of faculties entered into the composite genius of Mozart—the universal Mozart."[19] Shaw penned this accolade to Mozart while impersonating Lee, who once seemed to Shaw to embody a Mozartian genius. Shaw wanted to link his genius with Mozart, the musician he claimed as spiritual father, and not with Lee, the musician he both dreaded to claim as biological father and wished to claim.

In drama as in life, Shaw would pursue disembodiment through literary techniques and staged scenarios, exorcising the guilt and shame that followed him from Dublin. The protective armor of disembodiment exacted a price, setting him adrift without a sheltering space. Instead of rooting himself in his adopted land, the sojourning Shaw floated unanchored, extravagant creations his only ballast. Homesick for the "broad fields and delicate airs of France," the Swedish lakes and Norwegian fiords where he had been only in imagination, he made of himself both a fatherless and a "fatherlandless fellow" as he deserted George Carr Shaw and triumphed over Lee. Shaw quickly learned that acting in his own character was impossible on the great stage of London. His challenge was to transform the Complete Outsider into the Complete Insider. Although it was not yet true, he set out to convince London that, with the arts, "it was I who was the Insider."[20] The second strategy, like the first, was designed to demonstrate his superiority over the false father and over the social world. It was to out-humbug Lee, a fateful decision for the life history. The artist as insider was possible, but the humbug made the man as insider impossible.

The defiance that had been present in his boyhood grew increasingly established as a basic structure of his existence. From the first, Shaw struggled subversively but actively as the Complete Outsider. In the world of his fellow human beings the *Hornet* critic took pleasure in covertly and defiantly stinging the music profession. At the same time, from the vantage point of his inner, private world, the outsider disguised himself as a false Lee and reveled in being false to Lee. In the natural world he was the uneasy sojourner stained with guilt and shame, longing for imagined vistas; in this mode of existence as well, he would choose stealth and defiance. Rather than opening himself to life, he was eternally locked in opposition to it, so that his existence bore the marks of rigidity, inflexibility, willfulness. Given such leaden manacles, how did he spin out that golden web of comedy? How did he triumph over his very self?

7

Passion's Progress

The more I try to solve it
The more perplexed my future fate appears.
—Jesus, *Passion Play*

With the loss of the *Hornet* column in October 1877, Shaw's brief career as an employed writer ended. It was a blow not to see his pieces in print any longer and to have it underscored that *The Hornet* had purchased Lee's reputation and not Shaw's essays. Weighed down by dashed hopes, Shaw slept away the next two months. Bessie's charges of procrastination were the nagging echo of his own self-accusations. To counter them, he rushed about as if trying to make up for lost time. Within a few years Shaw's frenetic schedule would be a wonder, forcing even dubious observers to praise his energy. Yet the combination of dawdling with a drivenness to defeat time marked more than the activist making the most of life. They indicated a temporality unable to accommodate quiet contemplation, a temporality with an uneasy relation to the future and the realm of Becoming. When in December Lee arranged an introduction at the East India Docks, the roused Shaw dutifully went for the interview, but it came to nothing. A terse memorandum for the month sums up his state of mind: "Not worth anything." Later Shaw thought he had been lamed by the lack of a religious theory of life.[1]

Reclusive by day, Shaw became a creature of the night. Like the fictional Robert Smith, he might wander about Kensington Gardens until nine and then walk toward the theater district surrounding Leicester Square. The cheapest ticket to the Alhambra music hall allowed him admission but no seat. Notorious for staging ballets meant to display the charms of the dancers, the Alhambra was known as a wicked place. Well into the twentieth century, the back of the circle would be recognized as a meeting ground for homosexuals, just as the Promenade section of the Empire music hall was lined with gorgeously dressed prostitutes. The huge circular Alhambra was filled with a milling, drinking crowd, and the air was hot and heavy with the odors of cigar smoke and gas lamps. It was to go up in flames one December night in 1882, then be rebuilt. Shaw the pyromaniac would watch the old Alhambra "burn gloriously."[2]

The split between daytime and nighttime personalities paralleled the split between Shaw's private self-abasement and the pose of the all-knowing literary persona he had forged for *The Hornet*. He continued to refine this persona while his secret self surfaced in his continuing compulsion to satirize organized religion. The satiric view undoubtedly owed something to George Carr Shaw's jocular assurance that the Bible was the "damnd-est parcel of lies ever written." And Uncle Walter had thrilled Sonny with an elaborate "Rabelaisian repartee" that supposedly passed between King Darius and Daniel in the lion's den.[3] Even poor Uncle Barney, the carpetbag suicide, kept his Bible firmly on his knees when spying on the women's bathing beach in Dalkey through an opera glass. In 1877, when Shaw considered writing "An Essay on Repartee, by Jesus Christ," he showed the family influence, the hold of Scripture on his imagination—and a certain comforting hubris.

In February 1878 he began *Household of Joseph,* a blank verse drama usually referred to as *Passion Play.* Shaw encoded his own passion in the play that he abandoned after a few weeks. But in startling clarity in this early fragment are images that reveal his interior world. It is a strangely romantic world whose underside is vulgar and domestic rather than evil and exotic. Present in embryonic form is Creative Evolution, the cornerstone of Shaw's mature thought. Jesus dreams of universal brotherhood, and Judas is a Faustian philosopher who trusts in a future in which knowledge conquers death. The dialectic between Judas and Jesus dramatizes Shaw's polarized world and shows his early inclina-tion to use long speeches and anachronism.

The apostate Shaw created his own version of the Bible story, but he avoided dealing with its most familiar parts—the birth, the teachings, and the crucifixion. Instead, Shaw sketched the adolescent Jesus at home, then moved behind the scenes for an unmasking, which would become a staple of his drama. Despite the title, Joseph is a minor character in his own home. He is a drunk and Mary is a shrew, as the blasphemous Shaw strips the household of dignity as well as sanctity.

As he transformed the one household he knew into an image of the holiest of families, Shaw suggests a self-portrait. John spies on his brother and reports that, instead of working, Jesus spends his time lying on his back in the stubble fields poeticizing. If the language is indebted to Keats's *To Autumn,* the autobiographical debt is even greater. Jesus, full of "mirthful rage" and longing to be a "son of fire and air," resembles the fantasizing Sonny cradled by Torca Hill. Jesus bemoans his illegitimate birth, derides himself for his ignorance, and hates being a mediocre tradesman like his father. The autobiographical parallels carry over to the figure of Judas as well, as Shaw splits, then mixes, the messianic with the diabolic. For Judas defines his plight exactly as Shaw described his plight during this period—as a "wanderer" and "sojourner." Similarly, Judas is torn between the "beastly world" and an "ethereal" and "sublime" realm of beauty.[4]

In characterizing women, Shaw paints a dark picture. Judas thinks that no woman can stand the "test of intimacy," instructing Jesus that the divine qualities he attributes to women are his own, a theme to be most eloquently expressed by Don Juan in *Man and Superman*. Mary, the worst of mothers, calls Jesus an "ingrate" and the "worst of sons," berating him for his idleness. Joseph thinks "carrion birds" kinder than his wife, and when she strikes him, he beats her but does not best her. She is a mother who would refuse dinner to her starving son, whom she calls a pig. When Jesus compares Mary's care to that of a "leopard for her whelp," and Mary calls Joseph a dog, the imagery dramatizes Shaw's view of his own family kenneled in an animal world.[5] Here begins the literary use of degraded animal imagery that would peak three decades later in *Heartbreak House* and continue unabated through *Buoyant Billions*, his last full-length play (1947). Moreover, the fable form suggested here would become Shaw's preferred form during his last three decades.

Provocatively for the life history, Shaw had begun charting his profound unease with the world. His Jesus swears he will not mourn Mary's death, and he finally deserts her. Having reversed the sequence in his own life—he was deserted by Bessie—Shaw lost interest in his narrative. Soon after, in the middle of act 2, the text breaks off. Although it had been more than a year and a half since he had been reunited with Bessie, his anger over his motherless Dublin years had not abated. By modeling the character of the unrecognized Christ after himself, Shaw revealed his own deep-seated wish to be identified as a savior-son and his parallel wish to punish Bessie for her neglect. The latter wish prompted enough guilt for Shaw to identify with Judas, the archetypal figure of betrayal. Though both Jesus and Judas are attracted to an ethereal realm, Shaw emphasized Jesus's flight from the vulgar, earthy Mary, just as he fled from any suggestion that there was anything vulgar about Bessie.

Later, Shaw would have it that Jesus was a socialist, making him over into his own image, and, chameleonlike, life would imitate art. In his middle years Shaw reported the compliment on his "strong resemblance to Jesus Christ." The great French sculptor Auguste Rodin exalted this likeness, calling it a true head of Christ, startling his secretary, who thought Shaw's photographs revealed sardonic features. Somewhat different corroboration was provided by Geraldine Spooner, a flirtation of Shaw's in the late 1880s, who described him as a "strange and very wonderful looking man, tall and thin as a whipping post, with a massive head. . . . one side of his face was Christ-like, although the other was Mephistophelian."[6] The second half of Geraldine Spooner's assessment was shared by more observers than the first. Shaw himself liked to insist that his visage was the very mirror of Mephistopheles.

Pygmalion's Power

Considerably less grandiose than Christ is the persona Shaw created virtually in concert with *Passion Play* during January and February 1878. *My Dear Dorothea: A Practical*

System of Moral Education for Females Embodied in a Letter to a Young Person of that Sex is a fictional letter to a five-year-old. This tiny moral treatise is chock-full of the sharp-edged fragments of mature themes. Biblical-sounding admonitions abound, but they urge Dorothea to be as selfish as she can. The Golden Rule is quoted only to be inverted. A quarter of a century later, an inverted Golden Rule appears as the very first maxim in "The Revolutionist's Handbook," appended to *Man and Superman.*

Shaw's persona in *My Dear Dorothea* is that of a wise and kind iconoclast ingratiating himself to his fictional charge. For the unemployed and dissatisfied Shaw relished the opportunity to issue his own rules—rules counter to prevailing mores—even as he warned Dorothea against taking advice. In creating a young female to instruct, Shaw gratified an ever more urgent need to dispense advice. Especially with women, he became a Victorian Ann Landers. But unlike Ann Landers, he never waited to be asked for his help.

The highly autobiographical treatise reworks memories even earlier than those in *Passion Play,* memories presumably stirred up in the writing of his religious drama. Ignoring her father, Shaw assures Dorothea that her mother thinks of her only as a "troublesome and inquisitive little creature." In advising Dorothea to hate her mother and to lie to her, Shaw subverted not only child-raising advice but also the reigning literary genre. The most famous example, Lord Chesterfield's *Letters to His Son,* then a century old, was a guide to the art of pleasing and worldly success. But Shaw, unsure of his place in society, identified with a young female rather than with a young male.[7] He had begun to play with gender roles in his female creations.

If *My Dear Dorothea* revealed only this much, it would offer an enlightening glimpse into those secretive first years in England and into how Shaw channeled his creative energy. But it is even more suggestive. The letter opens with the author, who had answered to the name Sonny for half his life, making a point that the little girl is Dorothea, not Dolly, the diminutive at odds with her ambition. She is closely supervised by her Aunt Tabitha, who tries to improve her by giving her tracts to read. Though reading would be something of a feat for most five-year-olds, it was easy for Sonny, the born reader. Nor would it be unreasonable for a nine-year-old—Bessie's age when first subjected to Aunt Ellen's program of virtuous improvement. The highly ambitious Bessie was known by the diminutive of her given name, Elizabeth, reversing what Shaw considered appropriate. Psychology teaches that the psyche often works by reversal. Shaw's insistence on a proper name for Dorothea shows him identifying not only with a young female, but also with Bessie, whose proper name was not used by family or friends.

Clearly implied throughout is a father-daughter relationship. Remaking Bessie into a very young girl, the author exchanges places with his own mother. He makes himself into the wise and affectionate parent of his longings, and, not incidentally, cuts Bessie down to size. The Pygmalion-Galatea theme, the artist fashioning the woman of his dreams, would figure prominently in the life and the art. Here, in a single cryptic footnote appended to the document, we can follow the thread back to its psychic origin: "'There is a way that seemeth right unto a man, but the end thereof are the ways of death.' Proverbs xvi:32; xiv:12. This cuts both ways."[8] As Shaw relentlessly sought the right way, the tensions and inversions intimated in *My Dear Dorothea* ran through his life. What provided the artist with fresh perspectives would wreak havoc on his encounters with women. It cut both ways.

Placed together, *Passion Play* and *My Dear Dorothea* form a kind of palimpsest, the partially visible tracings of one work intermingling with those of the other. In both, home is something to survive and escape, and grown women wield dangerous power. Whether a suffering Christ or a wise counselor, the Shaw surrogates are morally and intellectually superior, like characters in the new *Pilgrim's Progress* he longed to write. From the very first, the defiant and restless Shaw cloaked his private grievances with the mantle of higher social concerns. Too easily influenced by the world, he was excessively concerned with exerting his influence. Nor would Shaw disown the "priggish conscientiousness" of his early efforts, the early stages of a literary destiny that proved that "like Goethe, I knew all along."[9]

So all the while he lived at home and looked out on the gardens of Victoria Grove he was reliving the offenses and resentments of Dublin and Dalkey, weaving them into a deceptive scenario of his own making, the backdrop to a private drama of punishment and purgation, atonement and flight.

Life Among the Artists

There were many other rooms surrounding
the hall: painted, panelled, padded, tapestried,
blue, green, and gold rooms; with peacocks,
flamingoes, jays, and other gorgeous birds
depicted on the walls. Bowls, plates,
candlesticks, statuettes, and etchings were
everywhere.
—*Immaturity*

However conscientious, Shaw's early writings garnered little respect from possible publishers, for the superhuman self-confidence exuded by the literary personae were not matched by the author's. He submitted a short story, "The Brand of Cain," with the disclaimer that it was "altogether grotesque" and "too preposterous to be worth publishing." After the fourth rejection of *Immaturity*, he wrote the rejecting publisher to feel free to throw his book into the fire if he thought it a service to the author.[1]

Shaw's "maiden novel," the result of five months' labor in 1879, would not be published until 1930. Opening the old parcel a half-century later was "like opening a grave." Entombed in the fine script of the ex-clerk's hand were the hopes of the youthful Shaw. Originally the novel was titled *A Quadrille* because the two heroes and heroines change partners.[2] The quadrille, a modified court dance imported from Paris by English aristocrats, requires prescribed patterns of movement. Through its adherence to rules and appropriate deportment, the dance reinforces the social standards of those in power. The discarded title suggests Shaw's interest in the socially correct, an interest he never relinquished, despite his iconoclasm.

In *Immaturity*, the dissatisfied but conscientious Robert Smith leads a mostly solitary life, without parents, relatives, or close friends. A diffident youth of eighteen, he is attracted to an apprentice dressmaker, to whom he teaches French, and to an exotic dancer in the Alhambra music hall. But Smith learns that appearances deceive. While the prosaic dressmaker Harriet fascinates the artist Cyril Scott and his set, Smith is falsely led to believe that his "Southern Passion Flower" of the music hall is a forty-three-year-old Englishwoman who is respectably married and the mother of four. Actually, Erminia Pertoldi is twenty-eight, Trieste-born, and devoted to her craft. The narrator notes that the "chief objection to fictitious romance is that it is seldom so romantic as the truth."[3]

As it traces Smith's chaste amorous adventures, the novel includes a peculiar passage. At an Underground station Smith bids Harriet good-bye, uncertain whether they will meet again or whether it matters. He feels anew the "romantic delusion" of her "occult charm." Then, as Smith strolls away, he notices the "grime of the station" and wonders "how long it would take a single man to clean it." Worrying that the thought might recur in a nightmare, and wanting to think about Harriet, he thinks of "nothing else than giddily swinging on a ladder among the sooty girders, trying to clean them with a towel and a small basin of water."[4] The occult charm casts a sexual spell over the entire passage—the train snaking outward, the dirty underground cavity, the rising ladder, the giddy swinging. Beyond sexual attraction and repulsion, the passage suggests the danger of the depths. Here Shaw makes his first literary association between female sexuality and personal threat and revulsion, an association that would prove personally prophetic.

Also prophetic is Smith's instinct. When threatened with falling, he demolishes his former view of Harriet. Earlier she had evoked a "real harvest field, full of fresh air, noisy birds, and sunshine," in contrast with Erminia, who danced amid a "vile-smelling midnight vision of gilt sheaves, painted skies, and electric radiance."[5] Now Harriet becomes part of the nightmare world. In the polarized worlds of Shaw's life and art, one pole equaled its opposite, just as in Dalkey there had been the ironic contrast between those majestic skies that nurtured romantic fantasy, and the emotionless woman and his dark fears.

Meanwhile, Shaw knew how to wait for literary success, but he did not know how to "live on air in the interim." Only a few days after completing *Immaturity*, his cousin Mrs. Cashel Hoey, a popular novelist and the wife of the agent general for Victoria, introduced him to Arnold White, the manager of the Edison Telephone Company. Despite his desperate financial situation, Shaw was more ambivalent than enthusiastic over his cousin's concern and the chance for a job. His letter of application to White offered that he "might not be the right man." To distinguish himself from other applicants, Shaw noted that a former job interviewer thought him a lunatic.[6]

In spite of himself, Shaw got a job collecting way-leaves—trying to persuade East London residents to let the company put telephone poles on their roofs. It was a "most distasteful occupation" that exposed him to the rebuffs of "worried women." Working on commission, he resigned after six weeks, having gotten one permission and seen no money. Shaw's letter of resignation was rewarded with a salary, then, in February, a promotion. As the only Edison employee who knew the scientific explanation for the telephone, he became manager of the way-leave department.[7]

In a crowded basement office on Queen Victoria Street, Shaw marveled at the "ferocious energy" of the "skilled proletariat of the United States." Those workers, given to singing sentimental songs, had crossed the Atlantic because they adored Edison and reviled Alexander Graham Bell, dastardly inventor of a rival telephone. Much as he appreciated their good cheer, Shaw found his chief delight in sitting in for the official lecturer and demonstrating Edison's invention. That phone was a machine of such deafening tones that unsuspecting visitors thought that someone with a speaker-trumpet must be concealed nearby. The incredulous auditors, uncertain whether such a demonstration deserved a gratuity, always erred on the side of prudence. Shaw never got a single tip.

In spite of the romantic fervor of the singing Americans, Edison Telephone merged with its English rival just seven months after Shaw's promotion. He had quarreled with White and was "sick of telephoning," and on 5 June 1880 Shaw left the phone company. He celebrated the occasion by beginning *The Irrational Knot,* his second novel, on the same day.[8]

Shaw did not bother to seek work for more than a year. Then, egged on by his family, he sporadically and half-heartedly answered newspaper advertisements and briefly considered emigrating to America. But he had no interest in mundane employment. Later he boasted: "I did not throw myself into the struggle for life: I threw my mother into it. I was not a staff to my father's old age: I hung on to his coat tails." Supposedly George Carr Shaw's reward was to live long enough to see one of his son's novels reviewed. Regardless of whether it was a "handsome reward," it was his only reward. Whatever guilt Shaw felt about relying on his father's meager resources, he acknowledged no guilt toward Bessie. Instead, he gloried in his pose of the selfish artist leaning on a capable woman. His "one line of progress" was literary, and he called himself nothing less than a "vessel of the Zeitgeist."[9]

Shaw's experience at the phone company and his fascination with such men of science as Chichester Bell emerged in *The Irrational Knot.* His hero, Edward Conolly, is an electrical engineer and inventor. As an Irish-American, Conolly is an outsider, but he moves freely in society because of his musical ability. The novel reflects Shaw's entrée into an otherwise closed segment of society by virtue of his ability to play piano accompaniment "congenially," if not well. It also reflects his distrust of the sentimental—the irrational knot of the title is the matrimonial knot. In calling the novel an "early attempt on the part of the Life Force to write A Doll's House in English," he meant to counter charges of having been influenced by Ibsen.[10]

Shaw creates recognizably Shavian characters in the controlled Conolly and his wife, Marian. The pregnant Marian has had a romance, left her husband, and, at novel's end, refuses to return even after he tells her that she may "have ten love romances every year with other men. . . . Be anything rather than a ladylike slave and liar." Marian's determination to remain independent is fueled by the death of Conolly's sister, Susanna, from the ravages of alcohol. An actress in musical theater who has made a name for herself as the seductive Lalage Virtue, Susanna resembles Shaw's own sister, already seen as Primrose in the pantomime *Beauty and the Beast*.[11] Susanna dies in a cheap boarding-house in New York City, but Lucy's star was rising.

At the time he wrote *The Irrational Knot,* Shaw was not part of the world he described. His peripheral position was represented by his attire. Shabby morning clothes transformed the seemingly gregarious man of the evening into a retiring creature. During this period Shaw tried to expand his intellectual and social horizons, but he suffered from extreme shyness, sometimes needing a good walk to work up the courage to present himself as a guest. Once on the scene, he compensated for his shyness by becoming insufferable. The drawing room was at once too small and too large a stage—too small because it did not allow him to draw on the fantasy that sustained his dreams but too large because its unforgiving space exposed his social failings. It would take almost two decades, but Shaw would redesign the drawing room into a glittering theatrical showcase where he had all the lines, all the wit, all the adoration.

Shaw learned to act the part appropriate to the well-born and moneyed classes. He gathered all the books of etiquette that he could find at the British Museum and studied their elaborate rules of arcane conduct like a script, including minute prescriptions, such as the precise number of cards to leave when calling on a married woman. But he was plagued by more than inadequate training in manners. For he had carried with him from Dublin the legacy of body shame that had haunted his boyhood, and he thought few men could have suffered more than he from "simple cowardice" or have been "more horribly ashamed of it."[12] Faced with the unbearable flippancy of young men and the pain of being compared with more successful men his own age, he retreated into a solitude that he remembered as lasting eight years. In reality, it lasted no more than three, his false memory underlining the way time dragged in those early London years and the constrictiveness of his world. Shaw would soon spread himself out, charting an ever-widening social arena for himself, even as he maintained a tiny private living space. The social arena would be the stage for the manufactured image so that a dialectic would remain—between the constriction of his private world and the expansiveness of his social world, between his concealing shame and his manic exhibitionism.

The Sweet Taint of the Salon

To get the attention of Victorian London was no easy matter. Entrenched convention and social routine made it virtually impervious to the struggles of an unknown outsider. Shaw's relative position, no less than his actual hardships, were galling. A case in point was Henry James, another writer and immigrant to England, whose terms of residence corresponded at times to Shaw's. His engagement book recorded that he dined out with the influential and important 140 times during the 1878 to 1879 social season. While the

Irishman walked the streets in disintegrating boots, the American visited private clubs to sip tea and nibble buttered toast presented by liveried lackeys. During one social evening James met Shaw's cousin Mrs. Cashel Hoey, a "curious and interesting specimen of the wondrous type—the London female literary hack." In evaluating his most literary relation, who wrote such works as *A House of Cards, Falsely True,* and *A Golden Sorrow,* Shaw concurred with James in almost identical language, suggesting that he had read James's assessment. He called his cousin a "first-rate literary hack: one of the great Victorian specimens of those indefatigable maids-of-all-work of literature." Again, in what seems to be more than linguistic coincidence, the already celebrated American writer called himself a "complete outsider" long before Shaw applied that term to himself.[13]

Though Shaw's "diary" entries for 1879 to 1880 are spare, summing up a month's activities in a sentence or two, they reveal how important new acquaintances were to him. In fact, the diary is largely a list of the people he met, such as J. Kingston Barton, a physician at whose home Shaw regularly spent Saturday evenings, and Pakenham Beatty, a minor poet and an amateur pugilist. At the home of Chichester Bell he met Bell's father, Alexander Bell, author of the *Standard Elocutionist.* The senior Bell had been a professor at Shaw's old school, the Wesleyan Connexional, and perhaps for that reason Shaw judged him to be "by far the most majestic and imposing man that ever lived on this or any other planet." Aileen Bell, Chichester's sister, was one of many young women who came to think that Shaw sought her hand in matrimony.[14]

At Bell's he met the clerk and phonetician James Lecky, who grounded Shaw in "Temperament," systems of tuning keyed instruments. Shaw then claimed to be "probably the only living musical critic" to know what the term meant. At Lecky's, Shaw met Richard Deck, an Alsatian basso profundo opera singer. Deck, who thought he had discovered a method of bel canto capable of producing song so beautiful that it would regenerate civilization, taught Shaw how to articulate his consonants explosively. Through Lecky, Shaw met the philologists Alexander J. Ellis and Henry Sweet, who fostered his interest in spelling reform and his ensuing battle for a new English alphabet. The latter's character, deficient in sweetness, can be glimpsed in Henry Higgins.[15]

Through Lucy, Shaw met Lady Wilde, lately arrived from Dublin, where the Wildes were of higher social status than the Shaws. Sir William Wilde reputedly knew more about surgery of the eye and ear than anyone in Ireland. Lady Wilde wrote under the pen name Speranza and presided over an extravagant salon on Park Street on Wednesday and Saturday afternoons. She was tall—just under six feet—and bulky, and she mounted huge headdresses on her black wig and dressed variously in white robes, purple brocade, train-dresses of silver-gray satin, or outdated scarlet costumes flounced and hung with great strings of beads, lace, and brooches. To conceal her age she conducted the afternoons behind heavy drawn curtains and in the forgiving illumination of candles and red-shaded gas jets. Among the long-haired artists and bejeweled women Lucy mingled easily, having made both Oscar and his older brother, Willie, into two of her many conquests. Shaw was less comfortable, chafing under the knowledge that everyone in attendance was famous or assumed to be nearly so. His diary records his meeting the popular novelist Mrs. Lynn Linton during his first afternoon.[16]

Oscar, less than two years Shaw's senior, was undeniably the chief attraction at the salon. He had advantages Shaw lacked—money, an Oxford education, acquaintance with the right people. (The Prince of Wales himself would seek an introduction: "I do not know Mr Wilde, and not to know Mr Wilde is not to be known.") At this time, the dandified Wilde took pleasure in dressing the part, delighting observers with a bronze coat that he had seen in a dream—it was cut to resemble a cello—or knee breeches and lace or clothes that were white from head to foot, accented with an ivory cane. When Wilde came over to introduce himself to the seedy looking and mortified Shaw, the gesture was doomed to failure. Shaw thought Wilde a snob, recalling that "we put each other out frightfully; and this odd difficulty persisted between us to the very last."[17]

Without a doubt, Wilde made Shaw feel uncomfortable, and the "odd difficulty" was based on more than aversion to Wilde's privilege. In his flamboyance, his self-advertisement, his wit, his fame, his literary skill, Wilde reflected what Shaw cultivated and coveted. He also resented Wilde's reputation as an apostle of art. He thought Wilde a "humbug" when he compared his own understanding of music and art with Wilde's. It was disturbing—that dandyism, that languid flesh, that supercilious extravagance, all flaunted as if to dare a charge of extreme aestheticism, in context virtually a euphemism for homosexuality.[18] Self-protectively, Shaw converted his own unease into a philosophic artistic difference.

Although he would revere William Morris and the cult of the beautifully useful, Shaw deplored the merely aesthetic and became a militant utilitarian. Battling the art for art's sake creed espoused by Wilde and the aesthetes, Shaw declared that great art can never be anything but didactic. His stand diverted attention from his own deep-seated aesthetic sensibility and the view that he shared with Wilde—but expressed differently—that the artist was a privileged creature. He saw Wilde "very seldom, as I avoided literary and artistic society like the plague." An uncanny mirror of what Shaw desired and loathed, Wilde himself was the plague to be avoided. Shaw's discomfort regarding Wilde extended to Walter Pater, Wilde's Oxford mentor, who glorified male friendship and who seemed to Shaw to take a "genteel walk up Parnassus." Later, however, Shaw would congratulate himself on his charity toward Wilde's notorious "perversion."[19]

Shaw would place the blame for Wilde's homosexuality on Lady Wilde—adored by *her* son. The incriminating clue lay in her large hands and hips. Consumed with curiosity, Shaw downplayed his interest, gleaning information, he said, from an encyclopedia. With no medical support for his theory, he diagnosed her as suffering from gigantism and somehow passing on to her son a hereditary taint. In dealing with Wilde's "weakness," which Shaw maintained was "pathological," Shaw concealed his own feelings behind those of others. He reminded Harris of the "disagreeable impression he made on you physically" and quoted Lady Colin Campbell, who described Wilde as "that great white caterpillar."[20] Connecting the son's sexuality with the mother allowed Shaw to attribute his own fastidious distaste for the fleshly to Bessie, the ever-stainless mother. It would take nothing less than self-creation to escape the sticky web of heredity and environment that held his own gender identification hostage.

The Wilde salon might have been the most outrageous, but it was not the only one Shaw attended. Bessie's musical activities included singing in the chorus of the Gluck Society, conducted by Malcolm Lawson. As a result, Shaw was invited to the Lawsons' Sunday evening salon in an elegant old house on Cheyne Walk in Chelsea. Shaw, a "dispiriting object in a drawing room," occasionally showed up. But he begged off an invitation from Elizabeth Lawson, Malcolm's mother, to attend a dance, on the grounds that "I could not accomplish a waltz for the sake of the most attractive partner you could offer me. . . . I should be an envious and gloomy wallflower."[21]

Unlike the stately quadrille, the waltz had scandalized the guardians of morality as it swept across Europe into the English court earlier in the century. The open eroticism of the public embrace, the galloping tempo of the dance, and the lush music of Johann Strauss, elder and younger, struck a Dionysian chord. Shaw's own unease at the waltz was related to its perceived erotic character. Moreover, it was danced under the scrutiny of spectators in little gilded chairs lining the dance area, spectators ever alert for missteps. Perhaps most daunting was that the waltz demanded strict role differentiation—the appearance of strength and dominance in the male, vulnerability and submissiveness in the female. In calling himself a wallflower, Shaw used a colloquial term that in 1880 was used to describe women. Henry James reflected conventional usage in *The Portrait of a Lady*, completed the following year. To Lord Warburton's "Are you not dancing?" Isabel Archer replies, "As you see, I'm a wall-flower."[22]

At Cheyne Walk, Shaw met Malcolm's brother Cecil, a well-known landscape painter and one of the models for the artist Cyril Scott in *Immaturity*. The other model was Shaw himself. Scott's posturing, conceit, and talent suggest the self-image Shaw was laboring to construct. Ready "to revenge himself on the world for its neglect of him," Scott had "both diffidence and self-confidence," and he divided women into various negative categories. The poet Hawkshaw articulates the tragedy of characters and author. As artists they are "unique and beyond class," but they all have middle-class relatives.[23]

Suffocated by the cloying sweetness of the salon, the budding artist now regularly sought out the more astringent air of the British Museum Reading Room, a good place to study Italian. It was also a favorite meeting place for young radicals of various dispositions, providing a comfortable spot to work. To that enormous circular space designed by Antonio Panizzi, Shaw brought the large sheets of cheap white paper he purchased for six pence and cut into quarto. There, physically encircled by books, spiritually encircled by the ghosts of the immortal dead, he served his apprenticeship under the great domed ceiling: "I steadily wrote my five pages a day and made a man of myself (at my mother's expense) instead of a slave." Though he had no master, the unemployed Shaw viewed England as a "slave state" where the slaves were so plentiful they could be gotten for nothing.[24] Wishing to eradicate his identification with the slaves, he would be unable to resist the magnetic power of dictators.

Writing, dreaming, longing, he was sustained by reading William Blake, that Romantic apostle of freedom and extravagant individualism, and his beloved Bunyan. These poets of the soul formed half of a mighty quartet whose "peculiar sense of the world" was similar to his own. The other half was composed of the eighteenth-century artist William Hogarth, whose famous series of engravings satirized British institutions so savagely in *A Harlot's Progress*, *The Rake's Progress*, and *Marriage à la Mode*. Completing the quartet was the great Romantic landscape painter J. M. W. Turner, whose fascination with the elements of fire and water can be seen in *Rockets and Blue Lights*, in the large sketch *A Fire at Sea*, and in the two pictures *Burning of the Houses of Parliament*. The pantheon swelled: Goethe, Nietzsche, Shelley, Schopenhauer, Wagner, Ibsen, Tolstoy, Morris all cast their spell. Specifically excluded were Dickens and Shakespeare, who were too concerned with the diversities of the world instead of its unities, though there were other more compelling reasons why Shaw refused to fall into Bardolatry.[25]

In October 1880 he applied through James Lecky for membership in the Zetetical Society, a debating club. Having a forum, Shaw let Richard Deck teach him how to speak intelligibly in public; then he forced himself to speak in every debate. Invited to chair a meeting, he could not keep his hand from shaking so violently as he signed the minutes that the secretary noticed.[26] Now Shaw's calendar overflowed as he raced from meeting to meeting, chasing literary, debating, and political societies of every description. In a striking development for the life, he actively sought to make a mark on the social world. Collecting affiliations like status symbols, he announced his taste and talents. Even as he validated himself through the exciting new milieu, his private world remained guarded and reclusive.

Marked by Mortality

> [The body] imprisons us on this petty planet
> and forbids us to range through the stars.
> —The He-Ancient, *Back to Methuselah*

During December 1880, Shaw finished *The Irrational Knot,* and the Shaws left 13 Victoria Grove for unfurnished lodgings at 37 Fitzroy Street. From one perspective, Shaw's life in 1881 seemed hardly distinguishable from his life in earlier years. He spent his days reading and writing in the British Museum, looked for a job without success, worked on his shorthand, and went three nights a week to Richard Deck's lodgings, where he exchanged English lessons for French. Yet that year there were two events momentous for the life, one the result of chance, the other of will, the two fatefully connected. In January, Shaw became a vegetarian. In May, he contracted smallpox.[1]

Despite infant vaccination, Shaw succumbed to the epidemic that raged across England. Once the quarantine was over he traveled to the outlying district of Leyton, Essex, on the border of Epping Forest, to regain his strength under the care of Uncle Walter, his medical "father," now respectably married and practicing there. During the summer Shaw resumed work on *Love Among the Artists,* begun in the weeks before his illness. He also corresponded with potential publishers of *The Irrational Knot,* with members of the Zetetical and Dialectical Societies, and with Lee. In October, healed but harboring a lingering ennervation, Shaw returned to the city and the routine of his life.[2]

While at Leyton, Shaw seemed to treat his bout with the dread disease stoically. In August, accepting a challenge to lecture in support of capital punishment, he reassured J. M. Fells of the Zetetical Society that he was "well and safe," meaning not contagious. All too casually he noted that since he usually read in bed anyway, "the chief objection to varioloid is the expense."[3] This was a peculiar objection, since Shaw's only expense was in sterilizing infected personal belongings, and since he had no job, he was out no wages. With punctilio, Shaw referred to the disease as varioloid, meaning the modified, mild form of smallpox occurring in the vaccinated or in those who previously had the disease. He avoided using the familiar and dread term *smallpox.* But he did not find the disease nearly as insignificant as he let on, and he was furious that vaccination failed to protect him.

Although a vaccine was discovered almost a century before, the disease that had felled the Aztecs and terrorized Europe still inspired fear. It was highly contagious, cutting a wide swath of death, blindness, and disfigurement. Its mandatory quarantine publicly marked its victims as dangerous. Though Shaw endured the inevitable course of the disease, he failed to recognize its onset, as the typical rash does not appear until the third day. His friend and colleague Henry Salt recalled that Shaw, "feeling ill, but not knowing what was the matter," decided "to spend a day or two riding round London on the top of an omnibus."[4]

Not helped by the bus rides, he went to a doctor who quickly diagnosed him in a sudden and awful sentence. It was impossible: "I was a fully vaccinated person, guaranteed immune from smallpox for the whole of my natural life."[5] Atop the swaying omnibus, soothed by the rhythmic sound of horses' hooves, Shaw could pretend that his illness was inconsequential, a wisp of affliction that might be carried off by the unsalubrious London air. But once legally and medically confined to 37 Fitzroy Street with his mother, he was forced to submit to the authorities, to the disease, to his fate. Not quite twenty-five, he was no closer to literary success than he had been six years earlier. At the same age, his hero Shelley had already established himself as an important poet. Compared with the drama of Shelley's life—which included the suicide of his first wife—Shaw's outward life had been uneventful, with nothing to intimate immortality. Not at all certain of the Christian version of events, Shaw could find little to sustain him from that quarter. Rather, there was Agnes, dead at twenty-one, briefly mourned by his mother, no trace but a grave marker.

Shaw watched as the disease ate away his skin. Surviving the worst effects, he falsely claimed to have been left unblemished. But his chin and jaw were pockmarked. His understandable regret at seeing scars on his face—the part of the body most closely identified with self—degenerated into something else: disgust with his entire body. He felt scourged by his scars, somewhat in the way that twentieth-century Mayas of the Chiapas highlands view face-marring illness. For them it is punishment by the gods, a visible sign of personal failures in the social, moral, or religious realm, a view Western medicine labels superstition.[6] While the Mayas' views are steeped in their culture, Shaw's irrational anger—it boiled for seven decades—was psychically rooted.

"Shaw has nailed the Red Flag to the point of his chin," fellow Fabian Sidney Webb would comment later.[7] Nurtured in extremis, the famous beard, hypocritically fashionable, defended and diverted. But the beard was inevitable, smallpox or not, for the face mirrors the inner self. The beard masked face, feelings, stigmata. The timing was fortunate, because Shaw had only a sprouting of hair on his face before he was twenty-four. If he could not manage an Old Testament beard, he could willfully play up his beard's Mephistophelean aspects. Habitually stroking and combing it with his fingers, he gloried in its defiance as he strutted and preened. Then, too, what could be more masculine?

Not yet psychologically recovered from his illness, Shaw was back at Leyton the following February, under quarantine from a slight attack of scarlet fever, apparently caught from infected milk. Once again there was sudden and unexpected contagion. He was luckier than Lucy, who, his diary notes, "suffered severely." Though the body's frailty was frightening, scarlet fever did not carry the stigma of smallpox. He could write about it to Fells, this time lingering Job-like over his ailments, personalizing his fate: "I have overtaxed the patience of the Almighty, and he has smitten me" in the throat, in the joints, in the lungs, "reverberating with the first hollow cough of phthisis, of which disease one of my sisters had the bad taste to die."[8]

If a cough brought Agnes to mind, as Shaw's bad taste shows, he could be cavalier about consumption because it was the most romantic of nineteenth-century diseases. The aesthetics of consumption endowed its sufferers with periods of elevated vitality and spiritualized passion, in contrast with smallpox, which signified putridly declining life. While the consumptive might be admired, the smallpox victim was shunned. In smallpox, Shaw found much too close a fit.

Shaw vented his fears through Owen Jack, the hero of *Love Among the Artists*, written during this period. Jack's most distinguishing physical feature is his black-grained face pitted by smallpox, the dirty color reminiscent of Wilde's complexion, a strangely resonant inspiration. A genius of a composer, the Welshman Jack is an outsider of Olympian ego and eccentricities, suggesting both Lee and Shaw. Shouting and roaring, his rotted face mirrors his plight and his creator's. Here is the unregarded Shaw "rotting unheard in the midst of a pack of shallow panders."[9] Here, too, is comic exaggeration that conceals inner torment. Jack is a veritable one-man orchestra who accompanies his raucous piano playing with hoots, whistles, and hisses, a volcanic transformation of Shaw's own pianistic efforts. Just as Conolly's absolute rationality drives his wife away, Jack's erratic genius frightens away Mary Sutherland. That sensible art aficionado chooses Hoskyn, a red-bearded American businessman. The two novels show Shaw moving between the poles of his restless personality, uncertain how to appeal to women.

While Uncle Walter administered his own boisterous brand of medicine, Shaw sought more sedate avenues of comfort during his convalescences. At Leyton the first summer he met Jane Lockett. During the siege of scarlet fever Jane reappeared with her twenty-three-year-old sister, Alice, a nursing student. Physically and emotionally vulnerable, Shaw succumbed to Alice's attentions, contriving to stay in Leyton after his symptoms subsided. His first real romance took root in the shadow of illness, but it never blossomed into mature love as Alice and Shaw toyed with each other for three years.

Once recuperated, Shaw returned to London and his new routine of writing novels—a routine spiced by writing love letters to Alice. On 22 April 1882 he moved with

Bessie from their inadequate Fitzroy lodgings to a respectable house at 36 Osnaburgh Street. There they rented the second floor and a room on the third where Shaw slept, recalling the old pattern of spatial distancing amid intimacy. Life seemed placid enough, but Shaw differed from his fellow Victorians, who found illness an occasion to meditate on the vanity of life. For him there could be no serenity, because body and self had been thrown out of alignment, breaching his fragile psychic defenses. Until smallpox struck, Shaw had seen no doctor since Dr. Newland, who had so ambitiously administered cathartics in Dublin. He had been a fixture in the household until Lee successfully treated the ill Bessie.[10] Now Shaw added a new twist to Lee's skeptical view of the healing powers of doctors.

Like Schopenhauer, Shaw believed sickness was a sign of an infirm will, an intolerable thought for him, so he blamed the doctors for the disease. Even more specifically, in one of the strangest and most sustained of his vendettas, Shaw attacked vaccination. As he fortified his position throughout his life, he put himself ever more at odds with the world. Since he had survived smallpox virtually unscathed, his behavior is puzzling and has been dismissed as mere eccentricity and superstition.[11]

Like Molière, Shaw declared doctors fair game. The Shavianized physicians are less likely to be knaves than fools, however, as more than twenty doctors parade through his works. Yet Shaw counted physicians among his friends, including the controversial bacteriologist Sir Almroth Wright from St. Mary's Hospital, where Alice studied and worked. In *The Doctor's Dilemma* (1906), Wright is the model for Sir Colenso Ridgeon. The dilemma of choosing to save one life over another was one that Wright had faced.

As long as art mediated, Shaw's attacks lost their edge. In *The Philanderer* (1893), Dr Paramore, a portrait of ideological excess, is a vivisector who makes his reputation by discovering a microbe in the liver that means certain death. When his discovery cannot be confirmed he is inconsolable, even though the misdiagnosed father of the woman he adores now appears to be in perfect health. In *Too True to Be Good* (1931), Shaw satirizes the doctor who admits he cures no disease yet persists in blaming the microbe. His microbe appears on stage as a character who has caught the measles from the patient. When the microbe laments that humans "infect us poor microbes" with their horrid diseases and the doctors pretend "it is we that infect them," it sounds a comic note, but Shaw was dead serious.[12]

Without the transforming qualities of art, Shaw's prose attacks were uniformly virulent, the wit biting, not benign. From an 1887 book review attacking vivisection through the one-hundred-page Preface to *The Doctor's Dilemma* and the 1932 collection of articles composing *Doctors' Delusions* right to the 1944 summary comments in *Everybody's Political What's What?* the controlling theme is victimization.[13] Doctors, pawns of the system, are the perpetrators. Shaw's unrelenting outrage pencils in a section of shadowy biographical landscape, a chiaroscuro mapping out otherwise inaccessible psychic terrain.

Shaw scoffed at the belief of Victorian intellectuals in total health or wholeness, that harmony of mind and body dependent on physiological health known as *mens sana in corpore sano*. This concept of the sound mind in the sound body—as important to the Victorians in shaping thought about human conduct as nature was to the Romantics— simply meant that training the body resulted in a vigorous mind. Only the reverse would do for Shaw, who had his own agenda: "it is the mind that makes the body and not the body the mind."[14]

Though less than robust by nature, and overly sensitive to body ills, he wanted to be regarded as healthier than most. In part he achieved this by converting tension into an air of electric energy. Away from the public eye, a vital current was switched off, and vitality gave way to discipline and anxiety. After his father's death from pneumonia, Shaw would worry about his own lungs. He spent many mornings singing in a deceptively strenuous fashion in hopes of strengthening them. He recorded aches, pains, colds, and headaches in the journal he kept from 1885 to 1897, taking stock and summing up his health for the year in a separate entry. Beginning in 1906 he kept a file on his headaches, noting the date, their effect on him, and the relief provided by medication. "I am in a most hypochondriacal state," he cried out during the throes of one headache made unendurable by the pain from a lacerated gum.[15] Over the course of his life he issued constant advisories, public and private, on the state of his health—on everything from neuralgia to nettle rash. Like the sickly Sonny, the man was always in want of sympathy.

No aspect of health or sanitation was beneath his notice. He recommended using the fingers instead of handkerchiefs, the refuge of germs. When he became a vestryman in the district of St. Pancras, where he served from 1897 to 1904, he labored devotedly on the Health Committee. As a champion of free public lavatories for women Shaw shocked the bourgeois vestrymen, but he was not as radical as he pretended. The clergyman, novelist, and Christian Socialist Charles Kingsley, writing in 1859, declared: "Of sanitary reform I shall never grow tired."[16] In her 1888 novel *Robert Elsmere,* the popular Mrs. Humphrey Ward (Mary Augusta) portrayed her clergyman hero as zealously interested in drains. Whatever the motivations of either Kingsley or Ward, Shaw's sanitary zeal, awakened by the sights and odors of the Dublin slums, marked the deepening cleavage between the earthward pull of the decaying body and the ethereal realm of purity and sunshine.

Shaw obsessively envisioned the human body plagued by blindness, cancer, and pestilence. Contagion spread into all modes of his world. In his social world, the metaphor of a diseased body politic ran through his thinking, and corrupt or inept doctors were themselves carriers of moral disease. Fearing assault from the natural world, like a patient in acute denial, Shaw refused to accept the germ theory of disease. The most spectacular medical advance of the nineteeth century was nothing but "superstition." Vaccination was merely Edward Jenner's "stunt." Shaw, far from conceding that the stunt probably saved his life, said that vaccination was "nothing short of attempted murder." He went even further: it killed one baby a week.[17]

The risks from vaccination and inoculation were not outweighed by the benefits. From his vantage point, inoculation never had the slightest success, including the "alleged military conquest of typhoid fever." Citing the "mathematical doctrine of chances," he ridiculed inoculation in which people deliberately contracted disease to protect themselves from it. He claimed that his grandfather managed to be inoculated, vaccinated, and to catch the disease as well.[18]

His dazzling display of partial truths isolated him in a moated tower from which he staged offensive forays against the medical world. Just as young Sonny felt the Dublin ascendancy to be united against the Shaws, the grown man felt the medical profession to be conspiring against him. The seeming lucidity of his arguments—what he needed to believe—was at odds with what he understood of his own motives. A bit too aphoristically he declared a self-controlled profession a "conspiracy against the laity," as he moved from the personal to the social sphere. It was simple greed. Vaccination was a way doctors could "make money out of people who were quite well."[19]

And yet did he not proudly claim *two* medical fathers—one a legitimately sanctioned, cheerful surgeon, and one a Faustian, vivisecting, mysteriously healing charlatan? In the depths of his psyche did he transform Lee into a darker Uncle Walter, even into a distorted mirror of the very medical establishment he accused of conspiracy?

Shaw's suspicions set the doctor against the patient: "We are all in the doctor's power when we are ill." Mephistophelean rebel, Shaw bowed to no one's authority and sought to usurp the priestly power he accused doctors of wielding, the power he secretly coveted. Himself a shaman weaving words into spells, he equated his private superstitions with the public good. He argued that there was no such thing as a typical bout of illness, citing ever-new strains of parabacillus as evidence. What he revealed was his fight against being reduced to his symptoms, his dread at being typified and objectified.[20]

Shaw singled out three men for attack: Edward Jenner, Louis Pasteur, and Joseph Lister. All three had become famous by controlling microorganisms—Jenner vaccinated, Pasteur used heat to destroy microorganisms in food, Lister used carbolic acid to to kill germs during surgery. For this Shaw mocked their reputations as "saviors of mankind," denouncing the three as impostors and murderers. Shaw echoed Almroth Wright's belief (which earned him the label Almroth Wrong from doctors) that microbes are vehicles of disease but not the prime cause. Lister's surgery was "far more incurable" than that of his competitors because his antisepsis killed the defensive cells as well as the aggressive ones. Shaw based this claim on the 1898 "vivisection" of his foot, for which he wore the "stigma on his instep." Contradicting himself, he argued that "microbes are so fond of carbolic oil that they swarm in it." Intellectually, he might believe, like his character Blanco Posnet, that the "croup bacillus was an early attempt to create a higher being," but the personal meaning to him was the threat of being metamorphosed into a breeding ground for bacilli. He fought back with biblical strength. His body was a battlefield in which his blood, fortified with "defensive hosts of phagocytes," killed microbes "more irresistibly than Samson slew the Philistines."[21]

Because he was acutely sensitive to odor, he could not black his boots. He scrupulously washed and aired every article of his clothing after it was exposed to tobacco smoke (in Dublin he had lived with George Carr Shaw, a smoker). His cry against "Listerics" was a cry of oppression, as every building on every London street "stank of carbolic acid." The world was "drenched, poisoned, nauseated" by this poison masquerading as a cure. The noisome odor violated privacy as it was carried by the air, violating the air itself. Fortunately, the sun's rays emitted an invisible curative. Exposing germs to sunshine "for a fraction of a second" killed most of them, because germs flourish "only in damp and darkness."[22]

His views resembled those of pythogenesis, the outdated notion that disease is generated spontaneously from filth and spread by a vile gas. During the Great Stink of 1858 and 1859, the odor from the polluted Thames so alarmed Londoners that they refused to cross the bridges or ride the riverboats. Similarly, Shaw argued that sanitary procedures, not vaccination, had lowered the mortality rate in hospitals and on the battlefield. He attributed almost all immunity from ancient plagues to sunshine, fresh air, soap and water. The triumph of sanitation was a "triumph of aestheticism," the mind-healing effect of "sweet sootless air."[23] Shaw moved the theater of action from an unseen, repulsive world of living organisms upward, to a brightly lit, clean, and deodorized incorporeal world, the only world his psyche could tolerate.

Shaw considered vaccination a "revolting practice" to be "repudiated with disgust."[24] He was repulsed on more than aesthetic grounds. It was the meaning of vaccination: its mark was the mark of mortality as it blended animal and human substances, the healthy and the diseased, the visible and invisible. The act itself—penetration by a substance representing the animal world—threatened body integrity by disturbing the boundaries between his natural world and his private world. The isolate and resisting Shaw was particularly susceptible to this rather feminine fear of penetration.

His antipathies showed other signs of having a sexual edge. In one of his strangest outbursts, he claimed that the worst effect of the vaccine was to produce "some of the most horrible results of human venereal contagion," indistinguishable from those of syphilis. Uneasy, he looked toward the sun, that mythic source of healing. He felt drawn not just by its fiery heat but also by its symbolic associations with the male and the intellect. As a force, the sun was held to be in opposition to the earth, the latter associated with the female and with matter. Shaw's affinity for these feelings surfaces artistically in *Man and Superman*. In the play's mythic deep structure, John Tanner functions as Jupiter, the Sun God, and the ever-changing Ann Whitefield as a predatory lunar goddess.[25] The long-incubating battle between the higher life and the lower instincts, between male and female, was to be fought with murky psychic material.

Shaw's was not the valetudinarianism of so many Victorian intellectuals like Darwin, Meredith, Ruskin, or Tennyson. Nor was it simply a civic-minded interest in hygiene. His revulsion against dirt and disease emanated from the deepest psychic levels. Decay penetrated his private world, where his self became dangerously entangled in threats to the bodily sphere; the world of his fellowman, populated by scheming doctors and diseased victims; and the natural world, a squalid landscape harboring armies of invisible lethal organisms.

He felt threatened by nothing less than the uncanniness of existence. To protect himself from that hostile, impersonal power, he personalized his enemies. He imagined a conspiracy plotted by the likes of Jenner, Pasteur, and Lister, and carried out by stupid and unsuspecting doctors. Shaw boldly battled his unseen antagonists, safeguarding himself by cleansing his body with ritualistic care. Even the adulatory Henderson thought that Shaw's "passion for cleanliness" was "almost fanatical," calling him the "cleanest man I ever saw or knew." It was a cleanliness that emanated powerfully and strikingly. To Henderson, Shaw seemed like an advertisement for sanitary underwear and Pears soap. To gay playwright, novelist, and critic Beverley Nichols there were other resonances. Nichols, himself quite sensitive to scent, observed Shaw at the first Malvern Festival in 1929: "I could never keep my eyes off him. For really, he was very good to look at. The cleanliness of the man! He was like snow and new linen sheets and cotton wool and red apples with the rain on them. One felt that he must even smell delicious, like hay or pears."[26]

Shaw's was an ever-lasting defense against dirt, poison, and contamination—whatever symbolized to him the form-destroying potencies of existence. It made him into an immaculate living mannequin. The mannequin would deploy his prophylactic defense ever more widely and strategically.

Yearning for Fragility

> I want to be ethereal.
> —Bernard Shaw

When the portly Alfred Hitchcock remarked, "One look at you, Mr. Shaw, and I know there's a famine in the land," the lean and unflappable Shaw retorted, "One look at you, Mr. Hitchcock, and I know who caused it."[1] This comment by the king of the macabre reflected the world's fascination with Shaw's eating habits. At Leyton, under Uncle Walter's care, Shaw abandoned his vegetarianism after only a few months. The connection between vegetarianism and illness that Uncle Walter posited would be psychologically endorsed by his nephew, but in an entirely different and a far more complex way.

Certainly Shaw found vegetarian cuisine easier to swallow than the badly boiled eggs served at home, and it was cheap. His favorite haunt was the Wheatsheaf, but he could also be found at the Pine Apple, the Orange Grove, the Porridge Bowl, the Cyprus, the Alpha, or one of the Aerated Bread Shops. There, among the radical artists and chic intellectuals, Shaw ordered his macaroni and rice, his wheatmeal porridge and lentils. He washed them down with Van Houten's cocoa, ginger beer, lemonade, or soda water, munching on penny candy from automatic machines—sweetmeats, butterscotch, toffee—or chocolate on the run. Like his Caesar, whose drink of choice is barley water, he avoided alcohol and tea, giving up even his occasional coffee at the Austrian Café or the Hampstead Room.[2] Vegetarianism was the latest vogue in Victorian England, and Shaw was always in vogue, whether writing novels or joining societies. But vegetarianism was no passing fad for Shaw.

There were, however, nondietary resonances. "Why not bait a bear, burn a village atheist, flog a Quakeress, pillory a dissenter, duck a scold," he wondered on hearing of a proposal for an ox-roast. He made his most thrilling pronouncement when the infant Shelley Society convened for its first large meeting in 1886. Shaw played to his audience, jammed with avant-garde women, by trumpeting that he was "like Shelley, a Socialist, Atheist, and Vegetarian." Playwright Henry Arthur Jones nudged his companion: "Three damned good reasons why he ought to be chucked out."[3] By invoking Shelley, Shaw veiled his private needs with romantic élan, his belated announcement yoking the artistic, the political, and the religious. Speaking as if he alone had discovered its benefits,

he credited vegetarianism with fueling his temperament and talent, as well as his ferocious energy.

Noisy about his vegetarianism, Shaw seems to have provided his biographers with
statements that can be taken at face value. Unlike the biographers, psychoanalytic critics
have sought explanations for the vegetarianism, discussing it in Freudian terms.[4] Freud's
view tells only part of the story, however, and not the most important part. What was the
meaning of vegetarianism to Shaw?

Long before his conversion to vegetarianism, Shaw had the model of dietary awareness in Lee as well as the cautionary examples of the alcohol addictions of Uncle Walter
and George Carr Shaw. There were other personal reasons for his vegetarian diet. One
incentive had been his hope of alleviating the migraine headaches that afflicted him in
monthly female fashion. Here the diet failed. The headaches would last until age seventy,
the result, he would decide, of too much protein in his diet, even without meat. When the
headaches finally disappeared, just after the publication of *The Intelligent Woman's Guide
to Socialism and Capitalism*, he could jest that he had transferred them to his readers.[5]

A more powerful incentive to vegetarianism was the revulsion evoked by the "horrible sameness" of meat. He grew tired of the "steam and grease, the waiter looking as if he
had been caught in a shower of gravy and not properly dried, the beer, the prevailing
redness of nose, and the reek of the slaughterhouse that convicted us all of being beasts of
prey." The waiter, the beer, and the beasts of prey combine to depict meat-eating within a
filthy, disgusting, and threatening landscape—one with a decidedly masculine edge.
Seeking refuge, Shaw "fled" to the "purer air" of the vegetarian restaurant, a dialectic
casting the vegetarian landscape at the feminine pole.[6]

Character traits have been called secret psychoses. That Shaw just might agree with
such a view is suggested by his sleight of hand in flourishing his own peculiar character
traits, which were irrevocably established during his first decade and a half in London.
Secret psychoses or not, Shaw thought that idiosyncratic elements revealed the inner
man. In his unfinished assignment on *The Voice* is a passage on Mozart's genius. Shaw
calls Mozart's skill at arithmetic, billiards, dancing, and acting more significant than his
sense of absolute pitch, for his musical endowments are obvious from his compositions.
But in the "other elements of his complex personality" lies the "secret of the difference
between him and the other composers."[7] Here, Shaw believed, was the key to unlocking
the secret man, that scant half-percent that distinguished one man from another.

More than just an aficionado of a somewhat exotic menu, he was convinced that "the
usual conception of the function of food is wrong." Investing food and eating with
ritualistic meaning, he became a missionary whose creed was celebrated with barley
water. He called vegetarianism the "occidental form of Yoga," or Jainism, and like the
yogi he sought purification through abstention. He embraced vegetarianism the way

saints embrace vigils and fasts. But no silent yogi or saint, he attacked meat eating as a form of cannibalism—a diet that the cannibals of the Upper Congo merely carry "to its logical extreme." Erasing distinctions, Shaw hyperbolically claimed that he had been a cannibal for twenty-five years. His zealous vegetarianism, with its elaborate rationale, was not a legitimate forerunner of twentieth-century ecology. Nor was it sentimental affection for animals. For chillingly coupled with his extraordinary aversion to meat eating was a dread that transformed the mouthfuls of his daily bread into a dark sacrament.[8]

His dread erupted in unexpected places. Because incest and inbreeding produce degeneration, he worried that animal feeding on animal might have the same effect. Paradoxically, to emphasize vegetarianism was to emphasize what Shaw wanted to forget—the body, the essence of the material world. His "objection to carnivorous diet" was "partly aesthetic, partly hygienic," suggesting the polarities that sundered him, but not their violent hold. Despite envisioning a race of long-livers, and achieving an almost legendary longevity himself, in the end he did not believe that diet affects the length of human life. His vegetarianism had other roots. All along his body had been troublesome. In *Man and Superman*, Don Juan recoils from the "two greasy commonplaces" of flesh and blood with their filthy baggage of disease and death. By the time of *Back to Methuselah* (1920), the vileness of the body burdened with the "horrible residues" left by digestive systems was "intolerable."[9]

Shaw longed for another order of existence: "Some day, I hope, we shall live on air, and get rid of all the sanitary preoccupations which are so unpleasantly aggravated by meat eating." He was sure that in a hundred years, cultivated people would "no more dream of eating flesh" than living, "as Pepys' contemporaries did, in a house with a cesspool under it." In the fourth of his *Farfetched Fables*, written in 1948, Shaw describes the advent of a superrace sustained by air. Hunger and thirst no longer mean the need for bread and beer, but become a "search for knowledge of nature and power over it, and a desire for truth and righteousness." The supergorilla becomes the "soldier and servant of Creative Evolution." Here is a Faustian alchemy that converts biological dross into spiritual and intellectual gold. Meanwhile, reality inhered in a beefsteak. In the last months of his life the old man warned a friend to avoid meat. His own evacuations were "entirely odorless," but eating meat would make them malodorous, "and I should give myself up for dead."[10]

In this world of violence and decay, where the primitive quality of odor assaulted and nauseated, it was a short path from the reeking slaughterhouse to the dinner table fouled with "murdered animals" to the stench of cesspool and grave. In the act of eating animal corpses, the line between life and death blurred as dead flesh became vital. But it conjured up the opposite process as well: we are what we eat. What masqueraded as fastidiousness was really a desperate revulsion from body and biology, a flight from a nightmare engulfment—the world as abattoir. As Shaw fled past reminders of mortality, appetite sank into animal greed, the ordinary and healthy menaced him at every turn: "What people call health—appetite, weight, beefiness—is a mistake. Fragility is the only endurable condition."[11]

The pursuit of fragility became paramount. He watched his weight so scrupulously that he could not tolerate an increase of even a few ounces. Among the meager diary entries of November 1879, he had carefully recorded, "On the 19th I weighed 10 st. 13 lbs. [153 pounds]. Only 1 st. 12 lb gained since Novr. 72." The crux of the issue was this: "You can be Sancho Panza on any food provided there is enough of it. If you want to be Pythagoras, you have to be more careful." At times his self-discipline faltered. During a summer stay at Monmouth in 1895, he complained to Janet Achurch that he was pursued there by a "horrible appetite," and was becoming a "gross and pig-like person." Sometimes he pleaded for help in curbing animal greed. Faced with the heartiness of a village dinner, he asked that Mrs. Girdlestone not provide too much milk, "as when I like anything I have a doglike habit of taking as much of it as I can get."[12]

Nor could he ever get enough of good bread and fruit. Yet he was satisfied with cocoa and porridge for breakfast, stewed corn or haricot beans "in place of the cow" for dinner, perhaps eggs at teatime. He was an accommodating guest. Not only was he satisfied with just the trimmings of the meal, but there was no need to cook for him at all—brown bread, cheese, and an apple made him feel as indulged as Mark Antony. Later he would prefer raw foods, having decided that roasting, boiling, and distilling were harmful. By 1938 his "most distressing complaint" was "anorexia, or dislike of food."[13] But even then he never lost the craving for sweets that plagued him as a boy, gobbling chocolates, ices, sweet biscuits.

Using his vegetarianism like a weapon, he assaulted his fellowmen and established his isolated beachhead: "Cannibalism with its best dish barred is good enough for the rest of you." Yet macaroni alone would not guarantee eminence. "There are millions of vegetarians in the world, but only one Bernard Shaw." Meat eating was repugnant to his nature—the higher nature. Like the love of Sergius and Raina in *Arms and the Man* (1894), the higher nature needed proof, and in a whirl of circularity, vegetarianism supplied that proof; he was too spiritually intense to sup on "stewed skeleton." Underlying this Calvinistic insistence that outer appearances reveal inner reality was Shaw's sense that he experienced a different order of existence than ordinary human beings. He would explain to Ellen Terry that as a vegetarian things happened differently to him: "pain is different, pleasure different, fever different, cold different, even love different." Separated from both the world of his fellow human beings and the natural world by his antipathies to the bodily side of his existence, a bite of meat or a sip of tea filled him with "vague apprehensions." But he could be "stoked up to a passable manliness" by the "terribly vital" vegetarian diet.[14]

He longed like Don Juan to escape the tyranny of the flesh. A "white-blooded man," wanting to live on air, he pressed on to the "goal of redemption from the flesh, to the vortex free from matter, to the whirlpool in pure intelligence" that Lilith envisions in *Back to Methuselah*. The airy, pure, unobtainable world that he wished for contrasted absolutely with the dread animal world of decay and death, symbolized by the cesspool. Indeed, the dread animal world overpowered the vegetable world as well, rooting out all signs of flowering, ascending life. Hesketh Pearson recalled that Shaw confessed to "'a bog-trotting hatred of agriculture,' and shuddered as he spoke of 'weasels, stoats, rabbits, worms, and all the other subterraneous horrors.'"[15] Recoiling from this rank, crawling, subterranean world, he obsessively sought the ethereal world.

Dreading his real future, he consumed himself with greed for life—labeling the Life Force itself Evolutionary Appetite. And he posited a false future without death: "Even prehistoric man dreamed of what he called an astral body, and asked who would deliver him from the body of this death." From the mire of his dread worlds arose his militant antivivisectionism. The butcher uses animal bodies as an end, the vivisector as a means, and both kill animals in the service of human desires. To the cheers of assembled antivivisectionists at their annual meeting in 1900, Shaw explicitly equated experiments on animals with those on human beings. If you think like the vivisectionist, you will "soon prove that you are justified not only in vivisecting dogs and guinea-pigs, but in dissecting every human being you can get into your power."[16] Not from high-minded love of animals was Shaw against vivisection, but from some buried fear that the hand that smote the guinea-pig might smite him.

In his outrage at vivisection, Shaw never cast a stone at the one vivisector he knew so well. Nor did he use that label in referring to Lee, who "trained himself" through "actual dissection." The resulting Method was so closely associated with Bessie, Lee's star pupil, that the ancient Shaw was not sure whether he had written some of *The Voice* for her, because she once thought of describing *her* method. Nor did Shaw mention that Lee's quest for the secret of beautiful singing—the reason for his vivisections—was part of the bel canto tradition. That tradition originated in the dazzling vocal art practiced in seventeenth- and eighteenth-century Italian opera houses and churches by the castrati, men who had been castrated before puberty to preserve their soprano voices. The castrati were vivisected physically and psychologically for art. All too mildly, Shaw called it the practice of sacrificing oneself "completely to his profession . . . at the cost of his virility." In 1885, Shaw wrote that all the private singing teachers he knew had rediscovered the method of the legendary Porpora, singing-master of the castrati.[17]

Like a mantra endlessly chanted, Shaw warned that there are certain things one should not know: "'for instance what it feels like to see your mother boiled to death.'"[18] This ghastly example of seeing what should not be seen was a geyser exploding upward from a deep well enclosing his own forbidden knowledge. Was Lee still vivisecting when Sonny knew him? Did Sonny ever watch the vivisector at his grisly task? Was Bessie an accomplice? Some things Sonny did know. Knowing is a kind of devouring, an assimilation that suggests both the alimentary and the sexual. George Carr Shaw's alcoholism had clashed with Lee's dietary abstentions—the alimentary. It was an unequal match. The alcoholic husband had defaulted. His wife had run to the blood-drenched ascetic, as the alimentary stream mingled with the sexual, a foul pooling observed by the son's devouring eyes. The demands of the singing-master, which threatened the son, overpowered the alcoholic's virility, a castration in effect, if not in fact.

Shaw harped on his father's alcoholism, but he never mentioned his father's lack of manliness, which he despised. Manliness and alcohol are tied together culturally—how much a man can drink is a measure of his masculinity. Here the father failed in the eyes of his son as he was contemptuously banished from his wife's affections. In that little room where George Carr Shaw changed his clothes and Sonny slept, the boy had smelled the nauseating odor of sickness and seen the miserable creature in filthy clothes running out to the privy, unable to hold his liquor or his bowels. It would be surprising if the boy did not connect his father's use of alcohol with his failures as a man.

Shaw continually advertised his abstinence from alcohol, drawing attention to himself and achieving a social reward from alcohol without drinking. Abstinence seems to have had further significance for him. As it protected him from the public humiliation of drunkenness, it also protected him from the loss of manhood that he had witnessed in his drunken father. Abstinence was a way of safeguarding his own virility. Like the turn that is the heart of wit, once again inversion insinuated itself into the fabric of his life. But this inversion was specifically tied to his sense of masculinity, and it had a distinctly sexual undercurrent.

From the small boy's abrupt and terrifying plunge into knowledge at the edge of the canal near Dolphin's Barn to the impenetrable mysteries of the ménage à trois, Shaw had learned from his fathers that there are some things you ought not to know. But still, in some of the things that he knew and did he surpassed his models with a Mephistophelean glee. In his relations with women, the artist, fist raised to the skies, claimed the right to be "half vivisector, half vampire."[19] As knowing became appropriation, the metaphorical blood of vivisection and vampirism was transformed into ink, and so the artist managed to accomplish what was impossible for the man—to reconcile the subterranean and the ethereal worlds.

Meanwhile, as a "mere artistic machine" he reduced his body to its market value with talk of solvency, overdrawing his account, and using himself economically. Ultimately, he wished to defend his body by eliminating "this machinery of flesh and blood," the ethereal wish stemming from a secret existential anxiety at having to accept the human condition.[20] His was the insoluble dilemma: willing not to be himself and stubbornly willing to be himself. The perspective of vegetarianism and antivivisection shows Shaw isolated once again. He was isolated from the animal and vegetable worlds, which surrounded and threatened him. He was isolated from the world of his fellow human beings, who experienced life differently, degrading themselves in greedy cannibalism. Most chillingly, he was isolated in his personal world as he was repelled by his own body.

And yet the flesh is neither matter nor mind nor substance. Rather, it has been called an element of Being. Seeking release from an element of his being, Shaw set his course on a perilous odyssey. He would navigate treacherous seas that threatened to swamp his existence—his compass, rudder, and sail, the transcendental powers of art.

11 The Noble Art

> A man that understands one art understands
> every art.
> —Cashel Byron

Unless called to the lecture hall, Shaw regularly spent Sunday evenings at the West Kensington home of Pakenham Beatty, a practice he continued until Beatty moved to Mill Hill Park, a remote section of London, in 1885. Shaw felt at ease with the Brazilian-born Beatty, who had passed part of his boyhood in Dalkey, though the two had never met there. Somewhat mischievously, Shaw drew a satiric portrait of the dilettante and poet as Chichester Erskine in *An Unsocial Socialist*. Part of the attraction of Beatty's hearth was the attention lavished by Beatty's wife, Edith (called Ida), who helped Shaw with his French and withstood his lectures on Jaegerism and child-rearing.[1]

An even more potent attraction than speaking French with Ida was sparring with Beatty. "Paquito" aspired to a boxing title and began coaching his visitor. To supplement Beatty's training, Shaw took to studying boxing at the British Museum. There he discovered the pocket-sized *Fistiana*, published by the editor of *Bell's Life in London*, jam-packed with lists of champions, sparring advice, and health hints. From the early decades of the century there were also zesty writings on "the fancy" by Jonathan Badcock, covering everything from female boxers to the best training breakfast (underdone beefsteak or mutton chops, stale bread, and old beer were recommended). Badcock's contemporary, the even more popular Pierce Egan, interlaced praise for cool judgment and elegant position with vivid, hard-hitting description in his classic, *Boxiana*.[2]

Immersed in boxing, Shaw sought out Beatty's instructor at the London Athletic Club. Ned Donnelly, author of *Self-Defense* and so-called Professor of Boxing, had developed a scientific approach to the manly art of glove fighting based on defensive parries for every offensive move. He achieved his modicum of immortality not for his system but as the chief model for Ned Skene in *Cashel Byron's Profession*, while Paquito would resurrect, in Black Paquito, the whispered nickname given the passionate half-Brazilian hero of *Captain Brassbound's Conversion*.[3]

Again the idea of isolating a method to execute a complex activity fascinated Shaw as it had fascinated Lee. There in Donnelly's gymnasium on Panton Street, only a few steps from the Haymarket Theatre, Shaw landed his first real blows against the upper class—

on the chins of the sons of the aristocracy sweating through Donnelly's method with him. With its emphasis on technique and form, the method was far above the slugfests common to pub house brawls and illegal prizefighting.

Soon the sessions with Donnelly consumed Shaw. Thin to the point of gauntness, he fought his body and the old fear that he had no courage, admitting that there is something in pugilism that "appeals irresistibly to the romantic coward that is in all of us." He put on the gloves when he visited writer and Fabian Hubert Bland as well as Beatty. He disciplined himself like a boxer, thought about boxing, and wrote about boxing. Then, one Saturday in March 1883 the author of *Cashel Byron's Profession* traveled to the Lillie Bridge Grounds with sparring partner Paquito to compete in the Queensberry Amateur Boxing Championships inaugurated only two years earlier. Beatty entered both the lightweight and middleweight divisions while Shaw, having won an "imaginary reputation" as a boxer and looking like a "tall man with a straight left," entered the middleweight and heavyweight ("Any Weight") divisions. The Fighting Irishman from the British Museum weighed in his six-foot, one-half inches at the bare minimum, posted as exceeding 10 stone (140 pounds), but his name was not drawn. Although he lost the chance to compete, he noted the winners and saved the program verifying his title aspirations. Hanging up his competitive gloves after this disappointment, he adhered to the opinion he aired decades later: "Boxing is only pardonable when it is very well done."[4]

Although the bell sounded on Shaw's hopes inside the ring, he became one of boxing's most astute observers, his comments a treasure trove of the practical and philosophical. He wrote both publicly and privately on the sport and its stars, analyzing, praising, blaming. Characters talk with their fists literally or metaphorically in *How He Lied to Her Husband* (1904), *Major Barbara* (1905), *The Fascinating Foundling* (1909), *Overruled* (1912), *The Millionairess* (1934), and *Shakes Versus Shav* (1949). When the American Joe Louis, the reigning world heavyweight champion, arrived in London in 1948, it was announced that the only people he wanted to visit were Shaw and Winston Churchill. Shaw answered the clamoring press by saying that both Churchill and he felt flattered. To Gene Tunney, the former world heavyweight champion, Shaw observed that Louis's tour made no money. The reason was clear: "our sporting crowds know nothing about boxing. What they pay for is bashing."[5]

Shaw attributed his interest in pugilism to the fads of the 1880s, a time when boxing was a favorite sport among the gentry. In response to gentlemanly fervor, the Amateur Boxing Association had been formed in 1880, becoming the world's first amateur governing body. Immediately the association revised the rules formulated by John Graham Chambers and given sanction by the Marquess of Queensberry in 1867, the revisions further separating boxing from the free-for-all of prizefighting. The latter had few rules—bouts lasted until one opponent could no longer continue—and its attractions included bare knuckles, power punches, and illegal betting. Like cockfighting, prizefighting was banned and ostensibly obsolete but still surreptitiously practiced.

Shaw's fascination with boxing was grounded in more than the merely faddish. Despite his ill-fated try for a boxing championship, in the spring of 1885 he was still avidly following the sport in such newspapers as *Sporting Set* and *Sporting Life,* and he bought himself a pair of five-pound dumbbells for modest bodybuilding. He and Beatty could be found ringside watching amateur and professional boxing competitions at Donnelly's gymnasium and at the West London Club, or making a day of it at a boxing show at St. James Hall. And Shaw still took the train to Blackheath to put on the gloves and spar with Hubert Bland.[6]

Shaw appreciated boxing as an ancient Greek art. Like the poet Byron, namesake of his own hero, he called it the "noble art." In addition, from Donnelly he had learned to value boxing as science. Touting his purely scientific interest, Shaw claimed to feel no sympathy toward either opponent. Yet caught up in the excitement of at least one match at Donnelly's, he tipped the loser.[7] As Egan had put it long before, it was the Sweet Science of Bruising, and Shaw was not without bias. He preferred the cool thinker to the passionate slugger, Gene Tunney discoursing during training on *The Way of All Flesh* to the likes of the Irish-American John L. Sullivan boasting in bars, "I can lick any son-of-a-bitch alive."

Shaw managed to divert attention from the mysteries of boxing's strange hold on him. Why did he pursue a sport seemingly so at odds with his mental, physical, and spiritual capabilities? Despite his interest in the sport, after the mid-1880s he avoided boxing matches and exhibitions for nearly thirty-five years because they did not measure up to his standards. Relenting for the Georges Carpentier/Joe Beckett match in 1919, Shaw was ringside to record his view of "The Great Fight" for *The Nation.* He had high hopes for Georges Carpentier. "Gorgeous Georges the Orchid Man" was born to move, like Cashel Byron himself. While Byron might complain that "it isnt right to be always looking at men and women as you look at horses," the debonair Gorgeous Georges, the "Pride of Paris," was an artist with the "kick of a thoroughbred horse."[8]

Shaw had not been fooled by an earlier stunt when Byron had seemed to appear in real life. In 1906, former world heavyweight champion "Gentleman Jim" Corbett played Shaw's boxer in an unauthorized American stage version of the novel. Only five years earlier Shaw had rushed to protect *Cashel Byron's Profession* from piracy by transforming it into his own play, *The Admirable Bashville.* Written in blank verse in one week, "so childishly easy and expeditious (hence, by the way, Shakespear's copious output)," its playful spoofing of the Bard delivers lighthearted jabs at the literary champion by the confident contender.[9]

A real-life Byron finally appeared in the person of Gene Tunney, a thinking techni-
cian who later cultivated resemblances to Shaw's fictional boxer. Yet shortly after his 1926
defeat of the hard-punching Jack Dempsey, Tunney declined to play Byron in a projected
film version of the novel on the grounds that it was an immature work. The unperturbed
Shaw, who had thought that the role of villain should be offered to Dempsey, politely
agreed with Tunney's literary assessment and suggested that since he knew so much
about boxing he should rewrite the book. Neither the film nor Tunney's revision ever
materialized. When Tunney visited London, Shaw invited him to lunch, listening with
interest as the boxer described a hotel on the Adriatic island of Brioni. Shortly after, Shaw
and his wife surprised the Tunneys by turning up at that very hotel. Tunney then played a
practical joke on the teetotaler by sending a case of cordials under an assumed name,
which Shaw returned unopened. From this beginning a warm friendship blossomed.
After Tunney retired, the only world heavyweight champion to retire undefeated as
champion (he lost only one bout in his professional career), the literate boxer wrote
several books and gave a series of lectures on the Bard at Yale University.[10]

What Shaw admired in Tunney was his "confidence in himself and his system."
Shaw stressed the mental and moral elements in opposition to "the seamy side of the
affair, the betting side." Shaw declared in 1946 that there are "no sports which bring out
difference of character more dramatically than boxing, wrestling, and fencing." All three
sports are one-on-one and were practiced in some form in ancient Greece, where athletes
fought naked. Within the context of symbolic combat, the masculine body is displayed in
all its muscular and agile glory—the cultural epitome of masculinity. All three sports
depend on pretense and strategy, on feints and parries. Victory often hinges on will and
mind. Shaw thought the punches and parries of the born prizefighter were as "instantaneous and unconscious as the calculation of the born arithmetician or the verbal
expression of the born writer."[11] Grounded in the wisdom of the body, such intuitive
knowing resembles the tenets of Creative Evolution.

In writing *Cashel Byron's Profession*, Shaw claimed to find his artistic material in the
comic contrast between the realities of the ring and the romance surrounding it. In
actuality, the novel is so full of romance that Shaw barely escaped the fate of a successful
novelist. "The world never did know chalk from cheese in matters of art," was his mock
disclaimer concerning the work that he viewed with particular fondness.[12] It is his best
novel, a joyous romp that makes good on the author's promise to provide a first-class fight
for the money.

Shaw's born prizefighter is an early sketch of the remarkable man of action, a
forerunner of his portraits of Napoleon and Caesar. Preaching the gospel of "executive
power"—"how to hit him, when to hit him, and where to hit him"—Cashel combines
the practical with the moral. Like his creator, he has spent a childhood fearing that his

cowardice would be found out. He fulfills many a boyish fantasy when he knocks his teacher down with a well-aimed blow and then escapes from boarding school by stowing away to Australia. Returning to his homeland years later, he finds that his profession has marked him as an outsider despite his gentle birth. When the hard-headed millionairess Lydia Carew sniffs that boxing is "wholly anti-social and retrograde," the indignant Cashel lashes out against the polite society that sanctions professional soldiers and vivisectionists. He finally wins over the priggish Lydia, reputed to know "forty-eight living languages and all the dead ones," not by his ideas but by his body, which intrigues her with its eugenic possibilities.[13] With comic irony, the union, entered into very scientifically on Lydia's part, turns out boys pure Carew and girls pure Byron. By investing Lydia with superior intellect and Cashel with godlike physique, and by having the lovesick Cashel give up his career for love, Shaw overturned cultural stereotypes on two fronts.

Autobiographical parallels are plentiful and playful. Shaw's warrior hero is a blue-eyed, auburn-haired, middleweight antivivisectionist who as a boy had exceedingly dirty hands—Sonny had thought "black was the natural color of nails." In contrast, Shaw endowed his pagan god with something he longed for: the classic form of Greek statuary. After his bout with smallpox, Shaw, worried about his looks, followed the advice of Richard Deck and modeled his hairstyle after that of the Greek statues, "brushed up from the brow" instead of plastered sideways. Combined with his upturned moustache and eyebrows, his new hairstyle changed his image from the priggish to the gloriously satanic—a suggestively sexual image. By entering the ring, Shaw sought to make an explicit statement of his masculinity. Writing about a masculine sport, he transformed the weakness of convalescence into the healthy strength of the self-assured artist. As Cashel insists that "every man has to grow his own style out of himself," Shaw's fantasy life surfaced. The pockmarked face of Owen Jack gave way to Cashel's classic form, the "visionary prizefighter as romantic warrior hero."[14]

Placing the novel alongside the play is unexpectedly revealing, for the burlesque treatment of material in *The Admirable Bashville* camouflages autobiographical elements. In both works, Cashel Byron has two secrets: his own profession and that of his mother, an actress. These secrets are covers for his real fear: that he is illegitimate. Both works have Cashel inheriting an estate in true Victorian rags-to-riches style. In the novel, he inherits from his uncle, in the play from his father, who is revealed to be the former "Sieur of Park Lane."[15] It can be no coincidence that at the time Shaw wrote the novel there was a Sieur of Park Lane—and that Sieur was Lee. Only after Lee's death, in the hastily written burlesque that jabs at Shakespeare, Shaw's literary "father," does Shaw insert this autobiographical fillip—a gleefully coded signal that has remained unbroken up to now.

The novel also reveals Shaw's masculine ideal. Unobserved, Lydia first comes upon him one May afternoon in the wooded park belonging to Wiltstoken Castle, her ancestral home. She has discovered him after wandering across a terrain rife with mythic-religious resonances—a swamp and a forest, even a toppling Druid's altar that reminded her of Mount Sinai threatening to fall on Christian in *The Pilgrim's Progress*. Lydia is "dazzled by an apparition" that she first believes is a beautiful statue—reversing the usual voyeurism of gazing on a female body. Since Shaw himself identified with Christian, Lydia's admiration of Cashel's "manly strength and beauty" is really Shaw's "strange glow of delight." The "glorious vision" of Cashel's idealized body, accented by his parted lips and rising color, is set amid the woodland sounds of birds and grasshoppers and is unlike any other in Shaw's oeuvre: "his bare arms shone like those of a gladiator. His broad pectoral muscles . . . were like slabs of marble. Even his hair, short, crisp, and curly, seemed like burnished bronze in the evening light. It came into Lydia's mind that she had disturbed an antique god in his sylvan haunt." She began to think she was seeing the Hermes of Praxiteles "changed by a daydream into the semblance of living reality."[16]

The idyllic setting, the season, the dreamlike atmosphere, and the portrayal of Cashel as Greek god—or Platonic beautiful boy—all mark the ethereal world. In *Lady Chatterley's Lover* (1928), D. H. Lawrence re-creates the scene almost identically as Connie Chatterley undergoes a "visionary experience" when, after emerging from the woods on her estate, she chances upon Mellors, the gamekeeper, and watches him unobserved as he washes himself outside his cottage. That Lawrence, the high priest of mystic sexual union, seems indebted to Shaw is all the more remarkable given his attack on "the Chief Dramatist" and his "tricks" of "counterfeit sex."[17]

Cashel in his sylvan haunt contrasts sharply with Shaw's description of the Carpentier/Beckett fight that drew him ringside that night in 1919. There he sat amid four thousand cheering fans packed into a "fearfully ugly" roofed enclosure that "calls itself a Stadium, probably to provide modern poets with a rhyme for radium." The atmosphere is "murky, stifling and fumesome." Right in the middle is a "scaffold, or place of execution, twenty-four feet square, fenced by ropes, and glared down upon so intolerably by arc lights that some of the spectators wear improvised brown paper hat brims to shield their eyes."

Two descriptions can hardly be more antithetical. Instead of a wooded clearing, there is the ugly enclosure; instead of birds singing, four thousand fans cheering; instead of a sunlit May day, a murky, harshly lit night; instead of an idyllic daydream, the nightmare associations of radium, whose X-rays invisibly penetrate human flesh to treat cancer and to photograph the body's secrets. When in 1922 Carpentier exhibited X-rays of the broken bones in his hands to prove that he had fought hard despite a stunning loss to the flamboyant Senegalese fighter "Battling Siki" (Louis Phal), Shaw refused to accept them as evidence. If the metaphor is the ring as scaffold, then the match is a descent into hell.

Even more remarkable is the aura surrounding the boxers themselves. As Lydia first took Cashel for an apparition, so Shaw was startled by Carpentier, who struck him as a "most amazing apparition: nothing less than Charles XII, 'the mad man of the North,' striding along the gangway in a Japanese silk dressing gown as gallantly as if he had not been killed almost exactly two hundred-and-one years before." The spellbound Shaw knew it must be "either Carpentier or the devil. Genius could not be more unmistakable."

From a sylvan god to the ascetic monarch rumored to love men to satanic warrior, Shaw's boxer seemingly had undergone a complete metamorphosis. But it was not so. Like a figure out of D. H. Lawrence, the vitalist Carpentier literally had ascended from the bowels of the earth. He was a miner who found in boxing a way to escape the coal pit. Symbolically linked with fire, coal represents the occult side of energy. The incendiary and Mephisphelean Shaw identified with the boxer-genius: "Being in that line myself I was under no illusion as to genius being invincible." But "genius is genius all the same, in victory or defeat."[18]

Shaw insisted that boxing was a trial of skill. Nevertheless, boxing was always performed partly as spectacle of violence, and Shaw was not immune to the spectacle. The paradoxical attraction of boxing lay in the tension between the pull to brutishness and the mystical power of elegant control. By offering a pathway to the ethereal realm, it was a playing out of Shaw's own psychodrama. Of Carpentier he marveled, "The transfiguration which takes place when he stands up to fight is amazing: he becomes a being of a different order." For after he set to work, a magical change occurred: "The unmistakable Greek line digs a trench across his forehead at once; his colour changes to a stony grey; he looks ten thousand years old; his eyes see through stone walls."[19]

Shaw implied that the boxing match was a reenactment of primitive rites. Admonishing the masters of ceremonies to attend to their duties, Shaw witnessed the "usual orgy" following Carpentier's win. While the Greek version had the male lover crowning and kissing the conquering boxer or wrestler, Shaw's orgiastic scene featured Carpentier being fondled by a woman as he was hung by his heels from the "scaffold." Nor could Shaw resist categorizing pugilists as a "sentimental, feminine species, much given to kissing and crying." He dared not exhibit such displays of emotion, signaling that his stoicism was linked to his sense of masculinity. Meanwhile, Cashel, like so many Shavian heroes, admits that "I'm no better than a baby at heart," and "I never cared much about women."[20]

Later, erasing sex lines, Shaw conceived of his millionairess Epifania Ognisanti di Parerga Fitzfassenden as a boxer, but that profession proved "unconvincing and unladylike" on the stage, so he made her a judo expert instead. Having married boxer Alastair Fitzfassenden because he "stripped well," she became infuriated on her honeymoon to discover that all his passion was in his fists, so she used her own fists on him. He responded with a knockout punch to her solar plexus, for which she "almost respected him."[21]

Boxing was a literal counterpart of Shaw's fight against convention and society, converting the quick jabs and parries of wit into their physical equivalent. The risk-taking satirist downplayed the risks of the ring. Apparently mindful of the ancient Greek practice of fighting without rounds and until one fighter admitted defeat, he argued that a boxing match was less arduous than a university boat race. Besides having rests every three minutes, boxers can always lie on the floor for nine seconds. Such rests startle the visiting African king Cetewayo in *The Admirable Bashville:* "Ye gods, what cowards!"[22]

Even on the most sensational aspect of boxing, the knockout, Shaw waxed romantic, claiming that the knockout was a perfect anesthetic. The knockout represents heroic strength, a strategic triumph over fate. It can be compared to the moment of truth in the bullfight, the union of matador and bull through the sword, what Hemingway calls the "emotional, aesthetic and artistic climax of the fight." In fact, Hemingway, the legendary man of letters as man of action, appears to reflect Shaw. In *Death in the Afternoon* (1932), Hemingway's matador, like Shaw's boxer, is an artist-genius practicing an impermanent art. Moreover, the saving technical device of this treatise on bullfighting—dialogue with an old lady—echoes the paternal tone of a self-interview that Shaw drafted to comment on the scandal evoked by the 1922 Carpentier / Siki match. In language that parallels and parodies Shaw's highly proper exchange with a naïve young man, Hemingway converts Shaw's young man into an old lady, substituting money and bullfighting for money and boxing.[23] Hemingway's vulgar exchange with his old lady appears to imply a comment on the virility of Shaw's young man and on Shaw himself.

The peculiar hold of boxing on Shaw can be traced to its temporality, a blend of predictability and suspense. The rules are clear and known in advance: a bout has a finite number of rounds, the violence of the action restrained by the clock. Even though suspense is a crucial element—where a punch will land, who will win—the unpredictable can occur only within a narrow range. By dint of discipline, training, and will, the boxer is master of his fate. The contempt Shaw felt toward the slugger emanated from a deeper uneasiness, the slugger's proximity to the chaotic fringes. The difference between a Dempsey and a Tunney was really the difference between unrestrained violence and choreographed scenarios, between brute strength and vital grace.

Not only in its temporality but also in its spatiality, the boxing match was psychically alluring. Within that microcosmic world bounded by flimsy ropes, action of mythic proportions might take place. As opponents faced off in single combat, male body against male body, the rare warrior-genius glowed incandescently—sweating, jabbing, dancing in that hyper-lighted realm. Without such genius, the landscape of the boxer deteriorated into a scaffold that might suddenly and lethally drop open. It recalled the ominous cast of the vegetarian's landscape, vulnerable to desecration by the meat eater's slaughterhouse, and that of the hypochondriac, populated by scarred faces and feverish bodies. Landscapes of soul barring the pilgrim's way to the Celestial City, they chart a dangerous topography of fetid sewers draining beneath the earth, poisonous microbes polluting the air, bloody slaughterhouses and ghastly laboratories defiling every corner, animalistic brawls degrading ring and public house alike. The inescapable view from such landscapes is man as crawling animal threatened by engulfment. Struggling against this nightmare vision, Shaw clung to his friendship with Tunney—"to plant my feet on solid ground."[24]

Through boxing, Shaw's inner self emerged in a strikingly romantic guise—supremely vigorous and powerful, moral and courageous—in short, as a superman. Meanwhile, the audience, shielding its eyes, made its gaze inscrutable in the very midst of that noisy communal drama. Finally, there was the boxing opponent, the male mirror. His look stripped away defenses and alienated when it called up memories of other aggressive looks. But when, rarely and miraculously, eyes could see through stone walls, then the gaze belonged to the clairvoyant and mystic.

In its mere physicality, boxing opposed the fragility Shaw sought. He claimed superiority to the boxer, cherishing his faith that the "pen is mightier than the dumbbell." Even so, inspired by a romantic vision of the bare-chested warrior hero, he sought to control his body, as if somehow he could be transformed into a higher being. In Carpentier he had proof that such a metamorphosis was possible: the artist-genius as boxer might punch his way to spirituality. It was more than wit that led Shaw to quip, "Paradoxing is a useful rhyme to boxing."[25]

Given the psychic allure of boxing, it is not surprising that Shaw had no interest in team sports. Instead, he channeled his restless energy more personally. A great walker and an intrepid, even reckless, biker, Shaw was passionately fond of swimming. Bracing air, frigid water, swimming naked at dawn—all were tempting: "I have an obscure fire within me that craves for cold water." But it was the sea itself that was the ultimate tranquilizer. It was "another world," one where his vigor was benevolently transformed. Actress Lillah McCarthy, a novice swimmer, remembered that as the land slipped away, he soothed and guided: "Have no fear, Lillah, gently and slowly does it."[26]

Immersed in the watery womb, rocked and lulled, weightless and cleansed, he could feel his body's boundaries dissolve. In forsaking the surface we normally inhabit for a space that has volume, like the airy heights, Shaw calls to mind the vision at sea that amazed Captain Shotover, the patriarch of *Heartbreak House:* the flying fish glittering "in the sunshine like birds."[27] Perhaps, as Shaw glided through the sea, he pretended he was serenely soaring.

Socialism and Salvation

For the right moment you must wait, as
Fabius did most patiently, when warring
against Hannibal, though many censured his
delays; but when the time comes, you must
strike hard, as Fabius did, or your waiting will
be in vain, and fruitless.
—The Fabian Credo

Promising a brave new world, socialism beckoned seductively to intellectuals and ideal-
ists in the 1880s. Enthusiasts gathered to argue and proselytize, hearts pounding, voices
rising, as they unfolded their dreams of universal brotherhood. The image of man trailing
clouds of glory had been shattered by Darwin's theory of evolution. Shattered, too, was
the religious faith that had vitalized the middle classes, leaving many in despair. But now,
in overstuffed parlors and bare-walled clubs across London, radicals and romantics were
finding a new creed as they sought personal redemption and the reconstruction of
society.

Insisting that he was a born communist even as he recalled being "drawn into the
Socialist revival of the early eighties," Shaw endowed his political sympathies with the
inevitability of destiny.[1] The first step was his momentous conversion to the economics
of Henry George. Inspired by his personal sense of injustice and the rhetoric of radical
and libertarian politics, Shaw had been pursuing radicalism from debating club to
debating club. But though he had read Ruskin and Proudhon, he had no real focus until
that September evening in 1882 when he wandered into the Memorial Hall on Farringdon Street.

Speaking there was a "born orator," a handsome romantic figure of a man with
"small, plump, pretty hands." Brilliantly the American Henry George, author of *Progress
and Poverty*, stirred the assembled with his vision of land nationalization through a single
tax on the use of bare land. Electrified by George's excoriations against privilege, it
"flashed" upon Shaw that the storm that raged around religion and science was a "mere
middle-class business." The "importance of the economic basis dawned on me."[2] It was a
crucial event. But what did it mean?

That flash, like Captain Shotover's annihilating mind ray, signaled the disruption of
continuity as Shaw's structure of beliefs was exploded. Like that long-ago splintering

presided over by George Carr Shaw—that dark physical scene at the canal—it revealed another reality amid its shower of sparks. Henry George's words illuminated the way to a higher vision. Shaw stood ready to fulfill the destiny he sought as saint and genius. With one saint at least, he had a fearsome bond. He would write that as a young girl Joan had been frightened by a "terrible father" and threatened with the "awful prospect of being thrown into the Meuse and drowned."[3] Significantly, Shaw linked Joan's early trauma to her later insistence on leading a man's life—that is, in forging her own gender identity and destiny.

A genius, he would write in the Preface to *Saint Joan*, is a person who, "seeing farther and probing deeper than other people, has a different set of ethical valuations from theirs, and has energy enough to give effect to this extra vision." Like Blake, Shaw felt the power of the mind's eye and naturally used visual images to indicate insight; meanwhile, he gloried in his own better-than-normal eyesight. Struck dumb by revelation, he soared from agnosticism to belief in a single shimmering instant. For the first time, Shaw's peculiar susceptibility to the disruption of continuity coalesced with both his unnamed desire to fly into the ethereal realm and his gnawing rage. He called it "conversion."[4]

All the old feelings rose up and flooded forth in a triumphant spiritual tide, cleansing and metamorphosing. From the mouth of Henry George, the paternal prophet, issued words of affirmation. Yes! the Dublin Sonny had suffered. Yes! the London Shaw had been exploited. Idle, greedy landowners were the villains. Land reform was the heroic remedy. Shaw felt empowered and called upon to join the newly sanctioned corps of the moral and righteous who were poised to participate in great events—even as he exacted private revenge. What was the boyish tearing down of gorse bushes compared to the thrill of tearing down the system of primogeniture or the entire capitalistic system? In an instant the torch that had set Torca Hill ablaze was traded for one far grander and more magnificent, transforming its bearer. The powerless Sonny was reborn as heroic warrior and world redeemer.

Through the Land Reform Union, a Georgite society, Shaw met others who felt as he did, men like Eton master, poet, and vegetarian James Leigh Joynes, who was "slaughtered" by doctors a few years later; Henry Hyde Champion, publisher of political pamphlets who would be tried and acquitted of seditious conspiracy for his part in the 1886 Trafalgar Square Riots; Sydney Olivier, a clerk in the Colonial Office who became governor of Jamaica; and Stewart Headlam, a Christian Socialist clergyman married to a lesbian, who would put up half the bail money for Oscar Wilde after his arrest. Shaw's acquaintance with the righteous, the disaffected, and the strong-minded expanded rapidly.[5]

A few months later Shaw attended a meeting of H. M. Hyndman's Social-

Democratic Federation. There, in the full pride of his knowledge of George's economics, the newcomer rose in protest against their dismissal of his prophet. Instead of winning his audience, Shaw was mocked on his ignorance of Marx. Shamefaced, he withdrew to the British Museum Reading Room to struggle with the French translation of the first volume of *Capital,* soothing his excitement and frustration by alternating his reading with the score of Wagner's *Tristan und Isolde,* which he kept propped open before him.

Observing Shaw's struggles in the British Museum was the Scottish drama critic William Archer, exactly Shaw's age and already well known. With a brief introduction by mutual friend Henry Salt, a lifelong friendship was launched. Unaffected and unpretentious, the seemingly dour Scotsman appeared to be Shaw's opposite. Actually, Archer's air of reserve hid a lively sense of humor. Shaw understood the phenomenon of presenting a contradictory mask and described Archer's reserve, in "modern psychopathological terms," as a "repression that had become a complex."[6]

The Marx-Wagner incongruity that caught Archer's eye was no aberration. Shaw's diary documents the constant juxtaposition of music and politics—attending concerts and speaking on socialism, penning music reviews and political tracts. When writing *The Irrational Knot* he often grew "tired of the sordid realism" of Edward Conolly, his electrical engineer hero, and would play Bizet's *Carmen* on the piano as a "safety-valve" for his romantic impulses. Surrounded by silent researchers in the great vaulted Reading Room, Shaw journeyed inside the sensuous world of *Tristan und Isolde,* its expressive chromaticism the melodic mirror of his disharmonious soul. Inside the dialectical world of *Capital,* he traversed intellectual chasms. Redemption through romantic love became redemption through Marx. He emerged from the experience a "furious Socialist," having undergone another "complete conversion." He was "saved" and ready to face his detractors.[7]

From that hour Shaw was a man with "some business in the world." His business was that of the keeper of public morals and ethics. He might talk of rent and wages, but his consuming interest lay in human relations. It was bitterness, not science, that led him to label capital a social relationship of a "peculiarly abominable kind." Discovering Marx was a "turning point." Marx opened his eyes to the "facts of history and civilization," giving him "an entirely fresh conception of the universe," providing him with "a purpose and a mission in life."[8] Once again the life had changed direction.

Marx's "jeremiad against the bourgeoisie" appealed to Shaw's feelings of being outside the various orders of privilege—the church, the academy, industry, and government. The Outsider concluded that the secret of Marx's appeal lay in the hatred of the respectable toward the middle-class institutions that had "starved, thwarted, misled, and corrupted them spiritually from their cradles."[9] Given a freshly conceived universe, the old alignments would change.

Shabbily dressed and clinging desperately to his self-esteem, Shaw was impelled to bear witness. On street corners and town halls, in parks and marketplaces, he brought the gospel to the people, always without fee. His widening circle of movement helped to stabilize his life, which threatened always to fly skyward or descend into dread. The verticality of the life broke through as he remembered speaking anywhere, at "the City Temple, a cellar or a drawing room," the three sites drawing on the axis stretching between the irrational depths, the civilized drawing room, and the upward-reaching temple.[10]

Joined by other penniless sons of the bourgeoisie, he "painted the flag red," waving Marx's banner: "We saw nothing for it but militant organization and revolt."[11] It was as if his deepest fantasies had surfaced, and with the whole weight of the intellectual vanguard supporting them. No longer was he Shaw the unsuccessful job applicant, unpublished novelist, impoverished immigrant, but Shaw the missionary, the prophet, the oracle. His pent-up frustrations erupted in a fiery shower as Marx's vision of ultimate conflagration shaped a future as dazzling as his own most daring dreams. Forged in the smithy of his soul was the adamantine link between political and personal longing.

That early socialism had a strong strain of religious fervor made it so much the better for Shaw. Now the "complete infidel" wanted to make a religion of socialism. Like his hero Trefusis, his calling was that of "saviour of mankind." Driven by moral passion, Shaw devoured economic treatises. Seeking sanction for his feelings, he found new labels to attach to long-held beliefs. Stating his case simply, he cut through the web of conflicting theories and abstract formulations. Dramatically, he portrayed the capitalist as a predatory highwayman stealing money to keep himself in velveteen and lace. Instead of abstractions, Shaw talked of trombones and tambourines, hothouse flowers and December strawberries. Instead of theory, he mourned a misspent youth.[12] There remained the memory of the Dublin rent collector and, years later, on inheriting Irish holdings from his mother's estate, the irony of becoming an absentee landlord.

Even apart from personal grievance and moral indignation, Shaw found Marx's dialectic of history psychologically appealing. The opposition of old versus new, evil versus good, idleness versus labor resembled his own compulsion to polarize life's possibilities. Just as laughter provided refuge from family tragedy, class war would resolve itself in harmony, exploitation in cooperation, isolation in community. Meanwhile, he moved from weakness to strength. Finding his calling, the alleged born communist proclaimed: "I was a coward until Marx made a Communist of me."[13]

In the winter of 1884, Shaw joined a circle devoted to the study of Marx and Proudhon. An invigorating walk brought him to Charlotte Wilson's luxurious Hampstead home, where the circle met until Charlotte and her stockbroker husband moved to the more socialistically appropriate Wildwood Farm, an idealized little cottage. The circle then convened at the Hampstead Library, where fierce discussions prodded Shaw the evangelical Marxist into becoming Shaw the apostate. There would be no mention of Marx in *Fabian Essays*, all of which Shaw edited and two of which he wrote.

Inserted in the minutes of the Fabian Society is the following note: "This meeting was made memorable by the first appearance of Bernard Shaw." This notation in Shaw's hand was made some time after that auspicious May evening in 1884. The small group calling itself the Fabian Society met for the first time on 24 October 1883 at the Osnaburgh Street lodgings of Edward R. Pease, another social-minded stockbroker. At that time, clerk Frank Podmore, who suggested naming the group for the Roman general Fabius Cunctator, became Fabian secretary (a job later assumed by Pease), and Hubert Bland acted as treasurer.

From the first, the Fabian Society had both practical and visionary elements. But with its hazy goals there was little to distinguish the group from other socialist groups or even from the numerous debating clubs that dotted the London landscape. But Shaw was attracted by the name and by a pamphlet that raised a question that long had troubled him: "Why are the Many Poor?" He soon discovered that the Fabian Society "lived by its wits, and by its wits alone," a description of his own ethos as well. He was also more comfortable with the intellectual discipline and humanity of the Fabians than with the "open intolerance" he found in Hyndman and his Social Democratic Federation. For Hyndman had no interest in women's issues or sexual reform, his stance consistent with that of Marx and Engels, who thought that social roles were biologically based and that heterosexuality was "natural" and homosexuality "unnatural."[14] On 5 September 1884, Shaw was elected to membership in the Fabian Society, two years to the day from his conversion to George's theories.

At the very next meeting, on 19 September, Shaw made his first written contribution to the cause that held so much personal meaning for him: *A Manifesto*, Fabian Tract no. 2. Among his propositions read to the Fabians that night and adopted was the following: "That the State should compete with private individuals—especially with parents—in providing happy homes for children, so that every child may have a refuge from the tyranny or neglect of its natural custodians." Shaw also convinced those that had come to Pease's pleasant lodgings that "Men no longer need special political privileges to protect them against Women, and that the sexes should henceforth enjoy equal political rights."[15] Thanks to Shaw's witty iconoclasm, the equal rights of women were firmly established as a Fabian tenet from the outset.

Significantly, his lasting commitment to the Fabians was ushered in not by disruption, but by a process of discovery. Within a few months he had persuaded Sidney Webb to join the Fabian ranks. Webb's first contribution, the pamphlet *Facts for Socialists*, marked the real beginning of Fabianism. It was Webb who voiced the memorable phrase, "the inevitability of gradualness." Shaw had met Webb, a civil clerk in the same office as Sydney Olivier, a few weeks after joining the Zetetical Society. That first evening Shaw had been struck by Webb's thick dark hair and Napoleonic profile. The twenty-one-year-old Webb not only knew more than the lecturer and everyone present, he had read everything on the subject and remembered all he read. He was "the ablest man in England," and Shaw claimed to have forced his friendship on him, so that the "futile" Shaw became a "committee of Webb and Shaw."[16] That committee accomplished an enormous amount of work and shared an enduring friendship.

"The talks after the Fabian meetings are very jolly," pronounced the excitement-loving Edith Bland, who was known to faint on cue. The meetings themselves were something else. Not given to the raucous passion of the Marxists, who scoffed at the "drawing-room Socialists," the first Fabians almost stifled themselves with dullness. For the minutes of one meeting, Shaw recorded: "Wilson yawning like anything—No wonder! . . . Coffin fidgeting—putting coals on the fire, distributing ipecacuanha lozenges. . . . Something making a frightful noise like the winding of a rusty clock. Mrs Bland suspected of doing it with the handle of her fan. Wish she wouldn't." Dullness aside, the Fabians persevered, Shaw enlivening their meetings by attacking invited speakers. "Did you see what sudden ruin overtook him?" he whispered to Salt after one such attack.[17]

Before joining the Fabian Society, Shaw had believed that the socialist economy was fatalistic, as Marx, like Darwin, called attention to the operation of huge impersonal forces. Freeing himself from fatalism, Shaw preached the "will to Socialism," conceiving will as creative energy and totally renouncing "Darwinism, Marxism, and all fatalistic, penny-in-the-slot theories of evolution whatever."[18]

Shaw had another change of heart. He entered socialism as a militant and an individualist, not a peaceful collectivist, but within five years he had reversed both those positions. When he finally accepted collectivism, the last of the "old gang" of Fabians to abandon individualism, he immediately turned on the Individual Anarchists. They saw laissez-faire as defending freedom, centralization as thwarting it—beliefs Shaw had largely shared. Now, recognizing the implications of the theory of rent as put forth by Sidney Webb, Shaw denounced the Individual Anarchists and Proudhonists for their "doctrinaire absurdities" on the subject. Even so, he retained the Proudhonist view that property is theft. Despite his conversion to collectivism, Shaw continued to be fiercely independent: "I object to the present system because it gives no scope for individuality."[19]

Shaw claimed that the Fabian Society was established under the "banner of Socialism militant," Charlotte Wilson's anarchism spreading like influenza through the society. More accurately, Shaw entertained "warlike" ideas at first. On a September evening in

Bloomsbury Hall two years earlier, he had provoked his audience of Fabians by voicing his alarm that the middle-class recruits might "taint Socialism with the ideal of self-sacrifice." Though the pigeon-livered Fabian lacked gall and made excuses for not fighting, Shaw's message was "one of rebellion."[20]

Shaw's rhetoric was not matched by his behavior. On Sunday, 13 November 1887, a huge illegal socialist demonstration for free speech was set for Trafalgar Square. The police and military were massed and ready for what came to be called Bloody Sunday. One procession of socialists formed at Clerkenwell Green, where Shaw and others spoke before advancing, banners unfurled, to Trafalgar Square. Marching alongside Shaw was Annie Besant, the freethinking author and orator. En route the procession was attacked by baton-wielding police officers, and the pair separated on Shaw's advice. Instead of heading for safety, Annie Besant commandeered a small wagon, wanting to break the charges of the police. But the driver was fearful, so she jumped out and rushed to the Square on foot. Undaunted by the "rattle of cavalry" or "Scots Guards with bayonets fixed," she identified herself, ready to be arrested. Then fearing a massacre, as she put it, "the people retreated as we passed round the word, 'Go home, go home.'"[21]

More militant than Annie was another woman who marched from Clerkenwell Green. Eleanor Marx, the fourth and youngest daughter of Karl Marx, reported being "in the thick of the fight," suffering blows to her head and arm, her cloak torn and slashed. But still she wanted to hold fast: "I had shouted myself hoarse calling on the men to stand and show fight." When Shaw arrived at the Square, he saw the mounted police and foot patrols, and the remnants of thousands of socialists retreating before the threat of baton blows. Like them, he "*skedaddled* and never drew rein" until safely home for tea. Belatedly, he looked for Annie. That evening, the heroine of the event, as he called her, chaired his talk on socialism at Farringdon Hall.[22]

While Eleanor Marx found it "sickening to see the men run," Shaw mocked the cowardice of a "band of heroes outnumbering their foes a thousand to one," breezily describing his own terror to William Morris. It tickled him to repeat a remark by the dashing R. B. Cunninghame Graham, whose conduct on Bloody Sunday earned him a bed in a prison hospital and Shaw's public praise for his heroism. Cunninghame Graham called Shaw "the first man to run away from Trafalgar Square on Bloody Sunday."[23]

Although he advocated revolution for little more than five years, he retained a militant streak. "If there is to be any shooting, [the Fabian] intends to be at the State end of the gun," he wrote in 1908. And by 1930 he would no longer be certain "that Morris was not right" in his revolutionary zeal.[24] But in 1889, with the appearance of *Fabian Essays*, Shaw, however noisy, was staunchly collectivist and apparently nonviolent. Notably, the Fabian credo with its cautionary strategy provided a remarkably close match to his psychic needs.

At the beginning of his Russian campaign, Napoleon remarked, "I feel myself driven toward an end that I do not know. As soon as I shall have reached it, as soon as I shall become unnecessary, an atom will suffice to shatter me. Till then, not all the forces of mankind can do anything against me." Fascinated by the military genius, Shaw profiled Napoleon in his 1895 play *The Man of Destiny*, his first portrait of a historical figure. As Shaw channeled his defiance into the task of regenerating man spiritually, like Napoleon he elevated his personal concerns to a greater theater. He identified his purpose with that of the universe, calling it an act of self-realization. Purpose is all-important, whether labeled "the will of God, or Socialism, or the religion of humanity."[25] Because capitalism relies on the planlessness of laissez-faire, chaos is implicit. In contrast, socialism promises a harmoniously ordered society—a vision psychologically more appealing to Shaw.

Nevertheless, Shaw did not follow Utopianism, one of the four chief streams of nineteeth-century socialist thought. The Fabian, Marxist, and Christian Socialist positions were all more desirable to him than the Utopian, which raised the specter of discontinuity. He feared a "catastrophic policy for simultaneously destroying existing institutions and replacing them with a ready-made Utopia." The revolution he sought would be "gradual in its operation," exactly what the Fabians advocated, exactly what his psyche demanded.[26] Moreover, the Fabian policy of "permeation," of infiltrating organizations with their members, also suited Shaw's need to overturn the status quo covertly. Permeation in the political realm paralleled the strategy he used in the personal realm— the strategy of the spy.

Like Blake, who created his own system so he would not be enslaved by another man's, Shaw envisioned his own psychologically stable system. Socialism merged with vitalism—that freely flowing spirit of life that he would call the Life Force and dramatize in *Man and Superman* before Henri Bergson had published his discourse on the *élan vital*. Politics and philosophy, biology and metaphysics evolved into Creative Evolution, a label declaring Shaw's affinity to Bergson's identically titled 1907 book.

Shaw's socialism was an effort to set things right, for the current respectability is "nothing but a huge inversion of righteous and scientific social order." Paradoxically, only through another inversion could Shaw find the stability he sought. This inversion at the heart of things accounted for the swinish behavior that Shaw abhorred. Human nature was "only the raw material which Society manufactures into the finished rascal or the finished fellowman." Everywhere—standing in the rain at Hyde Park, rousing long-shoremen at the docks, exhorting on streetcorners, arguing in drawing rooms—Shaw preached that human potential was being stymied and depraved by inequality.[27]

Demanding unceasing activity, promising an age of gold, socialism traded the present for the future. Eternally coiled to strike, Shaw struck a Faustian pact. "My hours that make my days, my days that make my years, follow one another pell mell into the maw of Socialism," he wrote the actor Charles Charrington in 1890.[28] As socialism insatiably swallowed him up, the abyss gaped open. His temporality was reduced to a pitiless numbing activity, and he became the machine Shaw. Sustained by the will to socialism, he rejected the status quo, making a commitment to things becoming, but not yet become, that was heroic in scope.

Couched in the gradualism of Fabianism was revolutionary action wedded to order. The envisioned socialistic world was but another version of Shaw's brilliantly lit, spotless ethereal world. Sojourner and actor, the alien and unnatural Shaw did not feel at home in the existing society he minutely observed, and so he looked ahead to a freshly formed society. There the Complete Outsider would stand revealed as the Complete Insider, directing and performing in nothing less than the drama of world reformation.

Although the wished-for future through socialism might offer him consolation, it could not promise transcendence. Moreover, just as he embraced the all-powerful state, he would for a while blindly endorse all-powerful dictators.[29] In 1885, however, he had not yet threaded his way through the Daedalus-like intricacies of his own spiritual labyrinth. The artist-genius was still to emerge.

13

The Jaegerized Butterfly

I want my body to breathe.
—To Ellen Terry, 1897

The 1880s, a period of frenzied activity for Victorian society as well as for Shaw, witnessed an avalanche of reform movements. For some, raising standards of public taste seemed as pressing a concern as socialism or women's emancipation. The fine and applied arts, fashion, health, and diet were all targeted by reformers. William Morris—artist, poet, and founder of the Socialist League—advocated the simple and natural in furnishings, textiles, colors, and fashion over the reigning fondness for bric-a-brac and generous ornamentation. The difference between the aesthetes and the philistines might be the difference between valuing hand-thrown pottery over delicate French china, as Morris did. Even in flowers Morris had his preferences: the honeysuckle and cornflower rather than the purple gloxinia or vivid blue convolvulus popular in contemporary wallpapers. In dress, Morris favored an indigo-dyed suit with a deep blue shirt. His wife, Jane, rejected the heavy, constrictive dresses dictated by fashion for flowing dresses that captured the romance of the medieval age. Daughter May devoted herself to art in the form of embroidery and to politics in the form of socialism, twin paths to a utopian life.

Meanwhile, Shaw found a circle of friends more inclined to celebrate Whitman and Thoreau than Marx and George. Henry Salt, Eton house master, vegetarian, and dress reformer, married James Leigh Joynes's sister and took up living in a laborer's cottage. Shaw's first visit to Henry and Kate in the Surrey Hills, exaggerated in the *Pall Mall Gazette,* pretended to confirm his "rurophobia" after he was drenched by rain during their walks in the countryside. An intimate of the Salts was Edward Carpenter, "the Noble Savage," who praised sandal wearing, linking liberation in dress to sexual liberation.[1] Like Carpenter's other visitors, Shaw wore sandals in the house. But for country hikes he preferred thick-soled boots, also just the thing for London pavements and the hard floors of art galleries.

These philosophically based approaches to the Simple Life contrasted with popular Victorian interest in cures. Some cures, like the hydropathy delivered at spas, depended on nothing but ordinary nonmedicinal water, unlike those offered at Bath or Tunbridge Wells. Visitors to the Grafenberg House in Hertfordshire could choose from an array of such plain-water cures delivered variously as the Wave Douche, the Cold Descending Douche, the Hot Spouting Douche, and Condy's Ozonized Sea-Salt Bath.[2]

The pursuit of health led in 1884 to the International Health Exhibition, the most comprehensive event of its kind ever before convened. Known as the Healtheries, it stirred Parliamentary interest in patent medicines, and Shaw wrote an article on the subject.[3] A large section of the exhibit was devoted to hygienic dress. One of the most prominent exhibitors was the author of *Health Culture*, Dr. Gustav Jaeger, a German physician who had developed the Sanitary Woollen System. His garments ranged from sheets to digital socks that resembled gloves for the feet. All garments were of un-bleached, knitted natural wool to encourage perspiration and the exhalation of poisons through the skin. Vegetable fibers were considered harmful because they absorbed and gave off noxious vapors, and silk was thought unsafe because it was the excretion of a worm. Virtually all dyes were forbidden. The natural colors and unconventional style coincided with the search for simplicity led by Morris. For Shaw, Jaeger's clothes would mean something entirely different from simplicity.

The importance of those clothes is suggested in the diary he began to keep in 1885. Written largely in Pitman shorthand, which Shaw had learned while convalescing from smallpox at Leyton, the diary was, appropriately, a cash account book. In it the former cashier kept track of his daily appointments as well as every pence spent. The cost to weigh himself, of a half-cent newspaper, a single stamp, rubber bands, train fare, a theater program, a red and blue pencil, an inkstand, a tip to a porter, alms to a tramp, a penny to a little girl at Bankside "for telling us about the alleys," a haircut, singe, and shampoo, chocolates, a tart, fourteen pounds of oatmeal, four pairs of colored spectacles ("as the reading of the *History of Music* had made my eyes a little sore"), the diary itself—all made their way between the bluish-gray covers of the *Court Diary and Engagement Book*.[4]

In February he began writing music criticism for the *Dramatic Review*, a post William Archer obtained for him. Archer also got him work as a reviewer for the *Pall Mall Gazette*, and by the end of the year he was writing pieces for the *Magazine of Music*. In addition, Shaw contributed art notes to Annie Besant's *Our Corner*. Having "slipped" into journalism, he recorded plaintively and prematurely: "this put a stop to my life's work."[5] During the year, Swan Sonnenschein agreed to publish *An Unsocial Socialist*, already serialized gratis in *To-Day*, Henry Hyde Champion's new monthly journal. Meanwhile, with Bessie teaching singing in high schools and Lucy touring with a stage company, Shaw raced across London haunting meetings on peace, on Marx, and on Fabianism, writing letters nonstop, beginning the correspondence that would balloon to a quarter of a million letters and postcards.

In January Shaw went to St. John's Coffee House to speak, but no one showed up because Morris was around the corner lecturing. Only a few weeks later Shaw attended a socialist meeting at Kelmscott House, Morris's wondrous home at Hammersmith Terrace overlooking the Thames. By March he was on social terms with Morris's neighbor, Kelmscott Press printer Emery Walker, watching the annual Oxford-Cambridge boat race from his back lawn. "(Oxford won)," Shaw parenthetically recorded. Having fallen getting off the bus at Chiswick Road, Shaw had muddied his clothes and then felt too dirty to stay for lunch at Hammersmith Terrace. But he was not too dirty to take the train afterward to visit Eleanor Marx to discuss *Love Among the Artists*. In his diary, Shaw circumspectly referred to Eleanor, who lived openly with the womanizing Edward Aveling, as Mrs. Aveling.[6]

The line between professional and personal activities blurred as Shaw rushed from tealess tea at the Cyprus to a meeting of the Shakespeare Society, from the British Museum to the Browning Society, from the Bach Bi-Centenary at Albert Hall to the South Kensington Museum, then on to the lodgings of J. Kingston Barton for his regular Saturday night dinner there (and an argument with a physician friend of Barton's over socialism). To Donnelly's gymnasium for boxing exhibitions, to the Crystal Palace for Berlioz's *Te Deum*, to the National Gallery for exactly ten minutes to look at Raphael's *Ansidei Madonna*, to the Industrial Remuneration Conference during the day to lecture, to Ladbroke Hall that same evening for his first London attempt at acting—the listing of events sketches a cross section of intellectual Victorian society and a seemingly indefatigable Shaw.[7]

All along observers have been struck by Shaw's myriad affiliations and his exploding list of commitments to journalism and politics. But even in his terse journal he periodically berated himself for sleeping late, recording a "desperate resolve to get up early—to buy an alarum clock."[8] Self-mockery aside, his desperation was neither exaggerated nor comic. Sometimes he slept until one in the afternoon in his third-floor room, undisturbed by Bessie downstairs or by Lucy, who still called Osnaburgh Street home even though she was often away touring in opéra bouffe. After rising, Shaw often did nothing but write letters or read a bit. Usually he did not go to the British Museum to work until after dinner, which he ate at two or three in the afternoon at the Wheatsheaf. Often he interrupted his attenuated workday by having tea with friends before beginning his evening round of meetings. When he managed to rise punctually, he ended up nodding over his books—a habit that grew into regular naps by the following year—right there in the middle of the Reading Room.

Disorganized and procrastinating, he still dispatched his reviews efficiently. They were more agreeable than some other forms of writing. He had little patience for editing jobs undertaken for the sake of a paycheck, having worked sporadically for more than a year and a half on an index and glossary for a new edition of the works of Renaissance author Thomas Lodge, finally abandoning the project. More palatable was editing Laurence Gronlund's *The Co-operative Commonwealth in Its Outlines: An Exposition of Modern Socialism* for the Modern Press.

But he was fooling himself when he complained in his diary that journalism left him no time to do any original work. His perpetual craving for sleep was a recognition at a deep level that he was forfeiting his own potentialities. Not even his devotion to socialism could compensate for his unfulfilled creativity. Ideology was not art. Encapsulated in a snaillike stasis in his room—a perpetually disordered space—he was besieged by a suspenseful waiting. Escaping to the streets, he became extremely volatile, leaping from task to task, roaming restlessly through London, evading the artistic destiny he had set out to claim.

Driven by the ambition he disdained, wearing defiance like a mask, his need to be recognized in the social world grew urgent. As literary success eluded him, he momentarily lost his bearings. He regularly forgot names and dates, sometimes showing up for appointments on the wrong day, sometimes missing them completely. To counter the disorderliness and emptiness he felt, he desperately tried to fill time—running away from himself with each new activity. His tense, jerky movements mirrored an experience of time overwhelmed by hopes and wishes, while his paralyzing lethargy reflected the sinking weight of anxiety.

He was in such a state of vague apprehension when he received the news of 19 April 1885. George Carr Shaw was dead. Shaw sent word at once to Bessie, who was in Leyton visiting Uncle Walter, and immediately wrote Barton: "Telegram just received to say that the governor has left the universe on rather particular business and set me up as An Orphan." Shaw embellished the note with two staves of music and the punning instructions, "Grave."[9] The seventy-year-old George Carr Shaw had died in his sleep while staying in a Dublin boarding house; he had congestion of the lungs, a complication of pneumonia. Since leaving Dublin, Shaw had seen his father only once, when he came to London to visit his family—the sole holiday he had taken in his life. No one from the immediate family attended the funeral, not even Lucy, who was in Ireland at the time. George Carr Shaw was ignored in death as he had been in life.

Writing to Uncle Frederick on 23 April, Shaw assumed a commanding tone, cautioning him against becoming depressed at the funeral: "Do not stand any of the family nonsense—they will do their best to keep down your spirits. You will find my way of looking at matters not half a bad one." This letter, like one written on the twentieth, was filled with detailed questions on the family finances. "I fear I have shocked you; but never mind—I have not humbugged you, which was the only alternative." There were questions not only about his father's estate, but also about the estate of his grandfather, Walter Bagnall Gurly, who would die that December at age eighty-five. Shaw even wondered how much Lucy would realize from his mother's estate. He told Uncle Frederick that

Bessie had once drawn up a will with the intention of excluding him, but he had pointed out to her that she had done the "very reverse."[10]

Significantly, he signed himself "yours philosophically G. Bernard Shaw," making this the first letter of record with exactly that signature. Up to this point he had signed himself GBS (beginning in 1880), G. B. Shaw, GBShaw, or G B Shaw. Only a month earlier, in a letter to Frances Archer, he had signed off with a flourish as George Bernard Shaw, "the name by which posterity will revere me." From first-name primacy, *George* was reduced to a vestigial initial, and Bernard was elevated to the status of a complete name, in effect, the first name—the legitimate name. In its new configuration, the name carried authority. A few days earlier he had chastised the socialist agitator J. L. Mahon, who had circulated a statement supposedly approved by "Comrade Shaw." "I am G. Bernard Shaw of the Fabian Society, member of an individualist state, and therefore nobody's comrade."[11] Unwilling to share fraternity, he craved the power and dominion of the father. At last officially fatherless, officially empowered, Shaw lost no time in asserting his identity and his authority over his estate. Every so often during the ensuing year George Bernard Shaw would spontaneously resurrect, until the old identity finally was laid to rest.

Shaw's diary during the week following his father's death shows a full round of attending concerts and meetings, writing articles for the *Dramatic Review*, and correcting proofs of *An Unsocial Socialist*, *Cashel Byron's Profession*, and *The Irrational Knot* (the last two to be serialized in *To-Day* and *Our Corner*, again with no money to the author), calling on friends, walking with Edith Bland, being smitten by the young actress Ethel Herbert. Except for Fanny Hoey calling to offer condolences, there is no mention of mourning. On the twenty-fourth he was "too sleepy to do anything" all afternoon, a condition he attributed to eating mushrooms for dinner.[12]

But Shaw had begun the process of mourning in his own way, uncharacteristically spending the greater part of 18 and 19 May "arranging my papers, tearing up rubbish"— trying to bring order into his life. He vented his feelings by going to Blackheath to spar with Hubert Bland. On 1 June, just before tea and a concert conducted by the Hungarian Hans Richter, Shaw walked with Archer to a shop in the West End newly licensed by Jaeger. Archer bought a pair of braces, and his companion browsed. On the nineteenth Shaw returned to the shop. As noted in the Harris biography, George Carr Shaw's death precipitated not grief but sartorial splurging. Shaw ordered clothes that adhered to Dr. Jaeger's Sanitary Woollen System but that were conventionally styled and appropriate for theatergoing, as he readied himself for the leap into Jaegerism. Then, on 10 August, he ordered the knitted one-piece wool suit that buttoned up to the neck and along one side, the suit that would cause a sensation.[13]

Without question, Shaw's wardrobe needed refurbishing. He had been reduced to lining his baggy trousers with brown paper for warmth, trimming frayed cuffs, and wearing his tall hat backward to prevent it from flopping over. After the daily humiliation of wearing such a wardrobe, any improvements would have been welcome. But Shaw's eye-catching new clothes took on political, social, and moral dimensions. Even as they formed a special kind of cultural document they were enveloped in a web of psychological meaning. Not only were they "the first new garments I have had for years," they were to be paid for "out of the insurance on my father's life."[14]

As he made clear in the tale of the drunken George Carr Shaw crushing his tall hat, Shaw associated his father with his clothes. And had he himself not paid a guinea, a steep price, at a fashionable hatter's for his own top hat, now limp with age? When his father's death released him from the relationship of impotent son to impotent father, Shaw donned the clothes of freedom and triumphantly faced the world on different terms. It was the sartorial equivalent of his victory over the fool of a clerk Smyth—*"I was right."*[15] In flaunting his defiance of his father's clothes, he also defied strict mourning customs on the attire for and length of the mourning period. He aggressively displayed the very feelings of mourning that he wanted to deny, as young children often do. Garbed in yellow, he flamboyantly bid farewell to his father and to his own earlier existence.

Harris (or Shaw posing as Harris) focused on the clothes but not their meaning, mocking the "Jaegerized butterfly."[16] But the clothes were the outward manifestation of an inner metamorphosis. They were more than clothes; they were the heart of Jaeger's system. Clothes, like memories, collect the past and represent continuity. In donning his Jaeger clothes with such bravado, Shaw severed his ties to the past and thereby ruptured continuity, ritualistically marking the end of an epoch. The mourning period became a baptism, a public witnessing of rebirth and transformation.

There is one piece of evidence that suggests Shaw was not as blasé as he let on. The day after visiting the Jaeger shop he tested his lungs on a spirometer, a device for determining the breathing capacity of the lungs, and recorded the amount as 230 cubic inches in his diary.[17] The specter of lung disease added to his general hypochondria. As his father dissolved into his fantasy world, he shed no tears, and he found no cleansing relief. Though the dust on the butterfly's wings glittered, it was mixed with the foul clay of earth.

Yet there he was in his one-piece suit of knitted wool, resembling a "forked radish in a worsted bifurcated stocking." Looking something like a gymnast, Shaw took a trial trip to the Marble Arch without being molested, his costume intimidating spectators, according to Harris / Shaw. The walk to the Marble Arch was just one of many events in which he waved his suit like a matador's cape. It was in a Jaeger suit of soft stockinet that he mounted the stage after the first performance of his first play in 1892, the very suit he had primed his audience to expect in a self-interview in *The Star.* Similarly, in a tongue-in-cheek account of the rehearsals for *You Never Can Tell*, ostensibly written by the actor-manager Cyril Maude but actually written by Shaw, he blamed the power of the author's new clothes for sabotaging the production.[18] With comic hyperbole he deflected from the obvious. Clothes send clear-cut signals. "Clothes make the man" and "Dress for success" are axioms in the social world. But Shaw's clothes exceeded their usual meaning, for he used them like a weapon.

Though the impulse persisted, Shaw would give up the extreme style of the combination suit and return to somewhat more conventional tailoring. Nevertheless, he favored knee breeches instead of trousers, a style advocated by Jaeger as preventing harmful drafts up the leg. The trousers were held up by Dr. Jaeger's Sanitary Woollen Braces and were worn with the Sanitary Woollen Shirt and the Sanitary Woollen Coat. Jaeger further advised that underwear be discarded, the Sanitary Woollen Shirt filling that function when the tail was pulled between the legs and pinned in front. (Later Shaw claimed to wear "some head-to-foot under-garment" and no shirt, although he certainly bought and wore soft shirts earlier.) Shaw wore a broad-brimmed rough-textured slouch hat (wool, felt, or horsehair were the approved materials) and a green, brown, or red tie, the latter too brilliant a color to be appropriate on any but political grounds. Completing his outfit, Shaw wore gloves—to keep his hands clean in the streets—and carried an umbrella. He was Jaegerized from boots to hat.[19]

Many stories circulated regarding his dress, and he was at pains to deny them, preferring those he originated. One story has Shaw promenading down the aisle in his shirt sleeves after the theater attendant objected to his velvet jacket. "Won't do?" cried Shaw to the dismayed attendant. "Do you think I am going to take off any more?" Apocryphal or not, the story illustrates the public perception that Shaw delighted in flouting dress codes. Yet he advocated formal evening clothes for men as hiding genteel poverty and once was mortified at finding himself the only one not in evening clothes at a dinner party.[20]

Wearing wool, like writing satire, was a cunningly aggressive act. Shaw sang the praises of wool to the histrionic Edith Bland, who chopped her hair short and waved a long cigarette holder to accessorize her newly adopted woolen clothing. Nor could children escape his zeal. A short time after his successful walk to the Marble Arch, Shaw urged Ida Beatty to dress her four-year-old son in wool: "The costume will probably expose him to insult from the youths of Mill Hill Park, with whom he can exercise himself in the art of self defence." A decade later, when the actress Janet Achurch lay ill with typhoid fever, the alarmed Shaw urged her husband, Charles Charrington, to put woolen sheets on her bed.[21]

Shaw's Jaegerism was part of the attack on fashion launched by contemporary reformers, like Salt and Carpenter, who wanted to free society from the unhealthy, the irrational, and the ugly in dress. Shaw carried that attack to the theater, denouncing the parade of fashion that turned the stage into advertisements for milliners and dressmakers. At the same time, he remained extraordinarily interested in costume. His stage directions precisely detail his characters' modes of dress, and he personally advised on costume during the production of his plays.

Criticism of fashion is often inspired by moral indignation, like that of the fifteenth-century Italian Girolamo Savonarola. Though Shaw saw clothes as having a moral component, he was no Savonarola. Yet in its more or less permanent form, its brownish tones, its texture, its austerity, the Jaeger suit resembled a monk's habit, protecting him from moral danger. Despite the unconventionality of the attire, it carried a reassuring element of imitation with it, thereby serving a dual purpose. For the suit not only linked him to an elite group, it also separated him from the masses. Dashing around London with wool rubbing his skin, Shaw felt and looked like an initiate.

Meanwhile, even Oscar Wilde had forsaken artistic dress for the suave appeal bestowed by impeccable and more conventional tailoring. The editors of *Punch* had mocked Wilde's change with an 1883 notice announcing the retirement of a successful aesthete. For sale was a "large Stock of faded Lilies, dilapidated Sunflowers, and shabby Peacocks' Feathers, several long-haired Wigs, a collection of incomprehensible Poems, and a number of impossible Pictures."[22]

If Wilde was the dandy, Shaw was the ascetic, but both used clothes to advertise themselves—and with feminine display. Since the end of the eighteenth century, men had dressed uniformly, allowing women the privilege of striking dress. Shaw's clothes exposed with a vengeance, but they also hid subtly, craftily. Shaw had always favored a reddish-brown color—his color—its mixed tones so soothing. There was the orange of flames, the yellow of sunlight, the muted red of sublimation, the brown of earth.

Even ordinary clothes incorporate the protective function of the mother. How much truer for Shaw, self-encased in womblike knitted wool whose comforting color matched his hair and beard. He was reassuring himself against lack of love much as we reassure ourselves in a strange environment by instinctively clutching our coats closer. To Thomas Carlyle, author of *Sartor Resartus* ("The Tailor Re-Tailored"), it was natural to use a clothes analogy in remembering his deceased wife, Jane: "She wrapped me round like a cloak to keep all the cold and hard world off me." Shaw always longed for such a cloak. He would cry out to the maternal Ellen Terry, "I should like to get away from this wretched place to some corner of heaven, and be rocked to sleep by you."[23]

In an 1885 diary entry Shaw placed woolen clothing and vegetarianism under the category of fads. Despite the telltale psychological connection, the innocuous heading has thrown biographers off the trail. Like vegetarianism, Jaeger's clothes had deeper meanings. Their crucial property was the capacity to protect Shaw from assaults launched deep within his body. It was to Ellen he wrote that the curse of London was its dirt and "lack of *light*." For a moment the defiant mask slipped. His "much ridiculed Jaegerism" was an "attempt at cleanliness & porousness." He resigned himself to dust and squalor in his rooms, but he kept the window wide open day and night for ventilation. Why did he avoid cotton, linen, and all fibrous fabrics? They "collect odors."[24]

He found body odor, the sensory representation of personal wastes, even more offensive than environmental odors. For here the revulsion was directed against internal decay and contamination. By wearing the suit he tried to nullify the curse of dirt, the inexorable reminder of matter, earth, and body. He could open his room to cleansing air, but interior, invisible dirt lurked like microbes inside his body, inaccessible to light and air. Paradoxically, the suit that buttoned up to the neck opened the skin to the air. His Jaeger clothes provided a sanitary conduit that drained away filth, forming an antiseptic barrier against anxiety. In donning those clothes, Shaw recoiled from the dirt and decomposition most recently evoked by his father's death, but also evident in his violent reactions to smallpox, meat eating, vaccination, and vivisection. Garbed in his Jaeger suit, Shaw sought the cleanliness and air that universally signify spiritual renewal and to him represented the spotless ethereal realm.

Once he adopted the system, he never abandoned it, carrying his Jaeger sheets with him when he traveled, wearing his socks knitted right- and left-footed, as Jaeger prescribed. Physical garments had been transformed into psychic garments, magic talismans and disguises to protect him from threats launched from within his body, from the surrounding natural world, and from the social world. Wearing his clothes like a suit of armor he camouflaged himself as the Jaegerized butterfly. So accoutered, he readied himself for his most perilous adventure: following the mysterious and terrifying siren calls of romance and love, passion and desire.

PART III

Don Juan in Heaven and Hell

The Victorian theory about Woman is ludicrous delusion. She is the most dangerous of
all the animals.
—To Matthew Edward McNulty

14

Overfed on Honeydew

> I will make you fall in love with me merely to
> shew you how clever I am.
> —To Alice Lockett

By his late twenties Shaw had begun to make his way in the intersecting realms of art, theater, literature, music, and politics. A recognizable man about town, the tall, lean figure in yellow wool seemed to materialize in every hall and club, on every platform and street corner. An air of irreverent intensity accentuated the obvious: he was a most eligible bachelor. Given his psychic ambivalences and intellectual searching, what kind of woman would attract him? It was a question Shaw himself energetically pursued for more than a decade as he defiantly tried to craft his fated male role into one more personally palatable.

In romantic stories—mythological or real life—Woman guides Man to sublime and sensuous revelation. Whatever his conscious desires and beliefs, it is within the secret recesses of the hero's heart that love takes root, fed by fantasies of perfection and promises of bliss. While Shaw cultivated his feminist intellectual convictions, his heart and psyche betrayed and blinded him. Woman appeared to him in a multitude of impenetrable guises, sometimes garbed alluringly, sometimes protectively. Worshipping the reflected glory of his own visions, he came, like his Don Juan, to believe that "in her voice was all the music of the song, in her face all the beauty of the painting, and in her soul all the emotion of the poem."[1] Enchanting and enigmatic, she was the forbidden temptress and the unattainable goddess, the punishing fury and the nurturing virgin. As his artistic imagination pursued Woman into ethereal realms, physical desire opened the gaping trap of flesh and blood and mortality.

Shaw's earliest romantic adventures are encoded in cryptic diary entries. Although terse, they represent a sizable proportion of the few lines he penned to sum up his early years. In Dublin there had been "the L*** Episode," ending in 1871, which was "food for mirth and mocking." Not until 1875 was there another episode worth recording. During "the Calypso infatuation," he and Matt McNulty both wrote verses to the same young woman. The infatuation ended in "Catastrophe."[2]

In London, Shaw's romantic adventures began with the "Terpsichore episode." Terpsichore was none other than Erminia Pertoldi, the gifted prima ballerina who danced her way into the pages of *Immaturity*. At the Alhambra, where ballet was viewed as pornography, not art, she cast her spell night after night, under an artificial moon, over the romantically naïve Shaw, who fancied she danced just for him. On stage, announced by the hushed and mysterious music of *Yolande*, the dancer was enveloped in "blood-red poppy lightening into gorgeous orange," cornflowers and golden ears of wheat "twisted fantastically in her black hair." Dancing and spinning on her toes, she was a "transcendent being" glowing with "supernatural fire . . . elfin fancy and ethereality."[3]

When the fictional Smith realizes that the ballerina is a human being and not a goddess, his love evaporates. In 1879, Erminia Pertoldi evaporated in Shaw's similarly imaginary lovelife, but she was not forgotten. Meeting her by chance nearly a decade later at Stewart Headlam's, Shaw remembered her as the dancer "I used to admire so much." Preparing the novel for publication some forty-five years after seeing her at the Alhambra, he hoped to "rescue her from oblivion" by substituting her real name for the fictional one. "I fell head over ears in love with her on the stage; but off it I found I had no use for her," he wrote Headlam. Shaw added that this reversed his usual practice, which was proof "against all the seductions of the footlights but susceptible to the unpainted private woman," a disclaimer that is fanciful.[4] He was continually seduced by the footlights, and especially by glamorous performers.

With the "eclipse" of Calypso and the "repose" of Terpsichore, "La Carbonaja" achieved the ascendant, where she flickered until 1879, when the "star of Leonora" gained the ascendant.[5] The romantic code names preserving privacy and the astrological metaphor contrast with the matter-of-fact language of the rest of the diary. The language of astrology is the language of romance, used to chart the celestial ebb and flow of romantic destiny. Its use reveals Shaw's inclination to bracket love. Calypso, seducer of Odysseus, Terpsichore, goddess of dance, and La Carbonaja, suggesting the drama and grace of a Mozartian heroine—all three names flowed from a romanticizing vision, an ethereal quest for Woman that was doomed by the flesh, not inspired by it.

The Heartless Man

When Shaw left the Leyton countryside after his bout of scarlet fever, he carried a piece of Alice Lockett's heart with him. So began a recurring motif in which his vulnerabilities evoked a response from a sympathetic woman. Once he was restored to health, Alice conveniently became Bessie's student. The romance was played out in train stations, through the mail, and after Alice's weekly vocal lesson in Bessie's cluttered drawing room—with tea, Shaw at the piano, his mother hovering nearby. As the respectable house on Osnaburgh Street became a semipublic trysting place, Shaw watched and waited for time with Alice, and Bessie watched the young lovers, inverting the spying games of Hatch Street and Torca Cottage.

In sooty, fog-shrouded London, the romance struggled to maintain its freshness. A photograph of the twenty-three-year-old Alice shows a healthy looking woman, not at all fragile or dainty, her fan held fashionably rather than flirtatiously. Though she inspired only the most perfunctory of diary entries, Shaw played the role of the smitten swain. He sighed for "Darling Alice!" and dared "with ink to rain Alice, Alice" eighteen times running. Inspired by paper passion, he jotted down shorthand verses in a pocket note-book. He scribbled letters while yawning over his books in the British Museum or at all hours in his room, lacing his epistles with wit, advice, and real or pseudo-rage over Alice's transgressions. His ambivalences and her prissy temperament and middle-class views destined the love affair to be unconsummated.[6]

In small and large ways, this romance set the pattern for future relationships. Shaw the pedagogue lectured Alice as if she were the fictional Dorothea. Her behavior was a misplaced effort to be a "grown up person of the world." Her handwriting was "the vilest," criticism he repeated to her sister. Jane Lockett retorted that *his* handwriting needed "a microscope it is so small." Shaw the psychologist analyzed Alice as having a schizoid personality. Shaw the satirist mocked, making her "dual entity" into Gertrude Lindsay in *An Unsocial Socialist,* originally titled *The Heartless Man.* Against the thousand Miss Lindsays in the world, "formal and false," his Sidney Trefusis posited only one Gertrude, the "ethereal" Gertrude.[7]

As Shaw transformed his frustrating and often antagonistic relationship with Alice into a paper love affair, he endowed it with a greater degree of playfulness than the real thing. Chafing against Alice's power over him, he provided Gertrude, "as a protection against tramps," with a St. Bernard that she treated more kindly than human beings. The impish Shaw always delighted in drawing analogies that played on his name—both the dog and the namesake saint. "Bernard is the trade mark," he insisted years later.[8]

He was a quick-change artist playing many roles. Sometimes he was the courtly lover bound to his beloved by golden chains. Sometimes he was a knight in shining armor prepared to save her from herself. "Well, let Miss Lockett beware, for she is the dragon that preys upon Alice, and I will rescue Alice from her." Sometimes he was a biblical hero, full of scorn and daring. "Aha, wretch, I am too strong for you. I snap your chains like Samson." He was a rebelling slave, she a "sorceress" and "coquette." One moment he was a "saint," quoting scripture to a "wicked" Alice, the next moment a "detestable, hardhearted, heartless, cynical, cool devil" was seated in his chair telling lies.[9]

He betrayed her. Having parlayed his skills at the piano into jobs as amateur accompanist and stage manager, he played at various operatic performances, including

Gounod's *Faust* at the Victoria Theatre. Rehearsing at 13 Park Lane for *Don Giovanni*, his adolescent fantasies flowered under Lee's baton and the spell of the "artist-enchanter" Mozart. Hearing the music reveal the hero's spirit "in magical harmonies" set him ranging "on a transcendent plane," tempting him to play a real-life version of the Don. Like the supreme Mozartian hero, he fell in love with the Donna Anna "for a week or so." Whether or not he also mocked exquisitely at slavery to love and morality, he conquered Katie Samuel so completely that she felt he was affecting her peace of mind. She would have been gratified to know that years later he remembered her as an old flame.[10]

Meanwhile, Alice was none the wiser. Shaw was used to the attentions of more than one female. Already he was several years into a correspondence with the novelist Elinor Huddart, his confidante on things literary and romantic. The forty-year-old unmarried woman, also Bessie's student, seems to have been a little in love with Shaw. He gave her his photograph, and she complimented him on being "almost as sharp as a woman." Shaw made sure Alice knew of the friendship. "PS Heavens! I nearly put this by mistake into the envelope of the other one, which is to Elinor Huddart!" he appended to an abusive letter.[11]

Using "transparent flatteries," he broke the code of lovers that praises the beloved's unique charms while promising eternal fidelity. Instead, Alice heard, "I have often said that to women," Faustian words to be mouthed by the statue in hell in *Man and Superman*. Sadistically, he told tales about her. Having missed Alice at the train station, where he waited, read, moped, slept, and developed a laming cramp, he lied to Bessie, pretending he had been with Alice until one in the morning. "'Well, upon my word!'" exclaimed the outraged Bessie, only a moment later calling Alice "'old enough to take care of herself.'" Reporting Bessie's reaction, he dared Alice look her in the eye. The affronted Alice complained that his behavior was unfair. Besides, it was his fault that he had missed her, because no definite appointment had been set: "You never are decided."[12]

His feminine indecisiveness irked her, and her masculine assurance prodded him to pseudohysterical outbursts: "Demon! Demon! Demon! Not a statement in your letter is true except the wicked and heartless one that you went home by the 8:32 train, which was the act of a fiend." Carried along by the flow of his own words, he raged: "I am not offended: I am only furious," the tone and rhetoric looking forward to the great catalogue in *Man and Superman* as Don Juan jousts with the Devil. Alice, however, whose sense of humor was imperceptible, did not appreciate her correspondent's wit: "How dense you are!"[13]

On paper he could control her. But if he created a "private fiction" it was because he too had a "dual self," an egotistical George Shaw goading him. The egotist flaunted his technique: the trick of "swordplay and lovemaking combined." He taunted her, telling her he was enjoying the sight of a pretty woman even as he wrote her, informing her he had consoled himself for her odious ways by taking a walk with another woman.[14]

Alice was wrong to think that individuality was anything but illusion, wrote the master of illusion. He discounted the sex differences so important to other Victorian males, saying that at least nine-tenths of him was a "simple repetition of nine tenths" of her.[15] Writing this letter at age thirty, he still felt young and inexperienced. His existential age would never be synchronized with his chronological age. By middle age he felt old. Meanwhile, the blurred sex line posed problems he would not admit.

He confessed that sometimes he did not like himself and that sometimes he did not like her. But then his fluctuating psyche waxed romantic: "there are moments when our two unfortunate souls seem to cling to the same spar." He had acted this part before, in the letter bursting with braggadocio he had written to McNulty two months after arriving in London. It was a confession more intimate and more complete: "You are the only person in the world to whom I am a person with an identity and a soul. That is why I cling to you."[16] There was more than a difference in intensity—with McNulty, he meant it.

Shaw's boyhood friend had married secretly in Dublin in 1883, with George Carr Shaw his witness. Informing him of the news, McNulty advised Shaw to get married and in a tone of regret recalled "another dream"—of the two men secluded together in a cottage with their books. Indeed their friendship had suffered only one breakdown, when their correspondence was halted during a nine-month period in 1876 and 1877. At that time Lucy had visited Dublin, and McNulty became instantly enamored. It seems likely Shaw was jealous that she had stolen his friend's affections and was annoyed that McNulty agreed with Lucy that Shaw should get a job. But with that one exception, the friends continued to write one another once or twice a day for years, Shaw asking McNulty to burn his letters and he, in turn, promising to burn McNulty's.[17]

Alice could not match McNulty's sympathetic understanding. What could she make of a man who admitted that his heart was a "machine" that put him "in *suspense*, which is the essence of woman's power over man"?[18] For here he revealed a psychic connection between his temporality, his relation to women, and Shaw the machine—a machine susceptible to the disruptive power of Woman.

But Alice cared nothing for his temporality or his revelations and the two traded insults: "All people are not machines" and "you are one of the weakest men I have ever met; and in spite of your cleverness I cannot help despising you." "It is false," he retorted: she did not despise him, she feared him. She accused him of considering himself irresistible. He pointed out that she misspelled irresistible.[19]

Shaw grew up watching his mother belittle his father. His attacks and counterattacks against Alice were a ritual testing of his manhood. He proved himself a better man than his father in subduing one saucy young woman. He would learn how to transform his infuriating ripostes into dramatic dialogue that harked back to the stage of Shakespeare and the Restoration and eighteenth-century dramatists. From a lover's quarrel with Alice to Don Juan's quarrel with the Devil, Shaw would expand the landscape of the sex duel to encompass the universe, the combatants nothing less than the Life Force and the Death Force.

Shaw might treat Alice as an adversary, but he knew how useful she could be in guiding him across the unfamiliar landscape of love. She was a novice at letter writing, he an expert. He was a novice at lovemaking, she an expert: "Let us then improve ourselves by practice. Write to me, and I will make love to you." A self-confessed buffoon and dancing bear who bribed people to listen to him by "silly tales of lovemaking," his motivations were decidedly mixed.[20] Meanwhile, the caprices of the romance with Alice allowed him to pillage autobiography for art, a reward rich enough to goad him on a more dangerous treasure hunt.

Shaw grew tired of Alice. She wanted to see him in October 1885. He had not "the smallest fraction of a second" until the following July. He was neither subtle nor kind. "Love making grows tedious to me—the emotion has evaporated from it. This is your fault." Tired of "moral death" with her, he was remorseless: "I hurl the truth about like destroying lightning," as others would discover as well. It was also with Alice that he first envisioned the lovers as a "pair of children."[21] Playing opposite her, he rehearsed the part he would play to perfection: the writer as lover masquerading as the lover as writer.

The final chord in the duet with Alice was struck neither in harmony nor cacophony, but in quiet decrescendo. Acrimonious exchanges aside, the two stayed on friendly terms and met each other occasionally. After Alice married Dr. William Salisbury Sharpe in 1890, Shaw saw them socially and engaged Sharpe as his physician. Surely Alice would have been surprised to know that her letters, tenderly encircled with a ribbon, were never discarded. But she would not have been pleased to know that while busy hurling the truth at her, Shaw neglected to add one small point. In the fall of 1885, as she pleaded for time with him, he was enmeshed in a torrid love affair.

Seduced and Betrayed

> What people call love is impossible except as a
> joke (and even then one of the two is sure to
> turn serious) between two strangers meeting
> accidentally at an inn or in a forest path.
> —To Ellen Terry, 1900

Like the Don Juans of literature and legend, Shaw had entertained himself as a child by daydreaming about women. Like them, he claimed that his blood boiled with sensuality from birth. But as much as he luxuriated in his imaginary adventures with women, as he approached twenty-nine he still lived as a "continent virgin," running away "even when the handkerchief was thrown" to him.[1]

During 1885 another of Bessie's students began to look forward to visits to Osnaburgh Street for chance meetings with the teacher's son. Jane Patterson, known as Jenny, was an Irish widow, a close friend to both Bessie and Lucy, living on properties left to her by former lovers. Shaw, who was "not attracted by virgins," found her experience in love a comforting quality: "I preferred women who knew what they were doing." Over the course of several months, friendship between Shaw and the considerably older Jenny turned "gallant." A crescendo mounted to "supper, music and curious conversation, and a declaration of passion." On 10 July he departed from Jenny at three in the morning with "*Virgo intacta* still," the Latin phrase primly distancing him from the situation, the adjective more appropriate for a woman. Needing a Leporello, he wrote McNulty.[2]

Shaw made a number of sorties and retreats over the next two weeks, his inability to be forthright with Jenny compounding the awkwardness of the situation. At home a few days later, he saw her briefly: "Blush etc." Self-incriminated by his blush—so characteristic of Victorian women—he sat up late to write her. The next day he purchased contraceptives, whose cost he punctiliously noted in his diary. Unsettled by his purchase, he forgot his ticket for a concert of ancient Netherlands music and had to go back home for it, where he found it in the pocket of his other coat. This gave him the opportunity to examine his "charges," which "extraordinarily revolted" him. When Shaw returned to the concert, he was surrounded by women—Bessie, Aunt Georgina Shaw, and May Morris. He left with May, and then went briefly to Jenny's. "Forced caresses" were all that he could manage. He then went on to a gathering at Lady Wilde's, then to Barton's to discuss socialism. Then he went back to Jenny's. She was not in and he did not wait.[3] He had been granted another reprieve.

Shaw had become increasingly forgetful. Why might his forgetfulness have peaked just prior to his sexual initiation, and why would it continue to plague him as his affairs multiplied? Forgetting is a kind of loss, and in sex one loses oneself in secrecy, in mystery, in matter. On the brink of the irreversible loss of innocence that is the price of sexual experience, Shaw was hesitant and fearful. Jenny's body promised the sensual and the forbidden, but he was hindered in accepting erotic knowledge by fears of losing himself in desire and of being swallowed by female flesh, fears he never resolved.

On the day after the concert, a Sunday, he took the train to Tilford in the Surrey hills to bathe and cycle, walk and sing with the Salts and Joynes. In the evening he called on Jenny, now discreetly identified in his diary as JP, but she was going to bed, so he walked home. The next few days he focused on other women, spending an afternoon with Elinor Huddart, escorting May Morris from Socialist League choir to coffee at Ludgate Hill Station, and writing Annie Besant. Meanwhile, he kept McNulty informed of the latest developments.[4]

On the afternoon of the twenty-fifth Shaw went to Brompton Square and to his embarrassment found Bessie visiting there, the women preparing to go out together for the evening. Shaw returned to Brompton Square after eleven only to meet his mother again as the women returned from their evening out. He walked along Brompton Road with them, put his mother on the bus, and escorted Jenny home. At last alone with her, he again stayed until three in the morning, but this time his virginity did not survive the hour. He celebrated his twenty-ninth birthday with a "new experience." Willingly seduced by a woman a good fifteen years his senior, he passed himself off as an innocent victim and gentleman. A later diary entry summarizes in a matter-of-fact but not exactly accurate way: "This was my first connection of the kind. I was an absolute novice. I did not take the initiative in the matter."[5] In the 1887 short story "Don Giovanni Explains" he romanticized the encounter to his advantage. Only Shaw's inability to sell the story prevented him from publishing this humiliating exposé of Jenny until years later.

If art imitated life, life imitated art as Shaw embodied the youthful Byronic hero in his first sexual encounter. The outline of Lord Byron's *Don Juan* shows a young man longing for goddesses. He comes to the attention of a dark-eyed fiery older woman, who visits the young man's mother. She determines to have the blushing son and succeeds in seducing him. There are certain arresting differences. Although Shaw pretended to be naïve, Byron's hero, at sixteen, really is. Significantly, the seduced Shaw, who had staved off assault for years, sounded more like the heroine, Donna Julia, who consented while whispering that she would never consent. Donna Julia, an unfaithful mother figure, is herself married to a jealous husband more than twice her age—a classic triangle. In *The*

Philanderer, Shaw's second play, Julia is the name given to the character who figures in a love triangle, and in several places he explicitly equated Julia with Jenny. Of the fictional hero created by the bisexual Byron, Shaw thought he should be left out of the history of true Don Juans: he was just an adventurous young sower of wild oats. At his age, Shaw might have done the same unless saved by "fastidiousness."[6]

It suited Shaw to think of himself as the innocent novice, for he felt ambivalent from the first and habitually refused to take responsibility for his sexual complicity. He submitted, he said, not out of desire but out of curiosity, and because sexual experience "seemed a necessary completion of human growth." But sex was fraught with danger. "He will be in your power through his desire," the Serpent tells Eve in *Back to Methuselah*. Putting himself in Jenny's power was gambling with his identity, giving her the chance to bend him to her will. Yet the path of manhood lay through the woman's body. To assure himself of his masculinity, it was necessary to take the risk. Self-protectively, he separated himself from his actions. In acting the part of the youthful virgin so coyly, he appropriated the Victorian female role of inexperience, surprise, and lack of desire. "I did not pursue women: I was pursued by them" was his line from beginning to end.[7]

His ambivalence is reflected in his flawed memory and failure to thank Jenny immediately for his birthday present. Though surely she was waiting to see him, he did not pretend to play the role of the gentleman. Instead, he spent the next day, a very warm Sunday, doing "nothing particular" until William Archer came by in the afternoon and they walked along the Thames embankment and stayed to talk on the Waterloo Bridge. On the twenty-seventh and twenty-eighth, he wrote her. On the twenty-ninth he found her waiting for him at his lodgings—she had responded to him by role reversal.[8]

On the thirtieth he walked along the Thames embankment with May Morris, then went to Hammersmith with her the following day and accompanied her to Blackfriars station on 1 August. Again he found Jenny waiting for him on his return, hoping once was not enough for her evasive young lover. Not until 2 August did the skittish Shaw again succumb to her sexually. Casting aside any consideration of Jenny's privacy or reputation, he rushed like a schoolgirl to write a "full circumstantial account" of the "affair" to McNulty. Brimming over with sexual secrets, he spent that evening with Sidney Webb, from whom he drew a tale of a disappointing love affair, feeding his own sense of anger and manipulation.[9]

Where was the fair goddess of his dreams demurely giving herself to him in some richly adorned chamber or idyllic meadow? Having hoarded his virginity, he had been cheated out of it. Somehow he had been made into an object, his defenses penetrated— raped. He lashed out. Instead of his love, he sent Jenny a "rather fierce letter." To make up for his sexual submission, he initiated the first "explosion" of an affair that was marked by explosions. The following day he called on Eleanor Marx, an object of sympathy as she endured her common-law husband's notorious promiscuity and a confidante to Shaw on the subject of sex. Then he had tea with Mrs. Lecky and resolved to begin writing a new *Pilgrim's Progress*. Further motivated by a visit from Alice Lockett the next day, he began (never to finish) his moral treatise.[10] He began playing a double role: the vengeful, violated beloved and the perfidious, sadistic lover.

As he was leaving Jenny's house after his birthday celebration, Shaw had been observed by "an old woman next door, whose evil interpretation" of the late hour "greatly alarmed us."[11] Whether or not Jenny was alarmed, his reaction suggests projected guilt. Two weeks earlier the late hour had not worried him. Instead of savoring his new-found pleasure, Shaw focused on the old woman. Then there was all the awkwardness of sending Bessie home by herself—Bessie, who would put her own correct interpretation on the late hour.

Bessie could hardly have been oblivious to her late-blooming son's new interest. Shaw's feeling that he had been seduced by a woman of the world reflected a range of ambivalences, not the least of them toward his mother's role in the "intimacy with a lady of our acquaintance."[12] If Bessie did not instigate Shaw's first sexual encounter, undoubtedly she knew about it and sanctioned it. It took place in Jenny's rooms on Brompton Square, a female space where the two Irish women, close in age to one another, exchanged confidences. Coincidentally, the difference in age between the experienced Jenny and the novice Shaw was the same as that between the experienced George Carr Shaw and the innocent Bessie, the roles neatly reversed. Much later Shaw gave out that Jenny admitted to being thirty-four. But forty-four seems a better estimate of her age, as surely Shaw knew—older than the so-called "elderly" Bessie when she had followed Lee to London. Alarmed at being observed on Jenny's doorstep, he took the offensive. Like the most profligate Don Juan, immediately he began spreading the news himself all over London and Dublin. It appeared that a precondition for loving was an injured third party. The old woman that worried Shaw that first night and afterward was his mother.

Just as Shaw meticulously and tersely recorded in his diary everything from buying postage to drinking cocoa, he recorded when he had sex—one more item for the clerk to enter into the register. Unlike Samuel Pepys, whose diary details his delight in the senses, Shaw was as squeamish as a girl about the subject. To deal with it, he devised a simple code to indicate sex—(o), (1), or (2). The (o) appears to indicate impotence and is scattered throughout the diary. In making his entries, Shaw committed several faux pas, misplacing the code meant for Jenny. On a couple of occasions it was entered alongside the wrong woman. The very first instance of Shaw's carelessness appeared shortly after Shaw began his affair. In that initial juxtaposition, which would be repeated several times, the code indicating sex was entered after—"Mother." Later, to Greek scholar Gilbert Murray, he wrote: "I very seldom dream of my mother; but when I do, she is my wife as well as my mother. When this first occurred to me (well on in my life), what surprised me when I awoke was that the notion of incest had not entered into the dream: I had taken it as a matter of course that the maternal function included the wifely one."[13]

In "Don Giovanni Explains" the hero enjoys the pleasure of his widow lady for almost a month. Then tedium sets in. Even at his most passionate, Shaw never found sex especially compelling, putting "everything else before it."[14] Nevertheless, complications from his dalliances, consummated and unconsummated, ate into many afternoons and evenings. During the month following his "seduction" he sought happy returns only a few times, complaining about being tired, sleeping badly, having nightmares, worrying about his health. These responses to lost virginity, suggesting guilt and remorse, are more typically female than male. It was only two weeks into the affair when he ordered the hygienic Jaeger suit to protect him against bodily dirt and odor, much as women have been culturally trained to eliminate what Shaw, like Don Giovanni, called the *odor di femmina*. He might assume the clothes and role of a liberated male, but his feelings toward his body were filled with disgust. While Mozart's hero found the scent of woman exciting, Shaw found it repulsive.

After Jenny confronted him with gossip he had been spreading about her, he went home with her, placated her with sex, then stayed away for more than a month, writing her, keeping her dangling, and aggressively pursuing platonic flirtations elsewhere. He found time to coach Agnes Consuelo for the lead in a musical burlesque, and she was charmed enough to send him a box of silk handkerchiefs, which he returned. A few days later, he introduced her musical into a review of historical instruments, Miss Consuelo faring better than anyone else mentioned.[15] The delicacy of her approach was more to his taste than were Jenny's fevered caresses. In the meantime, Jenny's ardor intensified as he withheld sex. It became his favorite sexual stratagem, and it was quintessentially feminine.

He had more than Jenny on his mind. William Morris had been arrested for his part in a free speech protest by socialists. Perfumed with the aromatic oil he had purchased that day at Jaeger's, Shaw went to a meeting of the Socialist League, where he was relieved to find Morris and "delighted to see Her," the adored May Morris. Shaw pledged to speak the following Sunday and get himself arrested, but the prospect put him in a "state of terror." That Sunday, 27 September 1885, tens of thousands streamed to the docks to demonstrate their right to free speech and public assembly; there were no arrests. As Shaw would have it, "the police capitulated" when he volunteered to defy them. Basking in the glow of his heroism, that evening he called on May.[16]

While he cultivated numerous women, he demanded constant availability from Jenny. "Be faithful to me or I will kill you by mere intensity of hate," vowed the unfaithful one, threatening desertion.[17] Counting on her affection, he courted her jealous wrath, strengthening his feelings of masculine sexual control and justifying his ill treatment of her. Though her jealousy was based on his actual philandering, his was the projection of his own fickleness onto her.

Desperate for glimpses of him, she stalked him on the streets and followed him to political gatherings. He regularly found her waiting at home for him, though he preferred to drop in on her without notice, giving an air of spontaneity to his carefully scripted performance. It seemed too calculating to make a date for sex. Sometimes he found Bessie there, making it a cozy threesome for tea. Sometimes he found Lucy. During an attack of pleurisy, she stayed with Jenny to convalesce, creating "confusion" but not deterring him from sex under his sister's nose, as his sexual code indicates.[18]

Then and later, sex was always at the woman's home, where he did not stay the night, making sex a furtive late-night act in a feminine realm—accentuating the split from his everyday life and guaranteeing him the sanctity of his cluttered room. It was not discretion that made him prefer sex in the woman's sphere, as Lucy's presence and Bessie's knowledge shows. He lured women to him and encouraged them to expose their vulnerabilities in front of his mother, then he recoiled from them. There is no evidence that Shaw ever had sex in his own bedroom, either before or after marriage. For him, the sexual was garbed in the taboo, veiled rituals of assault and defense conducted only within the boundaries of the other's territory, away from the psychic constrictions of home.

Rather than satisfying him, sex increased the frantic pace of his platonic pursuits, allowing him in some measure simply to escape Jenny's demands but also providing the suspense of ever-new encounters. As she beckoned to him out of a dark fantasy-world of midnight trysts and voyeuristic women, he shuddered. He found her "sexually insatiable." Since his visits to her were infrequent, this charge reveals more about his sexual appetite than hers, and very likely conceals his inability to satisfy her and his resulting insecurity. Six months into the affair he stopped in to see Lee, having just written an advertising prospectus for him. After a cup of cocoa, he went on to a tryst with Jenny, the first time he had followed that pattern since the affair began. Lovemaking evoked a one word response: "Revulsion." Its onset that night suggests the tangled web of Shaw's sexual and emotional ambivalences, the intersection of his past with the present. He returned to Jenny three nights later to find the journalist T. Tighe Hopkins there, "bent on seduction." The sexual competition motivated Shaw to outstay Hopkins, who was forced into surrender to catch his train. It was not the only time he outsat his rivals.[19]

Increasingly revolted by Jenny's demands for love and sex, and after "violent scenes" at Brompton Square a few months later, Shaw declared that in the future their relationship would be platonic. The distraught Jenny called on him and made another scene, which ended in "much pathetic petting and kissing," but Shaw remained aloof for almost two months. Jenny's delight in her young lover's embrace as they reconciled would have been greatly diminished had she known that his ardor was not the result of her charms. He had just spent a "memorable evening" with Edith Bland, after a day devoted to her. Although he was forced to borrow a florin from her to pay for dinner, tea, and first-class train fare, his diary entry is punctuated with an exclamation point, a form of admiration that Jenny never evoked.[20] In fact, Edith had been pursuing him in the months before his submission to Jenny, months in which he had been platonically involved with numerous other women—not only Alice Lockett, May Morris, Eleanor Marx, and Annie Besant, but also several Fabian women.

The charmingly histrionic Edith, who wrote children's books as E. Nesbit, attracted Shaw. She paraded happily in her "*deliciously* pleasant" woolens and her boyish haircut, the appropriate costume for a bohemian woman whose intimate attachments extended to the South African novelist Olive Schreiner. To Shaw, Edith was one more platonic flirtation, though she persisted in having other ideas. Physically, she thought him "*very plain* like a long corpse with a dead white face—sandy sleek hair and a loathsome small straggly beard," and yet he was "one of the most fascinating men" she had ever known.[21] They met at the British Museum or at various cafés for tea and talk. He escorted her home after Fabian meetings and dropped in to play piano duets. Finding Shaw eager to elicit intimacies, she confided in him about her life, which read like a sensational nineteenth-century novel and featured her handsome womanizing husband, Hubert, whose numerous infidelities included the family governess, Alice Hoatson. The forgiving Edith allowed Alice to continue to live with them, treating Alice's two children by Hubert as her own. Alice, like others, pretended to despise Shaw, but, like Edith, she had a weakness for heartless men. At least Edith thought Alice in love with Shaw.

Shaw offered Edith relief from the illicit ménage à trois in her home in the form of a nicely cautious triangle. More than once he missed the last train from Blackheath and was forced to travel the distance on foot, a journey of two and a quarter hours. Now "passionately attached" to Shaw, Edith "would not be denied" coming to tea. He blamed her for the attachment, and since she was a married woman with children, "she had to live down her fancy." Her "fancy" persisted, however, aided not a little by him. One May day after a visit at the British Museum they had tea at the Austrian Café. She wanted to go home with him. He let her accompany him to his new lodgings at 29 Fitzroy Square (Bessie was out), and the visit got out of hand. Circumspectly, Shaw noted an "unpleasant scene" after he asked Edith to leave, fearing the visit would "compromise her." But as Edith saw it, "You had no right to write the preface if you were not going to write the book," the complaint that men have often lodged against women. Once again Shaw had aroused female passion only to make a scene, not to make love. Although they remained friends, Edith remembered him as the "grossest flatterer" she ever met, as "horribly untrustworthy" and ready to repeat everything he heard without sticking to the truth.[22]

Edith Bland's assessment of his untrustworthiness is verified by the single surviving letter from Shaw to Jenny. It suggests Shaw's callousness toward the woman who was "laid low by crying & pain" for love of him, his lack of sympathy for his sister, and his deviousness with women. He wrote two letters of interest on 10 March 1886. One was to Ida Beatty. Her husband had been forcing himself on Lucy for some time and had harassed her at Jenny's during her stay there. To the "young, charming, and neglected" Ida, Shaw ingratiated himself by calling Beatty a rascal and an unmasked Don Juan. To Jenny, however, he reversed the blame. Poor Beatty was an "exceptionally nervous mouse" in the presence of "a pair of vigorous and experienced cats." It was the latter view that underlay his own cavalier treatment of women. Jenny longed to see him, but his calendar was full for the next two weeks.[23]

As the affair jumped from scene to scene in dramatic but plotless fashion, surprise and suspense gave it structure. Entry after entry in the diary records "scenes"—in the square, at the bus stop, in his home. The scenes were noisy, chaotic, abrupt, and performed. Relying on the impromptu sometimes backfired. One New Year's Eve, Jenny's lights already out, he lingered alone, watching wraithlike from the other side of the square as Jenny's neighbors came out on their doorsteps to welcome in the new year.[24]

Jenny acted the part of a woman driven to jealousy. She read his mail and spied on him. She swore at him, threw things, and pounded him with her fists. Laconically he observed, "JP came, raged, wept, flung a book at my head etc." He thought of her as a bad actress botching her scenes, while he boasted of acting the lover "diabolically well." He recalled to Ellen Terry, "You can't act things perfectly until you have got beyond them."[25] In his role as lover, art passed for reality. Whether cynical or idealizing, he played his part to perfection.

Sometimes the mask slipped. In October 1891, jealous over the actress Florence Farr, Jenny stormed into Fitzroy Square, where Shaw was finishing a paper for the Fabian meeting that evening. The day turned "desperate" amid "scenes from JP. Very tempestuous whilst I was at tea. At last pretended to throw her out of window." Pretense or not, the Shaws were living on the third and fourth floors. To assert control, he used physical violence to threaten the life of a woman driven to hysteria by his blatant philandering. His room had become a stage where he played at being the forceful male. Discarded mistresses torture their former lovers into violence, he wrote not long after, when a police constable murdered his prostitute lover. Sex inside or outside of marriage should not give anyone a lifelong claim on another.[26]

relationship with her emerged. All along it had been a form of aggression. The plot of the scenes, rehearsed with many women, depended on a "womanly" loss of control that empowered him. There were more of these scenes than there were actual sexual encounters. What was important was to act the male. Though he hated hypocrisy, he was the arch hypocrite. Adding spice to the drama of Jenny's sufferings was the dangerous thrill of being observed by Bessie, the trysts often taking place after Bessie and Jenny had spent the evening together. The entire affair was a form of exhibitionism that invited Bessie's voyeurism. With other women as surrogate Bessies, Shaw flaunted his conquests.

Jenny brought out his darkest feelings toward women, those flickering between masochism and sadism, sealed off from the liberating intellect of the feminist. Jenny did not know it, but the epitaph for the love affair had already been written. The year before, Shaw had lectured to the Fabian Society on Ibsen, an exposition that horrified some of the audience members with Shaw's insistence on will and self. By mid-1891 he had turned the lecture into *The Quintessence of Ibsenism*. Whatever his chapter on "The Womanly Woman" said about Ibsen, it spoke volumes about Shaw as he described the "repulsive effect" of the complete self-surrender that transformed "womanly love" into the "caresses of a maniac."[27]

What solution did Shaw propose for the Womanly Woman? Woman must repudiate "her womanliness, her duty to her husband, to her children, to society, to the law, and to everyone but herself," or she cannot emancipate herself—one way to read Bessie's conduct.[28] Ironically, given its background, *The Quintessence of Ibsenism* has meant nothing less than the quintessence of Shaw the feminist. Indeed, Shaw saw his essay in just that light. Yet beneath the visionary prose, the wonder of its logic and rationality, lies the tangled swamp of his ambivalences toward Bessie, his disgust with Jenny, and his antipathies toward the body.

These antipathies drove him to abuse Jenny psychologically as well as physically. He taunted her by dropping by her Brompton Square flat only to leave minutes later. He wrote letters of vitriol and of indifference. He began to pursue other women with a vengeance. So ungenerous was Shaw to Jenny, who loved him wildly, that he called her "no better than a woman of the streets" in a letter to Annie Besant, as Jenny found out by reading his mail. "My boy you got it all for nothing—it was not to be bought at any price," was her anguished cry. She pleaded with him not to leave her letters around for Lucy and Aunt Georgina to read in that house that respected no one's privacy. It was the vengeance of Sonny, the unwilling witness. No wily Alice or intellectual Annie, Jenny was all heart, but she understood him better than they. Her lover was becoming less her lover every month, thinking of her only "as a sucking baby does of its Mar when it is hungry!"[29] Sex with her was sex with a mother/whore. It was misogyny masquerading as sex.

In her fiery temperament, Jenny contrasted absolutely with Bessie, who "never made scenes; never complained; never nagged; never punished nor retaliated nor lost her self-control."[30] It was the single and crucial point of difference—in age, ethnicity, and independence there was all too close a fit. She was Bessie exposed and vulnerable, while he assumed Bessie's granitic surface, allowing pleas and protestations to wash unfeelingly over him, thereby revenging himself on the cold, uncaring mother. In Jenny's jealous rage he found a substitute for the show of feeling he had always secretly hoped to arouse in Bessie.

Just as Jenny and Bessie were associated psychologically in life, they formed part of a composite portrait in art. In *Getting Married* (1908), St John Hotchkiss, whose calling card identifies him as the Celebrated Coward, is involved in overlapping triangles with married women who go by male names: Leo and Mrs George. The latter, wife of an unseen coal merchant, is a clairvoyant who talks to Hotchkiss "like a mother" and recalls Bessie, who communed with spirits via a Ouija board. A woman of passion and ravaged beauty, Mrs George is *"certainly 40, and might be 50,"* Jenny's age during her affair with Shaw.[31] Hotchkiss, called Sonny in the bosom of his family, is twenty-nine and the only character given a specific age—the age of Shaw's induction into the mysteries of life. Sonny's resurrection suggests Shaw's wish to return to his former state of innocence. Through the transforming vision of art, the haunting portrait of Mrs George alludes to the mysteries of female power.

Those mysteries are also alluded to in *The Dark Lady of the Sonnets* (1910), a playlet that purports to show what Shakespeare was really like but actually shows what Shaw was like. There is a trio—Queen Elizabeth, a physically abusive Dark Lady, and Shakespear—reminiscent of the Bessie / Jenny / Shaw relationship. Shakespear, the subject, is under the dominion of Elizabeth, a relationship analogous to that of son to all-powerful mother, and, of course, the middle name of Shaw's mother *was* Elizabeth. As Elizabeth insists on her status as virgin queen, Shakespear insists he is not "baseborn."[32] If Elizabeth suggests Bessie as uncontaminated virgin mother, behind the Dark Lady hovers a forbidden Bessie—a fatal seductress.

In the sordid affair with the all-too-earthy Jenny, fantasies nurtured by art—wonderful amours in a gorgeous ethereal realm—collided with biology and psychology. As life imitated art and art imitated life, two trajectories were traced: an ascending one of art and aesthetics, and a descending one of violence and flesh. The toll exacted by their opposition would become unbearable. For Shaw's ethereal longings were mocked by degrading affairs set against a disordered landscape peopled by exhibitionists and voyeurs, sadists and masochists—the distorted images of his own impulses. Overwhelmed by "horror" and "disgust" at lust, he would finally decide that "neither the origin nor the destination of the spermatazoon should be known to the parties."[33]

As to professional and personal relations with Lee, Shaw never completed his revision of *The Voice* because Lee's heart stopped one night in 1886 when he was "in the act of undressing himself." He was found dead on a Sunday morning, at age fifty-five. Shaw heard the news Tuesday evening from Lucy, who had just heard it herself. He went to 13 Park Lane the next day to verify the death before telling Bessie. Angina pectoris was the official cause of death, but Shaw claimed that Lee's "brain was diseased and had been so for a long time. I was glad to learn that his decay was pathological as well as ecological, and that the old efficient and honest Lee had been real after all." Given Bessie's devotion to the Dublin Lee, it was necessary for Shaw to believe that the days of Lee's London vanity were also the "days of progressive decay." There is no corroborating evidence on brain disease, and Shaw did not attend the inquest, nor did the family take part in the burial proceedings. Earlier in Dublin, according to McNulty, Shaw had been diagnosed as having "'chronic congestion of the brain'" and that, strangely enough, Shaw seemed to be "rather proud of this diagnosis."[34]

Shaw downplayed Lee's death, asserting a bit too strongly that it had not had the least effect on Bessie but that it had seemed odd to her that other people buried him. Having mentioned the oddity, Shaw disposed of it. Once idolized in life, Lee was unmourned in death. Torn by wrath and resentment, mother and son wished to forget Lee and his charisma, not memorialize him through public or private rites of mourning.

Through the years Shaw would remain defensive about Lee, although he made sure that he entered his own version into the record. University of Pennsylvania English professor and would-be Shaw biographer Thomas Demetrius O'Bolger struggled for years to produce an account of Lee's relationship with the family that Shaw would approve. At each succeeding attempt, Shaw became more irritated, descending into the abusive in letter after letter. "You are suffering from what the psycho-analysts call a Resentment Complex"; "You really are the most complete duffer at this kind of work I have ever come across"; "you are a Godforsaken lunatic," a "buffle head." Shortly after Shaw's last denunciation, O'Bolger died, his work unpublished. Not knowing "whether to be glad or sorry," Shaw took responsibility for the lethal effect of O'Bolger's pernicious anemia. He had "helped to worry" O'Bolger into his grave.[35]

Shaw's accounts of Lee are either spare or anecdotal tales embedded in other narratives and built around his professional prowess. Shaw repeats essentially the same tale, shaping and reshaping Lee's history. The hubris that led to Lee's fall is attributed to a failure in teaching methods. From energetic genius to "a quack & a humbug," the sordid ending makes of Lee's life a cautionary tale, with Shaw besting Lee. Yet, as far as being Lee's ghostwriter, the nonagenerian Shaw confessed that he could not guarantee the accuracy of his account: "my imagination has always rearranged facts into stories."[36]

The rearranged facts produced at least two overt tales of guilt and shame built around Lee, that of *The Hornet*, set in London, and that of the Model School, set in Dublin. There is also Shaw's narrative of the decaying Lee, an account inexplicably interrupted by a digression on Pavlov, whose followers have learned "many things that no decent person ought to know." Shaw illustrates: "Our forefathers had the knowledge and experience gained by seeing heretics burnt at the stake and harlots whipped through the street at the cart's tail." Shaw then derives a "moral": "Mankind is better without such knowledge and experience." This moral, forcefully interjected into the narrative about Lee, suggests that Pavlov's experiments were associated in Shaw's mind with Lee's unmentioned vivisections of birds, creatures "so extraordinarily superior" in love and beauty. For Shaw, who as a boy "had sung like a bird" until his "voice broke," then returns to his "tragic" tale of Lee, the "damaged Svengali" at whose bidding he had endured the guilt and shame associated with *The Hornet*. Shaw—who mockingly referred to himself as Svengali—reiterates his point about forbidden knowledge, climaxing in the overtly sexual and phallic example of whips at the cart's tail.[37]

In his revision of *The Voice*, the single chapter Shaw did not touch was "Physiology of the Vocal Organs." An account of the registers by a woman, the chapter describes those mysterious, unseen organs given feminine characteristics by voice culturists. Shaw knew what the laryngoscope revealed and from Lee's Method had learned to control those organs: how to keep his tongue flat and to round up his pharynx and soft palate, how to make the "involuntary pharyngeal muscles" become "active and voluntary." He could then exercise his voice as much as he wanted without damaging it. Citing "private satisfaction," Shaw gladly used the knowledge that Lee had gained by forbidden methods—in trying to unlock the secrets of the vocal organs, Lee had used the throat for his own purposes. Whether the "genuine fecundity" that Shaw saw swirling in Lee's whirlpool of energy and the obsessively identified shame that Lee evoked carried a homoerotic charge, his hypnotic power persisted to the end, as Shaw's final reluctant tribute shows: "He was a genius in his way; but not in my way."[38]

Don Juan's Revenge

> I had no love affairs. Sometimes women got
> interested in me; and I was gallant in the
> oldfashioned Irish way, implying as a matter
> of course that I adored them; but there was
> nothing in it on my side.
> —To Frank Harris, 1930

Like the mythical Don Juan, Shaw considered all women fair game. Like his own Tanner, he wanted women to view him as an enigma and a possibility. Dashing at top speed across London, he encountered the brilliant avant-garde women—the feminists, writers, and artists—who vitalized Victorian society. He flirted with all of them. His insouciance, a disadvantage with women of more conventional expectations, ignited the passions of women dedicated to overturning Victorian strictures. Drawing on a "stock of fantastic complaints" whenever a woman did something for him, he surprised and disarmed those primed to reject delicate compliments.[1]

This technique was brandished so artfully that it worked even with women who disliked him. He clashed with Mary De Morgan, novelist and sister of the stained-glass artist-novelist William De Morgan. Mary was a woman whose mischievous gossip and talent for infuriating her hosts "wrecked every household she entered" (the irony of his description was entirely lost on Shaw). They met at William Morris's home, where Mary bore the "outrage" of being introduced to Shaw with minimal civility. Plotting revenge, he decided to fascinate her. Fascination consisted of this: one afternoon as they chatted over tea in the garden, Shaw asked her how she could tell "such a monstrous string of lies." Morris, drinking his one cup of the day from an "enormous vessel," looked stricken. Everyone else "sat paralyzed." Then Mary smiled. The tactic was so pleasingly unconventional that later in the evening, according to Shaw, the now complaisant Mary surreptitiously squeezed his hand as she went to her room for the night.[2]

His technique with Geraldine Spooner was also typical of an approach in which his pockets were "full of the small change of lovemaking," although what he spent on women was "magic money, not real money." Geraldine was a "pretty girl" he met at an afternoon entertainment at the Socialist League at 13 Farringdon Road. Playing the gallant gentleman, he immediately escorted her to her train at Blackfriars. Three weeks later he gave her his private view gallery ticket. She turned up at a lecture, became a Fabian, and soon they were dining at the Wheatsheaf. Over the course of two years, he would decide he was "rather in love" with her, and she would follow the route of many of Shaw's conquests by taking voice lessons from Bessie to be near her son.[3]

The Black sisters, Grace and Constance, both thought themselves in love with Shaw, with Grace openly declaring her feelings. Their first appearance in the diary is a joint one, on 23 February 1885. Even after becoming engaged to someone else, Grace wrote Shaw, lamenting that her love for him was a "waste of force." Years later, Constance told her son that Shaw said he wanted to marry her but was too poor to take a wife.[4] That he made such an avowal while retreating behind the often-invoked poverty excuse seems likely, but his feelings toward both sisters appear to have been nothing more than flirtation.

In the "Gilchrist affair," his open exploitation of the affections of Grace Gilchrist aroused gossip and anger. They met in March 1885 at a Marx reading in her Hampstead home. Grace joined the Fabian Society to see him, and he returned the favor by flirting and being charming. At the last meeting of the Hampstead Historical Club held at her home, he sang "The Wearing of the Green." He trifled with her, escorting her from the Orange Grove restaurant but lying in Jenny's arms later that night. He wrote her letters and paid her the romantic compliment of trying to compose music to the Browning poem *I Go to Find My Soul* for her. Grace became hopelessly enamored of him, and in a tortured letter she confessed to "childish jealousy of other women."[5]

All this infuriated Emma Brooke, who, acting in Grace's interest, "heaped abuse" on Shaw, as a heartless Don Juan who preyed on young Fabian women. On 12 April, most of his day was occupied with Emma Brooke over Grace Gilchrist. At Marjory Davidson's two weeks later, there still was "great gossip" about Grace. A letter on the affair took up all afternoon on the twenty-fourth. He might have put everything before sex, but not before intrigue. Uncomfortable feelings persisted. Meeting her by chance one day on Hampstead Heath, they passed each other without speaking, and he was "astonished" to see her turn up at a Fabian meeting some time later.[6]

In addition to the endless stream of interchangeable young Fabian women, Shaw courted and admired powerful and famous women. In the British Museum Reading Room, Shaw observed Eleanor Marx working for pennies an hour on various literary assignments. An impassioned socialist and feminist, she translated Flaubert's *Madame Bovary* and two Ibsen plays, and joined the Shelley and Browning Societies. Eloquent on the "great cause of the uplifting of humanity," on one bitter cold night she gave "one of the finest speeches" H. M. Hyndman had ever heard. Shaw admired the dark-haired Eleanor from afar but not at all silently. "I hope I may be excused for confessing that the daughter of the great Karl Marx so interested me that I made a speech solely in order to make an impression on her," he reported one Friday evening to assembled Fabians.[7]

His first try at acting, at Ladbroke Hall in January 1885, had been alongside Eleanor Marx and May Morris. Then the radical chic Socialist League presented *Alone,* by Palgrave Simpson and Herman Merivale, a "third rate comedy" complete with a request for an audience sing-along of "The March of the Workers," with words by none other than William Morris. Shaw would act with Eleanor again, in William Archer's translation of *A Doll's House.* During a private reading he would play the part of Krogstad opposite Eleanor's Nora, chattering and eating caramels in the back drawing room of a Bloomsbury lodging house.[8]

Whatever Shaw's intentions toward Eleanor, he was too late. Eleanor had fallen under the spell of the corrupt and clever Edward Aveling, living with him in hopes that he would divorce the wife he had deserted. On Eleanor's part, their relationship was meant to be a living example of the honesty possible in relationships between men and women under socialism and which the two espoused collaboratively in *The Woman Question.* But Aveling, translator of Engels and Marx, in part the model for the unscrupulous artist-genius Louis Dubedat in *The Doctor's Dilemma,* amused himself by swindling his friends and seducing his young female students. His very presence inspired "a fear and a horror" in Olive Schreiner, Eleanor's friend. Olive astonished Shaw by writing that *he* was the only man she was ever afraid of: "Why, God knows!"[9]

In her misery, Eleanor turned to Shaw. He dropped in unannounced for private tête à têtes after working at the British Museum or responded to desperate notes from her. While Aveling was out seducing other women, Shaw sat with Eleanor dispensing advice and sympathy—he urged a career on the stage and elicited the most personal details of her relationship with Aveling. So successful was he in assuming the feminine role of confidential friend in his talks with Eleanor and other women that he believed that a "woman will let a man deeper into her intimacy" than another woman.[10]

In spite of the private nature of their conversations, Shaw was not at all bothered if Aveling came home to find the two of them together. Because Eleanor was another man's woman, her charms were enhanced for Shaw, who sent her a "long promised" photograph in the spring of 1889.[11] Nor did he ever forget whose daughter she was. His relationship with her was based on two triangles: one with Aveling, the other, more significant one, with the ghost of her godlike father, who died in 1883, before Shaw had a chance to meet him.

When Aveling's wife died more than a decade later, Eleanor expected their union to be legalized at last. Instead, Aveling secretly married a woman half her age. Learning of his betrayal via an anonymous letter, she swallowed poison like Emma Bovary. Hearing of her suicide, Shaw recoiled from writing the obituary, wanting to write about Aveling, blaming him not for deserting her but for having squandered all her money. He stayed away from her cremation, but a few years later, perhaps with Flaubert in mind, described her suicide as "romantic tragedy."[12]

Another friendship that developed deeply personal implications during the mid-eighties was that with Annie Besant, famous disciple of Charles Bradlaugh, leader of the National Secular Society. Tutored by an ardent feminist educator and herself passionately evangelical, she was married at an early age to a mean-spirited country clergyman. After illness led her to question the Scriptures, she incurred her husband's wrath. In a "wild swirl of agony," having lost her Christian faith, she fled with her daughter, finding refuge in her mother's London home.[13] She was in desperate financial straits but was able to impress Bradlaugh with her views. He offered her a job writing for the *National Reformer*. Soon gossip linked her romantically to the handsome and compelling Bradlaugh, but their relationship remained platonic despite his unhappy marriage to an alcoholic.

In the country, behind the locked doors of her husband's church, she had tested her voice and thrilled to its sound as it resonated from empty pew to empty pew. In London she had the chance to thrill an audience. When the petite, delicate-looking woman stepped to the podium to speak on the political status of women in her clear low voice on September 1874, a great platform speaker was born. Shaw, who thought her perhaps the greatest orator in all Europe, later vouched that he heard her say " 'A rose is not a violet' with such quiet force" that it seemed a "revelation of a new truth."[14] But in 1877 her advocacy of so-called Malthusianism for the working class ran afoul of prevailing mores and of the Lord Chief Justice, who equated birth control with corruption. She was prosecuted along with Bradlaugh for publishing and aggressively distributing a tract on contraception. The resulting trial, sensationalized by the press, prodded Annie's vindictive husband into suing for custody of their daughter. He won his case and dragged the child, screaming and racked with scarlet fever, from her home. Martyred, Annie believed that she had helped society recognize that a father's absolute right over his children deprived the mother of legal claim.

At a socialist meeting in 1885, Annie heard Shaw flippantly call himself a loafer, by which he meant he was not of the working class, just as his Tanner would mockingly add the initials M. I. R. C. after his name to indicate Member of the Idle Rich Class. Not recognizing the self-satire, Annie attacked him in print, deciding this explained why he was so "marvellously shrewish and 'crooked' " in discussions. Learning the truth, she printed a retraction, though she felt that she had been trapped by the Irishman. In January 1885 she came to a meeting of the Dialectical Society, where Shaw was lecturing on socialism. Tension mounted as everyone waited for the great orator to demolish Shaw.

Instead, she demolished the opposition, asked the amazed Shaw to nominate her for the Fabian Society, and invited him to dinner, eloquent testimony to his wit and intellect— and the powerful charm of his personality.[15]

The triumphant Shaw submitted to the worshipful attention of the conquering woman nine years his senior, a victory especially sweet coming after the two previous men she had admired. When Annie had tired of Bradlaugh's atheism she became a disciple of Aveling's scientific secularism, espoused in his presocialist days. Shaw and socialism were now her twin causes, as she officially became a Fabian by early summer. She offered Shaw the pages of her socialist magazine, *Our Corner,* as an outlet for his unsold fiction, and made him her art critic, an easy enough task since he was already gallery-hopping for *The World.* Savoring his victory over Aveling, Shaw spent Monday evenings playing piano duets at Annie's Avenue Road home. True to the tenor of the relationship, Annie practiced faithfully for those evenings while Shaw made impromptu attacks on Hayden. The relationship was also marked by Annie publicly smoking cigars and Shaw carrying her handbag.

Eventually cacophony overpowered the personal as well as the musical elements of the relationship, for Annie demanded more emotional security than her advanced views suggested. Shaw saw it as an intimacy "of a very close and personal sort" that did not go further than friendship. Annie disagreed, and the relationship "threatened to become a vulgar intrigue." In 1887, a month after her courageous actions on Bloody Sunday, the irrevocably married Annie drew up a legal contract setting down terms by which she and Shaw might forever make beautiful music together. At this Shaw bolted, the two return- ing their letters, Shaw burning his. But not before Jenny, still very much in his life at the time, absconded with some of them, returning enraged to pound on his door early Christmas morning.[16]

Yet how could Shaw confuse Annie's legal document offered to him, a professed feminist, with a vulgar intrigue? It was the prospect of a sexual liaison that was unsettling. Moreover, Annie's independence, take-charge attitude, and disregard for conventional mores resembled the pattern Bessie had traced. In abruptly breaking off the relationship, Shaw treated the professionally esteemed woman no better than the young Fabian women who swarmed around him. Revealingly, his diary records that having read over Annie's letters before destroying them, he was "disgusted" with "the trifling of the last two years or so with women."[17] The period of his trifling equaled the period since he had become sexually active (but only with Jenny) and ignored earlier flirtations. Sex with women threatened and disgusted.

Boarding at Annie's house had been John Mackinnon Robertson, a Shakespearean scholar and journalist who had come from Edinburgh to assist her with *Our Corner.* On at least one occasion Shaw had visited Annie specifically to put on the gloves and spar with

Robertson. Undeterred by the Scotsman's obvious attachment to her, Shaw insouciantly played the piano and the lover. By the time of Annie's written proposal, Robertson had left England—heartsick at being neglected for the Irishman, or so Shaw thought. Now Annie was alone, and the story arose that she became suicidal over Shaw's rejection and that her hair turned gray with grief.[18]

Whether Annie's agony in 1887 was entirely because of Shaw, as he believed, or aggravated by her involvement in political issues, she continued her socialist activism. Ironically, after Shaw sent her Madame Helena Blavatsky's *The Secret Doctrine* to review for the *Pall Mall Gazette,* Annie abandoned Fabianism—rewarding Shaw by making him virtually invisible in her autobiography.[19] Embracing the book's occult doctrine of theosophy derived from Hindu thought, she became a disciple of Madame Blavatsky. Somewhat inevitably, given the older woman's strongly masculine appearance, rumors circulated that theirs was a lesbian relationship. When Madame Blavatsky died in 1891 the anointed Annie ascended the altar to preside as the high priestess of the secret doctrine.

"I am your Mahatma," declared Shaw, but she ignored him and moved to India. There she combined politics and religion, founding the India Home Rule League and promoting Jiddu Krishnamurti, her adopted son, as the messiah. "I know too little of her Indian career to say whether she achieved anything original theosophically," was Shaw's comment on that stage of her life. But of Krishnamurti, whom Shaw met in Bombay, he was the "most beautiful human creature I had ever seen. . . . I have never read anything of his doctrine that I disagree with."[20] Nor did he finally disagree with Annie's approach to marriage. The action of *Getting Married* consists of the characters attempting to draft a partnership contract to take the place of traditional marriage, the clairvoyant Mrs George offering advice on love and life.

As the relationships with women expanded geometrically, even the usually laconic Sidney Webb exclaimed, "My! you do warm both hands at the fire of life!" It was a welcome comment from another male, reassuring the reluctant Shaw that he had mastered his part. But it was not the fire of life that warmed him, but the fire of art. "I am a fiend, delighting in vivisectional cruelties," he wrote Bertha Newcombe in 1896. Tanner describes the unscrupulous nature of the artist, who gets into intimate relations with women "to study them, to strip the mask of convention from them, to surprise their inmost secrets," for women have the power to make the artist "see visions and dream dreams."[21]

Nor were sisters exempt from use. Georgina Sime, Lucy's friend, reported that Lucy complained to her that "'George listens to all I say and then he takes down the good bits and writes them down as his own, and everybody laughs and thinks how clever he is.'" Lucy's revenge was to mock the author of *Man and Superman* by referring to him as the "Super-One." Another memory of her brother's cleverness may have added to her annoyance. He once reviewed her performance in the comedy-opera *Dorothy* for *The Star* as "desperately vapid," and her husband Charles Butterfield, who appeared opposite her, as "cherubically adipose" and "evidently counting the days until death should release him from the part," the reviewer himself skipping out before the third act.[22]

All the women who interested Shaw, young and old, advanced and conventional, had one quality in common—a highly assertive personality. Such a personality traditionally has been regarded as masculine, and it is often identified with militant feminism. The women's interest in socialism and feminism branded them as sexless or lesbian, just as actresses were branded as whores—a holdover from the theater that flourished after Charles II was restored to the throne in 1660, a period when actresses were mistresses to nobility and royalty. It was to the socialists and actresses that Shaw looked for excitement.

Katie Samuel and his mother's pupils notwithstanding, the music critic and lover of opera showed little amorous interest in professional female operatic artists, another group of female performers relying on costume, makeup, and role-playing. Opera is an art form based on vocal aggressiveness, the equality of male and female voices. Whatever their fate, operatic heroines must be musically equal to hero and villain alike. In their characterizations, dying or oppressed operatic heroines are paragons of strength, often exhibiting a fierce will as they disregard conventional codes of female conduct. As he sang their parts for his own amusement in Dublin, Sonny had reveled in the mystical power of the great heroines. Alive as they were to him in his imagination, the son and brother of singers was not attracted to their flesh-and-blood counterparts. Compartmentalizing women, he sought out the "masculine" socialists and the "feminine" actresses, admiring the intellectual, elevating the whore.

Ironically, in view of his treatment of women, Shaw's overreliance on his cold and selfish mother played an important role in his identification with the feminist cause, certainly a politically correct one for a Fabian. Faithful to his mother, Shaw proved personally treacherous to many women. His admirable fidelity and shameful treachery grew out of the knotted roots of childhood pain. For long before, Sonny had identified himself with the parent who had inflicted the most frustrations. That parent was Bessie.

Tailoring the New Woman

I am a first class ladies tailor.
—To Mrs. Patrick Campbell, 1912

Shaw's writing from the mid 1880s consisted largely of sparkling short pieces that eclipsed the journalism of his peers. Chock-full of anecdotes and insight, the writing still crackles with freshness and wit. There were book reviews for the *Pall Mall Gazette* from 1885 to 1888, art criticism for *The World* beginning in 1886 and continuing sporadically for years, and music criticism—for *The Star* as Corno di Bassetto from February 1889 to May 1890, and then for *The World* as "G. B. S." from 1890 to 1894. There was the appearance of *Fabian Essays,* various Fabian tracts, and *The Quintessence of Ibsenism.*

Summed up, the writing seems prolific enough. But his diary makes clear that he felt he wasted most of his time. Day after day he arose at noon or one and amused himself by playing the piano and singing before going to the British Museum, where he might talk the afternoon away. Often he picked up conversations with strangers encountered during the course of his day. Sometimes only by escaping his lodgings could he write.

Stymied by a *Star* article, he left his room to write in the street, finishing the piece "on a coping of the Embankment near Blackfriars Bridge." He wrote while waiting for women, on train rides to the country, on the top deck of city buses, lying on the sand at Broadstairs just outside London. Being in transit, changing the scene, and writing in public were more dramatic acts than writing at home. He acted the part of the writer, and so he wrote. But even away from his fourth-floor study his space remained relatively constricted, as he traced and retraced his steps around London. He did not even cross the English Channel until 1889, when he spent a week with Sidney Webb. Then he was squeamish on the way over, disgusted at the Hague by the smell of the canal, and sick on the way back.[1]

What is missing in the summary of Shaw's output is any purely artistic writing, although there were a couple of desultory attempts. For two months in 1887 he attempted a novel about doctors. *Rhinegold,* the collaboration he had begun three years earlier with William Archer, appeared abandoned as well, Archer having defected when Shaw demanded more plot. The so-called cup-and-saucer comedy, was to have been based on the French formula popularized by Eugène Scribe in the early part of the century and still used by Victorien Sardou, a formula Shaw derided a little later as "Sardoodledom." Shaw read the play fragment to Henry Arthur Jones, whose 1884 play *Breaking a Butterfly* (with Henry Herman) was a perversion of *A Doll's House*. One of the two most popular playwrights of the period, the melodramatist wondered: "Where's your murder?"[2] Ignoring Jones and Archer, reacting against Scribe and Sardou, Shaw took until 1892 to complete the play. *Widowers' Houses* emerged finally as a bitter satire on slumlandlordism, the first in a trio he labelled Unpleasant Plays and a far cry from sentimental comedy.

Widowers' Houses was followed in 1893 by *The Philanderer*, which satirizes the new cult of Ibsenism, the New Woman, vivisection, and the medical profession, all somewhat precariously balanced on a "real basis of clandestine sensuality." *Mrs Warren's Profession* written that same year, was banned for thirty years in England because Mrs Warren was a successful (and unremorseful) entrepreneur in the world's oldest profession. Earlier that year the censors had not objected to Sir Arthur Wing Pinero's tragedy of a "woman with a past," *The Second Mrs. Tanqueray*. Pinero, who shared the honors of success and fashionability with Jones, relied on the conventions of the French *pièce bien faite*—the so-called well-made play—which used the formula of exposition, situation, "great scene," and disentanglement. In dramatizing his delicate subject, Pinero took the precaution of condemning Mrs. Tanqueray to suicide once her past as a prostitute is revealed. Outraged at treatment of sexual material he found blatantly exploitive, or "Pinerotic," Shaw came up with his own version as he turned to playwriting in earnest.[3]

Then what accounts for the almost decade-long lacuna in Shaw's artistic output? Was he really too busy or too poor or too discouraged or interested only in success by any means, as his biographers variously contend? Unlike Mozart, whose father's death as he began *Don Giovanni* unleashed an artistic volcano of such strength that a single night's labor yielded the overture, Shaw seemed to have buried his artistic impulses with his unartistic father. Strutting around town in yellow wool, he seemed like a caricature of an artist more interested in labor laws than aesthetics. But the theme that would engross his art had taken hold of his life. He had first to work it out there before he could transform its elements artistically. For more than a decade it simmered underground, sending forth strange plumes of steam, first surfacing artistically in *Immaturity* as the longing of the autobiographical hero to be known as Don Juan Lothario Smith, and more obviously in "Don Giovanni Explains." In a tremendous artistic eruption, it would find its most compelling expression in the figure of Don Juan in *Man and Superman*, whose third act, the dream symposium in hell, furnishes an oblique spiritual biography of Shaw.

For the creative artist, the death of the father can stir deep feelings of ambivalence. For Shaw, that meant working through feelings of loss and guilt, anger and betrayal at the drunkard who had seduced the young Bessie into marriage, the spineless husband who was an accomplice in his own usurpation, the father who never measured up. Long preoccupied with feelings of guilt and punishment, Shaw now fused them with the feelings of sensuality natural to his aesthetically sensitive nature. He would never write an operatic masterpiece like Mozart, nor was he ready to write a dramatic masterpiece. First he had to prove to himself that he was his father's son, the man who had seemed "very safe company" until he scandalized society by carrying Bessie off. The son, "fastidious and proud," began to woo with a vengeance.[4]

In this chapter of his life, the man touted as a great feminist mistreated women, the Jennys and Geraldines and Annies mere conveniences or ornaments. He had internalized the elements of sexuality, punishment, and damnation, the very elements composing the Don Juan legend.[5] The most influential theme in Western literature, a symbol of Western culture since 1600, it underlay the generic roles Shaw admitted to playing, such as author and man of the world. Inverted and expanded, it became the vehicle for working out his personal destiny as he incarnated the arch-seducer of women, at last transcending that role to epitomize the artist as hero.

Such a destiny seemed a far remove from his first play, in which Shaw projected his own anger and disillusionment onto the stage. Admittedly, *Widowers' Houses* is "a propagandist play—a didactic play—a play with a purpose."[6] The informing principle of the play, which is structured as a satire, is the ridicule of institutions and manners outside the world of the play. As the play points up the discrepancy between the ideal and the actual, Shaw subverts the conversion pattern common to Victorian literature—and significant in the playwright's life. The play turns on the propriety of using rent from slum property to maintain a comfortable bourgeois life. In the morally diseased society depicted, the physician cannot heal, for the hero himself, Dr Harry Trench, falls victim to the corrupting epidemic. His expected marriage to Blanche Sartorius, daughter of the slumlord, reveals Shaw's view—lust seduces, then money seals the marriage contract. The unpleasant subject, the satiric form of the play, and a dramatic method that attacked expectations and misled his audience—all reflected Shaw's view of the world and his way of dealing with it in everyday life. But while life was subject to enfeebling vicissitudes, art offered empowerment. He soon decided that it was infinitely more exhilarating to manipulate the minds and emotions of an amorphous theater audience than the body and emotions of an audience of one. The playwright as lover would move between seduction and assault.

Even before *Widowers' Houses* was produced Shaw was trying to arrange publication on the grounds that a successful production of any play is virtually impossible.[7] His play ran for only two performances, opening 9 December 1892 at the Royalty Theatre. It was presented by the acting company of J. T. Grein's Independent Theatre, whose initial production the year before had been Ibsen's *Ghosts*, proving it a company able to weather controversy. Dramatic history was being made.

Opening night was noisy. As *Widowers' Houses* assaulted a complacent society, the offended, near-riotous audience hooted in protest, encouraging the socialists to applaud wildly in a vain effort to drown them out. Then Shaw stepped before the curtain to make a political speech, a feat he found so agreeable that he repeated it for the final performance. The Jaegerized Shaw embodied the message of his play—a new suit of beliefs is needed—a message alluded to through the associations of the slumlord Sartorius's surname (he is given no Christian name) with Carlyle's famous "Clothes Philosophy" in *Sartor Resartus.*

An uproar raged for a fortnight as the newspapers carried articles and letters that marked the play as an event. Shaw savored his notoriety as the critics attacked on two fronts. Most agreed that all "his *dramatis personae* are entirely selfish and despicable." Blanche especially horrified the theater reviewers, just as Robert Louis Stevenson had been horrified after reading *Cashel Byron's Profession* a few years earlier: "I say, Archer, my God, what women!" Even Archer, the one-time collaborator reviewing it for *The World,* thought the characters a "set of blood-suckers" who are "strangely bloodless." Shaw was not at all put out by Archer's "amazing exposition" of his "Shaw theory," affectionately calling him a "sentimental Sweet Lavendery recluse," a reference to Pinero's sentimental comedy *Sweet Lavender* (1888).[8]

A second critical camp dismissed the play as no play: "Mr Shaw wishes to utter a tirade against certain abuses; and he thinks the theatre a suitable pulpit for his utterances"; and "Mr Bernard Shaw is an amiable Fabian who believes that 'rent is robbery.'" Shaw answered that anyone who wanted to see the difference between an essay on rent and Widowers' Houses could buy Fabian Essays, containing exactly such an essay by him, for ninepence.[9] In some measure, both types of criticisms—characters as mouthpieces and discussion instead of action—would haunt Shaw's career. His great virtue, his unprecedented articulateness, would be judged a flaw by those blind to the complex way his characters *used* words dramatically.

There was another complexity. Shaw had so little taste for the "horrible artificiality of that impudent sham the Victorian womanly woman, a sham manufactured by men for men," that he had his heroine beat the parlor maid. Yet even as he challenged the "whole rotten convention as to women's place and worth in human society," an entirely personal drama was being played out between the playwright, his leading lady, and another woman. How much more scandalized the critics might have been to learn that the vilified, darkly melodramatic Blanche had a real-life counterpart.[10] Moreover, the actress who played Blanche relished the part because she believed herself first in the playwright's affection. With its subversive message and its autobiographical resonances, Shaw's maiden play gave him a thrilling taste of power.

The Philanderer

Shaw's deceitful treatment of women became public spectacle with *Widowers' Houses*. The episode stands out like a Pirandellian drama, blurring the line between actors and spectators, life and art—as Shaw cast one woman in the role inspired by her rival, the latter was a spectator at the impersonation. The flesh-and-blood model for Blanche was none other than Jenny. Still his faithful mistress after seven and a half stormy years, she had been jealous of Shaw's attentions to the leading lady for some time.

Acting the role of the sultry Blanche was Florence Farr. The thirty-two-year-old actress was the daughter of Dr. William Farr, a famous sanitary reformer who, having "survived his wits," consequently "lost most of his means by senile speculations." A New Woman, Florence Farr rebelled against the sexual and domestic roles assigned to Victorian women, pursuing feminism with unrelenting vigor. Safely married to the absent actor Edward Emery, she was admired by William Butler Yeats for her beauty of face and voice. The Yeats connection aroused Shaw's competitive instincts.[11]

Seeing her perform one May evening in 1890 in John Todhunter's *A Sicilian Idyll*, the critic for *The Star* was impressed by her striking good looks and her intelligence. He met her not long afterward in the company of May Morris, who was teaching her the fine art of embroidery. Then in October he ran into her at a private gallery viewing of arts and crafts, and they had a good talk. A week later he escorted her to an afternoon concert at the Crystal Palace, and they lingered over tea (beer for her) at the Pine Apple before going on to her rooms for "playing and singing" and talk of Ibsen. He stayed so late that he missed an evening appointment and had to write a letter of apology. Entranced by the "*amiable* woman, with semicircular eyebrows," he began to squire her around town and to show up at her Dalling Road lodgings, whose walls she had adorned with Egyptian gods and goddesses she herself had painted.[12]

Sometimes he found her more independent than amiable. When she took brandy to cure a headache, he quarreled with her and left in a huff. He pushed her artistically, trying to rescue her from mediocrity. He persuaded her to play Rebecca in Ibsen's *Rosmersholm* and Beatrice Cenci in Shelley's verse drama, *The Cenci*, working with her on elocution, coaching her for her parts, even giving costume advice as she tried on Rebecca's dresses for him. The Ibsen play he found personally intriguing—a female intruder moves in with a couple, destroys the marriage, and drives the wife to suicide. As Rebecca, Florence was uncertain in voice and action, but she "got through by dint of brains and a certain fascination and dimly visible originality."[13]

Her uncertainty was nothing compared with her fascination. Writing Charles Charrington, Shaw declared himself in love with Florence Farr, but "for Heaven's sake do not tell Mrs Charrington." This was typical grandstanding, given the actor's marriage to

Janet Achurch. After seeing *her* play Nora to Charrington's Dr. Rank, Shaw sat next to her at a dinner for the cast and friends of *A Doll's House.* As if Nora, the New Woman, had become flesh, he was "suddenly magnetized, irradiated, transported, fired, rejuvenated, bewitched by a wild and glorious young woman," immediately writing her to that effect and sending her copies of *Cashel Byron's Profession, An Unsocial Socialist,* and a lecture of his on acting. Within a week of meeting Janet, his "going on about Miss Achurch" had so offended Archer's wife, Frances, that Shaw was "terrified" she would "have it out" with him.[14]

The letters to Florence are beautiful and extravagant but too histrionic to issue from deep feeling. Similar ones were being written to Janet at the same time. Having stopped by to see Florence, finding her home in darkness, according to his diary, he "wandered about disappointed for a time," and then came home and read a tract on anarchism. To the actress he ranted: "Tears have dropped from my heart—tears of mortal disappointment." And then, "Wretch! selfish, indifferent, heartless wretch! A million reproaches on you for ever and ever. Farewell: all the happiness I owe you is cancelled and the balance is now on the other side—a huge balance, incalculable, unliquidatable."[15]

Only days earlier, carried along by such melodrama, he had cried out in self-conscious adoration: "oh my other self . . . my very self." Less than a month later, on 2 June 1891, an evening visit to her evoked one word: "Disillusion." Yet the next day he wrote verses to her, "being more deeply moved than I could have imagined."[16] It was not Florence the flesh-and-blood woman that moved him but the image of her that his own romanticizing imagination could still conjure. The intimacy had run its course from excitement to disillusionment—as swiftly and inexorably as that with Jenny. But Florence had not outworn her usefulness to him as an artist. She radiated an aura of the beautiful and the artistic, putting him in touch with emotions he could release creatively.

Meanwhile, Jenny was racked with uncontrollable jealousy. Shaw felt no compunction at all in seeing both women, dividing one August evening neatly in half, one part Florence, one part Jenny. Then, one evening when Shaw was calling on Florence, Jenny burst in at Dalling Road, "being violent and using atrocious language." Shaw kept her from physically attacking Florence by brute force, then spent the next two hours coaxing her out of Florence's house. Back at Brompton Square at one in the morning, it took another two hours to coerce a letter of apology out of her to reassure the unnerved Florence. The episode left him "horribly tired and shocked and upset." The following day he went for a walk with May Morris, persuading her to deliver Jenny's letter to Florence.[17]

No longer was the Jenny/Florence triangle possible. Its coup de grâce occurred onstage in the first act of *The Philanderer,* a play Shaw began writing a month after Jenny's unforgivable scene. In transferring the affair to *The Philanderer,* Shaw conceived of Julia

Craven as a "study of jealousy." Beautiful and tragic looking, she enters the play raging. Like Blanche Sartorius, she is dynamically sexual, a stereotypical dark-haired temptress. Nevertheless, the transformation into art endowed the character with more dignity than Shaw allowed for the original, who was "without a single redeeming feature" and a "perfect idiot." That Jenny could still sometimes be lovable was a "great lesson" to Shaw. The resulting play, a "detestable thing" combining "mechanical farce" with "realistic filth," disgusted him.[18]

This closely autobiographical play opens with a fictional scene depicting the actual final scene of his love affair with Jenny. Julia breaks in on Leonard Charteris making love to Grace Tranfield in her drawing room, with Charteris as coolly cavalier as the author wished he had been. When Grace beams with love, Charteris feels a *"sudden revulsion."* In this fictional world of icy lust and delicate savagery, the fate of the philanderer is to go on philandering. "Coquettes and Philanderers are incorrigible," the author later warned.[19] Just as Shaw's affair began in a triangle, it ended in a triangle. As the personal became the public, reality became illusion and the sordid became art—finally giving Shaw the power to extricate himself from Jenny's too earthy clutch. Now the plays flowed from his pen. Art was a way to live on the earth while transcending it.

Flaunting the label *philanderer,* Shaw advertised his manliness. The label hid the fact that he engaged in sex far less frequently than appearances suggested. Protected from sex by multiple relations, many with married women, he retaliated in a hundred ways against those women who relentlessly offered their bodies. Obsessed with bloodlines, his trademark was bloodlessness even as he established the desired lineage. It was, he told O'Bolger, "the outcome of the Shaw taint" in him, since the Shaws were "all philanderers." Yet in 1890 to Jules Magny, who had translated a socialist paper of his into French, he wrote, "As to 'les séductions de la femme,'" opinion was divided between those who regarded him as "a saint or a statue" and those who suspected him of being an "Irish Don Juan." Both opinions were "equally romantic."[20]

Having satirized the lust of the philanderer, Shaw turned to the female prostitute—the first mother he portrayed dramatically. He was prodded by Janet Achurch's suggestion that he write a play using Guy de Maupassant's *Yvette,* a story of a prostitute mother who passes her profession on to her daughter, a story Shaw called "ultra-romantic." "Oh, I will work out the real truth about that mother some day," he told Janet. In August 1893 he traveled to Monmouth to stay with Sidney Webb and his bride of one year. The former Beatrice Potter was the daughter of a well-to-do businessman and the author of *The Co-operative Movement in Great Britain* (1891). She and Sidney would form a remarkable intellectual partnership as they worked together for social and economic reform. At Beatrice's ancestral home, Shaw, like the Dalkey Sonny, lay outside, sometimes on a deserted bank of broken ground, sometimes in a field commanding a view of the Wye

River, and he imagined a story. Working on a play begun a few days earlier, he blended *The Second Mrs. Tanqueray* with *The Cenci*, Shelley's tragedy about incest and victimization in an evil society. He introduced a "real modern lady of the governing class" to please Beatrice, ending up with Vivie Warren and *Mrs Warren's Profession*.[21]

Shaw has the matter-of-fact Mrs Warren take to the streets in the same way Cashel Byron takes to the ring. Both choose professions considered immoral as the best way to capitalize on their special talents—just as Bessie and Lucy brazenly sang on the stage. Mrs Warren is not the sentimental whore with the heart of a virgin so beloved by men from Alexandre Dumas *fils* to Eugene O'Neill. From her perspective, marriage is prostitution, a view her creator never relinquished: "The only way for a woman to provide for herself decently is for her to be good to some man that can afford to be good to her." If the woman and the man are social equals, she should make him marry her, "but if she's far beneath him she cant expect it."[22]

The play revolves around the relation between Mrs Warren and her daughter Vivie, a cigar-smoking, whiskey-drinking mathematician. When Archer called Vivie a "Shaw in petticoats," Shaw derided the possibility but repeated it in print. Beneath the surface of the play flows the hint of incest between Vivie, who is not sure who her father is, and her suitor, Frank Gardner. Writing Archer, who shuddered at the horror of the Vivie/Frank courtship, Shaw wondered why he had not also noticed the incestuous overtones between Mrs Warren and Frank, the son of Sir George Crofts, her former lover, and between Crofts and Vivie.[23]

More than literary influences like Shelley or Ibsen account for Shaw's "unholy fancy" for incest. There was the case of a man Shaw personally "watched," a friend of his mother in her younger days, he wrote Archer. "When my sister grew up he became infatuated about her and wanted to marry her." That this is an oblique reference to Lee becomes obvious in a long letter, written a week later, devoted to the subject of incest. Shaw thought societal taboos regarding sexual intercourse were really convention masquerading as instinct or morality. Of the taboos necessary as a "point of honor," the "most important case" was the childhood housemate, whether blood relative or "stranger in blood." Incest should be redefined to mean "intercourse between housemates."[24]

The last of his Unpleasant Plays completed, on 26 November 1893 he began a new play, a "romantic one," for Florence Farr. Had he not already certified her to be "my best and dearest love, the regenerator of my heart, the holiest joy of my soul, my treasure, my salvation, my rest, my reward, my darling youngest child, my secret glimpse of heaven, my angel of the Annunciation"?[25] Then on 29 March 1894 she appeared in John Todhunter's *A Comedy of Sighs,* a pseudo-Ibsenite play that failed disastrously.

The next day Shaw hurriedly put the finishing touches on the play he called *Arms and the Man*. He immediately offered the "romantically beautiful" lead to Alma Murray, the actress acclaimed for her performance as Beatrice in *The Cenci*. It was to Alma that Shaw had first appealed before promoting Florence as Beatrice for the later Shelley Society production of the play. He had no qualms about revealing to Alma that Florence still expected to play the lead.[26] Alma was enticed by the invitation, and Florence was persuaded to give up Raina to play the role of the aggressive servant Louka. The obliging Florence even underwrote the production, having been given money by Annie Horniman, who would become the patron of the Abbey Theatre in Dublin.

With Yeats's *Land of Heart's Desire* as a curtain raiser, *Arms and the Man* delighted an opening-night audience that included Oscar Wilde and Henry Arthur Jones. Satirizing the false heroics of war while gently mocking class pretensions and romantic ideals, Shaw's candy-coated Pleasant Play ran for fifty performances, making it his first commercial success. Its setting in a storybook Bulgaria and its trappings of military romance would inspire Viennese composer Oscar Straus and lyricist Stanislaus Stange in *The Chocolate Soldier*, a popular operetta that was a travesty in Shaw's view.[27] Not until after his death would another Shaw play be set to music, the *Pygmalion*-inspired, hugely successful *My Fair Lady*.

However enchanting *Arms and the Man*, disenchantment had taken its toll in real life. Once he had written Florence: "Cubits high and fathoms deep am I the noblest creature you have yet met in this wood of monkeys where I found you straying." Having ascended to a poetic plane, he challenged any analyst to find "one base ingredient" in his regard for her. But he was her taskmaster more than her lover: he refused to allow her to do her work badly. It was the taskmaster who would finally pronounce the verdict to actress Elizabeth Robins: "She can't act."[28]

Like Don Juan himself, Shaw advertised that Florence "set no bounds to her relations with men" and already had "a sort of Leporello list of a dozen adventures" when they met. The gender reversal inherent in the Leporello epithet was a pointed one, the unnecessary revelation about her sex life clearly implying that he had been added to her list. Shaw reported that the good-natured Florence seized hesitant admirers by the wrists, pulling them to her with the cry, "Let's get it over." At least it was the kind of behavior he often evoked from women. [29]

The intimacy Shaw brags about probably had much less sex than Shaw let on, and may have been sexless. For Florence, no hot-blooded Jenny, viewed sex as a form of hygienic gymnastics. She preferred to bar it from her "serious relations." Then there is the report of Sidney and Beatrice Webb to Hesketh Pearson. Sidney credited Shaw with "'one divagation,'" to which Beatrice added, "'And that one forced on him.'" Pearson decided afterward the escapade "must have referred to his married life only," since the Webbs knew about Jenny and Florence—Pearson assuming the relationship with Florence was sexual. But the forced relationship more closely describes that with Jenny than any other before or after marriage. It seems likely that Shaw meant to mislead on the nature of his relationship with Florence. In fact, she wrote an article that seems to have been insidiously aimed at him, denigrating "Man," who at night avoids passion, fearful of the emptiness and depression that follow ecstasy.[30]

Shaw's diary is of slight help here—except negatively. There is no corroborating evidence that he had sex with her. Possibly because the novelty had worn off, he had discontinued his sexual bookkeeping by 1888, when the single diary headnote was devoted to his health and his spirits, both more absorbing topics for him (both health and spirits suffered until sunlight returned the following spring). Although Florence retained Farr as her stage name, in his diary Shaw referred to her as Emery or FE as long as she was married, noting always the man's claim on the woman. The initials suggest a special closeness but not necessarily sexual intimacy—he had used initials immediately after their Crystal Palace rendezvous. Other than Jenny, she was the only woman regularly indicated by her initials. There was one man so designated—McN for McNulty.

Shaw claimed that society was "full of people" who flirt and "conceal nothing but the humiliating secret that they have never gone any further." Even to the womanizing braggart Frank Harris he admitted that the women who had conquered him physically could be counted on "less than the fingers of one hand." To those "occasions," he attached "no importance; it is the others which endure." So in addition to revulsion at the sex act itself, he denigrated the worth of those "occasions," the term itself suggesting infrequency and reduction of the woman to the act. He always believed what he wrote in *The Quintessence of Ibsenism:* "Love, as a practical factor in society, is still a mere appetite."[31] Although he had sexually charged relationships with a number of women and appreciated female beauty, it is possible that during his lifetime Shaw had sex only with Jenny. That would not make him unique. Groups of men who incline to such sexual constraint include the religious, the ascetic, and the homosexual.

He urged Florence to divorce her husband, not because he wanted to marry her, but to prevent legal problems should Emery return. She followed his advice, but once her divorce was final, he avoided her. When she wrote him at last, it was "rather bitterly." They met, strolled around the park one March day in 1895, chatted and laughed, stopped at the Swiss café, took the tram to her sister's Bedford Park home, but there was nothing left to say—all of which he reported in full to Janet Achurch. Even so, Florence still could be used to taunt Janet, whom he accused of never writing him. If Janet did not write immediately, then "F. F. shall be Mrs Bernard Shaw at the earliest date."[32] But Florence would not even be mentioned in his diary for another seven months. It was over as far as Shaw was concerned.

She consoled herself with Yeats. More and more she immersed herself in mysticism, occultism, and the secrets of the Order of the Golden Dawn. She devoted herself to what she called "elaborating the art of speaking to the psaltery," accompanying herself on a thirteen-stringed lyre, made for her by French musician Arnold Dolmetsch. Shaw, who mocked Yeats's belief that "cantilation" was anything other than intoning, complained to her about her recitations. He had "never been able to knock enough articulation" into her, and he wanted "to throw things" at her when she let the final consonant wither.[33]

Florence's revenge for Shaw's Higgins-like bullying came in the form of an unflattering portrait written in 1907 in *New Age*, a socialist journal that had hired her at Shaw's recommendation. Then she, the New Woman nonpareil, compared his method of understanding women to a dentist putting a gag in his patient's mouth and ruthlessly probing a tooth. Florence emancipated herself, just as Shaw recommended in *The Quintessence of Ibsenism*, and the two forgave each other, remaining faithful friends. Her path led eastward, like Annie's, to a Vedantist seminary for females in Ceylon, where she died in 1917. In the last months of her life she wrote Shaw twice about her breast cancer, and he replied "as gaily as I could." Florence's older sister Henrietta Paget informed Shaw of Florence's death because "you worked for a long time together & she was fond of you."[34]

While Florence had flourished on her own, Jenny, for all her fury and vitality, was no match for Shaw, who succeeded in transforming his longest and earliest relationship into an aesthetic slice of life in *The Philanderer*. In 1912, Shaw, who had seen Jenny only once and in passing since that fateful night with Florence, denied her written demand for money supposedly spent in caring for the recently deceased Aunt Georgina Gurly. A year later, "in affectionate remembrance and honor," he altered his will, leaving her one hundred four pounds per annum, money she did not live to inherit.[35] Jenny is the only woman friend to have her photograph included in *Sixteen Self Sketches*, published the year before his death.

G. J. Vandeleur Lee, center, encircled by Lucinda Elizabeth (Bessie) Shaw (left) and George Carr Shaw (right). Courtesy of Beineke Rare Book and Manuscript Library, Yale University.

The author approaching 33 Synge Street, Shaw's birthplace, second door up, with plaque. Photograph by Rosalind Schnyder.

Secluded Torca Cottage, Dalkey, as it looks today. Where the ménage à trois flourished and the moral passion was born. Photograph by the author.

The Rabelaisian Dr. Walter John Gurly, Shaw's "third father."

Shaw and Robert Moore Fishbourne, a fellow clerk at the Townshend Estate office, Dublin, 1876.

Shaw and Lucinda Frances (Lucy) Shaw at Ventnor after the death of Elinor Agnes (Yuppy) in 1876. Courtesy of the Shaw Collection of Dan H. Laurence, University of Guelph Library.

Oscar Wilde and Lord Alfred Douglas at Oxford, about 1893.

AMATEUR BOXING CHAMPIONSHIPS

FOR THE

QUEENSBERRY CHALLENGE CUPS,

LILLIE BRIDGE GROUNDS,

SATURDAY, MARCH 17th, 1883.

Managing Committee.

MARQUIS OF QUEENSBERRY.	C. W. L. BULPETT, Esq.
SIR J. D. ASTLEY, Bart.	D. GIBSON, Esq.
H. J. CHINNERY, Esq.	E. B. MICHELL, Esq.
GENERAL G. F. GOODLAKE, V.C.	E. C. STREATFIELD, Esq.

Judges.

C. W. L. BULPETT, Esq. | E. B. MICHELL, Esq.
D. GIBSON, Esq.

The Winner in each Competition will hold the Cup for One Year, and receive a Champion's Medal. If four compete, the Winner will receive a Silver Cup in lieu of a Medal, the second man a Bronze Medal.

LIGHT WEIGHTS.

Not exceeding 10st., to weigh and draw at 1.30 p.m.
Challenge Cup (25 Guineas).

1	P. BEATTY	..	London.
2	C. LACEY	..	London.
3	W. H. HEATH	..	Hungerford.
4	H. J. HOWLETT	..	Cobden Club.
5	GEO. MAUDSLEY	..	Manchester.

MIDDLE WEIGHTS.

Exceeding 10st., not exceeding 11st. 4lb., to weigh and draw at 2 p.m.
Challenge Cup (30 Guineas.)
To Box after the First Rounds of the Light Weights.

1	P. BEATTY	..	London.
2	G. B. SHAW	..	London.
3	W. DENNISON	..	East London B. & A. C.
4	J. ANDREWS	..	Hackney.
5	F. FRANCIS	..	Twickenham.
6	R. ELSTON	..	Fulham.
7	S. H. REED	..	Eastbourne B. C.

HEAVY WEIGHTS.

To Box after the First Rounds of the Middle Weights.

Any Weight. Challenge Cup (35 Guineas) To Weigh and Draw at 2.30 p.m.

1	G. B. SHAW	..	London.
2	A. F. SOMERSET	..	Farnboro'
3	H. MURRAY	..	Oxford.
4	F. FRANCIS	..	Twickenham
5	C. PHILLIPS-WOLLEY	..	Fairford
6	H. J. STEVENS	..	Salisbury
7	*Montgomery*		

WINNERS OF BOXING CHAMPIONSHIP CUPS

Since the Commencement of the Competitions.

	Heavy Weights.	Middle Weights	Light Weights.
1867	J. C. HALLIDAY.	H. J. CHINNERY	R. CLEMINSON
1868	T. MILVAIN.	H. J. CHINNERY	No Competition
1869	No Competition	H. J. CHINNERY	H. L. JEYES. w.o.
1870	H. J. CHINNERY	E. B. MICHELL	R. V. CHURTON
1871	H. J. CHINNERY	E. C. STREATFIELD	R. V. CHURTON.
1872	E. B. MICHELL	H. J. BLYTH	R. V. CHURTON
1873	F. B. MADDISON.	A. WALKER.	C. T. HOBBS.
1874	D. GIBSON	F. R. THOMAS	L. DEVEREAZ
1875	A. L. HIGHTON	J. H. DOUGLAS	H. S. GILES.
1876	R. WAKEFIELD	J. H. DOUGLAS.	A. BULTITUDE
1877	J. M. R. FRANCIS	J. H. DOUGLAS	H. SKEATE.
1878	R. FROST-SMITH	G. J. GARLAND	G. AIREY.
1879	G. H. VIZE.	H. G. BRINSMEAD	G. AIREY.
1880	R. FROST-SMITH	W. B. BARGE.	E. HUTCHINS.
1881	G. FRYER.	T. P. BELLHOUSE.	E. B. MICHELL
1882	A. F. SOMERSET.	F. FRANCIS.	C. H. KAIN.
1883	*Montgomery*	*J. A. Reed*	*H. J. Hewlett*

Shaw's personal program, Amateur Boxing Championships, 1883, showing him entered in middleweight and heavyweight ("Any Weight") categories, with winners noted in his hand. Courtesy of Harry Ransom Humanities Research Center, University of Texas at Austin.

William Archer in 1891. Courtesy of the Elizabeth Robins Papers, Fales Library, New York University, and Mrs. Mabel Smith, trustee of Backsettown.

Shaw in 1885, soon after he purchased his first Jaeger woolen suit (without knickers). Photograph by Emery Walker. Courtesy of the Shaw Collection of Dan H. Laurence, University of Guelph Library.

Mrs. Jane (Jenny) Patterson in 1885. Under the label "My Lady Friend," Shaw included this photograph in *Sixteen Self Sketches*.

May Morris, Henry Halliday Sparling, Emery Walker, and Shaw during the time of his "Mystic Betrothal" to May, which began in 1885 and ended in 1893 in a ménage à trois with Sparling. Photograph by Walker.

Ellen Terry and Henry Irving in the sentimental *Olivia*, which Irving first presented at the Lyceum Theatre on 27 May 1885.

Edith and Havelock Ellis in 1896.

Edward Carpenter at Millthorpe in 1905.

Charlotte Shaw on the beach, photographed by Shaw shortly after their marriage in 1898. Courtesy of the Shaw Collection of Dan H. Laurence, University of Guelph Library.

Harley Granville Barker on the beach, near Studland Bay, Dorset, 1901, photographed by Shaw.

Shaw on the beach near Studland Bay, Dorset, 1901, photographed by Harley Granville Barker.

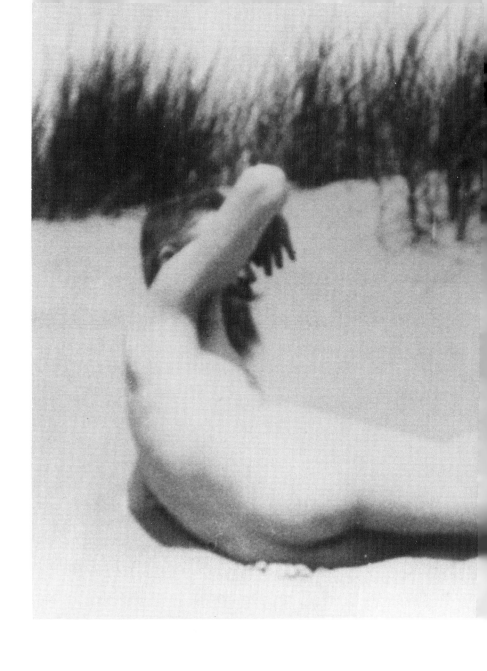

Shaw on holiday, reclining on the sand. Photographer believed to be Harley Granville Barker. Courtesy of the Shaw Collection of Dan H. Laurence, University of Guelph Library, and the Royal Photographic Society.

A revealing shot of Shaw and Harley Granville Barker. Photograph by Charlotte Shaw (generally dated 1901, but more probably 1904 at Harmer Green). Courtesy of the Shaw Collection of Dan H. Laurence, University of Guelph Library.

Harley Granville Barker and Charlotte Shaw, photographed by Shaw, 1901. Courtesy of the Shaw Collection of Dan H. Laurence, University of Guelph Library.

Harley Granville Barker, Lillah McCarthy, and Shaw rehearsing *Androcles and the Lion,* 1913. Courtesy of the Shaw Collection of Dan H. Laurence, University of Guelph Library.

After his legendary World War I exploits, T. E. Lawrence (Lawrence of Arabia), an ardent admirer of Shaw, assumed the name T. E. Shaw. Photograph by Howard Coster, 9 October 1931.

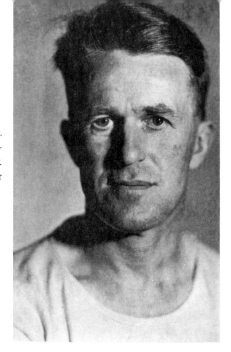

A domestic Shaw at a Fabian Summer School. Courtesy of Burgunder Shaw Collection, Cornell University Library.

Shaw and Gene Tunney on the Adriatic island of Brioni in 1929. Courtesy of International Newsreel.

At his hut at Ayot St. Lawrence with Vivien Leigh and Gabriel Pascal. Shaw discusses his screenplay of *Caesar and Cleopatra*, which Pascal filmed during 1944 and 1945. Vivien Leigh played Cleopatra opposite Claude Rains as Caesar. Courtesy of Valerie Pascal, *The Disciple and His Devil* (London: Michael Joseph, 1971).

At Ayot St. Lawrence shortly before his ninetieth birthday. Courtesy of the Private Collection of Sidney P. Albert.

18

The Imaginary Lover

> The ideal love-affair is one conducted by
> post.
> —To Hesketh Pearson

"Janet *recreates* me," Shaw wrote Janet Achurch as his love affair with Florence was winding down in March 1895. "I become a saint at once and write a drama in which I idealise Janet." The play he referred to was the recently completed *Candida,* which would premiere in 1897, with Janet as Candida and husband Charrington playing her stage husband, the Reverend James Mavor Morell. Idealizing women was a direct path to art, but creating art required a certain life. Trying to rescue the drug-dependent Janet, Shaw advised her that "you do not lead the heavenly life by abstaining: you abstain because you live the heavenly life."[1] More and more for him, art and abstentions crowded out mere sensuality. As for his relationships: the more ethereal, the more appreciatively and artfully remembered.

He recalled the Jenny / Florence triangle with disgust. There in the sexual extreme of his triangular relationships, flesh gaped and life pressed down. At the opposite end of the spectrum was another triangle, one thoroughly idealized by art and charged with the spiritual and aesthetic yearnings that fired both his drama and his socialism. It had begun in soulful adoration a decade earlier, antedating his affair with Jenny by some months and lasting a lifetime in memory. The object of Shaw's worship was May Morris. Admired for her virginal beauty, she was drowned in the scent of art, fame, and power, an aphrodisiacal blend for Shaw. Around her he fabricated a magical tale. It resembled those medieval romances that poured forth from William Morris's Kelmscott Press, tales Shaw disparaged as troubadour trash but read for pure escape. Appropriately, the setting for Shaw's romance was May's splendid home on the Thames.

There, as in the namesake Kelmscott Manor, Morris's medieval country house in Oxfordshire, the faithful came to pay homage to their "one acknowledged Great Man," as Shaw called him. Those who came were inspired by utopian visions, and some were convinced that Morris, in his dedication to the handsomely useful and the beautiful in itself, had already created a version of that earthly paradise he longed for in verse and prose and pursued in ideology. Much was designed by Morris himself, a statement against the ugly materialism of industrial England and an avowal of devotion to the

145

aesthetic ideals he had pursued as a member of the Pre-Raphaelite Brotherhood. Everything in this "magical house" was beautiful, from the hanging Oriental carpet to the gorgeous tapestries to the big cupboard Edward Burne-Jones had embellished with a scene from Chaucer.[2]

Shaw gained the older man's respect. It was Morris who labeled Shaw's wit "Shavian," after a Latin signature in a manuscript by some medieval Shaw.[3] The contemporary Shaw came to spend Sunday mornings with the great man, helping him offer up socialist gospel on street corners. On Sunday evenings workmen and poets alike dissected socialist thought in the converted coach house adjoining Kelmscott House. After those intense meetings the lecturer would be invited into the house to dine. The incongruity of favoring armed insurrection in this setting, as Morris did, was politely ignored. Burning with visionary fire, the one-time clerk who still dreamed of rending Ireland's social fabric found himself seated around a long, unpainted trestle table in a room of otherworldly splendor.

The magnificently maned Morris, garbed in intense blue—given to expressing his annoyance at trivial or offensive statements by pulling single hairs from his moustache and muttering "Damfool! Damfool!"—presided and poured fine wine. In total silence, Jane Morris, immortalized in Pre-Raphaelite Dante Gabriel Rossetti's portrait *The Blue Dress*, offered meticulously prepared meat dishes. Languid and remote, with her dark hair and flowing garments cut from wondrous cloth, she appeared to Shaw to have just emerged from an "Egyptian tomb at Luxor."[4]

Amid this voluptuous setting sat Shaw—the ascetic, vegetarian, teetotaler wearing the impossible woolen suit that crackled and chirped when he moved, like some giant yellow insect unaccountably fluttering around Jane Morris's impeccable dining room. Having accepted the supper invitation, Shaw managed to decline most of the supper, disappointing both host and hostess. Shaw himself was ill at ease, but on one occasion Jane Morris avenged the slight to her cuisine by pressing two servings of pudding on the unsuspecting Shaw. She then triumphantly announced that the pudding had been cooked with suet. It was the only remark Shaw remembered her addressing to him.

So Shaw gained the frequent, sometimes intimate, company of the beautiful May. The irresistibly attracted Shaw advertised his admiration. He wrote playfully of May to Mary Grace Walker in January 1885, creating a miniature drama revolving around a stolen handkerchief at the rehearsal of *Alone,* the production that also featured Eleanor Marx. In September he praised the "divine profile of the most beautiful of women" to Ida Beatty. The theme of May's beauty runs through the letters and lends credibility to his account years later. The shape and aura of a fairy tale permeate the telling: "Now it happened that among the many beautiful things in Morris's two beautiful houses was a very beautiful daughter, then in the flower of her youth. You can see her in Burne-Jones's picture coming down *The Golden Stair*, the central figure."[5] The once upon a time tone, the unnamed maiden, the thrice repeated "beautiful" (three being the magic number of myth), the unassailable proof provided by art—all create a vision of supernatural youth and loveliness.

The ineligible Dublin outsider, although not at all inclined to marriage, found May infinitely desirable and untouchable. One Sunday evening he turned to say farewell. At that moment May appeared in the hall and, according to Shaw, made a "gesture of assent with her eyes," as a "Mystic Betrothal" was registered in heaven. With that description, like Burne-Jones, Shaw immortalized an image of May. Surely part of the heavenly aura surrounding her was reflected glory from her powerful father. The very fact that a half century later Shaw included the tale of the Mystic Betrothal in his introduction to a volume devoted largely to Morris's politics attests to this. At the time, Shaw's romantic longings swirled around May so that in true fairy tale fashion he made no sign to his beloved, claiming the Mystic Betrothal was "written on the skies for both of us."[6] The celestial imagery was an effort to transform a real woman into a goddess. But once he associated the flesh-and-blood woman with his longings, she may as well have been impenetrable marble.

Since May represented Shaw's personal ideal, he regarded her possessively and was stupefied when suddenly she married "one of the comrades." Then Shaw needed rest and change, and the young couple invited him into their home: "Everything went well for a time in that *ménage à trois*," reads Shaw's romanticized version. "It was probably the happiest passage in our three lives." But then the ménage à trois took on another cast. When Shaw left the following January, the marriage was in ruins, fired by rumors that his continued attentions to May did nothing to extinguish. Shaw told biographer Holbrook Jackson that the stricken May remained an "iceberg" as far as her husband went. Even Lucy fanned the flames of scandal. At an Arnold Dolmetsch concert she cried out: "'There goes Mrs Sparling. . . . She's just divorced her husband, because she wants to marry George.'"[7]

Shaw's diary paints a somewhat different portrait. On 4 April 1886, Shaw learned from Henry Halliday Sparling, a socialist colleague, of his love affair with May. On 8 April, at the Wheatsheaf Restaurant, there was talk about May and Sparling. During the next four years, Shaw saw May frequently, but though he might dine with her or walk with her, he was not interested in marrying her. Tired of waiting, May married Sparling in June 1890. Then, on 1 November 1892, Shaw, unable to bear the odor of paint at Fitzroy Square, asked the Sparlings to put him up "for a few nights" at their small Hammersmith Terrace home, close to her father's great one. There in the little house with all the Morris charm, Shaw watched May embroider by day in the drawing room, the art critic having praised her "great curtains covered with glowing fruit-forests" in the pages of *The World*. In that elegant haven Shaw was sheltered from the odor, grime, and disorder of his own rooms. The days stretched into almost three months. Shaw, worried about sanitation, would not return home because the drains were up in Fitzroy Square. It was time enough to turn his unhappy surprise at Sparling's success to his own advantage.[8]

Years later May would scoff at Shaw's description of the Mystic Betrothal, suggesting that it was pure fantasy. Of course she could not have been pleased at this dredging up of her unhappy marriage to Sparling, whom she so soon forsook, restoring her maiden name. Still, the story is a long digression in Shaw's account of Morris's socialism and only tangentially appropriate. Why then did Shaw include it?

Shaw's fairy tale is peopled by a king and a queen (Morris and Jane), a princess (May), a knight (Shaw), and an opponent (Sparling). The action plays itself out in an enchanted setting with a test of moral strength and wit. The knight gains entrance by guile, insinuating himself by weakness rather than heroic strength. He remains an intruder in the castle while time passes peacefully. Then the mystic marriage asserts itself "irresistibly." In Shaw's world without a middle ground, he was faced with polar options: "to consummate it or vanish." The knight, having won the heart of the fair princess, selflessly vanishes, but the "rupture" leaves the marriage in "pieces." Demonstrated is a masculinity so potent that despite pure intentions it ruptures a marriage. Coloring everything is the knight's passive relationship to the unseen powerful king, making it more like a ménage à quatre than like the Dublin ménage à trois to which Shaw pointedly alludes.[9]

Whether Sparling thought May physically unfaithful, he believed Shaw controlled enough of her affections to make the marriage a travesty, so he vanished too. Still, there was a fairy tale ending of sorts. The lovely maiden, having been rescued by the wily knight, could now live in the little Morris house as serenely as she had lived in the larger one, and it would come to pass that her last years were to be lived out in the medieval splendor of Kelmscott Manor.

This little tale was a version of the one Sonny, the psychological orphan, had consoled himself with long before as he roamed from kingdom to kingdom in his imagination. Like a fairy tale, which is the truth of imagination, Shaw's tale, told in 1936, presents certain truths. As he selected details from the conscious and unconscious residue of memory, he reconstructed his past, viewing May through the glass of idealized femininity, her father through the glass of visionary masculinity.

When Morris died on 3 October 1896, Shaw reacted far less stoically than he had to the death of his own father. Inundated with requests for articles about Morris, Shaw cried out to Ellen Terry, "Oh, I can't write, I can't think, I am beaten, tired, wrecked." He did not attend the funeral, Jane Morris's disdain toward the comrades reminding him too much of Bessie. Consoling himself in his own way, he argued with William Archer over

Ellen Terry's interpretation of Shakespeare, and he wrote a eulogy. In Morris, the "complete artist, who became great by a pre-eminent sense of beauty," Shaw rejoiced: "You can lose a man like that by your own death, but not by his."[10]

Shaw's initial infatuation with May balanced the erotic with the ethereal as it ran in tandem with his affair with Jenny. Similarly, the triangle formed with May and Sparling ran parallel to the one with Jenny and Florence—the romantic and sexual extremes existing simultaneously. In his reminiscence of May, Shaw created an idealized version of a love triangle, assigning a celestial motive to both May and himself. In blaming the broken marriage on a violated Mystic Betrothal, he invoked a romanticized fate, casting himself as love's fool and not its villain. In so doing, Shaw artfully rewrote history.

A Paper Courtship

The Mystic Betrothal, Shaw's most romanticized in-the-flesh love affair, still was not his most ethereal romance. That distinction lies elsewhere. When he began to woo the world-famous Ellen Terry, she was his superior in fame and fortune. Beginning tentatively, their correspondence culminated in the great flow of letters between 1895 and 1900, the celebrated "paper courtship" that Shaw designated "perhaps the pleasantest, as it is the most enduring, of all courtships." Forged by pen and paper, fantasy and art, it was Shaw's most imaginary courtship, too fragile to withstand the brutal realities of the flesh. Despite extensive scrutiny, the underlying meaning of the correspondence remains veiled in the mundane. More than a vehicle to transform lusterless biography, as with May Morris, it was a laboratory allowing Shaw to liberate himself from the body.[11]

Universally loved and admired, Ellen Terry was "born with a property spoon in her mouth" into a family of itinerant actors. She made her stage debut in April 1856 at age nine, three months before Shaw's birth. By 1906, the time of her jubilee celebration of a half century in the theater, Ellen Terry had achieved the stature of a beloved queen. Shaw, never susceptible to mere prettiness, always appreciative of older women, described her as a wise and witty woman, "interesting and singular" in her youth, "astonishingly beautiful" in later life.[12]

Undeniably, the fair, statuesque actress radiated a bountiful femininity. Her likeness was everywhere—adorning dress shops, art galleries, theater posters—and everywhere women copied her dress, her walk, her hair. Lucy adopted her look successfully enough to make people stop short in the streets. Ellen Terry's taste in clothes popularized the avant-garde trend toward artistic dress—flowing gowns of russet brown and salmon pink or apple green adorned with yellow ribbons. Like Jane Morris, she favored a loose scarf and shade hat in summer, a circular cloak in winter. Also like Jane Morris, she had been influenced in her dress and love of beauty by famous men who loved her and who subscribed in some measure to the Pre-Raphaelite Brotherhood vision of "truth to nature."

First married at sixteen to the painter George Frederic Watts, almost three times her age, Ellen sat for him as an armored Joan of Arc and as the flower-bedecked, loose-tressed image of femininity in *Choosing*. The marriage to Watts proved as ephemeral as spring and scarcely longer. At the urging of his wealthy patroness, Watts cast her out after ten months. Not to receive a divorce for another dozen years, Ellen assuaged her heartbreak with the aesthetic architect Edward William Godwin. Out of that six-year pastoral idyll, in seclusion from the stage, she bore Godwin two children: Edith Craig (Edy), actress, feminist, and costume designer; and Edward Gordon Craig, actor, producer, and theatrical designer. There were to be two more marriages to actors. But by far her most celebrated liaison, offstage and on, was with Henry Irving, the great tragic actor and manager of the Lyceum Theatre, whose leading lady she became in 1878.

Shaw, reshaping events, claimed that during the height of their paper courtship a clever Ellen toyed with "two dolls," both "incorrigible actors." One was the mountebank Shaw, the other Irving. Long before in Dublin, Shaw had seen Irving act at the Gaiety Theatre. Under the spell of Irving's personality, with its strange and sinister edge, he had felt that the tall, gaunt man with the nasal voice was the harbinger of a new drama. Although he did not know it then, it was the drama that he declared himself "destined to write." But Irving heeded a different call, one that exalted the actor-manager into heroic primacy on stage. In the 1880s he transformed the Lyceum Theatre in London's West End into what Shaw denigrated as a grandiose "temple of pleasure," with its dedication to gorgeous productions, pictorial glory, and Irving's own enshrinement[13]—the antithesis of the pristine antibourgeois morality that anchored the Shavian vision of the theater. Irving's staged spectacles were curtain raisers for postperformance parties legendary in their opulence, themselves grand theatrical scenarios thronged by the rich, the famous, the fashionable.

Dominating the English-speaking stage during the last quarter of the nineteenth century, Irving triumphantly reinterpreted Shakespeare to suit his oddly introspective style of acting—one that led in 1895 to his being knighted by Queen Victoria, the first actor so honored. Shaw granted that the actor had become the preeminent man of the theatre but lamented the cost: Irving was retrogressive in his art. In Shaw's eyes, the great actor squandered his own talent and that of the great actress by condescending to melodrama and committing "Bardicide"—mutilations of the greatest playwright: "Shakespear at his highest pitch cannot be set aside by any mortal actor, however gifted."[14] Irving's crime was to look backward to an actor's theater, one that placed the actor's interpretation of role at the apex of the theatrical ziggurat. For Irving had no interest in upsetting that hierarchy in favor of an author's theater.

Shaw, however, took up the sword brandished by Wagner and Ibsen. Envisioning a godlike role for the prophetic artist, he sought to usurp Irving's power. Even as he put the relationship entirely in the context of theatrical history, he gloried in his victory over Irving, making Ellen aware of having "her possibilities sterilized by him." Equally an avenging patricide and an obsessed Pygmalion, he sought to impregnate Ellen with his own vision. Admittedly the theater was his "battering ram."[15]

The correspondence opened fitfully and by chance. Ellen, wondering about the potential of a young composer-singer, had written to Edmund Yates, editor of *The World*, a letter that his music critic answered for him. A few letters were exchanged. Shaw dared to chide her for wasting her talent on melodrama, sending her a copy of *The Quintessence of Ibsenism*. Three years passed. Then, prompted by a newspaper announcement that Shaw was to lecture, she picked up her pen. With the correspondence under way, Shaw attacked Shakespeare, telling Ellen that the Bard offered no challenge for a modern woman. Even Eleanora Duse, the celebrated Italian actress whom Shaw admired and Ellen idolized, "could do nothing with Cleopatra."[16]

Shaw had his own agenda, having set to work training audiences in his new drama, railing against pre-Ibsen plays that were, according to his standards, "womanless." There was also a seeming coincidence. Knowing that Ellen was slated to appear in Victorien Sardou's Napoleon play *Madame Sans Gêne*, he lost no time getting to the point. He had just finished a a "beautiful little one act play for Napoleon and a strange lady." To entice Ellen to his "Napoleonad," Shaw placed her second in competition with Gabrielle Réjane, the French actress known for her role as Sardou's washerwoman: "your place is not *after* Réjane."[17]

Ellen read *The Man of Destiny* and pronounced it "delicious." Shaw now wooed her for his play in earnest. In March 1896 he tried to snare her by threatening to take his blarney to the beautiful Mrs. Patrick Campbell: "Farewell, faithless Ellen!" The extravagant farewell, coupled with the threat of a younger actress, had the desired effect. Ellen pressed Irving to produce the play, for Shaw had complimented her even more extravagantly in the play itself, making his heroine's description a description of Ellen. His Strange Lady is *"very feminine, but by no means weak: the lithe tender figure is hung on a strong frame."* She is taller than Napoleon, but *"her elegance and radiant charm keep the secret of her size and strength."* In a culture that associated the feminine with daintiness and vulnerability, Shaw's affirmation of a femininity not bound by size was an instinctively correct response to the woman, and the elegance of his heroine contrasted with the perceived vulgarity of Sardou's heroine.[18] Moreover, his first cross-dressed female character exuded other flattering resonances, because the young girl had impersonated boys on the stage, and the young woman had built her career in breeches roles.

His strategy appeared to work. He confided to the sculptor Bertha Newcombe, hopelessly love-sick over him, that the "blarneying audacities" of his correspondence with Ellen Terry—which would make Bertha envious could she read them—had resulted in an offer from Irving for the Napoleon play. Bertha then had to put up with his "wild stories and extravagances and adorations" of Ellen, her own letter having opened with "Heavens! I had forgotten you—totally forgotten you."[19]

Ellen became the intermediary as *The Man of Destiny* was put off and Shaw struggled with Irving over control of his own play. Convinced that Irving had no intention of presenting it, Shaw interpreted an offer as a bribe to buy a literary courtier. As Irving resisted, Shaw wondered whether Irving was blind or deaf or no actor at all, "but only a Shakspere-struck antiquary" that he passed by the "great chances of his life as if they were pieces of orange peel laid in his path expressly to capsize him." Antagonism between the two men heightened as Shaw criticized Irving from the pages of the *Saturday Review*. This prompted Laurence Irving, Henry's son, to relay the message: "'All my people think you the most appalling Yahoo.'"[20]

When *The Man of Destiny* was presented the following year, it was at the Grand Theatre, not the Lyceum, with Florence West playing the Strange Lady, not Ellen. Maintaining a certain aloofness, Ellen found amusing Irving's pronunciation of the playwright's name, which he spat out as "Mr Pshaw." Perhaps Shaw would have found some solace in knowing that Henry James was to endure a similar neglect, sending Ellen a copy of his play *Summersoft* in 1895, not getting it back "for three mortal years," as he complained to H. G. Wells, James then salvaging his labor by turning it into the short story "Covering End."[21]

In *The Quintessence of Ibsenism*, Shaw illustrated his belief that the advent of the New Drama was inextricably entwined with the advent of the New Woman. Insistently a living example of life imitating art, Shaw claimed that his own urgent interest in the new drama formed the central theme of the correspondence. Meanwhile, he wove a cautionary tale, telling Ellen she had been "sacrificed to the egotism of a fool."[22] Even considering Irving's refusal to honor his promise to produce *The Man of Destiny*, neither Shaw's ambition for himself nor his hope for the theater accounts for the peculiar revelations. His actual scenario was a far more personal one that theatricalized fantasy. Immersed in the role of heroic savior / son, he determined to rescue the great Ellen Terry from emotional and professional bondage to Irving, to Shakespeare, and to the Victorian theater.

In his desire, Shaw was motivated only incidentally by outright ambition. Far more powerfully, he was impelled by a romanticized vision of masculine heroics. Embedded in his scenario were the boyhood rescue fantasies that had infused the youthful Sonny's imaginative life and that were a continuing leitmotiv in his relations with women. An 1886 diary entry records him going after "a young rough beating a girl" on the street,

Jenny Patterson a witness to his manliness. But the devotee of boxing confessed to Ellen, "I've no courage: I am, and always have been, as timid as a mouse."[23]

Meanwhile, his rescue fantasies found a congenial habitat in the magical landscape that formed the backdrop of his paper courtship, for the stage is a "fairyland" and a "secret paradise." As Shaw blended hope with fantasy and vision with desire, the half-saved Mephistopheles wove an artful fable in which he pitted himself against the ogre Irving, his senior in years (twenty-two) and fame (immense). He imagined Ellen imprisoned in "the Ogre's castle," the Lyceum, and she accommodated him by playing a familiar part, the vulnerable woman. In a variation of the fairy tale starring May Morris, he fashioned a "little world apart," an imaginative space walled off by fiat where the physical was forbidden to intrude. Here he could put aside his fear that intimacy with a "disagreeably cruel looking middle aged Irishman with a red beard" would "rub the bloom off" the courtship.[24] Yet in love there is a look that makes all the world bloom, and Shaw cut off any possibility of discovering the look of love. For him, the look of another alienated. Even within the closest embrace woman remained the *other*.

Shaw's language resembles that of the high romantic who thrives on the thrill of obstacles. His solicitousness toward Ellen's health calls to mind the near-legendary epistolary romance of Robert Browning and the older, ailing Elizabeth Barrett, which climaxed in the daring rescue from a tyrannical father and her miraculous restoration to health. Such romance has an aesthetic element that thrives in a world of delicate ladies, locked bowers, and secret letters. For Shaw, believing that marriage is "not the man's hold on the woman, but the woman's on the man," the romantic fantasy of fearsome obstacles and unmarried lovers defined a sphere where the man played an active and artistic role. Ever searching for someone who could use him to his utmost capacity, he romanticized himself as "the Wandering Jew"—surely an alien, irrelevant, and tragic figure.[25] In such a guise, he craftily concealed a feminine self-image—one that appropriated woman's threatening role as *other* and her submissive role in *being used*.

He wielded his pen deftly, lovingly, treacherously. Paying homage to his lady, he was both the devoted troubadour and the uncrowned king seeking the holy grail of art and love. The letters trace his quest, a pilgrimage in which words were so devotedly substituted for flesh that in an act of transubstantiation the words themselves were enshrined, coming to stand for both love and the beloved. He invested the letters with religious awe, keeping them "because her handwriting made pictures of them which I could not burn: it would have been like burning a mediaeval psalter or a XV Century French Book of Hours."[26] Her powerful hand contrasted with his superfine feminine script that allowed him to squeeze hundreds of words onto a single postcard.

His letters were little scenes. He was "a liar and an actor," assuming she understood that. He told her she was not a "slave of love," because her abandonment was entirely voluntary, artistic, and *willed*. Decades later he described a romantic comedy "without ulterior motives."[27] Shaw and Ellen were simply acting to please the other. At first he imagined himself a powerless and raging god, unable to prevent her from wasting her sacred fire. Obscured by the smokescreen of posturing and hyperbole was the dark flame fed by the thrilling, terrifying attraction of female power. As the correspondence wore on, her power appeared to increase, his to diminish—he was needier. But all the while he continued to steer the relationship from the safe harbor of his writing desk.

Denouncing the paternalistic Irving, her stage husband, he played the part of demanding son. "Ellen Ellen Ellen Ellen Ellen Ellen Ellen Ellen Ellen Eleanor Ellenest," he cried, "no man ever does anything for a woman's sake: from our birth to our death we are women's babies, always wanting something from them, never giving them anything except something to keep *for us*." And then the tormenting thought was sounded: "I do not know whether women ever love. I rather doubt it: they pity a man, *mother* him, delight in making him love them; but I always suspect that their tenderness is deepened by their remorse for being unable to love him." The man who boasted to Alice Lockett that he was "hardhearted, heartless, cynical" here revealed his stance to be armor donned to protect him from women's pity and lack of love.[28]

Having run off with Godwin, Ellen had long been a woman with a past—the opposite of the Victorian ideal exemplified by the title of Coventry Patmore's popular poem *The Angel in the House*. To thwart possible attacks on her character, Shaw emphasized that Ellen was not a *"grande amoureuse."* Rather, she was a woman of "very exceptional virtue" without any respect for the law, a distinction that allowed him to praise her character despite her "transient fancies" and "five domestic partnerships." Because the older Ellen bore certain resemblances to Bessie, he followed a familiar and necessary pattern in stressing Ellen's virtue: he defended her as he defended that other ladylike bohemian. But unlike Bessie, Ellen had "the wisdom of the heart," which made it possible "to say deep things" to her.[29]

He confessed to "philandering follies," and in a great show of intimacy described his initiation into sex with Jenny. But there were signs that the relationship would never break the bonds of "dead matter—linen rag and printer's ink." He began mentioning the Irish lady "with the light green eyes and the million of money." Then, having inspected Ellen's photograph, he relapsed into the lover, his nerves and heart glowing with the impulse to have her in his arms. But the sound and fury of professed physical attraction signified nothing but a stratagem to enhance the virility of his image. His strength was strictly literary: "my letters will always be a little bit original; but personally I shouldnt be a bit original."[30]

One night she managed to glimpse him through the theater curtain: "I've seen you at last! You *are* a boy!" Then, "how deadly delicate you look." Her excitement was not reassuring, and he replied with a sexual metaphor: "I don't ask that the veil of the temple shall be rent." He was afraid to come stumping in his "thickbooted, coarse, discordant reality, into that realm where a magic Shaw, a phantasm, a thing who looks delicate and a boy (twelve stalls and a bittock off) poses fantastically."[31]

She called him "bountiful Bernie," "Sweetiken," "my charming darling," "Dearest silly-billy," and on reports from Edy, a "flirting girl"—for though he feared to meet Ellen, he met her lesbian daughter often and without fear. Ellen was "Dearest & beautifullest," "Dearest and Everest," "my Ellenest Ellen." But he also pretended she had the very traits he knew to be his own. She was "inhuman Ellen," a "fickle, faithless wretch," a "jealous, exacting, jilting Ellen." Mostly their signatures were initials only, especially his. For it was he who insisted on the attenuated nature of their relationship but swathed it in bravado and urgency—"I love you *now*."[32]

The nuanced, compelling language of Don Juan was his native tongue. He could be ardent: his regard for her was "on all planes, at all times, under all circumstances, and for ever." He could be erotic: "love me hard, love me soft, and deep, and sweet, and for ever and ever and ever." He empowered her: "my soul is shrouded in mists and my heart clogged." If she would just touch the spring, "tender things" would "flow fast enough." He toyed with her, spinning verbal magic. She was nearby; they could meet "if only I dare. Don't let us break the spell—*do* let us break the spell—don't, do, don't, do, don't, do, don't." He promised her everything: "You may chop off all my fingers and toes for a necklace, and have my heart as a locket." He sacrificed himself to art and love: "Now I have finished my play, nothing remains but to kiss my Ellen once and die." More ominously, he damned (and praised) the power of her femininity. She was worse than Lilith, Adam's first wife.[33]

Male and female, yin and yang, they were in complementary opposition: she was earth; he was air. Ellen craved the transformation that occurred onstage, never feeling like herself when acting but like someone else, always "in-the-air, light, and bodyless." When that did not occur, as in *Cymbeline,* she was *"all earth,"* with no inspiration, *"hide-bound."* Shaw chided her for wanting inspiration: "set your heart like iron, Ellen, and fight for your side tenderly—that is, strongly."[34] For to him Ellen was of the earth, and the iron heart, tender and strong, recalled another woman of the earth—Bessie, strong but not tender, the woman of granite.

He thought of Ellen "as warm as a summer island lying fast asleep in the Mediterranean," an image of fecund earth, tranquil and tropical. No matter that she protested: "I am not a bit of the South. Not a bit. Northy, Northy-Polish." For Shaw boasted of his opposing qualities, icy and aerial: "I was born to bite the north wind" and "I am by complexion & constitution a Northman." Claiming not to understand it, the Northman repeated Beatrice Webb's comment on his love affairs: "You cannot fall in love with a *sprite;* and Shaw is a sprite in such matters, not a real person." Was it more than an odd coincidence that Ellen had written *"A Sprite"* underneath a merry-looking photograph he had sent her? The sprite had other meanings for Shaw the Shelleyan, for he specifically connected the aerial creature to the realm of thought and truth, a realm he later described as having "something spritelike" about it.[35]

Sprite, Northman, phantasm, delicate boy, flirting girl—the magic Shaw confessed to descending to the level of a "treacherous brute in matters of pure affection." But Ellen, whose "soft side was her mothering side," soothed and elevated. Exhausted, making a midnight train journey across a ghostly country, Shaw apologized for a love "knit into an infernal intellectual fabric." Longing to unburden his heart, he imagined the consequences of sleeping with her: the next day at noon in the woods she would give birth to hundreds of babies who would fly her away to some heavenly country. There "they would grow into strong sweetheart sons with whom, in defiance of the prayerbook, you would found a divine race. Would you not like to be the mother of your own grandchildren?"[36]

Shaw's fantasy cannot be regarded simply as a wish for incestuous or infantile love, as has been assumed. Focusing on the result of love and not the ardor of love, it was a conscious effort to please Ellen, who wanted him for her lover. Through this fantasy, laden with heroic and mythic overtones, he told her it could never be, spinning out another skein in the intellectual fabric of his romance. Indeed, Ellen herself had called him "my dear dear Son" and signed herself "Your Sweetheart-Mother." It was to Ellen that he had spoken of the fate of the male spider—"killed by the female the moment he has succeeded in his courtship"[37]—sex as suicide-homicide. In his midnight fantasy, he escaped the devouring sexuality of earth as his longings streamed upward like butterflies in flight.

Forever susceptible to the dizzying pull to the heights, Shaw later recalled the impossibility of planting the "goddess-like" Ellen "on the solid earth."[38] Rather than being pulled down by the taboo, Shaw carried the Ellen of his imagination to a heavenly country. Meanwhile, he vanished safely—having been of great use to Ellen, the all-powerful goddess and submissive lover who murmured the language of love ever so comfortingly, in babytalk.

The winged babies, so at home in Shaw's world of soaring wishes, resemble Eros, the Greek god of love, whose youthful guises culminated in his depiction as an infant, the little hovering Cupid. But the meaning of eros is love's insistent drive to create and procreate, and in Plato is the drive toward union with truth. Similarly, Don Juan describes Life as the force that unceasingly "strives to attain greater power of contemplating itself." Don Juan fights the Devil and the forces of Death—the forces of chaotic instinct that for Freud took on the meaning of eros. Shaw ever in dread of the instinctual forces was ever seeking the joy of "helping Life in its struggle upward."[39]

Shaw's fantasy contains one other curious element: "If you were my mother, I am sure I should carry you away to the tribe in Central America where—but I have a lot of things to say," he breaks off. Was he referring to the legend of the Amazon women, mythical warriors who ruled over a land where all roles were reversed? For by virtue of being a woman, even Ellen was a "huntress."[40] Perfectly able to broach the idea of incest, Shaw stops himself short at the point where his deepest fantasies surrounding sexual roles threaten to erupt. Literally, his fantasies of love become unspeakable.

Shaw's vision is reminiscent of the Virgin Mary carrying the child and being encircled by baby angels. "One does not get tired of adoring the Virgin Mother," swore the author of *Candida*, "THE Mother Play," to Ellen, swearing also that he wanted "to reincarnate" the Virgin Mother in yet another play especially for her. In *Candida*, Shaw exposes patriarchal assumptions surrounding marriage as Shaw's heroine builds a "castle of comfort and indulgence and love" for her husband, Morell, who confesses, "You are my wife, my mother, my sisters: you are the sum of all loving care to me."[41] But Shaw the feminist gave way to Shaw the romantic fantasist in erecting the castle holding a captive Ellen.

Behind his recurring rescue fantasies, the bravado in whisking Ellen away from her ogre, was his own wish for rescue and spiritual restoration—a decidedly feminine wish. Clearly discernible is the shape of his own ogre—his sorrow and submission in love, his terror of physical love, his desire for love as sanctuary. What he feared was true. They were all feelings his culture labeled feminine. What he dreaded was their power to challenge his manhood.

Never to be united in life, the pair would be united through art. To establish copyright on *Captain Brassbound's Conversion*, Shaw asked Ellen to appear in the necessary performance and also to oversee the legal arrangements. On 10 October 1899, Ellen read the part of Lady Cicely Waynflete, a woman *"of great vitality and humanity,"* opposite Laurence Irving as the vengeance-seeking smuggler-hero dubbed Black Paquito. Ellen initially thought the part not right for her and was not at all assured by Shaw's avowals that the play had been "deeply written" for her and that it was the only play in which he had not "prostituted the actress" by adding sexual interest to the character. Shaw's "melodramatic comedy" set in Morocco is shot through with themes of adventure and romance, fantasy and rescue. Lady Cicely, showcased as the sole woman in the play, intrepidly instructs the brigand, whose "power and purpose" as a man are consequently "restored and righted." Converted from his passion for revenge, he proposes marriage. But at the last moment the heroine resists, holding on to a "mad little bit of self," making a glorious escape from the marriage fate.[42]

Shaw was absent from that reading of his play. He was off sailing the Mediterranean on a "godless cruise with godless people"—and with his wife. Eventually the play did bring the pair together. When the paper lovers met at last, it was ever so briefly, at a performance in December 1900, with Laurence Irving again playing Captain Brassbound but with Janet Achurch playing Lady Cicely. For Ellen remained wary of the part, and she became even more wary of Shaw after their meeting. Then Shaw's fears seemed confirmed. The correspondence, at times daily and averaging every three days in 1897, broke off for fifteen months, never to resume on the old footing. "He was quite unlike what I had imagined from his letters," Ellen recalled. She repeated to Shaw the rumor that "you could not bear me, when we met, that one time," apparently believing it herself.[43]

In 1906, a year after Irving's death, Ellen finally appeared in *Captain Brassbound's Conversion* (labeled Ellen Brassheart's Obduracy by the author), playing the part written for her years earlier. But those years and the weight of all those feelings, spoken and unspoken, had taken their toll on her. As Lady Cicely she was nervous, hesitant, and forgot her lines, paining those who loved her. In reviewing the play Max Beerbohm felt obliged to note that she "marred Mr. Shaw's conception." Yet he affectionately defended her against even harsher critics, celebrating the actress over the role, the woman over the actress: "Nothing can obscure for us her sense of beauty and her buoyant jollity." The jubilee testimonial being prepared for her was a "tribute not less to the great actress than to the 'great dear.'"[44]

The play did bring Ellen Terry a triumph issuing from her youthful vitality. During the rehearsals she set her sights on James Carew, an actor half her age, and carried him off. Shaw watched "awstruck." She played Lady Cicely as she toured America, with young Carew moving up from the role of the blunt American, Captain Hamlin Kearney, to play an immature Brassbound and a temporary husband. But the time would come when the aging actress would humbly ask the playwright for a "fine part written by you." Instead he wrote *Pygmalion* for Mrs. Patrick Campbell, plying her with the "most wonderful love letters," even while vowing then that "there is only one Ellen" and later that "nobody replaces you in my heart." Ellen mourned that an "old woman would not attract as a centre piece in a play."[45] No longer needing her, Shaw flickered in the distance like an unreachable beacon as Ellen Terry's star dimmed. Long extinguished was his dream of lighting up the theatrical skies with the glorious triumvirate of Shaw, Terry, and Irving.

Believing that "literary ghouls" made publication "inevitable," Shaw encouraged Edy in her desire to sell the letters after her mother's death—but with a preface by him as a way to control the damage. Although T. E. Lawrence (Lawrence of Arabia), a friend whom Shaw consulted, wondered why disturb the legend, Edy, an ardent feminist, preferred the truth about her mother over a sentimental legend. When the correspondence appeared in 1931, three years after Ellen Terry's death, edited by Christopher St. John (Christabel Marshall, Edy's lover), it was immediately controversial. There were the endearments and extravagant pledges of devotion, the casual, conspiratorial revelations about the famous, including their own partners. Most outrageous to Ellen's son, Edward Gordon Craig, was the language laced with erotic babytalk. The man Shaw addressed as "Teddy the Tramp" and the "Man who Vamped Isadora" (Craig had fathered two children by Isadora Duncan) accused Shaw of misrepresenting Ellen and attacked his motives. Like a naughty child, "G. B. S. pouted ever so pretty, and so E. T. 'loved' him." Shaw countered that the resentment was Craig's "desperate denial of the big woman he ran away from and his assertion of the 'little mother' he loved."[46] Shaw, of course, understood the sensitivities of sons all too well, having contended with his own version of the big woman–little mother syndrome.

Shaw's version of the relationship closed in a tribute to the woman: "she became a legend in her old age," but "she was never old to me." Indeed in the last line of his last letter—literally his last word to her—he bragged of his encroaching age, 63 ¾ to her 72 [73].[47] Whatever Ellen Terry's personal disappointment in the man, Shaw the paper lover finally did what he promised: he revealed the woman behind the roles played onstage as a great instinctual actress and offstage as handmaiden to Irving. Willingly sustaining damage to his own image, like the entirely selfless knight of his imagined fable, he bestowed on his lady the double gift of personal authenticity and literary immortality. So famous did the correspondence become that it subsumed not only the actress but her daughter. When Edy died in 1947 the *New York Times* headline proclaimed: "Daughter of Dame Ellen Terry, to whom George Bernard Shaw Wrote Love Letters, Dies."

For Shaw, as he assured Hesketh Pearson, the correspondence remained a "wholly satisfactory love-affair." To have met would have complicated their "delightful intercourse." Ellen "got tired of five husbands; but she never got tired of me." Never once did they meet in private, and the only time he touched her was on the first night of *Captain Brassbound's Conversion*, when he kissed her hand. The letters, the paper-and-pen substitutes for flesh and blood, were offered as proof positive that sex was an undesirable complication. "Let those who may complain that it was all on paper remember that only on paper has humanity yet achieved glory, beauty, truth, knowledge, virtue, and abiding love."[48]

The letters of the paper courtship fluttered along the path leading toward the ethereal realm. But Shaw's route was still obscure, winding past secret way stations, circling dark temptations. The most hazardous part of his journey lay ahead.

PART IV

The Secret Life of the Superman

> What a man believes may be ascertained, not
> from his creed, but from the assumptions on
> which he habitually acts.
> —"Maxims for Revolutionists"

Triangulating Desire

> I became the subject of fierce jealousies: in
> spite of my utmost tact there was not a
> married friend of mine with whom I did not
> find myself sooner or later within an ace of a
> groundless duel.
> —"Don Giovanni Explains"

It was not only as Sonny that Shaw lived a secret life. By December 1894 he was willing to reveal to Janet Achurch his conviction that "love is hopelessly vulgar and happiness insufferably tedious to those who have once gained the heights." But he was not yet ready to drop the Don Juan mask. Writing from the windswept cliffs of Folkestone he stubbornly declared that the "material heights" made him "robustly vulgar," so that he boiled with "ten-philander-power cynicism." In vain did he look around for "some new inspiratrice," another Janet to inspire another *Candida*. Instead, there he was, braving the cliffs, reveling in the ozone with Graham Wallas, the sea air racing through "clothes, flesh, bone, spirit and all, so that one walks against it like a naked soul, exhilarated."[1]

By clinging to the heights he could avoid the abyss. Like Don Juan, he saw pursuing women as having a single goal: "to throw down my fortifications and gain my citadel."[2] The military metaphor captured his anxiety about sex. In sex all three modes of his world were drowned in violence. In his world of sexual drives and needs he was trapped in his body, repelled by odors, repulsed by uncontrollable physiological processes. In his private world he was swallowed up, reduced to animal flesh, cut off from communion with the ethereal realm. In his world of social relationships he was stalked and attacked. He defended himself by masquerading as Don Juan and trafficking in calculating and sadistic sexual encounters; he was fixed in a hypocritical pose that he despised.

Only two weeks before taking the sea air with Wallas, Shaw had completed *Candida*. The subtitle, *A Mystery*, alludes to the medieval religious dramatic form; his "modern pre-Raphaelite play" was in part an effort to link himself with the artistic aura of the Morris paradise. Calling *Candida* a "counterblast" to Ibsen, Shaw claimed to show that in the typical doll's house "it is the man who is the doll."[3] At least it was his experience that the man was the weaker spouse. In the play, a ménage à trois revolves around the youthful poet Eugene Marchbanks, who enters the home of Candida and her clergyman husband. The fictional triangle dissolves when Marchbanks, having provoked a domestic crisis, emasculates the husband, who collapses in sobs: he has been living all along in a fool's paradise. At this turn of events the triumphant poet, like his creator, vanishes into the night rather than consummate the love affair.

At first Marchbanks wants nothing more than a love that transports him to the "highest summits." For Candida is woman encompassing three common roles raised to the level of exaltation: domestic maid, enchantress, and angel. At the last moment, "standing outside the gate of Heaven, and refusing to go in," Marchbanks, feeling "heroic," sees that sex with Candida, fifteen years his senior, is "really the gate of Hell."[4] The apocalyptic imagery conjures up the dread toothed vagina of psychoanalysis and myth, the devouring sexuality of woman. Meanwhile, the opposition between the heavenly and the hellish pits the possibility of transcendence against the threat of spiritual damnation. In Shaw's secularized religious drama, art offers salvation, sex damnation.

To interest actor-manager Lewis Waller in *Candida*, Shaw told Janet that he was going to read Marchbanks "for all he is worth," for the play hinged on that character. Fortified by art, Marchbanks holds tight to the secret in his heart. The unrevealed secret continually aroused speculation, annoying Shaw, who insisted that the secret is that "domestic life is not a poet's destiny." Yet in 1903 Shaw wrote Siegfried Trebitsch, his German translator, that the "whole point" of the play is the "revelation of the weakness of this strong and manly man, and the terrible strength of the febrile and effeminate one." Similarly, in 1895 Shaw described Marchbanks as "rather fragile and effeminate."[5] The emphasis on effeminacy, the caricature usually applied to the male homosexual, was there from the beginning.

Moreover, Marchbanks, called variously a "good little boy" and a "bad boy," cries with rage at being brutally handled, while Candida admires him despite his "queerness." The latter is a quality that the stage directions label *"unearthliness,"* and it seems *"noxious"* to the prosaic and *"angelic"* to the poetic. The ambiguity of "queerness" is compounded by its date of appearance, in December 1894. Just one month before, the Marquess of Queensberry had used the term "Snob Queers" to designate homosexuality, and the meaning would be firmly established in slang by the end of the 1890s. Adding to the ambiguity surrounding the character is the fact that Marchbanks originally had been written as Majoribanks—and *marjorie* was known as an abusive term for a male homosexual.[6]

The circumstances under which *Candida* was written support this view of Marchbanks. In July 1894, Shaw was on assignment in Bayreuth to review the Wagner festival for *The Star.* While in Germany he saw *Parsifal* twice, writing his *Star* piece from the highest point in Bayreuth, atop the tower at the summit of the hill on which the Wagner theater was built. In October he lectured on the opera at the Church and Stage Guild the day after finishing the first act of *Candida. Parsifal*, like *Candida*, features a triangle: the castrated villainous magician Klingsor, the seductress Kundry, and Parsifal, who renounces sexual temptation in order to preserve the brotherhood of the Grail. There is no doubt that the playwright had the opera in mind. "The passage where you put your hand on your heart" in sympathy is "cribbed from Wagner's *Parsifal*," he advised the actor Richard Mansfield, who was rehearsing Marchbanks. The Wagner connection was not confined to *Parsifal*. Playing with gender, Shaw described Candida to the American critic James Huneker as "as unscrupulous as Siegfried."[7]

Shaw studiously read the literature and attended lectures on Wagner. There were discussions with experts like William Archer, who had written on the composer's life and works. Shaw also was friendly with William Ashton Ellis, the translator of Wagner's prose works into English, whom he praised lavishly in an 1892 column for *The World*. Shaw knew the Wagner correspondence and would have known that Wagner's patron—the homosexual "Mad" King Ludwig II of Bavaria, whose beauty Wagner admired—wondered about the meaning of Kundry's kiss of seduction, and that the composer had replied, suggestively and ambiguously: "Darling, that is a terrible secret!" Shaw thought that kiss one of the "pregnant simplicities" of the world.[8]

Surrounded by ambiguities, *Parsifal* inspired a veiled homosexual literature at the turn of the century, even as Shaw celebrated the Wagnerian superman in his manifold guises. And why, after Shaw read his play to an assembled group at Henry Salt's London lodgings, did homosexual poet Edward Carpenter strenuously declare: "No, Shaw. It won't do."? The mystery of the subtitle infuses the play. Through the poet's unknowable secret as he slips away into "Tristan's holy night," Shaw created a vaguely allusive atmosphere that bathed Marchbanks in a coded homosexuality—a character with auto-biographical parallels to the playwright.[9]

Much later, critic Beverley Baxter alleged that it was an "open secret at the time" that the characters were based on Henry Irving, Ellen Terry, and Shaw. Shaw claimed that the allegation gave him a "shock that would have killed any other man" of his age. Conveniently forgetting the nature of his relationship with Ellen, he insisted that she was hardly the model for Candida because of her five discarded husbands: "I had no models for Candida." Yet in an 1898 letter to Archer, Shaw mentioned some of the people who had been or might have been models. For Candida, he headed a list of three prominent women with Ellen Terry. But in 1944 he dwelled on the absurdity of Ellen and Irving as Candida and Morell, making more plausible the absurdity of Shaw as Marchbanks: "I certainly never thought of myself as a model. Heaven forgive you, Beverley Baxter!"[10]

The strength of Shaw's denial at age eighty-eight suggests that Baxter hit close to home. In Marchbanks, Shaw created an explicitly effeminate character on a secret quest—one that keeps him uncontaminated by woman's flesh. Having completed the play, Shaw feared that *Candida* was the "beginning of weakness and mollycoddledom." A mollycoddle is a pampered weakling, specifically an effeminate man. The similar term *molly* was applied to homosexuals, especially those with effeminate or transvestite attributes.[11] What was the relation between Marchbanks and his creator?

For Shaw, sexuality was highly compartmentalized and ultimately expendable. In his body consciousness there was a strict line of demarcation. It was an unequal separation: above the neck and below it. In *Too True To Be Good* the autobiographical Aubrey explains that we all have "our lower centres and our higher centres." The lower centers act with terrible destructive power, but "they dont talk." The higher centers speak in all the great poetry and literature of the world, "even when they are saying nothing or telling lies. But the lower centres are there all the time: a sort of guilty secret with every one of us."[12] From the streets of Dublin to the ghostly desk of *The Hornet* to an imaginary British outpost on the fringes of the empire, the guilty secret festered, and it was explicitly sexual.

Shaw's mystic betrothal and his paper courtship had each been an effort to conduct a worldly relationship as if it were part of the higher centers. But the lower centers screamed for attention. He found "irritating" the sentimental cliché that "'love is enough'" and claimed that he was "raging for justice, not for love," yet triangles continued to beget triangles. In velvet-draped drawing rooms all over London he sat, strutted, and played the exhibitionist, his talk volatile, dominating, intimate. Yet not even the seductive vigor of Edith Bland and her "scenes as usual" could transform the platonic into the sexual. Shaw's restraint was based on more than loyalty to the husbands, as he claimed, for he rather casually disrupted households. Later he admitted, "I have no scruples about breaking up marriages that are mistakes, (perhaps all marriages are, by the way)."[13]

What motivated Shaw to create triangles? As a boy with three fathers, Sonny learned that "it takes all sorts to make a world." In such a world he shrank from his father's humiliations and sought protection from powerful male rivals, all of which played havoc with his own gender identity. In his seemingly passive identification with the Bessie of his imagination he found a refuge and a special vantage point from which to fashion his experience. Shaw's ability to "convert his own youthful rebelliousness into an image of rebellious womanhood" has been cited by Eric Bentley as "one of the most productive things" in Shaw's whole life. The remarkable ability that created a vast gallery of strong female characters was based on one method: "I always assumed that a woman was a person exactly like myself, and that is how the trick is done."[14]

The trick involved more sleight of hand than Shaw let on, but the double male triangles offer a behind-the-scenes view of his juggling act. There was the little harlequinade of sexual preference and revulsion with Henry and Kate Salt. The couple appeared to accommodate themselves to a companionate marriage while devoting themselves to the higher calling of Salt's Humanitarian League and the Simple Life. Their cottages, first at Tilford and later at Oxted, offered Shaw a refuge from the dirt and odor of London, and he liked to hike and bicycle in the fragrant Surrey countryside. Typical was a moonlight walk to Oxted Village with Salt and Sydney Olivier. In the morning, after sleeping "very badly" on a bed that was too short for him, Shaw "lay down among the thistles on the brink of a sandpit," his mackintosh keeping off the rain as he wrote letters. That evening the group was joined by a soaking wet Edward Carpenter, who stayed overnight.[15]

Of those visits, Salt recalled a tired Shaw sitting at breakfast turning the pages of the Army and Navy Co-operative Society's Catalogue. An exemplary houseguest, Shaw helped with household chores and had "his own way of making his bed: no one else might touch it." During these interludes with the Salts, Shaw relished the chance to sing and play duets with Kate on a thunderous grand piano. Once, when he was "in a destructively electrical condition" and "hardly safe without a chain and muzzle," Kate complained that he had been practicing scales, an "unheard-of accusation," he assured Janet Achurch (although his diary variously shows him doing exactly that).[16]

While Shaw looked forward to long intimate talks with the raven-haired Kate, all was not pastoral in that little cottage. Shaw learned that even though Henry was "normal," Kate would not let him touch her. She became distraught and tottered on the verge of a nervous breakdown. Shaw, the family confidant, prescribed factory work, since "factory girls cannot afford nerves."[17] It seemed natural for a man with a machine for a heart to prescribe working with machines as a cure for a sexual problem.

Kate followed his advice, going to work at Emery Walker's engraving works. It took Edward Carpenter to figure out what really ailed her. He recognized that Kate's constant infatuations with women were rooted in lesbianism. Like the German Karl Heinrich Ulrichs, Carpenter believed that Urnings, or Uranians, formed an intermediate sex whose love was of a higher order than ordinary love. (In Plato's *Symposium*, pederasty is praised as Uranian, from *Uranos* for heaven.) Noting the mental prowess of many "inverts," Carpenter thought they might represent a higher stage of evolution. In this vein, the special function of their love was in social and heroic work, to propagate "children of the mind," those ideals that transform society. Enlightened by Carpenter, Kate excitedly told Shaw that she was an Urning. She then "dropped the factory and sublimated her desires into harmless raptures about music and poetry and platonic adorations of Carpenter and of me," Shaw wrote years later.[18]

But Shaw did not like being on the short side of any triangle. At least once he sent advice to Kate via Carpenter. Despite tranquil professional relations with him, which included writing "The Illusions of Socialism" for Carpenter's *Forecasts of the Coming Century* (1897), his defiant homosexuality made Shaw nervous. In January 1889, Carpenter addressed the Fabians on "Civilization: Its Cause and Cure." Arguing against respectability for the homosexual, he proclaimed that "The Outcast of one age is the Hero of another." Upset by Carpenter's portrait of the outcast hero as homosexual, Shaw was instantly on the offensive: "Attacked Carpenter rather strongly over his lecture—perhaps too strongly. I believe my nerves are getting too high strung." After the unsettling lecture he passed up supper at Gatti's restaurant, going home alone. The next day he felt so dispirited that he talked Frances Archer and Jim Archer into spending the afternoon together. His wife and brother occupied, William Archer was free for Shaw. The two men walked through frost and fog to Hampstead talking about *Macbeth*, Henry Irving, and little Tom Archer's education, but Shaw's spirits failed to rebound.[19]

Shaw claimed he had not recognized Carpenter's homosexuality at first. Only after reading his epic Whitmanesque poem *Towards Democracy* and realizing that the "works give you the man" did Shaw understand that "all Carpenter's ideals of noble companionship were unisexual." Then Shaw had all the "usual thoughtless horror" of homosexuality and called Carpenter an "ultra-civilized impostor," not a genuine noble savage, as he had been dubbed.[20] Shaw's professed horror may have been reinforced by several of Carpenter's beliefs: that Urnings were chiefly attracted to literature, that Uranian men were likely to identify with women's causes, and that Urnings were more highly evolved than their fellows—the latter coinciding with Shaw's self-conception. It was also true that most of the radical thinkers on sexuality were socialists and feminists, thereby linking political liberation for women with that of homosexuals.

Even though Shaw politely mocked Carpenter's "sandal making village set," Carpenter, like Shaw, was devoted to feminism and vegetarianism, and he had a mystic belief in an evolving consciousness. Shaw recognized the man's vision, closing *On the Rocks* (1933) with the singing of "England, Arise," for which Carpenter wrote the lyrics. Shaw credited Carpenter with clearing the air on homosexuality but could not condone his way of life. On this point Henry Salt agreed. Despite Kate's delight at playing duets with Carpenter on the kitchen piano, Salt's friendship with him became strained in the 1890s when he allowed his young lover to move in with him at Millthorpe. There, in Carpenter's house outside Sheffield, the two men raised flowers and vegetables and spent evenings together mending their shirts. The latter activity at least would have met with Shaw's approval, because he thought all boys should be taught mending and cooking.[21]

Years later Shaw claimed that the overlapping triangles with the Salts and Carpenter gave him a "serious and humane view" of homosexuality. Carpenter, "understanding his condition scientifically and poetically, was not degraded by it." Neither Carpenter nor Kate were in the least danger of falling into "debauchery." Shaw's neat account neglects to mention Kate's flirtation in London and his part in preventing its consummation when she was serving as his temporary secretary. Kate became enamored of Sydney

Olivier's wife, Margaret, and Olivier came to Shaw for help. Shaw wrote Charlotte Payne-Townshend that in five minutes it was settled that the women's "romantic arrangements" were not to be carried out, although appearances were to be kept up. "Thus are women deceived: thus do men stand by one another in the war of the sexes," boasted the iconoclast. As he embraced the conventional he exercised patriarchal control, upholding his manly front at the expense of the women. Maybe, too, Shaw was annoyed. Only two days earlier Kate had flattered him with the news that Mrs. Olivier wanted him to take her husband's place at home while he traveled to America with the Webbs.[22] To play the husband was one thing, but to be asked to play the eunuch was too close for comfort.

Claiming that Kate—whom he called "a queer wife," "a queer hybrid," and "a homo"—loved him "as far as she could love any male creature," Shaw was willing to let her "be a mother" to him. For her part, she remained loyal to Carpenter and Shaw, her "'Sunday husbands.'" It was a loyalty that withstood her being "rather mad" about May Morris one evening at the Hygeian restaurant, although whether the focus of her jealousy was Shaw or May is not clear from his diary entry.[23] From Kate in her raptures and Carpenter in his vision of Urnings, Shaw learned that the impulse to romanticize love affairs was not limited to conventional male-female relationships.

Often when the woman in the triangle was attracted to Shaw the husband or lover was a womanizer, leaving the woman especially vulnerable to attention. With the steady, hard-working Webbs, the tensions were different. Before Beatrice Webb entered the scene, Shaw and Webb so enjoyed each other's company that a rainy night's entertainment consisted of playing Patience and Beggar My Neighbor. But Beatrice despised Shaw's trifling with women and would not tolerate any "stupid gallantries" or personal flatteries from him. Although Shaw would forge a working relationship with her, she remained jealous of the intense friendship and fruitful collaboration between her husband and the man she described as "agile, graceful and even virile."[24]

There were other friendships with married men whose wives were less resentful as Shaw filled their drawing rooms with music. Sometimes Shaw went to Fabian Robert Dryhurst's home to play duets beside him at the piano, an activity he enjoyed with Edgar F. Jacques, editor of *The Musical World,* and also with socialist Andreas Scheu. At home, Shaw usually preferred to play and sing alone for hours at a time, although occasionally there was an impromptu duet with Bessie. One morning when Bessie was gone, Scheu stopped by for a "little singing."[25]

The geometry of the sexually constructed triangle made Shaw the "centre of the household," the husband supposedly consoling himself with the superior cuisine inspired by the guest. Shaw's seemingly symmetrical relation to both partners gave him a semblance of family life and encouraged him to take liberties. Under the guise of awakening Janet Achurch's emotions, he stage-managed Janet and Charles Charrington, like characters in a play: "I do brutal things—put money into her pocket secretly in order purposely to produce a scene with her husband."[26]

Sharing a triangle with another male had a special advantage. He could arouse the woman's sexual expectations, toy with her—and be protected from her. When he shrank from Edith Bland's embrace he could focus on loyalty to her husband and concern for Edith's reputation, and avoid facing his own revulsion. And yet it was exciting to have access to all those vital women—Ida Beatty, Eleanor Marx, May Morris—living with their forceful men. Their drawing rooms became an erotically charged landscape where he faced off against male sparring partners in pseudo-intellectual combat. Energetic in the parlor games of talk, music, and charades, Shaw (always a touch paranoid) masked his feelings of pursuit and persecution. He aimed verbal blows at his opponents—the monocled, frock-coated Bland, the boyish moustachioed Beatty, the lizard-eyed Aveling, the tall, thin-necked Sparling. It was a dangerous game. Elinor Huddart, friendly with a neighbor of the Beattys, warned Shaw of Pakenham's violent behaviour—he had thrown a servant boy down the stairs and broken his arm, and Ida herself was "in terror of her life and limbs."[27]

Those double male triangles, so endlessly seductive to Shaw, show him reducing his rival to the humiliating role of cuckold. His victory lay in winning a secret—and sexual— relation to him.[28] Drawn to playboys and power brokers, Shaw sought to triumph over them, to impress them with his masculinity. And what better way than through their women? Half-wooing the wife, he half-wooed the husband. With its sudden inversions and rapier thrusts, his wit was the perfect weapon. Friendly with the man, he stole the woman's affection, waving his conquest like a banner.

Shaw might disdain the "eternal triangle of the Paris stage," calling adultery the "dryest of subjects," but the triangle itself never ceased to fascinate him. He went back to the very first ménage à trois, that in the Garden of Eden. In *Back to Methuselah*, Part 1, *In the Beginning,* the laughing Serpent reveals *the* piece of forbidden knowledge, *the* guilty secret to the incredulous Eve, who, overwhelmed with repugnance, *"buries her face in her hands."* Adam feels as if the "ground were giving way" beneath his feet. The Fall is a dirty joke, a dizzying sentence. Adam faces world collapse, but as the curtain drops on the first act of the first play of Shaw's "Metabiological Pentateuch," the focus is on Eve. [29]

The view of sex presented here was not just the feeling of the aging playwright. In a letter to St. John Ervine, Shaw uses the language of economics and medicine to explain that the reason for Eve's wry face lay in the "indelicacy with which Nature, in a fit of economy, has combined a merely excretory function with a creatively ejaculatory one in the same bodily part," so that Eve "is to allow herself to be syringed in an unprecedented manner by Adam."

After sex, Shaw always felt obliged to apologize to his partner for his "disgraceful behaviour." His apologies did not stem from the instincts of a gentleman, as he claimed. Rather, they expressed his disgust at being reduced to his "bodily part" in order to perform the medicalized syringing. The apologies also suggest identification with the woman. Shaw, the man with the extra sensitive eyes, recalled sympathetically the woman who told him that she left her husband "because sexual intercourse felt, as she put it, 'like someone sticking a finger in my eye.'" Defensively, he insisted to Ervine that "I am the normal heterosexual man describing, in Eve, the normal heterosexual woman," much as he would insist to Frank Harris that "I was not impotent; I was not sterile; I was not homosexual; and I was extremely, though not promiscuously susceptible."[30]

To Ervine he generalized that "we would all like to detach the ecstasy fom the indecency," from the "ridiculous and disgusting acts and postures."[31] Although Ervine did not agree, could Shaw have resurrected Swift, Shaw could have counted on the self-proclaimed misanthrope to express savage disgust at Nature's arrangement. Yeats, intrigued by the antinomies of body and soul, in *Crazy Jane Talks with the Bishop* explored the paradox that "Love has pitched his mansion in / The place of excrement." But unlike Shaw, the aged poet defiantly vowed to think on his deathbed of all the nights he had wasted in his youth.

Shaw, ever fastidious, often used the term in sexual contexts, and he thought men naturally more fastidious than women. Hesketh Pearson, who knew Shaw personally, put it in a slightly different way, observing that he had a "strain of feminine fastidiousness in him that frequently prevented him from realizing in the flesh what was ideal in the spirit."[32] This quality seems to have been physically noticeable, recalling the deadly delicate look that struck Ellen Terry with wonder.

Writing Hugo Vallentin, who was translating *The Philanderer* into Swedish, Shaw defined a philanderer as a man strongly attracted to women: "He flirts with them, falls half in love with them, makes them fall in love with him, but will not commit himself to any permanent relation with them." Shaw's philanderer "often retreats at the last moment if his suit is successful." He loves women, but "loves himself more—is too cautious, too fastidious, ever to give himself away."[33] Just as the word *aesthete* had layers of meaning, *fastidious*—defined as "demanding excessive delicacy"—seems to have been a loaded term for Shaw, who here freely admits his narcissism to Vallentin.

Eve's turned-up nose was that of her earthly creator, who consistently linked sex with the excremental, desire with contagion. Marital relations made the British home an Augean stable "so filthy that it would seem more hopeful to burn it down than to attempt to sweep it out." While he thought of the "sex problem" in terms of "social sanitation," the reverse was also true: he thought of sanitation in terms of sex. Centuries earlier, ashamed to face sanitary problems, people brought the Black Death upon themselves, and a "similar policy as to sex problems has solved itself by an even worse plague," sexually transmitted diseases. The remedy was not medicinal powder, but "sound moral hygiene."[34] For Shaw the sexual plague was worse than the horror of the medieval epidemic spread by rodents and rotting corpses. Viewing sexually transmitted diseases in this light is to equate the visitation of disease with moral judgment, and sex with sin.

To guard against libidinous contamination, Shaw walled himself into triangular fortresses, but they were not roomy enough to contain either his dread or his desire. For Shaw's inner journey traced a tortuous path through sexual anxiety and ambivalence, one in which asceticism and art were his twin beacons.

Scandals and *Siegfried*

> I appeal now to champions of individual
> rights . . . to join me in a protest against a law
> by which two adult men can be sentenced to
> twenty years penal servitude for a private act,
> freely consented to and desired by both,
> which concerns themselves alone.
> —To the Editor of *Truth*, 1889

Shaw's arrival in London coincided with the rise of campaigns to control vice. As he walked the streets he heard the shrill voice of social purity advocates venting their outrage at sexual decadence. They were especially inflamed by a series of homosexual scandals, including one in 1884 involving officials at Dublin Castle. Typical was the speaker who mounted the platform on 22 August 1885 during a huge demonstration in Hyde Park for Irish land reform. He demanded purity in public men and expressed the view, commonly accepted by the moral evangelists, that male lust was the breeding ground of both prostitution and homosexuality. Standing side by side in the noisy, belligerent crowd that day were Shaw and Pakenham Beatty.[1]

Among those addressing the Hyde Park crowd was William T. Stead, the crusading editor of the *Pall Mall Gazette*. Although labeled a conventional idealist by Shaw, who was a reviewer for his newspaper in the mid-eighties, Stead's style made him hugely successful, and he was then riding the crest of his popularity.[2] In July he had written a sensational series of articles entitled "The Maiden Tribute of Modern Babylon," an exposé of the forced prostitution of young girls that featured the muckraker himself being hauled off to jail for pretending to buy the services of one young girl. In the ensuing hubbub an uneasy coalition of socialists and clergymen formed to fight the sexual abuse of children.

Putting the blame on male lust, Stead sent a report on male prostitution to Henry Labouchere, a radical member of Parliament dedicated to exposing fraud and abuse. Although laws long on the books threatened life imprisonment for male homosexuality, juries rarely convicted. But with Stead's report in hand, Labouchere said he had the proof needed to force a change in the laws. Amid an atmosphere of protest meetings and "vigilance" committees, the Labouchere Amendment to the Criminal Law Amendment Act was rushed through during the first week of August. This landmark amendment imposed up to two years' imprisonment at hard labor for men who committed any homosexual act, public or private. Called the Blackmailers' Charter, it was the law under which Oscar Wilde would be convicted a decade later, an outcome that alarmed Stead himself, who feared the law endangered the "freedom of comradeship now possible to men."[3] Unquestionably, the Labouchere Amendment ushered in a period of increased control and reprisal toward male homosexuals.

One result of the morally turbulent summer of 1885 was closer scrutiny of male friendship, especially emotional relations between men, which had been considered normal in Victorian society. By the time of the Labouchere Amendment this scrutiny had already exacted a toll. Driven by sexual politics if not sex, amid an atmosphere of moral vengeance, suspicion, and outrage, Shaw chose to prove his manliness to the world—and to himself. Less than two weeks earlier he had reluctantly and defensively surrendered his virginity to Jenny Patterson.

Thanks to Jenny and the dozens of women who pursued him, Shaw's numerous intense friendships with other males have not been questioned. But even as his high-visibility affairs fostered an image of masculinity, his less than passionate responses filled him with a doubt that was reinforced by the noisy debate over the relative sex drives of men and women. The influential Dr. William Acton, whose 1857 book on the functions and disorders of the reproductive organs went through many editions, believed that women were rarely bothered by sexual desire. Dr. Richard Freiherr von Krafft-Ebing agreed that men had greater sexual needs than women and went even further in his authoritative *Psychopathia Sexualis* (1886, English translation 1892): he labeled as abnormal those men who flee women. Feeling unable to satisfy women sexually, Shaw admitted that "except perhaps on one occasion I never felt quite convinced that I had carried the lady more than half as far as she had carried me."[4]

Krafft-Ebing voiced the widely held belief that physiology relegated women to the role of the sexually passive. Recoiling from unwanted advances like a proper Victorian female, Shaw ungraciously pointed his finger at his pursuers. Nevertheless, the lover manqué was susceptible to the seductions of female beauty. A latter-day Pygmalion, Shaw glorified women, ritualistically worshipping his own creation. Whipped to and fro by the opposing poles of desire and dread, he glibly neutralized them via the parable of the gulf—"the difference between the angelic and the diabolic temperament." But Shaw, no less than his oily Devil, found the "gulf of dislike" to be "impassable and eternal"[5]— at least as far as sex was concerned. More purposefully than Kate Salt and her raptures, Shaw used art as disguise, convincing himself that his superman meant more than the mere personal sublimation he diagnosed in Kate.

At times he ventured to play a discreet role in expanding public tolerance toward the homosexual, usually under cover of freedom of the press. What he called, in the privacy of his diary, the "sodomy scandals" is a case in point. In 1889 a scandal erupted over a male bordello at 19 Cleveland Street, near Shaw's lodgings on Fitzroy Square. Allegedly among the bordello's aristocratic clients was none other than Prince Albert Victor, elder son of the Prince of Wales, heir to the throne. The ensuing trial of the bordello operator was belatedly mentioned in *Truth* by its founder–Labouchere himself. Amid cries of a coverup, the scandal heightened when Ernest Parke, proprietor of the weekly *North London Press*, reported the names of the alleged Cleveland Street clients. One of those he named sued Parke for libel, and Parke was found guilty and sentenced to a year in jail.[6] Shaw knew Parke, who was also deputy-editor of *The Star*, and came to his defense. Twice, in January and in June 1890, Shaw drafted a petition and sought signatures on Parke's behalf, appealing to Henry Matthews, the Home Secretary.

But Shaw did more than support Parke personally. On 26 November 1889, Shaw drafted a letter to the press in which he took a stand on "what everybody declares unmentionable" but that a "majority of the population" mentions "at every sixth word." Shaw's letter, rejected by *Truth* as well as *The Star*, was written under the banner of "moral responsibility" to protest the "principle of the law" and its "outrageous penalties." In his letter Shaw showed familiarity with both current thinking and the historical tradition concerning homosexuality, using the examples of Norfolk Island, an eighteenth-century penal colony in Australia, as well as the Greek philosophers. He cited the poet Sappho to show that "this abnormal appetite is not confined to one sex," a reference to lesbianism that surely would have shocked Queen Victoria. (When it was pointed out to the queen that the Labouchere Amendment ignored women, she replied: "No woman would do that.")[7]

In his letter Shaw took care not to be explicit. He did not mention one significant aspect of Greek and Roman practice—that the sexual dichotomy was not male / female. It was active / passive and dominant / submissive, a piece of information that would not have escaped his notice. It is also likely that through Carpenter Shaw had seen, or at least knew about, John Addington Symonds's *A Problem in Greek Ethics*, privately printed in 1883 and part of Havelock Ellis's *Sexual Inversion* (1897). Shaw's constant complaint that he recoiled from sexual use *by* aggressive women may have concealed the feeling that he was being used *like* a woman.[8]

Shaw was well aware that no one wanted to speak out against the current law on homosexuality "lest they should be suspected of acting in their personal interest." His own unease can be detected in diary entries in the weeks preceding his letter. It was on 28 September that the *North London Press* broke the news that prominent aristocrats were involved, naming names six weeks later. On Tuesday, 8 October, Shaw went to lunch at Sweeting's on Fleet Street with H. W. Massingham, a Fabian who worked as Parke's assistant editor at *The Star*. Uncharacteristically, Shaw ordered fish. This departure from his vegetarian code, repeated on a return visit with Massingham, in itself suggests something amiss. On the train back Shaw began writing verses, to be published in *The Star*, attacking Stead. That evening Shaw went to the Blands' where he met a man "whose name I forget," then, on his way to a Fabian meeting, met Massingham at the train station, where he stayed to talk with him.[9]

The next day, feeling restless, Shaw sat at the piano playing *Parsifal* "with a very deep sense of it all." Thursday evening he went to the Salts' and played the score to Kate. He explained that the leading poetic theme was that of the "innocent greenhorn" who, guided by "compassion for suffering, finds the way of salvation." However much he may have identified with the greenhorn, he is on record as identifying with the greenhorn's seductress: "Like Kundry in Parsifal, I am the victim of the impulse to laugh at inappropriate moments."[10]

Not even the opera helped Shaw shake off his feelings of restlessness and preoccupation. During the next few days he tripped and fell on his way back from Jenny's, mistakenly substituted the word *Star* for Fabian in his diary, and wrote letters "about the Star affair" to socialist councilman John Burns and to T. P. O'Connor, who founded *The Star* in 1888. Shaw's mistakes continued: shortly afterward he got on the wrong train.[11]

Shaw found some relief with Robert Dryhurst, going to his home on 28 October and playing the *Eroica Symphony* with him, a duet the two would play again and the same piece he had played so intimately with Kate Salt. He spent most of a dark and gloomy 11 November with Dryhurst, taking a long walk with him, then singing ballads back at Dryhurst's, his friend's eyes "too bad for playing." On the following day Shaw wrote Parke and offered to do the political column in the *North London Press* for him until he was able to pay someone for the job.[12]

Shaw's agitation intensified, and he became unable to concentrate. He resorted to spending one foggy, chilly evening moving about in the streets, trying to write his *Star* column under lampposts. In the days immediately preceding his ill-fated letter to the press, he felt "so done up" that he made "no attempt" to work and continued to seek solace in music. He immersed himself in the score of *Siegfried* that he had borrowed for Kate Salt. Attracted to Wagner's evolutionary faith in life as a "tireless power which is continually driving onward and upward," Shaw found in Siegfried's intense vitality "a totally unmoral person, a born anarchist . . . an anticipation of the 'overman' of Nietzsche," as he put it later in *The Perfect Wagnerite* (1898).[13]

Shaw's intensity that November strained his inner resources as he sleepwalked through the days, unable to commit himself to composing the letter he felt compelled to write. There was a "mistake about the Haggerston Club lecture," as he rather cryptically recorded. On 25 November, he spent the day playing *Siegfried* and loafing about, going to Dryhurst's in the evening. On the twenty-sixth he went to a meeting of the Matchmakers' Union, only to find he was a day late. It was during his travels back and forth on the train that he finally began to write the letter that had been germinating "about the sodomy scandals." His mind was elsewhere, and the very next day he forgot to attend the chamber music concert at Kensington Town Hall. (Although he was preoccupied, his wit remained sharp. As a reviewer for *The Star*, on the twenty-eighth, he attended the lecture "How to Fail in Literature." His verdict: "Many who went were quite capable of doing it without [the lecturer's] instruction.")[14]

Shaw's state of mind was reflected in concern for his health. In September he had worried about a "vibratoriness" around his heart, a sign, he thought, not to overexert himself. In October he caught a bad cold, which left him with a lingering cough. Modern medicine recognizes that physical illness can also be a psychological response to crisis or lack of power, a response once considered particularly female. Shaw himself recognized the connection between his physical and emotional health. He recalled that early in the year he had been "nervous, depressed, and in unsatisfactory health in general as far as my nerves were concerned." Even Bessie had noticed his hand shaking one morning while he was holding a letter. Shaw's self-consciousness about his nerves might have had another meaning. Those thought to be especially prone to nervous maladies were women and homosexuals, as both Ellis and Carpenter believed.[15] Extremely susceptible to the black and filthy fogs blanketing London, Shaw's spirits flickered with the intermittent sunlight of the winter, rising in the spring.

Perhaps adding to Shaw's anxiety was the memory of 14 October. On that evening, while visiting the Salts, Shaw sat up alone with Kate until past one in the morning. Then, "as Mrs. Salt was very curious about my sincerity as to women I thought it best to tell her—without mentioning names—about JP."[16] Given Shaw's reticence in his own diary, his "sincerity as to women" suggests a meaning other than Don Juanism as has been assumed. Kate, who saw Shaw often and intimately, asked a bold question that Shaw felt obliged to answer. Her question, coming in the midst of the furor surrounding the Cleveland Street scandals, might very well have been prompted by them. It seems likely that Kate, who celebrated her Urning nature, was wondering about Shaw's sexual preference—as to women, or as to men. For certainly Shaw could not justify his sincerity by the example of the ill-treated Jenny. But he could use her to demonstrate his heterosexuality.

Shaw's personal ambivalence was at odds with his progressive public stance. In 1898, only a few months after quietly discouraging Kate's romance with Margaret Olivier, he denounced public hypocrisy on the subject. The case in point was that of George Bedborough, secretary of the Legitimation League (founded to legalize illegitimate children), who was being prosecuted for selling Havelock Ellis's *Sexual Inversion*, published the year before. Shaw, a member of the newly formed Free Press Defence

Committee, wrote Henry Seymour, editor of *The Adult*. Shaw praised the book as being the only "authoritative scientific" treatment of its subject in English. Under the rubric of the "scientific," Shaw felt free to discuss homosexuality, emphasizing that there was no proof that the "morbid idiosyncrasy" was "necessarily associated with the most atrocious depravity of character." Years before he had been "shocked" when an elderly man had been sentenced to twenty years imprisonment for his "folly." Unsuccessful in getting the press to protest, he discovered that the fear of becoming suspect oneself made every Englishman an "abject coward." In a similar frame of mind in 1887, he had written Stead that in "branding an elderly voluptuary as a detestable satyr you have public opinion on your side."[17] Both earlier and later it was easy to brand and dangerous to be branded. Secret self-branding was also dangerous, carrying entirely different but equally inescapable consequences.

The Curious Reversal

> Do not do unto others as you would that they
> should do unto you. Their tastes may not be
> the same.
> —"Maxims for Revolutionists"

In remembering his boyhood, Shaw claimed that Uncle Walter, that veteran of sea life and lover of the scurrilous tale, was "astonished and horrified by the homosexualities of English public schools." Shaw here reveals that he learned of homosexuality at home, where there may also have been advances from Lee. Did such a memory also deflect onto Uncle Walter his own disturbing experiences in Dublin schools? It would be another reason to hate those boy prisons and their vulgar charges, and Shaw made a point of distancing his experience as a "day boy" at an Irish school from the "deeper shames" of English boarding schools.[1]

Adding to such dark and fragmentary knowledge were Sonny's daily wanderings on the streets of Dublin, where he would have become aware of the homosexual underworld that had thrived since the mid-nineteenth century. He also made forays to the theater, where cross-dressed women acted alongside homosexuals, for homosexuality ran through the theatrical profession, according to *The Yokel's Preceptor* (1850). At the same time, underground pornographic works circulated. The most notorious were the anonymous *My Secret Life*, which included homosexual episodes (a number of its eleven volumes appeared by 1890), and *The Sins of the Cities of the Plain: or the Recollections of a Mary-Ann* (1881), the alleged autobiography of male prostitute Jack Saul. When Shaw called punishment by flogging a "ridiculous longing for this relic of the Cities of the Plain . . . a final triumph of the vice it pretends to repress," he invoked Sodom and Gomorrah to point to a homosexual element and may have been alluding to Saul's book. Outraged by the sensuality of the punishment, Shaw waged a campaign against "flagellomania," which he compared to nymphomania.[2]

"The Uranian life in London goes beyond imagination," wrote a German informant to Karl Heinrich Ulrichs in 1868. "In a luxurious cafe where concerts take place, whose busiest hours are from eleven to one o'clock in the morning, entire tables are occupied only by Urnings." As sexologists and homosexuals alike began to use terms like invert, for the first time homosexuality was viewed as a distinctive identity. The term itself was first published in an anonymous 1869 German pamphlet, the author identified by Havelock Ellis as Karl Maria Kertbeny.[3]

Kertbeny's term was adopted by his good friend, none other than Gustav Jaeger, in the second edition of his *Entdeckung der Seele* (Discovery of the Soul, 1880)—an aspect of Jaeger unnoted by either Shaw or his biographers. Yet Jaeger's name appears several times in Ellis's *Studies in the Psychology of Sex*, where he discusses Jaeger's belief that odor is the supreme influence in sexual instinct and agrees that some people have extreme olfactory sympathies and antipathies. In *Psychopathia Sexualis*, Krafft-Ebing, who uses the terms *homo-sexual* and *homo-sexuality*, refers to Jaeger and notes that the "'discoverer of the soul'" regarded perspiration "as being especially seductive."[4] Meanwhile, Shaw, highly sensitive to odor, wore the Jaeger suit that encouraged perspiration, claimed that he perspired profusely, and bathed himself ritualistically.

Shaw struggled with his own emerging sexual identity as he moved amid overlapping circles of radical thinkers and homosexuals, where sexuality was both a social and a personal issue. In trying to sort out his conflicting feelings and thoughts, he was influenced by his contact with two of the most important figures working to reform public opinion on homosexuality, Ellis and Edward Carpenter. Carpenter preferred the term *homogenic* (derived from two Greek roots) over *homosexual* (a "bastard word"). Nevertheless, he quoted Jaeger's comment that the "German penal code, in stamping homosexuality a crime, puts the highest blossoms of humanity on the proscription list."[5]

Carpenter's virtual deification of Urnings proved alluring to the romantically aspiring Shaw. Carpenter argued against the notion that love and sex were meant to be limited to childbearing. Exalting the body, he emphasized the distinction between sex and procreation. This challenge to bourgeois morality would be articulated differently by Shaw, who disdained the body.

Ellis, the leading theorist, also took a positive approach. While Carpenter praised spiritual union in works like *Love's Coming of Age* (1896), Ellis stressed the universality of homosexuality throughout history. Shaw met Ellis, a friend of Eleanor Marx, at a meeting at the Fellowship of the New Life in 1887. Shaw also met feminist Edith Lees there in 1890 when she lectured on "Woman." The lesbian Lees, who was thrilled by the prospect of emancipation that *A Doll's House* promised, married Ellis, who was not homosexual, in 1891. He had gone through a stormy, sexually unconsummated relationship with Olive Schreiner, later incorporating her sexual feelings during menstruation (corroborated by Eleanor Marx) into his *Studies in the Psychology of Sex*. Ellis, who appears to detail Edith's case history in *Sexual Inversion*, needed to look no farther than his own hearth to point to the respectability of most homosexuals. A quarter of a century later, Shaw called him "my friend." Meanwhile, the bearded Ellis, hair combed in peaks, was often mistaken for Shaw.[6]

When Ellis classified variations of homosexuality in *Sexual Inversion*, he concluded that homosexuality was inborn but not pathological, just as genius might be abnormal but not a disease. Ellis believed that homosexuals were divided into two types: the inverts, who were born that way, and the perverts, who acted out of lust. Rejecting Carpenter's view (based on that of the homosexual Ulrichs) that homosexuals formed a third, or intermediate, sex, Ellis thought of homosexuality as an anomaly.

On this point Shaw agreed with Ellis rather than Carpenter, accepting the idea of inversion and rejecting the theory of the third sex. He vehemently opposed Carpenter's attempt to induce homosexuality in "normal people"—creating perverts, according to Ellis's theory. Shaw insisted that only the abnormal person could fail to see "how frightfully disagreeable—how abominable, in fact—it is to the normal, even to the normal who are abnormally susceptible to natural impulses." But he did support Carpenter in his effort to make people see that the "curious reversal" is a "natural accident." It was absurd "to persecute it or connect any general moral deficiency with it."[7]

When in 1907 Ellis published an article in the journal *New Age*, he used the occasion of a German homosexual scandal to attack repressive English law, citing the findings of German sexologist Magnus Hirschfeld that "to be abnormal is not to be unnatural." Just a few months before Ellis's article appeared, when Alfred Richard Orage took over as editor, Shaw had helped finance the journal.[8] Shaw's silent sponsorship was therefore responsible for Ellis's message reaching a wider, more diverse audience than had his scientific treatises.

In his ideas, Shaw was indebted to both Carpenter and Ellis. But in his relationships with the two men, Shaw was dominated by the heterosexual Ellis, granting him the advantage. Meanwhile, Shaw asserted himself over the homosexual Carpenter, refusing to give him his due.

After her son Robert Gould Shaw (Bobby) was released from prison, having served time on a charge of homosexuality, Shaw offered Lady Nancy Astor some advice. Discreet and guarded, it sounded unmistakably personal: "A man may suffer acutely and lose his self-respect very dangerously if he mistakes for a frightful delinquency on his part a condition for which he is no more morally responsible than for color blindness." Behind Shaw's advice was Ellis, who considered sexual inversion a simple abnormality like "colour-blindness, criminality and genius" rather than a disease like scarlet fever.[9]

In discussing the curious reversal, Shaw reversed his skepticism toward science: the invert should understand his own case "scientifically and objectively." Yet elsewhere he mocked the "wide difference between common knowledge and the intellectual game called science."[10] Adding to his longstanding grievances against the scientific and medical establishment, Shaw rebelled against the determined effort to label homosexuality a disease. On homosexuality, the science Shaw alluded to was specific: it was the science of Ellis, the science that analogized homosexuality to genius.

Alongside the studies of the sexologists arose a coded homosexual literature. The suggestiveness of Oscar Wilde's *The Picture of Dorian Gray* alarmed John Addington Symonds, himself homosexual and fearful of retribution. Also in evidence, in print and about town, were the Uranian poets, many of them—like young Lord Alfred Douglas, who was linked with Oscar Wilde—becoming Uranian at Oxford University. Uranians idealized ancient Greek practices in man-boy relations but were sensitive to the stereotype of the male homosexual corrupting youth, using the word "shame" as a euphemism for homosexual love. The most notorious use of that word was by Douglas in his poem *Two Loves*.[11] Shaw, for whom the phenomenon of shame resonated powerfully, was compulsively intent on improving youth, appropriating the great nineteenth-century female role of teacher exemplified by Miss Caroline Hill so long before.

In his drama Shaw preferred to have his older male teach a younger woman. This arrangement, fraught with more conventional dangers than an older man teaching a younger man, was nevertheless doomed to an unconventional ending. In *Major Barbara* the diabolonian capitalist Andrew Undershaft teaches the gospel of money and gunpowder to his daughter Barbara, who chooses to battle for the souls of the well-fed in her father's factory town instead of bribing the starving poor with bread in the Salvation Army shelter. Henry Higgins does not marry Eliza Doolittle, nor does Caesar take Cleopatra for his mistress (Shaw thereby fictionalizing history), while the eighty-eight-year-old Captain Shotover enters into a spiritual "marriage" with the young Ellie Dunn.

Of the four young women, Shaw identified with three of them. Barbara learns how money can be a tool of enslavement or liberation—the lesson Shaw learned from Henry George and never tired of teaching. Eliza laboriously practiced proper speech, just as Shaw resolutely practiced public speaking. Ellie, genteel, poverty-stricken, and craving beauty, recalls the youthful dreaming Shaw, seemingly trapped by circumstances. In contrast, the childishness of character that Shaw ascribes to Cleopatra is his way of dealing with the mystery of female power she embodied, for the Serpent of the Nile is no match for the woman-impervious Caesar—who does resemble Shaw. Historically a man of monumental intellectual and physical vitality, Caesar was rumored to have had homosexual relations with King Nicomedes of Bithynia. Addressing the Sphinx, Shaw's Caesar identifies himself as a wanderer and an exile, a stranger to the race of men: "I am he of whose genius you are the symbol: part brute, part woman, and part god—nothing of man in me at all. Have I read your riddle, Sphinx?"[12] It is a reading of Shaw's riddle as well.

Shaw crossed paths with the Uranian poet Marc-André Raffalovich. Said to be so ugly that his mother packed him off to London to avoid looking at him, he became an enemy of Wilde. Raffalovich's survey of homosexuality in literature and history was published in France in 1896 as *Uranisme et Unisexualité*. His writings included collaborations with his companion, John Gray, who had been Wilde's lover and a model for Dorian Gray. Eventually Raffalovich, who thought everyone had a duty to understand the place of inversion in society, escaped social and personal turmoil by becoming Brother Sebastian, a Dominican monk. One evening in 1893, Shaw attended a performance of Raffalovich's *Roses and Shadows*. Perhaps the work piqued Shaw's interest in literature written by homosexuals, for Shaw went on to the lodgings of the ever-amiable Florence Farr, where they "read a lot of Walt Whitman and were very happy," until the late hour forced him to make a desperate dash for the train. Reading Whitman in no way compromised him, since Havelock Ellis maintained that Whitman was "strenuously masculine."[13]

The next day in the street, Shaw ran into Ernest Parke and Richard Le Gallienne, book reviewer for *The Star*. The handsome Le Gallienne was dubbed "poet and lover" by Wilde, who delighted in pointing to him as the angel Gabriel in *Annunciation*, the painting by Rossetti. To Le Gallienne the gas lamps lining the streets were "iron lilies of the Strand," the grotesque imagery capturing the decadent artifice he was to foster as editor of *The Yellow Book*. Like Raffalovich, Le Gallienne collaborated on sexually suggestive writings with a fellow Uranian (Robinson K. Leather). At the same time, the romantically adoring Le Gallienne was captivated by the "tall, lithe, boyish-girl figure" of Edith Bland and came close to eloping with the older woman—likely making him her first important romance since Shaw. A few years earlier Shaw had met Le Gallienne at the Wheatsheaf Restaurant. Reviewing the work of his fellow critic under his Corno di Bassetto pseudonym in *The Star*, Shaw thought Le Gallienne's poems dainty. This verdict prompted Le Gallienne to reply with a verse to "C. di B.," a "Galilean swine." Shaw defended his review to Pakenham Beatty, calling Le Gallienne a "poor little sensitive plant" who shed tears of "quivering sensibility" over valentines "crumpled . . . up in my horny fist."[14]

A similar comment on his own work later infuriated Shaw. Lord Alfred Douglas, reviewing *Getting Married*, thought the play should not have passed the censor, and he chided Shaw for preaching on morality, because he "does not possess a masculine intellect." Shaw, stung by this attack, angrily demanded that Douglas withdraw the article because of a mistatement of fact. Douglas called it "characteristic of the feminine quality of your intellect" to make "such an outrageous suggestion." The paper duel was fought publicly in the pages of *The Academy*, a literary weekly edited by Douglas and to which Shaw had contributed. The duel ended in a draw after five letters were written, the last a less rancorous one by Shaw. Silence ensued for more than two decades, until Shaw again wrote Douglas. They then began a revealing correspondence, reminiscent of the one Shaw had with Ellen Terry, with the pair not meeting but writing openly, playfully inventing pet names. Evoking romantic legends to one another, they were St Christopher (the saintly ferryman represented in art bearing the Christ child on his back) and Childe Alfred (as in *King Lear,* "Child Rowland to the dark tower came"). Douglas thought it "amazing" that Shaw should turn out to be a "sort of a saint. I never could love anyone unless he or she were good."[15]

Douglas confessed to putting Shaw "on pedestals," their relationship suggesting an older wiser man and younger questing man—an idealized paper reenactment of the Wilde-Douglas liaison. Indeed, the ghost of Wilde hovered over the correspondence, forming a spectral triangle. Despite thinking that Wilde's prayer to posterity might have been "'Read my works; and let my life alone,'" to help Frank Harris's widow, Nellie, Shaw wrote a new preface for Harris's biography of Oscar Wilde, first published in 1916. Collaborating through the mail with Douglas, Shaw agreed so completely with his notes that he thought the book should be issued as edited by Douglas. Meanwhile, in making emendations, Shaw assured Douglas that he was also rescuing his reputation. Nevertheless, Douglas was bewildered and upset that the published book retained Harris's "malignant lies and libels" about him. "How *could* you?" Shaw agreed to withdraw seven pages, requiring a new edition.[16] His willingness to placate Douglas contrasted with the unsuccessful Wilde-Douglas collaborative effort, when Douglas's inability to translate *Salome* satisfactorily from the original French resulted in a bitter quarrel between the two.

The single meeting between Shaw and Douglas had occurred in March 1895, long before any letters were exchanged, in the midst of the ill-fated libel suit that Wilde had brought against Douglas's father, the Marquess of Queensberry. The very same Queensberry who had codified the rules regulating boxing accused Wilde of breaking sexual rules by corrupting his son, who was twenty-one to Wilde's thirty-seven when the affair had begun three years earlier. Queensberry's charge, that Wilde posed as a sodomite, suggests the emotions that homosexuality aroused—mere posing was a punishable offense. On that March day Shaw, then drama critic at the *Saturday Review,* was lunching with Frank Harris, the editor, at the Café Royal; the meeting was part of a series of working lunches that Harris had set up. Shaw disliked those meetings, feeling that they wasted his time. Moreover, they were apt to degenerate into "bawdy talk," and Shaw admitted to being "old-maidish" in disliking off-color stories. This lunch proved memorable. At three that afternoon Wilde arrived with Douglas, wanting Harris to testify to the "high artistic character" of *The Picture of Dorian Gray,* as Shaw recorded in his diary. Appalled at what he was hearing, Shaw was cowed into silence while Harris warned Wilde of the terrible evidence the hotel servants would testify to in court and urged him to leave the country instantly. But Douglas, enraged at his father, "clearly dominated Oscar and was determined that the case should proceed."[17]

Years later Shaw wrote Douglas that if as a beautiful youth he had seduced Wilde into homosexuality, he might have saved him from his "wretched debaucheries with guttersnipes!" Yet to assure good care for Douglas when he entered the hospital for an operation, the ever-cautious Shaw wanted Sir Almroth Wright, the bacteriologist, to spread the word that Douglas was "not a homosexualist." Cultivating Douglas, Shaw took the Uranian high road, expressing disgust at casual street encounters and praising the ideal. Shaw's disparagement of Wilde notwithstanding, the most eloquent defense of the "love that dare not speak its name" (the line itself a quotation from the Douglas poem *Two Loves*) was uttered by Wilde himself at his trial: "It is that deep, spiritual affection that is as pure as it is perfect. It dictates and pervades great works of art like those of Shakespeare and Michaelangelo. . . . It is intellectual, and it repeatedly exists between an elder and a younger man, when the elder man has intellect, and the younger man has all the joy, hope and glamour of life before him."[18]

Conscious of male beauty, Shaw was careful to distinguish between homosexual inclinations and the admiration he felt toward the male body. He praised Douglas's youthful appearance as "that flowerlike sort of beauty." But then he insisted that the attraction of male beauty was "entirely distinct from the homosexual attraction" and that one was not evidence of the other.[19] It was a distinction, he wrote, that Wilde did not understand. Even so, it was a distinction that made Shaw uneasy.

Meanwhile, although Shaw found women infinitely fascinating, he felt no physical attraction to them. What he wrote to Max Beerbohm in 1903 summed up his feelings, both earlier and later: "Walk down Piccadilly, and ask yourself at every woman that passes you, could I bear to have her as my mistress? You will be astonished at your own virtue: 99.99999999999999999 percent of them will leave you cold—perhaps 100%."[20]

There is another recorded oddity in Shaw's response to women—his use of female pseudonyms, which has been regarded as a literary curiosity. In February 1881 he appears to be the "authoress, Miss Minnie Macmullen" of 13 Victoria Grove, who asked for return of a manuscript. He also appears to have written the unpublished 1880 essay "A Reminiscence of Hector Berlioz," which opens with the announcement "I am a woman." In 1888, under the names of two fictional women, he wrote letters to the *Pall Mall Gazette* on the London theater. On 8 June an offended Horatia Ribbonson protested against the current Gaiety Theatre production of *The Taming of the Shrew*. On 31 August Amelia Mackintosh wrote "In Praise of 'The Silly Season.'" For professional reasons, women have often assumed male pen names, so Shaw's reversal is noteworthy. His literary transvestism, despite its playfulness, suggests self-identification, especially because it occurred just as Shaw was struggling to establish his sexual identity. By this time

Ulrichs had recorded the use of pseudonyms and female nicknames in modern and ancient transvestites. Ulrichs also singled out the name George as one that Urnings commonly feminized among themselves as Georgina. By continuing to disavow the hated George, Shaw publicly asserted his masculinity.[21]

Pseudonyms used in a newspaper can be a safe means of assault, providing anonymity and refuge while bestowing a secret fame. Shaw also used a number of male pseudonyms in a similar way, including two with gender significance, "No Gentleman" and the punning, Greek-influenced "A. Donis." In a much odder use of pseudonyms, Shaw added to the avalanche of letters provoked by the Jack the Ripper murders terrorizing London women in 1888, especially those living in the dungeonlike warrens of the East End. At the height of the murders an estimated one thousand letters a week were pouring into Scotland Yard, hundreds from thrill-seekers claiming to be the murderer.

As fear gripped the city, the murders inspired a series of letters in *The Star* debating whether Christianity had failed. Shaw wrote two letters on that topic, neither of them published. On 19 September, under the initials J. C., listed as residing at "Sky Parlor," he wondered, "Why do you try to put the Whitechapel murders on me?" and repudiated eye-for-an-eye punishment for the "unfortunate murderer." On 20 September, as the foreigner Shendar Brwa, he observed that "only a very small proportion of the population have any religious beliefs at all." Also unpublished was another pseudonymous letter of 20 September. Shaw wrote as Jem Nicholls, an unlettered workman who had just heard the Bishop of Rochester preach on socialism—Shaw having gone to hear the bishop with Graham Wallas, who wrote a "serious report" when the men returned to Fitzroy Square.[22]

On 24 September *The Star* did publish a Shaw letter on the murders. Shaw wrote that public interest in the poor had been aroused only because "some independent genius has taken the matter in hand, and by simply murdering and disemboweling four women, converted the proprietary press to an inept sort of communism." Apparently incensed that Jack the Ripper had succeeded in pointing up the social problems of the East End, where law-abiding socialists had failed, Shaw thought that the anarchists would find that the lesson was the knife: "a single experiment in slaughter-house anatomy on an aristocratic victim" might bring in money and save four poor women. Even though he suggested that the solution to poverty might be the municipal rate collector instead of the charity bazaar, his rhetoric was inflammatory, especially given the nature of the murders. For Jack the Ripper—self-named in one of the letters the authorities believed to be authentic—hated women, hated their life-giving potential. Acting out his hatred and rage he slit women's throats and surgically removed their wombs, lingering over his victims as he carefully placed the organs in a precise arrangement outside their bodies.[23]

Having exploited the "greatest police sensation" of the nineteenth century, Shaw diverted attention onto himself. It is striking that this letter does not bear a pseudonym but is allowed to appear under his real name. He admitted that he wrote with a greater sense of personal responsibility when using his own signature, and he thought that all newspaper articles expressing the writer's private opinion should be signed. Two decades later he was tempted to accuse Emile Zola of using "Jack's hideous neurosis" to attract readers.[24]

There is an extremely strange sidelight to Shaw's involvement in the events surrounding the Jack the Ripper murders, suggesting how inextricably entwined Shaw was in the events transpiring in Victorian London. In 1882, the same year the bulk of *Cashel Byron's Profession* was written, Sir William Gull, Physician in Ordinary to the Queen and a vivisectionist, wrote an essay supporting Claude Bernard's invention of a stove that allowed him to watch dogs being baked alive. Apparently referring to Bernard, Cashel Byron pointedly inveighs against those who bake dogs in ovens "to see how long a dog could live red hot!"[25]

In late-twentieth-century journalistic investigations of the murders, Gull has been suspected of being Jack the Ripper. One investigator speculates that Gull was assisted by two other men, including the artist Walter Sickert. Rather ingeniously, connections are suggested to the Cleveland Street scandal and a coverup orchestrated by the royal family. A few of the decidedly melodramatic and sensational elements of the story include: Prince Albert Victor, his secret marriage to a young Catholic woman, her kidnapping by the royal family, her child's escape through the help of the nanny who then falls in with harlots, a blackmail scheme, the nanny's execution by the trio known as Jack the Ripper.[26]

Whether such bizarre allegations have any basis in truth, there is a Shaw tie-in, since he knew the Sickert brothers. His diary records that at a lecture on socialism "Sickert, the artist [Walter], took the chair for me at Walham Green" and afterward "walked with me as far as Gloucester Rd. station."[27] The date was 23 December 1888.

Pluck or Cunning?

Nothing is left but the frank avowal: "I did it because I am built that way."
—*A Degenerate's View of Nordau*

Along with Dr. Jaeger's woolens, among the many attractions at the 1884 International Health Exhibition was the Anthropometric Laboratory of Cambridge biologist Francis Galton. There Shaw paid threepence to enter a space some thirty-six feet long and six feet wide, separated only by lattice-work on one side, putting him in full public view. Amid a profusion of measuring devices, he submitted to having his physical proportions and characteristics quantified—everything from the color of his eyes ("blue-grey") to his color sense ("Good") to the span of his arms ("5 feet 11.7 inches") to his strength ("Of squeeze in lbs. of—right hand, 83; left hand, 80") to his breathing power ("Greatest expiration in cubic inches—298") to his height without shoes ("6 feet 0.1 inch"). He was issued a card containing the results, with a copy being retained for Galton, who used the results in developing a theory of statistics.[1]

It was no accident that Shaw had wandered into Galton's Anthropometric Laboratory, for he followed Galton's work with interest. In *Cashel Byron's Profession*, Lydia justifies her attraction to Cashel as a "plain proposition in eugenics," the latter term coined by Galton. Shaw's personal encounter with biometrics proved to be lasting. Three-quarters of a century later he reproduced a fantasized version of the Anthropometric Laboratory, making it the setting for the futuristic Third Fable in *Farfetched Fables*, placing it on the Isle of Wight, where sister Agnes had died so long before. In Shaw's little morality play men and women are classified according to their abilities. Agreeing to be measured are a "nincompoop who thinks he's a genius; and a genius who thinks he's a nincompoop"—at least so they are tentatively diagnosed. Proper classification awaits analyses of bodily secretions and reactions. The Anthropometric Laboratory is then transformed into the building of the Diet Commissioners in the Fourth Fable, itself a soliloquy on how a diet of air and water changed the supergorilla into a soldier of Creative Evolution. In yet another metamorphosis, the Anthropometric Laboratory becomes the Genetic Institute of the Fifth Fable, and it too is indebted to Galton. Both Rose (a female) and Herm (a hermaphrodite who wears the tell-tale harlequin pattern of the clown) voice the same wish: "to be a mind without a body."[2]

Galton's crucial influence on Shaw has escaped notice. This influence goes beyond Galton's beliefs that would have increased Shaw's anxiety about Lee—that both the musical taste and the energy of superior men were transmissible and that the male line assumed supremacy in producing artists and poets. In fact, Galton's investigation of artistic taste interested both Havelock Ellis and Edward Carpenter. Ellis found a 68 percent artistic aptitude in inverts, a finding he considered significant given Galton's figure of 30 percent as the average for the population. Carpenter cites Ellis, concluding that a "large number of the artist class, musical, literary or pictorial" were Uranian.[3]

Shaw makes only a few passing references to Galton. In the Preface to *Widowers' Houses*, Shaw defended himself against charges that he was an Ibsenite pretender. Before Ibsen was known in England, Shaw had been saturated with ideas of heredity prevalent in English culture—through Herbert Spencer, Darwin, Huxley, Tyndall, and Galton. More obliquely but more revealingly, in the Preface to *Saint Joan*, Shaw described Joan as a "Galtonic visualizer," a reference to Galton's *Inquiries into Human Faculty* (1883), specifically mental imagery and visionaries. Shaw had read Galton's work enthusiastically some forty years before *Saint Joan*, as indicated by an 1886 book review that explains visualization. In *Inquiries*, Galton writes of being astonished to discover that the majority of men of science viewed him as "fanciful and fantastic" in supposing that a visualizing faculty existed. Like the color-blind, they had not discerned their "defect."[4] As Galton's investigations branched out to various forms of visualization, they included musical scores, manuscripts, numbers, and landscapes, as well as experiments in hypnosis.

In describing Joan's visions Shaw follows Galton. Joan saw imaginary saints the way some others see imaginary diagrams and landscapes, allowing them to perform extraordinary mental feats. Shaw's defense of the sanity of the hallucinating genius was personal. He boasted of his abnormally keen eyesight and worried about his sanity in a world he saw mired in stupidity and ignorance. For the self-proclaimed genius saw visions in the magic lantern of his mind's eye. Ever wary, he took the precaution of transforming them into art, preferring to subvert the status quo instead of launching an outright military campaign as Joan did.

Galton made two other discoveries that would have been of particular interest to Shaw. He isolated a class of people who recalled scenes not from their own point of view "but from a distance," and they visualized themselves "as actors on the mental stage"— reminiscent of Shaw's sense of posturing on the stage of the world. Such people, Galton thought, possessed the "power of seeing the whole of an object, and not merely one aspect of it." The latter power resembles Shaw's admonition to know "*all* the points of view," a credo describing his approach to life and to drama. Scoffing at impartiality, he sought to get his case argued "with reckless bias for and against. To understand a saint, you must hear the devil's advocate."[5]

As much as Shaw would have been impressed that Galton's investigations disclosed something of his own interior world to him—and that he was not alone in his private visions—one of Galton's findings would have proved unsettling. For Galton found that more women than men regularly saw mental imagery. He also found the power and vividness of visualizing to be "higher in the female sex than in the male," so that it was "distinct" and "full of colour." Although not conclusive, Galton's findings could only add to Shaw's unease about his sexual orientation. When Sir Almroth Wright took a stand against woman suffrage, he cited the alleged inferiority of woman's mind, which "attends primarily to the mental images it evokes." Notwithstanding his friendship with Wright, Shaw countered that man's mind and woman's mind are "exactly like." He argued that "Man as he exists at present is what Sir Almroth Wright calls Woman." Adding a feminist twist, Shaw found it staggering that Wright's description of the "political disabilities of mankind" should be "ludicrously blind to the sex of the patient."[6]

When Galton argued in *Hereditary Genius* that mental as well as physical characteristics are inherited, it was an idea startling enough that two years later his cousin, Charles Darwin, quoted him in the *Descent of Man*. Galton thought extraordinary genius so rare that through all of recorded history the number did not exceed four hundred, and yet a "considerable proportion" of geniuses were related, a point not lost on Shaw. Suspicious of those who inherited money or position, as well as the working classes, Galton became convinced that selective parenthood was necessary to create the superior population he thought desirable. Having founded the science of eugenics, Galton stirred his followers into evangelicalism as they sought converts for their "virile creed." By eugenics Galton meant not only "good in stock," but "hereditarily endowed with noble qualities" and influences that would give the "more suitable races or strains of blood a better chance of prevailing speedily over the less suitable."[7]

Working with Galton was Karl Pearson. A "most attractive man" with an "engaging smile," Pearson was a mathematics professor and political activist whose intense commitment to women's issues had played its part in drawing Olive Schreiner passionately and hopelessly to him after her relationship with Ellis had sputtered. Now married, but not to Olive, Pearson invited Shaw to his home one evening, giving Shaw a chance to read aloud an early version of *The Quintessence of Ibsenism*, its evolutionary thrust and liberated stance no doubt finding a receptive audience. Shaw was close enough to Pearson that when he satirized Ibsen clubs in *The Philanderer* he welcomed his comments on the unfinished play. The friendship with the enthusiastic Pearson humanized Shaw's research into evolutionary questions. Pearson's work included founding and editing the journal *Biometrika* with Galton; Shaw dutifully scanned the journal despite feeling out of his depth, because mathematics was "only a concept" to him. Pearson, who charmed Shaw by laughing off attacks on his speciality by calling himself a mere credulous mortal, went on to establish the Eugenics Laboratory, then to occupy the chair in eugenics at University College, London. All along he adhered to the belief that "it is the stock itself which makes its home environment, the education is of small service, unless it be applied to an intelligent race of men"—exactly the view Shaw adopted.[8]

In 1887 Shaw attended Galton's lectures "Heredity and Nurture," lectures important enough to Shaw that he carefully noted rescheduled dates. That same year he read Samuel Butler's *Luck or Cunning?* Shaw lingered over the book, carrying it to the British Museum Reading Room in January, sitting up late on a cold, foggy February night, taking it with him as he walked in Hyde Park, finally writing a review on 7 and 8 March for the *Pall Mall Gazette.* In November 1889, Emery Walker introduced Shaw to Butler at Butler's Clifford's Inn lodgings. Shaw recorded noncommittally that they talked about music at their meeting. But Butler remembered that Shaw "did nothing but cry down Handel and cry up Wagner." It annoyed Butler, who had composed *Narcissus,* a comic cantata in Handel's style, the previous year. Later, writing stage designer Charles Ricketts, Shaw wondered whether he knew that Butler "actually wrote Oratorios in the style and with the most ridiculously complete command of the Handelian manner and technique."[9]

Perhaps that first evening Shaw felt uneasy with Butler, who was undoubtedly homosexual. For his part, Butler recorded finding "something uncomfortable" about Shaw and experiencing a "dissatisfaction" with him, of feeling simultaneously repelled by him and "attracted by his coruscating power." Whatever the reason, having aggressively asserted himself by celebrating the "passionate" and "sensuous" Wagner over "Handel the Imperishable," Shaw lost the chance to talk evolution or even to ingratiate himself with Butler. Invited to address a Fabian meeting, Butler posed the question "Was the *Odyssey* written by a woman?" believing that "anyone but a fool" would agree on female authorship. He was greeted with laughter until Shaw spoke up: "Why, of course it is a woman."[10]

Butler's thought proved instrumental as Shaw moved from the rationalism of his early days at the Zetetical Society to the growing mysticism of his evolutionary concerns. Shaw recognized that debt, and Henry Salt was struck one day at lunch at Shaw's Adelphi Terrace home to see Shaw treating Butler with "almost filial respect." Generously, Shaw helped Butler by introducing him to his own publisher, Grant Richards, who eventually published three Butler works, including, posthumously and with Shaw's help, Butler's autobiographical novel *The Way of All Flesh,* which Shaw called "one of the great books of the world."[11]

Butler rebelled against Darwin, who he thought "banished mind from the universe." Intellectually, Shaw was attracted to Butler's belief in purpose over Darwinian chance. But Shaw's philosophical arguments obscured his psychological motivation. Darwinian chance signified a massive disruption of continuity, a chaotic loss of control that filled him with dread. He preferred to believe that the power of the life force was lodged within and that he could wield it, thereby achieving dominion in an orderly universe. For the same reason Shaw preferred Jean-Baptiste de Lamarck's pre-Darwinian emphasis on will and purpose, with his famous speculation on functional adaptation: that giraffes have long necks because of their habit of reaching for leaves. Like Lamarck, Butler also believed that acquired traits can be transmitted, in Butler's case via unconscious memories—further clouding the intertwined issues of heredity, genius, and homosexuality for Shaw. Over the years Shaw's Lamarckianism targeted him for ridicule. Unnoted has been Shaw's alignment on this issue with Carpenter, who believed that *"desire precedes function."* Carpenter wondered poetically, "Who shall say that the lark, by the mere love of soaring and singing in the face of the sun, has not altered the shape of its wings?" But Carpenter also connected Lamarckian desire ultimately to the "longing for the perfect human Form," the careful language veiling a connection Shaw preferred not to acknowledge. Characteristically toying with the truth, one day at Millthorpe Shaw told Carpenter that the world would see the Shavian influence on him, a claim Salt found unreasonable.[12]

From Butler, Shaw derived a further rationale to develop Creative Evolution. But the personal side of Shaw's philosophical-religious system was there all along as he set about determinedly moving upward, self-consciously creating himself and his universe. Late in life he confided that Providence had preserved his life by taking care that he was "born a devout coward" and that some day he would write a book called *Pluck or Cunning.*[13] Whatever the significance of that little confession to Lord Alfred Douglas, for Shaw, luck was a four-letter word, the pluck of the coward a better bet than the luck of the Irish.

All the talk of Darwinian evolution had led to a new fear in the 1880s: that degeneration threatened. Some looked at the slum-infested cities and, equating genetics with class, saw ominous signs that a reverse natural selection was already taking place. Shaw's preoccupation with evolution and heredity reflected his society, but for him, degeneracy represented disruption, increasing the menace of the natural world. The actual Anthropometric Laboratory and the imagined Genetic Institute represented the natural world codified and civilized, a controlled scientific microcosm. The social world was represented by the efficiency-seeking eugenicists, in sharp contrast to the unpredictable dangers of sexually voracious men and women. Instead of the precariousness of a private world where he was both sexual subject and object, Shaw preferred a world where personal sexuality ceased to exist. From Jenny Patterson's hysterics to the practices of Ellis's pervert to the sterility of the eugenics laboratory—sex meant marginal realms.

Completely excluded was the large middle ground, the taken-for-granted realm of comforting, physically expressed love. Creative Evolution, heavy with intellectual apparatus and most elaborately dramatized in *Back to Methuselah*, was a creed to assuage the terror of the margins. Meanwhile, the focus on eugenics was a substitute for facing his own sexual anxiety.

For Shaw, obsessed with his father's drinking, one instance of the alcoholism and insanity that blighted his family, there was another fear: the legacy of damaged genes. Sexologists like Krafft-Ebing saw homosexuality as deriving from the neuroses and pathologies of parents and forbears, and the Russian Benjamin Tarnowsky thought that the children of alcoholic parents were born homosexual. For most of the biological school of sexology, to be homosexual was to be degenerate. Here Shaw was caught in a double bind. He could not countenance the biological school of degeneracy, with its emphasis on damaged genes. Yet as he worried about his sexuality, the issue of inheritance loomed large. It marked the difference between the invert and the pervert, according to Ellis. Indeed, an inherited homosexuality marked one as a superior being, according to Carpenter, and was congenial with Galton's theories of hereditary genius. Trying to sort it all out was a confusing and unsettling business.

A century earlier, the term degenerate had been applied to men who took on the tendencies of women, a process thought to be linked with coffee drinking (a good reason to drink cocoa). In 1895 the threat of degeneracy took on a greater urgency in reaction against Wilde and other writers considered decadent. That year saw the English translation and publication of Max Nordau's apocalyptic treatise *Entartung* (Degeneration). Relying on the theories of the biological school of degeneracy, Nordau depicted European civilization as decadent, attacking the "severe mental epidemic" he saw afflicting artists, themselves symptoms of the exhaustion of the race. The "black death of degeneration and hysteria" was evident in a general "sexual psychopathy."[14]

Nordau sounded a chillingly familiar note: he agreed with those researchers who thought that the degenerate may be a genius. He dedicated his book to the criminologist Cesare Lombroso, who viewed homosexuals and criminals alike as evolutionary throwbacks.[15] Nordau also followed Krafft-Ebing, who had documented case histories of sexual behavior considered peculiar or deviant in *Psychopathia Sexualis*. Meanwhile, doctors prescribed willpower to ward off homosexual temptation. Lack of self-control was itself considered evidence of such an inherited taint.

Shaw read Nordau's book at the request of Benjamin Tucker, anarchist and editor of the American weekly *Liberty*. In an open letter to Tucker, Shaw responded with a blistering attack on Nordau that swallowed the issue of 27 July 1895. Published as *A Degenerate's View of Nordau*, it would be slightly revised and a preface would be added when it reappeared in 1908 as *The Sanity of Art*. In *A Degenerate's View of Nordau*, as in

The Perfect Wagnerite, and *The Quintessence of Ibsenism,* Shaw linked evolution and art, genius and amorality. He specifically denigrated Nordau's reliance on psychiatry and "all the latest specialists in madness and crime." Nordau's attack on Wagner, Ibsen, Tolstoy, Whitman, Jaeger's clothing, and vegetarianism might as well have been an attack on Shaw.[16] Shaw's method was to reverse Nordau—to transform Nordau's degenerate artist into nothing less than the artist as superman.

First Shaw defined the great artist as one who supplies works of "a higher beauty and a higher interest than have yet been perceived" and who succeeds, "after a brief struggle with its strangeness, in adding this fresh extension of sense to the heritage of the race." Diametrically opposing Nordau's degenerate, Shaw revealed his own sense of suffering by exhibiting his superman as a martyred saint: "The Superman will certainly come like a thief in the night, and be shot at accordingly. . . . Every step of his progress must horrify conventional people; and if it were possible for even the most superior man to march ahead all the time, every pioneer of the march towards the Superman would be crucified."[17]

No less than Nordau, Shaw presented totalizing categories: degenerate or artist, crucifier or crucified, reactionary or pioneer. By definition, the superman was the ultimate outsider. Elsewhere in Shaw's writings, in varying guises, he could be glimpsed as the impostor, the saint, the artist, the genius—alien sojourners all. Under a panoply of similar self-appellations, Shaw, always the Complete Outsider, constructed romanticized images of himself, projecting them—grandiosely, satirically, covertly—onto the theater stage and the stage of the world. For the highly evolved outsider was an exalted version of Carpenter's already exalted Urning. Here, too, was an exaltation of anomaly. Beyond the anomalies of color blindness and criminality, of genius and inversion that Ellis described loomed the prospect of the ultimate anomaly, the supreme incarnation of the curious reversal: the superman.

By pursuing his vision of the purified Urning-invert as prototypical superman, Shaw counteracted the threat of degeneracy and decay that lurked for him in the dread either/or option on sexuality. Yet Nordau's view was never totally exorcised for him. In the Preface to *The Sanity of Art,* Shaw thought that criticisms of Nordau did not "dispose of the main question as to how far genius is a morbid symptom." A year before his death the old man could still ask: "Am I a pathological case?" and "Is literary genius a disease?" In answering these questions himself, he proudly asserted that followers of Freud, that "indelicate adventurer," could never understand the nature of his mind. For Shaw was nothing less than an "instrument of the Life Force," like Shakespeare, Michelangelo, and Einstein. Shaw was born a storyteller "because one was needed. I am therefore not a disease but a social necessity."[18]

Shaw's dilemma centered on what appeared to be a clear-cut distinction between the artistic, saintly invert and the degraded, sordid pervert. Carpenter stressed that the "special act" with which inverts are "vulgarly credited is in most cases repugnant to them," an act Shaw labeled "abominable." As Shaw wondered how much of the inner man could be revealed through actual behavior and physical attributes, he sought alternatives to more or less orthodox science. Having reviewed Dr. Francis Warner's *Physical Expression* for the *Pall Mall Gazette,* he agreed that the hand revealed as much about character as the face, and gravitated to palmistry, then enjoying a faddish popularity. On 14 September 1886, at the home of the Irish novelist and biographer Joseph Fitzgerald Molloy, Shaw met with a dozen men, including Oscar Wilde and chiromantist Edward Heron Allen. All watched as Allen "told my character by my hand very successfully." On 4 October 1887, Shaw returned to Molloy's for an evening devoted to fortune-telling, again having his hand read among a group that included Wilde.[19]

Shaw had been attending meetings of the Society for Psychical Research with fellow Fabians Frank Podmore and Edward Pease. There he listened to lectures that ranged from inexplicable phenomena to hypnosis. Defending the society from ridicule, Shaw wrote that it was divided into two opposing groups of "sikes": the soft-headed, who wanted to protect impostors, and the hard-headed, who wanted to expose them. Madame Blavatsky was one of those exposed some three years before Shaw sent Annie Besant *The Secret Doctrine.* Since the soft-headed sikes were afraid to sleep in haunted houses, one evening after a society meeting he instantly accepted Podmore's challenge to spend the night at a house reputed to be haunted. No ghosts appeared, but Shaw's diary records that his sleep was interrupted by a "terrific nightmare." Notwithstanding, on 6 September 1887, Shaw publicly mocked spiritualism, outraging certain members of the Society for Psychical Research. Sixty years later, intrigued by an article by science-fiction writer Arthur C. Clarke, the nonagenarian enrolled in the British Interplanetary Society as a life member.[20]

Although he called Molloy the dupe of shallow impostors, Shaw retained an interest in palmistry. In June 1895 he called on Mrs. Katherine St. Hill in Knightsbridge so she might take casts of his hands and study his palms from the casts. The same month his attack on Nordau was published, *The Palmist* published an "amusing study" of his character. Having asked them to send a copy to Janet Achurch, he could not wait to write her that the palmist "accuses me, as you do, of atrocious cruelty." Later he told Henderson that the palmist had mixed acute character-analysis with utter nonsense, one way of downplaying his embarrassingly unscientific excursion. The palmist thought Shaw's "long conical hands" betrayed him as to jumping to conclusions, which Shaw accepted. But he did not like the palmist's finding that he had "little if any faculty for attachment."[21]

The palmist aside, an 1891 photograph taken by Emery Walker shows Shaw standing on the balcony of Hammersmith Terrace. The photograph is arresting precisely because of the hands. Shaw, his body turned slightly to the left, stands with his weight on one hip, one leg extended. It is a feminine pose. His hands, strangely small for a tall man, are delicately poised on his hips, the fingers of the right hand arching upward like a dancer's; the fingers of the left hand are long and graceful. They are a woman's hands, displayed in womanly fashion. As Shaw undoubtedly knew, Ulrichs thought Urnings had feminine hands.[22]

Even more suspect than palmistry was phrenology. Phrenologists thought the shape of the skull reflected the brain's contours. They also believed that "adhesiveness," the instinct for friendship, could become excessive between men. It was from the phrenological school of psychology that the belief arose in the late eighteenth century that homosexuality was innate. Influenced by phrenology, Walt Whitman used the language of adhesiveness in his poetry. Galton, who loved to measure, was fascinated by phrenology, considering skull measurements significant and correlating remarkable energy with smaller heads.[23]

Shaw felt self-conscious about his ears, which stuck "straight out like the doors of a tryptich." He apologized to Ellen Terry with comic exaggeration: "I was born with them full size, so that on windy days my nurse had to hold me by my waistband to prevent my being blown away when the wind caught them." The connection between ears and phrenology surfaced later when he sat for a portrait by Dame Laura Knight. Instead of mentioning the size of his ears, he drew attention to the meaning of their peculiar projection at the base of his skull. Comparing himself in that respect to Catherine the Great, he said that he had been told that it meant "excessive sexual development."[24]

Shaw seems to be referring to the popular myth that equates large ears with large genitalia and lascivious tastes. His large ears link him not to another man but to a woman known for her sexual appetite, a woman he once called the direct opposite of Saint Elizabeth. Furthermore, Catherine was labeled bisexual and of a "homosexual temperament" by Havelock Ellis. Like Victoria and Elizabeth I, Catherine ruled over a decisive period in her country's history. To Maxim Gorki, Shaw described her as a "very shrewd" queen who used war to keep her throne secure. Nonetheless, in his playlet *Great Catherine* (1913), Shaw's main concern was providing a vehicle for the actress Gertrude Kingston. He did not explore either Catherine's extraordinary political or sexual power, the latter virtually impossible under current censorship laws. He did depict her as a person of wit who was subject to crippling headaches.[25]

Shaw liked to tell the story of a brush with phrenology during a chance encounter at a vegetarian restaurant. Supposedly the phrenologist had been amazed to discover that where the bump of romantic veneration should have been, there was a hole instead.[26]

Given his belief in a genetic basis for homosexuality and his willingness to submit to all sorts of bodily measurements, Shaw's boastful phrenological tale takes an unexpected twist. For this particular inversion was literally so, substituting a female hole for a male bump.

That was not the only time Shaw questioned a phrenologist about his missing bump of veneration—one way of indulging in phrenology while seeming to mock the proceedings. May Morris recalled essentially the same story, setting it in the garden at Kelmscott House, with the assembled group all "having our characters described by the bumps on our heads." On at least one other occasion, an evening in 1889 at Jenny Patterson's, Shaw submitted to Miss Annie Oppenheim, who "told my character from my face and we had a good deal of talk over it." Writing in 1907, Shaw declared feeling a man's head "as scientific a proceeding as feeling his pulse." His missing bump of veneration was an example of partial evidence, like microscopic examination of sputum to detect tuberculosis. Even so, he thought it worthwhile to consult a phrenologist when hesitating upon a boy's future vocation. What phrenology needed was a "psychologist of genius" to create more precise classifications devoid of moral connotations.[27]

Shaw's desire for neutral classification was a reaction to Nordau, who used phrenological criteria. Nordau cited asymmetry, the "unequal development of the two halves of the face and cranium," as branding the degenerate. Shaw was sensitive to the Christ/Mephistophelean facial asymmetry that the once-enamored Geraldine Spooner found so notable. The artist Augustus John, who painted Shaw, said his head had "two aspects, as he pointed out himself: the concave and the convex." In *A Degenerate's View of Nordau,* Shaw confessed that his two profiles were so different when photographed that the camera would prove him to be "an utter degenerate" if his case were exceptional. But he defended his face as being "as symmetrical as faces are ordinarily made."[28]

Shaw ridiculed Nordau's "'stigmata of degeneration,'" defending as always by attacking. Since his facial asymmetry was obvious, might not some people wonder whether his facial anomaly indicated sexual anomaly as well? It was not just Nordau who troubled him. Far more difficult to dismiss was Galton, who had studied physiognomy through composite photographs. Using facial characteristics, Galton charted health, disease, and criminality in a study that Shaw mentioned approvingly in an 1885 review of a handbook of physiognomy. His immersion in the subject was enduring. From the pugnacious high-bridged nose of Major Sergius Saranoff to Undershaft's long head indicating huge reserves of mental power to the great foreheads of the puppet figures Shakes and Shav, Shaw used physiognomy to delineate character.[29]

He took Nordau's attack as personal and dangerous. Feeling exposed by his face, his habits, his tastes, he went on the offensive, destroying Nordau and making himself the champion of art—including the fin de siècle art associated with Wilde, with decadence, and with homosexuality. With the change in title from *A Degenerate's View of Nordau* to *The Sanity of Art*, the focus was shifted away from the personal to the universal. Such a measure also assured that no one would take Shaw's original title literally.

Son of Shakespeare

> I am of the true Shakespearean type.
> —To Frank Harris, 1930

"I wish Cymbeline were 'cut,'" wrote Ellen Terry in August 1896 as she prepared for a production of Shakespeare's play. Shaw found it maddening that she was "slaving over Imogen," because Shakespeare is "as dead *dramatically* as a doornail," though "his music is unfailing." Responding to Ellen's plea, Shaw trimmed "the dead & false bits" from *Cymbeline* and coached Ellen in her part, advising her "to be a mother to Shakspere." Having cut one speech because Shakespeare, "like an ass," spoiled the scene, Shaw the reviewer singled out that exact scene (Imogen being summoned to "'that same blessed Milford'") as being executed "so perfectly" that it "might have been written" for Ellen Terry. Only half in jest, Shaw warned Ellen that "when you propose to cut *me*, I am paralysed at your sacrilegious audacity."[1]

Shaw's "blasphemy" of excision would be repeated forty years later when he was roused by an "actual emergency": the proposed production of *Cymbeline* at the Shakespeare Memorial Theatre at Stratford-upon-Avon. Believing the play "goes to pieces in the last act," then "the fancy" of fixing the last act began to haunt him until he "exorcised it" by rewriting the ending, which became *Cymbeline Refinished.*[2] It is perhaps no coincidence that Shaw began his act of exorcism on 3 December 1936, the exact date of publication of his memoir of William Morris, Shaw's myth-laden tribute to that intellectual father and his paradise.

Rewriting the act as Shakespeare might have had he been "post-Ibsen and post-Shaw instead of post-Marlowe," Shaw imaginatively traded places with Shakespeare. He retained eighty-nine lines from the original, none of them Imogen's, whose "affectionate docility" Shaw ridiculed. Shaw remade her character, modeling her into the bold and practical woman he favored for his own heroines, just as he admired the women of the Shakespearean love chases. Meanwhile, Posthumus remained virtually unchanged, Shaw keeping the entire bloody cloth soliloquy of the character who earlier in Shakespeare's play bitterly cries "we are all bastards."[3]

In putting himself in Shakespeare's artistic shoes, he elaborated on his own obsessionally expressed life theme of reincarnating the Bard: "I go back to Shaigh, the third

199

son of Shakspear's Macduff. Hence my talent for playwriting." Stratford-upon-Avon was almost a "supplementary birthplace." He might call himself a "born Shakespearean genius," but he complained that Shakespeare was "overrated intellectually." While Shakespeare was the yardstick he applied to himself, sometimes he pretended to care "not one single damn" about the rivalry. Still he was haunted by the "feeling that the real Shakespear might have been myself." In 1949 the aged playwright—who could quote Shakespeare as easily as Shaw—denounced the mistaking of his feeling as "mere professional jealousy."[4]

All along Shaw had been struck by parallels between Shakespeare and himself. Shaw thought it remarkable that both John Shakespeare and George Carr Shaw were failed businessmen yet their sons could keep a cash book. As to the playwrights' mothers, there was no evidence that Mary Shakespeare, a woman of "social pretension," was a "particularly nice woman" or that her son was "particularly fond of her." Artistically, both Shakespeare and Shaw were born dramatists and shared the same psychological impetus to comedy, having discovered comedy in their misfortunes. So, too, Shakespeare had an "irrepressible gaiety of genius."[5] Insistently, Shaw forged a dialogue with his powerful predecessor in which the pair became indistinguishable from each other artistically, biographically, and psychologically.

In addition to *Cymbeline Refinished,* the collaboration with the Bard across time, and *The Dark Lady of the Sonnets,* set in Shakespeare's time with Shakespeare as a character, Shaw fashioned a puppet play set in his own time, with characters meant to indicate both Shakespeare and himself. *Shakes Versus Shav* was written at the request of puppet master Waldo Lanchester for his Malvern Marionette Theatre. Written very late in life (January 1949), and very quickly (a mere three days, virtually a spontaneous response), this little play offers an unusual lens through which to view Shaw's preoccupation with Shakespeare.

In the play Shakes comes "raging" like a darker self to chastise the "infamous impostor" who pretends to "reincarnate" him, shortening his name to Shav. Tinkering with Shakespeare's name was nothing new for Shaw. From 1882 into the 1890s his preferred spelling was Shakspere—literally, "Shakes, the father." Coined during his apprenticeship period, that spelling suggests a wish to surpass the literary "father" he admired and envied. Under the rubric of "Shaxper or Shagsper the illiterate bumpkin," in the Preface to the puppet play, Shakes, *père,* still survived in the twilight of Shaw's life.[6]

In the tradition of puppet plays, the action of *Shakes Versus Shav* is physical. Challenging Shav to spar, Shakes knocks Shav down with a straight left, the punch that was Shaw's pride three-quarters of a century earlier. But then Shav, younger by three hundred years, knocks Shakes down and out. The absurdity of the physical battle veils the serious nature of the real battle, which is psychological: Shaw's unending duel with the ghost of Shakespeare.

The duel surfaces most forcefully in the play-within-the-play, a ritualistic reenactment of the Macbeth / Macduff legend that Shaw claimed as his own heritage. Projecting himself through layers of puppet characters, the nonagenarian summoned the psychic means to slay Shakespeare. At the climax of the contest between the young king and the old king, the phallic sword decapitates. Dramatically, the action of the play-within-the-play mirrors Shaw's verbal emasculation of Shakespeare, who has literally been de-*speared* via naming, so that he impotently shakes and rages. Is Shaw playing a little Freudian game here? Victory is elusive as a jealous Shakes puffs out the candle burning between them that bears Shav's "glimmering light."[7] The final dramatization in the duel with Shakespeare symbolizes the end of Shaw's line as fecund playwright and sterile progenitor. Darkness envelops the pair, but the intensity of the one-on-one encounter between puppets charges the landscape with a strangely cosmic mystery.

Shaw praised Shakespeare for having a "prodigious fund of that vital energy" found in the man of genius. The secret of that energy fascinated Shaw's contemporaries, a number of whom examined the old theory that Shakespeare was attracted to boys. The womanizing Frank Harris tried to dissuade Oscar Wilde from writing on that topic. Wilde went ahead, producing a short story with a special resonance for Shaw. "The Portrait of Mr. W. H." included an effeminate young man who took the role of Shakespeare's female leads in school plays. Samuel Butler also agreed with the theory, publishing *Shakespeare's Sonnets Reconsidered* (1899), which identified Mr. W. H. as the son of a sea cook. Lord Alfred Douglas in his *True History of Shakespeare's Sonnets* (1933) identified Mr. W. H. as a boy actor in Shakespeare's acting company. After reading Douglas's account, Shaw wrote him, praising his version as the "best of all those known to me."[8]

In "The Revolutionist's Handbook," appended to *Man and Superman*, the world is described as a "den of dangerous animals" among whom the "few accidental supermen"—the Shakespeares, Goethes, and Shelleys—"must live as precariously as lion tamers."[9] If Shakespeare was Shaw's literary double, Goethe, whose Faust seeks to transcend the human, and Shelley, restless poet of the heights, were also psychological kinsmen.

Shaw's accidental supermen had something else in common: all three artists were considered examples of great geniuses who were homosexual—a powerful reason for living as precariously as lion tamers. More than he would admit, Shaw was influenced by Carpenter's view that the artist's very homosexuality was the source of his greatness, endowing him with a cosmic consciousness. Of Uranian man, Carpenter wrote, "at the bottom lies the artist-nature, with the artist's sensibility and perception." Shaw, too, believed in the existence of an artist-nature. For him it operated unscrupulously. It simulated the procreativity of the mother as it operated in all geniuses as philosophic consciousness, in all women as fecundity. Shaw lets Tanner express the artist's ruthlessness, but it was Shaw's psyche that cried out that of all human struggles none is "so treacherous and remorseless as the struggle between the artist man and the mother woman."[10]

Shaw was irresistibly attracted to woman's multifarious guises: "No fascinating woman ever wants to emancipate her sex: her object is to gather power into the hands of Man, because she knows that she can govern him." Shaw, "disarmed and intimidated" by women, believed they could only be beaten "by brutal selfishness or by their own weapons." Defensively, he appropriated those weapons. He learned to use them "with more than feminine skill," enchanting his dangerously charming enemies by concentrating all his magic, "like the lady in Man & Superman." Carpenter also recognized the power of female fascination and thought that Uranian men were "by their nature drawn rather near to women." Because of their "singular appreciation and understanding of the emotional needs and destinies of the other sex," Uranian men were often the most faithful friends and defenders of women.[11] Truly ambivalent, Shaw defended himself against women as he defended women against a patriarchal society.

Like Shakespeare, he was third born after two sisters, a biographical correspondence bound to have impressed him. Satirically attributing his genius to his mother's invention—and implicitly disregarding Galton—he revealed her formula: "To make a man of genius you require practice. You practice on girls—say, two girls; and then, having formed the habit of making girls, when you try a boy, you start him as a girl before you recollect what you are about, and only get in his sex at the last moment, with the result that he is a monster who writes plays because he is a hero or a heroine on paper as he chooses."[12] Behind the protective satire lurks the self-identity of the genius-monster whose manhood is deficient because of his mother, the man who is essentially a woman. At the same time, free to move between the roles of hero or heroine, the artist exalted in gender fluidity.

Shaw defended Shakespeare against the charge of "perversion." Unlike Michelangelo, whose work is strikingly devoid of susceptibility to female charm, Shakespeare's "normality" could be confirmed "by the excessive susceptibility to the normal impulse shewn in the whole mass of his writing." To Shaw this was the "really conclusive reply."[13] It is the absence of just such a susceptibility that marks Shaw's writings.

Ascent of the Naked Skeleton

> On the mountains I revive.
> —To Siegfried Trebitsch

Shaw's enduring fascination with the heights reflected his inner landscape. One sunny August day outside Munich, an alpine peak dotted with edelweiss beckoned. "If you slip, you break your neck; and the Matterhorn can do no more for you than that," he boasted to William Archer of his cragmanship. The less daring Sidney Webb, Shaw's companion on a two-week excursion to the Continent, stayed below, sitting amid the trees and writing about municipal death duties. Then near Strasbourg, amid "agonies of terror," Shaw climbed to the top of a cathedral spire, ascending a "naked flight of steps" outside the steeple at a height that made him sick to remember. Stopped short by terror some thirty or forty feet from the "horrible apex," Shaw was forced to make a "fearful descent." Yet once safe on the street he had a "craving to try again—a remorse at having given in."[1] Having recalled the incident to Archer, Shaw devoted the remainder of his letter to Ibsen.

Shaw's craving to climb high resembles the similar craving of Halvard Solness, Ibsen's masterbuilder, who builds higher than he can climb, becoming giddy at the heights. But in 1890, Ibsen was two years away from writing *The Masterbuilder*. Ibsen continued his study of the relation between height and breadth—the unattainable and the attainable—for human existence in *Little Eyolf* (1894), through the road builder Borgheim. As much as he praised Ibsen's ideas, Shaw found a psychic mirror in the artistic creations of the tragic Norwegian, in 1897 referring to himself as a "contemporary of Master-Builder Solness."[2]

Shaw made actual aerial ascents. Going up for a stunt ride in a biplane in 1916, he seemed "chiefly interested in the fact that, when one is flying upside-down in the loop, there is no particular sense of invertedness," as pilot H. C. Biard recalled. "'The world is like that, young man!'" cried Shaw. A decade earlier there had been an ascent in a balloon. At nine thousand feet he peered through a hole in the boards, "which made him feel rather sick," remembered fellow passenger Robert Loraine. Shaw reported to Archer that the sensation of riding in the balloon was like standing "on the tip top of the Eiffel Tower on one toe," a vivid evocation of the acrophobia he invited. But for later publication Shaw pretended otherwise, describing his balloon ascent as so far from thrilling that it almost put him to sleep.[3]

Shaw's admiration of those who brave the heights erupted in *Misalliance* (1909). In that play Lina Szczepanowska, who enters the action by crashing through the glass roof of a country house pavilion, shines as the strong, valiant aviator and acrobat. Triumphantly, Lina affirms her independent womanhood—and scathingly denounces bourgeois marriage—in language so thrillingly charged that her speech is often hailed as one of the finest bravura pieces in Shaw. The playwright's self-identification with his proudly soaring heroine is strengthened by her appearance in male garb and by the initial mistaking of her for a man. For by the time of *Misalliance*, the heights and gender had melded even more personally and momentously for Shaw.

In *Sexual Inversion*, Ellis and Symonds present case histories in which inverts detail circumstances surrounding their dawning recognitions of their sexuality. These case histories were scanned by one group of readers in particular—those in search of secret but familiar scenes. The revelations are steeped in longing for male beauty and at times are bathed in an erotic mysticism. Ellis includes Raffalovich's observation that a moment arrives when the invert "discovers the enigma of his homosexual tastes" and "remembers that he has been what he is from his earliest childhood," with innocent dreams of brigands and savages, slavery and masters. Without "the least thought that is crudely sexual" he has "discovered his sentimental vocation." Such self-discoveries, possibly stimulated by accounts in Krafft-Ebing, became more likely after 1895, a watershed year in homosexual consciousness. Not only was it the year that Wilde was sentenced to prison, but also in January of that year Carpenter's *Homogenic Love* appeared, making it one of the first books defending homosexuality to be commercially published.[4]

On 30 March 1896, Shaw went to the country with Graham Wallas, spending the Easter holidays with him at Stocks Cottage, lent to Wallas by Mrs. Humphrey Ward. From this "lonely cottage on a remote hillside" Shaw realized the "full significance of the singular fate" that led him "to play with all the serious things of life and to deal seriously with all its plays," his very language playing with inversion. In mid-April, sitting up after midnight in that still and secluded cottage, Shaw sent Janet Achurch a "line to ponder" during the absence of her husband, who was coming down to the country the following day. In exuberant romantic language, Shaw revealed that he had undergone an ecstatic experience, though the exact nature of that experience was carefully veiled. Little can be gleaned from his diary, because comments on his health made two weeks earlier proved to be the last personal notes he would record, such entries having diminished for some time.[5]

Shaw wrote Janet that his growing certainty that he could be a dramatic poet might be a "symptom of decay"—odd enough in itself. Then he cryptically described a powerful self-revelation:

> But ability does not become genius until it has risen to the point at which its keenest states of perception touch on ecstasy, on healthy, self-possessed ecstasy, untainted by mere epileptic or drunken incontinence, or sexual incontinence. Well, in the rose valleys; on the plains of heaven, I was not incontinent; but I was ecstatic. For the moment I got far beyond any former rapture; and there was no rebound, no reaction, no bill to pay: for many days the valleys and plains were still in sight; and I never lost the ground I had gained afterwards. In a later experiment I threw all this away with such reckless, prodigal irresistible completeness, that I stood utterly drained of my ecstatic mood, only to find the naked skeleton of my force diabolically strong and resolute. I was not sorry.

The ecstatic experience, like his earlier, well-documented conversions, had changed the course of his life. At such a moment of heightened awareness, Shaw suddenly read his life in a certain way.[6]

Shaw specifically connected his ability as an artist with a fear of decadence, opposing sexual incontinence to untainted ecstasy—an ecstasy attained by genius. On the plains of heaven, Shaw's spiritualized garden of Eros, there were at least two rapturous experiments with no bill to pay. Later he would posit the "vital necessity to evolving society" of a "chronic ecstasy of thought" where there is "no reaction, no disgust, no love turned to hate," unlike the feelings evoked by "physically reproductive pleasure."[7] Now, from the perspective of the heights, Shaw attested to the transcendent and purifying power of art. To Janet, Shaw described his joyous recognition of his naked skeleton—the inseparability of the artist and genius—with all the accrued meanings of genius, including that of the noble invert.

Having made his candid but safely abstract revelation, he appealed to Janet to devote herself to art, confessing that the "step up to the plains of heaven" was made on her bosom, and it was a "higher step" than those he had taken "on other bosoms." As an artist, he had used her: "But he who mounts does not take the stairs with him, even though he may dream for the moment that each stair, as he touches it, is a plank on which he will float to the end of his journey."

Having chosen his path, there was no turning back: "I know that the floating plank image is false and the stair image true; for I have left the lower stairs behind me." He had transcended the peril described to Janet a year earlier: "But all we who are artists are rallied on a narrow ledge about the millionth of an inch broad, which yet makes all the difference between us and the others."[8] At that time, from his narrow base, he dwelled on the disproportionate relation of height and depth. Now stairs stretched continuously upward, guarding him from a sudden plunge from the ledge or a slip off the dangerous floating plank. As the revelation to Janet integrated crucial life themes of height and depth, disruption and continuity, all three modes of world—the biological, the social, and the personal—were integrated into an ethereal world of rose valleys and rapture, health and strength, art and genius.

As Far as Thought Can Reach—Part 5 of *Back to Methuselah*—is set in A.D. 31,920 but resembles Greece of the fourth century B.C. Against a pastoral backdrop of altar, glade, and dainty classic temple, the childish artist-biologist Pygmalion is accidentally slain by the beautiful artificial female he created, an automaton unable to control her human reflexes. It is Lilith, the female principle, who expresses the Platonic wish that concludes Shaw's metabiological pentateuch: that Man and Woman ford the "last stream that lies between flesh and spirit," disentangling their lives from the matter that has always mocked them.[9] From the vantage point of a world design structured on equilibrium and continuity, Shaw imagined an entirely cerebral universe free from the vulnerabilities and uncertainties of the body, including the special unpredictability of the male body.

Meanwhile, irradiated by art, either men or women—especially theatrical performers—could inspire his romanticized visions. Here, too, in the arena of eroticism, Shaw's uniquely configured rich inner life became a phantasmagoric structure separating him from the bulk of mankind—heterosexual and homosexual. His personal dilemma centered on Ellis's clear-cut distinction between the artistic, saintly invert and the degraded, sordid pervert. The quasi-religious and aesthetic aura surrounding Ellis's invert corresponded to Shaw's natural inclination to etherealize and elevate. But unlike those for whom the significance of the invert was to endow powerful erotic feelings with a higher meaning, for Shaw it was just the opposite. Full of dizzying ambivalences and romantic yearnings, fearing a plunge into the abyss of desire, he embraced the idea of the noble invert to give artistic sanction to his retreat from flesh. In this Shaw followed a familiar pattern of behavior. To forge a fleshless bond with the objects of his love and desire was consistent with his rituals of abstention and discipline: "the survival of the fittest means finally the survival of the self-controlled."[10] Such a bond guarded him against the unseen dark forces that forever assailed him and that he himself called the Death Force.

In the twilight of the twentieth century there is no agreement on whether self-definition—even with emotional commitment to one of the same gender—is sufficient for a *cultural* recognition of sexual identity. But psychologically for Shaw in his own fin de siècle, the cultural climate of sexual ambiguity and private revelation mirrored his uncertainties. Crucially, for his self-identity as man and artist, he now bore the secret brand of the invert.

"How did you respond to your sexual urges?" asked Frank Harris, author of a graphic autobiography. "It is a very wide and complex subject, on which a mere record of ejaculations, like that in My (Your) Life & Loves, throws no light," replied Shaw.[11]

The Accidental Bridegroom

> There is an old saying that if a man has not
> fallen in love before forty, he had better not
> fall in love after.
> —Preface to *Plays Unpleasant*, 1898

Shaw's letter to Janet revealing his ecstatic conversion was written in the spring of 1896. Just as the noise culminating in the Labouchere Amendment became the fanfare heralding his loss of virginity to Jenny Patterson, the overheated sexual atmosphere now sent him scurrying for cover. Before the end of the summer the wily philanderer had located the necessary camouflage: a suitable woman. Even so, it took him two years and a crippling injury to overcome his reluctance to marry.

At a luncheon in the autumn of 1895, Beatrice Webb was introduced to a wealthy woman, originally from County Cork, who had come to London some twenty years earlier. "Bred up in second-rate fashionable society and without any education or habit of work," Charlotte Payne-Townshend has "drifted about," wrote Beatrice, who unashamedly cultivated her "'for the good of the cause.'"[1] Within a year Charlotte had donated one thousand pounds to the Library of the London School of Economics and endowed a scholarship for women. So persuasive was Beatrice that the directionless Charlotte even rented the two upper floors at Adelphi Terrace from the school. For all this Beatrice welcomed her into "the 'Bo' family," the Potter family name for Beatrice.

Charlotte Payne-Townshend had long been accustomed to a life of serious social obligations. She was a fashionable woman who shopped in Paris and held a salon in Rome. An inveterate traveler, she journeyed back and forth to the Continent, to Africa, to Asia. In India she danced at the State Ball; in Egypt in 1894 she lunched with Horatio Herbert Kitchener, commander in chief of the Egyptian Army, and stayed aboard the yacht of Lord and Lady Waterford. In Rome she had a pastel portrait done by popular artist Guilio Aristide Sartorio.[2]

Charlotte also had a taste for fringe religious sects and charismatic cultists. Like many Victorians, she countered the rationalism of the times by dipping into spiritualism, though her practical nature prevented total immersion. Bessie Shaw, long a believer in the wonders of the Ouija board, would perspicaciously dub her Carlotta after their first meeting. Described by Beatrice Webb as a "large graceful woman with masses of chocolate-brown hair," Charlotte seemed a "pleasant, well-dressed, well-intentioned woman." She made so little impression on Shaw that he did not bother to note their introduction at the Webbs' on 29 January 1896. Charlotte, however, recorded the event in her diary. Compared with being magnetized and irradiated by someone like the glamorous Janet Achurch, Shaw's initial encounter with the thirty-nine-year-old Charlotte was decidedly low voltage. Her name first appears in his diary some two months later in a calendar notice that she was holding an "at home" for the London School of Economics. He did not attend. As he confided all too clinically to Ellen Terry later that year, Charlotte was a woman at whom "nobody would ever look twice."[3]

Despite her involvement with the London School of Economics, Charlotte's social life continued unabated. In August she joined the Webbs in renting a country house, a rectory in Suffolk, for six weeks. As was their custom, the Webbs invited Fabian friends to join them in hammering out socialist principles. Graham Wallas and Shaw were part of the small group that assembled amid the graying brick and austere greenery. Shaw found the sylvan setting with a purpose so invigorating that he stayed the full six weeks. After intensive intellectual exercise in the mornings, the group welcomed equally intensive physical exercise in the afternoons, hiking and cycling around the countryside. As the summer wore on and people came and went, Shaw frequently found himself alone on these jaunts with Charlotte. Everyone agreed that her station in life made her a "'great catch for somebody'" and Shaw declared his intentions toward the "Irish millionairess" to Ellen Terry: "I am going to refresh my heart by falling in love with her—I love falling in love—but, mind, only with her, not with the million."[4]

Pleased with Charlotte's not quite original, not quite conventional outlook, Shaw used the month and a half of long summer days and nights to woo her, and she openly accepted his advances. Each evening the company assembled to hear Shaw talk or read his plays. When the others retired, Shaw and Charlotte strolled outdoors. They took a bicycling tour with the Webbs for a few days. On returning to London Shaw shared a revelation with Ellen Terry: "the ideal woman is a man, though women lie low & let that secret keep itself."[5]

In the meantime, Beatrice felt a bit put out by the turn of events. She had invited Charlotte with the solemn and solid Wallas in mind. "Now she turns out to be an 'original,' with considerable personal charm and certain volcanic tendencies," wrote Beatrice in her diary on 16 September. "To all seeming, she is in love with the brilliant philanderer and he is taken, in his cold sort of way, with her." Of Charlotte, Beatrice wrote knowingly that she "bitterly resents her enforced celibacy but thinks she could not tolerate the matter-of-fact side of marriage." From Shaw, Beatrice gathered that the two were on "very confidential terms" and had "'explained' their relative positions." Apparently Shaw could safely woo Charlotte without worrying about sexual demands. Unlike so many of the women he knew, Charlotte was a "restful person," as he wrote Ellen, "very ladylike," and "not so very plain" once "you are in her confidence."[6]

The confidences that gave Charlotte a not-so-plain luster may have been those of her love life. Over the years Charlotte had refused the honorable advances of one Danish count, two barristers, and three military officers, men too predictably conventional for her. Shortly before Beatrice had befriended her she was rebuffed by the only man to rouse her somnolent passion, a dashing Swedish doctor with a fashionable practice in Rome. Axel Munthe, a hypnotist by personality and profession, as well as something of a local legend, specialized in charming every woman he encountered. Charlotte met him at a dinner party in Rome in 1894 and became instantly infatuated. Twice she consulted him about her nerves. He suggested a change of air in Venice, where he was going to attend the Swedish Crown Princess. Charlotte went to Venice and fell in love for the first time, but Munthe rapidly lost interest.[7] The timing of the Munthe episode explains the energy Charlotte unleashed on the London School of Economics and indicates a weakness for spellbinders.

Charlotte's solitary romance, more imagined than real, and dissolved against her will, contrasted with Shaw's thickly tangled relationships with women, each skein of many years' duration. In the fall of 1896, Ellen Terry hoped for more than a paper relationship, and the embers of the love affair with Florence Farr were being snuffed out that October. Just as in his previous year's complaint to Janet, Bertha Newcombe still wanted to tie him "like a pet dog to the leg of her easel & have me always to make love to her when she is tired of painting." Later the scorned Bertha described Shaw as "by preference a passionless man," writing that "he seemed to have no wish for and even to fear passion." His "talking, talking, talking of the pros & cons of marriage, even to my prospects of money or the want of it, his dislike of the sexual relation & so on, would create an atmosphere of love-making without any need for caresses or endearments."[8]

On 17 October, three days after renouncing spiritual intercourse with Florence, Shaw telegrammed Charlotte, now in Paris, "ALL CLEAR NOW YES A THOUSAND TIMES." Shaw then proceeded to stay in London and write tales of Janet, whom he still flattered as "unusually beautiful." He warned Charlotte that her worst theories of maternity were being carried out by the pregnant Janet: "all her animal forces are thrown into a sort of liquid suffusion & eruption, & she's stark mad." To illustrate, he insensitively described how Janet had tortured Bertha, falsely telling her that he and Charlotte were engaged. It was a lie he verified in writing, outrageously giving Bertha "full particulars" regarding the money Charlotte was settling on him and the house they had taken, so that the distracted Bertha raced over and bullied him face to face. When Shaw finally broke with Bertha, Beatrice consoled her: "'You are well out of it.'" But the forlorn Bertha, mocked by her own portrait of Shaw that dominated her wainscoted studio, quietly muttered that it felt like "'the peace of death.'"9

"Well, shall I marry my Irish millionairess?" he asked Ellen on 4 November. "You'd be all bad, and no good in you," answered Ellen, "if you marry anyone unless you know you love her." Feeling contrite after Sidney Webb lectured him about Charlotte, on 9 November, he was "still here," and "if it would do any good" to run away, "I'd do it." He was mortally afraid his "trifling & lying and ingrained treachery and levity with women" were going to make her miserable. One week later Shaw announced, "Cold much worse—fatal consummation highly probable." Then "like a whirlwind," he swooped across the channel and swooped back to London.10

Yet another question to the "heartwise" Ellen: "And must a woman who is nervous, and sensitive, and sleeps badly, and longs for healthy rest, be *honorably* charged for a very simple remedy the modest price of £5000 a year & her hand in marriage? What kind of swindler and fortune hunter do you take me for?" With immense bravado, he confessed to being a "mere bottle of nerve medicine, and riding gaily off." All this he claimed in a self-congratulatory letter to Ellen, who had not been spared by men, and who was not now spared by Shaw, insensitive to *her* feelings. "Ha! Ha! ha! ha!!!! In mockery for all illusions—in tenderness for my dear Ellen," he closed ambivalently, and as treacherously as he had feared.11

In spite of the assumptions of Shaw's recent biographers, it is unlikely that the fatal consummation ever occurred. What he wrote to Ellen he likely repeated to others. Shaw's inconsiderate announcement was a public relations device, incidentally making Charlotte appear more interesting to Ellen but especially shoring up his masculine image. Having invested so much public time with Charlotte and broken with everyone else, he needed to conceal his lack of ardor. Either going through with the fatal consummation or merely saying he had served the same purpose. Then, too, Shaw had an old-fashioned streak of gallantry, and Webb would have urged marriage, not sex. On her side, the ladylike Charlotte would probably not have been as willing as more bohemian women to lose her virginity without a ring. The macho pose was from the same man who only a few months earlier in the *Saturday Review* could not see why "it is less dishonorable for a woman to kiss and tell than a man."12

He played his toying games with Charlotte, his loving games with Ellen, and the months wore on. In March 1897, Shaw described a "ridiculous difficulty with Miss P. T." She insisted on turning up at his lectures in holes and corners and dock gates. Even though his "demagogic denunciations of the idle rich" lacerated her conscience, he was exasperated that she refused to stay away, although surely it was one way of showing her loyalty to him. "Was there ever such a situation?" he asked Ellen. In May, Beatrice recorded that Charlotte insisted on renting a country house with them to be with Shaw. In Dorking, a worried Beatrice saw signs that he was tired of Charlotte, despite his "cat-like preference for those to whom he is accustomed." "Poor Charlotte," whose eyes had lost their "dancing light," observed the working partnership between Beatrice and Sidney. Wanting to be useful, she resolutely acted as Shaw's unpaid secretary. She typed his plays while he wandered about in the garden, writing his articles, revising his plays, and correcting the Webbs' work.[13]

Shaw was at a crossroads. In June, while riding the night train from Dorking and then back again to the Webbs and Charlotte, he wrote two of his most intimate and revealing letters to Ellen. In August, after Graham Wallas announced his engagement, the astounded Shaw swore his undying faithfulness—to Ellen. Of the original Fabians, now only he remained unmarried. Perhaps emboldened by the Wallas news, Charlotte made a "generous & romantic proposal," but as ungraciously as John Tanner, Shaw felt "shuddering horror & wildly asked the fare to Australia." Charlotte was "inexpressibly taken aback." From her vantage point at summer's end, Beatrice found the relationship "disturbing" and verging on the "dishonourable," with Shaw bored but finding Charlotte necessary.[14]

In October, with Charlotte off for a very social week of riding and dinner parties with her sister, Mary Cholmondeley, at Keyham, Leicestershire, Shaw teased: "I think I shall fall in love with Mrs Phillimore." Two months later, when Charlotte and Lucy ("Lion") Phillimore planned a trip to Dieppe, Shaw was invited to accompany them. But he blustered on about going to a watering place in the dead of winter to be chaperoned by two women, each wanting the other to seduce him. Stung by his caustic rejection, Charlotte left for the Continent without a word to him, conduct he judged "inconceivable." He demanded that she report back for secretarial duties, but the "ungrateful wretch" was becoming less predictable, more independent.[15]

Never one for playing other people's games, Shaw fluctuated between bewilderment and fury. The relationship dragged on, threatening to become another inconclusive long-term affair. During March and April, Charlotte again went to the Continent with Lion, stopping in Rome to study the municipal services and to socialize (but not with Axel Munthe), her absence evoking harsh words from Shaw. Charlotte, like Ann Whitefield, was a spider and he the fly. She was the "terrible Charlotte, the lier-in-wait, the soul hypochondriac." Yet sometimes in dreams he missed "'die schöne grünen Augen.'"[16]

Shaw bombarded her with missives describing toothache, neuralgia, headache, fever, weakness. Having just had a "huge grinder dragged out" by the dentist, he complained to Webb, "I live the life of a dog." Not that the Webbs could offer much in the way of help. They were off on a nine-month world tour, researching English municipal tradition overseas. Wallas was in Devonshire, and Kate Salt, Shaw's sometime secretary, had gone to Millthorpe to spend the Easter holidays in the country with Carpenter. Shaw wrote Webb that all he could do was brutally exult in his "loneliness & freedom," as only Ellen remained faithful. Meanwhile, the theater critic touched on a matrimonial theme: "People marry for companionship, not for debauchery. . . . If I were to get married myself, I should resort to some country where the marriage law is somewhat less than five centuries out of date." Partners in marriage should be as responsible for their behavior to one another as partners in business.[17]

Then he suddenly developed an "unaccountably sore" left foot, which he attributed to his tightly laced shoe. By 21 April "locomotion" had become "very excruciating." He was a "fearful wreck." Needing a physician, he relied on Dr. Sharpe, Alice Lockett's appropriately named husband, Alice quietly waiting in the next room as her husband operated, then acting as nurse while Shaw "raved all sorts of love" to her. Sentenced to his chair, he began *Caesar and Cleopatra*. Solving the problem of locomotion, the celebrated critic and playwright, red beard to the wind, took to hopping around London. He hopped his way to a St. Pancras Vestry meeting, where his support of free "sanitary conveniences" for women was labeled "disgusting." Then afterward, in his role as theater critic, he hopped to the Avenue Theatre to see the farce *The Club Baby*, writing Charlotte: "Play with a baby in it. Might have been written by one." The reviewer vented his outrage at the exploitation of an infant on stage and thought the play should have been called *The Stage Baby's Revenge*.[18]

In May, after more surgery, Shaw diagnosed his condition to Janet: he was "overdoing the superhuman." As the foot became too great a hindrance to theater reviewing, he grew irascible, informing Bram Stoker that he had only one desire: to see the theaters of "this accursed metropolis," along with their actors, managers, and critics, all "plunged into the blinding white hot heat of hell." The previous November when he had suffered his "annual bicycle accident," which temporarily obliterated the left side of his face, he had described in the *Saturday Review* being stitched up by a country doctor. Now he regaled his readers with his experience under anaesthesia as "G. B. S. Vivisected." A week later, "nailed by one foot to the floor, like a doomed Strasburg goose," there was a valedictory to his readers. "I am off duty forever, and am going to sleep," he swore as he passed the torch to Max Beerbohm and ended the most brilliant reign of theatrical journalism in history.[19]

"By the way, would you advise me to get married?" he asked Henry Arthur Jones on 20 May. "Yes, I would get married if I were you," replied Jones a day after Shaw had dropped broad hints to director Max Hecht of an imminent secret marriage. On her return from Rome, Charlotte, horrified both at the squalor of Shaw's rooms at Fitzroy

Square and at Bessie's apparent indifference to her son, had taken to nursing him. Plainly he needed to go the country to recuperate. Plainly, too, Charlotte was the "inevitable & predestined agent appointed by Destiny."[20]

If Charlotte did not excite him, neither did she threaten to drown him in the *odor di femmina*: "she had none of the feminine traits that I had expected, and all the human qualities I had only hoped for." Nor did he have to arm himself against her in the fashion of Caesar, his "psychological woman tamer." The objection to his marriage had ceased with the objection to his death, he wrote Beatrice Webb. Similarly, Tanner, "the marked down victim, the destined prey," succumbs to Ann and the Life Force: "Let it kill us." The time to marry was at hand. Shaw had become "fleshless, bloodless, vaporous, ethereal."[21]

On 31 May, Shaw wondered whether Henry Salt could meet the next day at 15 Henrietta Street, Covent Garden, "TO WITNESS A CONTRACT." The marriage contract was dutifully signed at the West Strand Registry Office on 1 June 1898, with Salt and Graham Wallas the witnesses. Shaw had considered asking Kate Salt, but since she "violently" objected to the "whole proceeding," there was the danger of her "breaking out and forbidding the banns at the supreme moment." Now, why did Kate object so violently? Did she fear that Shaw's sexual orientation might bring grief to Charlotte? Certainly Kate had plenty of opportunity to discuss Shaw's love life with Carpenter, who was adept at recognizing the closet Urning. Moreover, her own marriage had strained under the weight of her lesbianism, despite the bohemianism of both parties. Nor had Shaw changed his perception of Charlotte, now a member of the Fabian executive committee: "Ladylike woman," he warned Archer of his forgettable bride, "remember that you know her already." And Don Juan mocks, "wherever ladies are is Hell."[22]

Gender roles were reversed for the wedding, conveniently aided by Shaw's self-described "disabled condition." Before the ceremony, the bride had gone to Henrietta Street to make the arrangments amid "shrieks of merriment," then suffered the "final humiliation" of buying the "symbol of slavery" from a West End jeweler. At the ceremony Shaw appeared in an old jacket worn ragged by crutches, foot swathed in bandages, boasting afterward that he looked like a beggar. In Dublin, the cashier had bought a tailed coat to announce his status to the world. Now the inappropriately dressed bridegroom, who had provided neither the license nor the ring, used his clothes to announce his sham status, an announcement underlined when the well-dressed Wallas was mistaken for the bridegroom.[23] The role confusion recalls Shaw's account of his christening, his very first ceremony, when the sexton took over the duties of his drunken godfather. Like his godfather, Shaw would not fulfill his role-defined duties; like the sexton, Shaw intended only to stand in.

In another description of his wedding ceremony, Shaw outflanked would-be satirists by doing the job himself, writing in *The Star* how a lady and a gentleman taking shelter from a shower at the registry office were married "in the confusion," making it the "second operation" the bridegroom had recently undergone.[24] With the information that the bride's income was many times that of Corno di Bassetto, Shaw, the invincible comic hero, evoked a version of the universal laughter that ends *Man and Superman*.

Pretending to be an accidental bridegroom, he refused to play the traditional role. What did the bride wear? What did she think of the ceremony? Shaw did not say. By publicly satirizing his wedding, he made himself—not the bride—the star of the occasion, reversing gendered expectations. By advertising his relative poverty, he did more than fend off accusations of being a fortune hunter: he put into practice his own disgust at a marriage tradition based on the economic and sexual slavery of women. The dependence of women on men made the difference between marriage and prostitution simply "the difference between Trade Unionism and unorganized casual labor," he would write in his nearly one-hundred-page Preface to *Getting Married*. The married man of 1911, the bridegroom, and the bachelor who wrote *Mrs Warren's Profession* spoke in one voice. Marriage was, and "still is, largely a survival of the custom of selling women to men." Then, too, three years before marrying a wealthy woman, he had written that the drive of the whole female sex toward either prostitution or marriage for money "accounts for some of the difference between a man and a woman." Now he flaunted the gender reversal. Even though the American production of *The Devil's Disciple* had brought him substantial royalties before the wedding, he would allow his wife to settle a sum of money on him.[25]

At the nuptial news, McNulty, who had named his son George Bernard, wrote a long letter with only a passing comment on the marriage—the irony of marrying a Townshend. Honeymooning in a rented house in Surrey, the accidental bridegroom became the accident-prone husband. The moment he felt any strength at all he rushed not to his bride but to Wagner. He had begun writing *The Perfect Wagnerite* on 28 April and was working on it when, two weeks into his marriage, he fell down the stairs and broke his arm. He was now confined to a wheelchair that he could not wheel. Thinking he heard a burglar, he jumped up on his bad foot. He was tormented with a bad case of nettle rash. He had a second major operation on his foot. Attempting to ride a new bicycle, he sprained his ankle, the first of three sprains. For more than a year he was on crutches, at one point clamoring to have his toe amputated against the doctor's wishes. Married "on one leg," he became a symbolic castrato, if not an actual one. He admitted that Mrs. Shaw's nice new husband was "all broken and damaged." Despite injuries that left him "helpless as a baby" during that first August, he wrote in defense of George Bedborough, who had been arrested after selling Ellis's *Sexual Inversion* on 27 May, just days before Shaw married.[26]

With the aid of servants and nurses Charlotte cared for him as they lived the country life, then sought to restore his health as they sailed the Mediterranean on the SS *Lusitania*. But he complained that the steamy sirocco air was unhealthy. Life aboard ship did not suit him at all. It irritated him to watch others "as they suck their pipes continually. It is a guzzling, lounging, gambling, dog's life." The protracted honeymoon-convalescence came to a close when husband and wife arrived back in London at the tail end of October 1899.[27] Shaw, who had maintained his address at Fitzroy Square, at last moved to Adelphi Terrace, trading Bessie's home for Charlotte's.

In *Man and Superman*, Tanner warns Octavius, who wants to marry Ann for inspiration, that he should keep a safe distance, that after a week she would be no more inspiring than a plate of muffins. In the comforting muffindom of the unglamorous Charlotte, Shaw found solicitous companionship and an ordered domesticity. Giving up any career plans of her own, Charlotte devoted her energies to her husband. Even before he achieved worldwide celebrity she deferred to him as "The Master" or "The Genius," implicitly urging guests to follow suit. Such deference to his intellect did not prevent her from stating her mind or openly disagreeing with him. Rather annoyingly, she wore fur, ate meat, and drank alcohol. Meanwhile, her husband practiced what he preached: the lady should be allowed to order her own dinner, he had declared in an 1897 review of *The Fanatic*, a play in which a vegetarian husband forced his diet on his wife.[28]

Shaw was publicly, even ostentatiously, chivalrous to his wife, whose manners, despite her advanced views, remained those of the 1880s. Observers were amazed at Shaw's courtly manners, which included opening doors with a bow and a flourish. Those manners concealed the boredom of a couple who did not mind dining in public with books propped in front of them. Boredom was also alleviated by Charlotte's love of travel—a restless roaming from country house to country house, from hotel to hotel. Despite his complaints about "these accursed holidays," with "no place to write—no place to bathe," Shaw gave in to her, often indulging in his own daredevil driving style on foreign roads (and reaping his share of accidents), as fiercely masculine driving an automobile as riding a bicycle.[29]

Man and Superman, begun three years after he tied the irrational matrimonial knot, reflects Shaw's domestic arrangement and shows his ambivalence toward women cunningly elevated to a cosmic plane. The play itself is based on inversions—the pursuing woman and the philosophical Don Juan. Having reversed the cultural stereotype of passive women and active men, Shaw nevertheless reinforces the conventional dichotomy of man as mind, woman as body. As the Life Force streams through the strong-willed Ann, she becomes Woman Incarnate, relentlessly seeking her mate. Trapped, Tanner reluctantly and comically submits, as Shaw apparently did. Meanwhile, Don Juan, Tanner's mythical ancestor, flees from hell to spend his eons in a contemplative heaven. There Don Juan, who hates "playing and pretending," can escape his sexual duties as husband and any pretense that he liked those duties, as Shaw actually did. Part of the allure of heaven lies in its women, who are so dowdy they "might be men of fifty"—that is, sexually indistinguishable and solidly middle-aged, like Charlotte.[30]

In autobiographical but abstract fashion Shaw integrates the unfolding Don Juan myth, which he long had associated with himself, into Creative Evolution, his private evolutionary myth—both myths dependent on the power of sex. But for all the glories of this wonderfully joyous play, the final scene does not ring true, for Shaw never endows the Life Force with living dramatic form. Like the machinery of melodrama that swallows his devil, it is Shaw's merely ideological interest in heterosexuality that forces Tanner into submission.

In the Preface to *Getting Married*, Shaw voiced his disgust at conventional marital arrangements: to be shut up with your wife for eight hours out of every twenty-four was unnatural, unhealthful, intemperate. To William Archer, he labeled sexual intercourse between husband and wife "arch-incest." He made a point of saying that his marriage was never consummated, obviously an unnecessary remark and certainly inconsiderate of the very private Charlotte. Shaw felt compelled to draw attention to the odd sexual arrangement in his house, blaming it on his wife. To Thomas Demetrius O'Bolger, he wrote: "There never was any question of breeding: my wife had a morbid horror of maternity; and as she was forty it was too late to begin without serious risk even if I could have converted her on that point." Later, more explicitly, he wrote Frank Harris that he was "too experienced to make the frightful mistake of simply setting up a permanent whore," nor did his wife make the "complementary mistake." There was "nothing whatever to prevent us from satisfying our sexual needs without paying that price for it." It was "for other considerations" that they married.[31]

Certainly Charlotte provided Shaw relief from the pressure of pursuing women and from some other suspicions of perpetual bachelorhood. Shaw referred those who were "curious about the psychopathy of bachelordom and spinsterhood" to the "monumental work" of his friend Havelock Ellis. If marriage provided a haven from pursuit and observation, it did not affect Shaw's self-identity. As with certain well-known homosexuals, the fact of marriage seemed irrelevant. Wilde had been respectably married and fathered two sons. Likewise, Symonds had married and fathered four daughters, explaining to Carpenter that homosexuality "does not interfere with marriage when that is sought as a domestic institution, as it always is among men who want children for helpers in their work and women to keep their households."[32] But for Shaw domesticity was one thing, fathering children another thing entirely.

At the end of 1896, despite their growing intimacy, Charlotte had not revealed her age to Shaw. Quite coldly, he estimated her to be "certainly not less than 37, & looks 40."

Charlotte, then two months away from her fortieth birthday, would have been less sensitive about her age had she realized that Shaw wanted a woman beyond childbearing age. During their almost two-year courtship she pushed and he dawdled as her biological clock wound down. Shaw insisted that theirs was a childless partnership "between two middle aged people who have passed the age at which it is safe to bear a first child."[33]

Publicly he drew attention to her age to explain the puzzling celibate marriage, but his language revealed something else as well. It was not merely that Charlotte was too old: as a couple—two middle-aged people—they were unfit to be parents. For the secret invert paid close attention to the findings of eugenicists and various sexologists. Ellis advocated chastity as he warned that "for the most part" the children of inverts "belong to a neurotic and failing stock," later reiterating that from a "eugenic standpoint," the marriage of inverts is "always very risky." It was a warning he heeded scrupulously in his own companionate marriage to the lesbian Edith Lees. There is an incestuous homoerotic edge to Shaw's eugenic fable *The Simpleton of the Unexpected Isles.* On a tropical island in the Pacific, the English clergyman Iddy agrees to marry the sisters Vashti and Maya, who fancy that they were "not to love oneanother, but that they were to be oneanother," and the three *"embrace with interlaced arms."* Iddy, a man fed on air from childhood, turns out to be of no use eugenically: he is an "impotent simpleton."[34]

More than wit lay behind the famous interchange with the Zurich woman who propositioned the famous playwright: "You have the greatest brain in the world, and I have the most beautiful body; so we ought to produce the most perfect child." Replied Shaw, "What if the child inherits my body and your brains?" The fear of fathering degenerate children was no joke, and it added to Shaw's revulsion at female flesh. Little wonder he maintained that chastity was an instinct so powerful that denying it "on the scale on which the opposite impulse has been starved and denied would wreck any civilization." Insisting that "intellect is a passion," like many women, he derided "as crude and barbarous" the "notion that passion means only sex." Inveighing against the "criminology" and "pathology" that festered under the "farmyard or slave-quarter conception" of marriage, Shaw aligned himself with women as he called for their increased rights in and out of wedlock.[35] Meanwhile, in his unconsummated union with Charlotte, he had found a protective but sterile womb that sealed him safely from the world.

A Woman Without Petticoats

> It is not necessary to wear trousers and smoke big cigars to live a man's life any more than it is necessary to wear petticoats to live a woman's.
> —Preface to *Saint Joan*

When Shaw aphoristically asserted that "a woman is really only a man in petticoats," feminists took note. The second half of Shaw's aphorism has been ignored: "a man is a woman without petticoats."[1] Shaw plainly says that a man lacks something a woman has: the petticoats. To make the petticoats the essential mark of gender is to reverse the way gender was determined by his ardently phallocratic society. In a society that conceived of woman as absence, Shaw conferred on woman the signifying power of gender, thereby abdicating the power traditionally reserved for the male. In a society where relations between men and women were hierarchical and vertical, Shaw advocated the horizontal, the equal, the similar.

Shaw's comment recalls the well-publicized 1870 trial of two male transvestites, the so-called "men in petticoats" about whom jokes abounded. Seen as a threat to traditional gender roles, effeminacy was the most stigmatized form of homosexual behavior, as it is today. Shaw evoked the charge of effeminacy, manipulating it into a feminist statement. Part of his satiric technique was to give his heroes "feminine" traits, metaphorically putting them in petticoats. Meanwhile, his heroines outwit or ignore societal codes and control men. Under the guise of comic reversal, Lina overpowers a whimpering Bentley, and Lady Cicely overpowers everyone. Millionairess Epifania talks like a man and gets what she wants, including the Egyptian doctor, who calls her sexless. With God's work to be done in this world, ideology more than love prompts Barbara Undershaft's last-minute conversion and her agreement to marry her "dear little Dolly boy."[2] For the charismatic Joan, who leads soldiers for God, virginity is a sign of strength, not mere Victorian purity. At the same time, women like Hesione Hushabye and Mrs George exude a frightening, even supernatural, sexuality.

Shaw's husbands and husbands-to-be are often vaguely foolish men like Hector Hushabye, Morell, or Tanner, helpless to defend themselves against women or to prevent their wives' indiscretions. Jealousy is out of place. By coolly and cleverly refusing to acknowledge his wife's infidelity, Napoleon shows that he is a leader and not a mere husband. The epitome of Shaw's foolish husband appears in *How He Lied to Her Husband*, written as a curtain-raiser for *The Man of Destiny*. A young poet-pugilist agrees to protect the reputation of the married woman he woos by denying that he is in love her. Her Husband, as he is diminishingly labeled, is so insulted that he physically assaults him. Once the lover admits to having addressed love poems to the wife and confesses that he hopes to whisk her away, Her Husband is so gratified that he begs the favor of printing the poems at his expense so he can show them off.

Shaw said he was interested in the truths that the unfaithful spouses tell each other and did not want to be bothered with the divorce cases, strategems, and lies that characterized the English stage treatment of infidelity. At the time of *Candida*, only the French considered adultery an appropriate subject for nonserious drama.[3] Shaw's lighthearted treatment of infidelity marks a departure on the English stage, away from both the moralistic Victorian fingerpointing at fallen women and the cruelly lascivious satire directed at the cuckold on the Restoration stage. Because the wife's flirtations stop short of the bedroom, Shaw's husband is not so ludicrous a figure as an outright cuckold. After Shaw, domestic comedy, with its sympathy for escapes from strict monogamy, was handed over to the gay playwrights, perhaps because gay men do not feel sexually possessive toward women or inclined to support the status quo in sexual relations. From Noel Coward, Somerset Maugham, and Terence Rattigan in England to Edward Albee in the United States, the adulterous drawing room ranges from the elegantly witty to the darkly absurdist.

Shaw's personal interest in the censorship of social behavior—one reason for his feelings of affinity to women and their causes—extended to stage censorship, namely the licensing laws. Out of eight thousand plays submitted to the Lord Chamberlain for approval between 1895 and 1909, only thirty were completely banned. Of that total, 10 percent were by Shaw. In addition to the "immoral" *Mrs Warren's Profession*, also banned were *The Shewing-up of Blanco Posnet* (considered blasphemous) and *Press Cuttings* (labeled an "offensive" representation of a living person). After the banning of *Blanco Posnet*, in a statement the parliamentary committee tried to suppress, Shaw identified himself as a "specialist in immoral and heretical plays." His continuing struggle stemmed from his belief that much of the current morality regarding sexual relations was "disastrously wrong."[4]

Shaw's artistic and political statements were skirmishes in a treacherous war, the costs luridly articulated by Oscar Wilde to George Cecil Ives in 1898: "I have no doubt we shall win, but the road is long, and red with monstrous martyrdoms." Influenced by Wilde and Carpenter, Ives worked for homosexual liberation, forming a secret society in the mid to late 1890s. The Order of Chaeronea, composed mostly of literary and professional men, was named after a battle in ancient Greece in which three hundred young

Theban soldiers, bound to one another in close friendship, were killed by the forces of Philip of Macedon.[5]

Only a few of the Order's members have been conclusively identified, but Ives's secret society formed the nucleus of the British Society for the Study of Sex Psychology (later the British Sexological Society). Established in 1914, the society, with Carpenter its first president, was generally dedicated to educating the public on issues of sex, and specifically to reforming the law on homosexuality. The society is historically important as the only official organization ever formed by Uranians. Havelock Ellis, a member ex officio, never attended a meeting and cautioned that the "usefulness of the Society will be largely destroyed if it comes to be regarded as simply a homo-club." In a similar vein, the society has been charged with being "little more than a cabal of homosexuals," an accusation that one social historian calls misleading, "at least" regarding the society's early days. Nevertheless, there is agreement that the society was dominated by homosexuals. Among its members were Vyvyan Holland (Oscar Wilde's son), E. M. Forster, whose autobiographical novel *Maurice* was published posthumously because of its homosexual theme—and Shaw, an early member who became a life member in 1930.[6] It is a membership that Shaw biographers have completely overlooked.

Shaw's relations with men were not confined to formal organizations. Quite visible on the fin de siècle scene were collaborators like Marc-André Raffalovich and John Gray. At the same time, an invisible collaboration occurred between the heterosexual Ellis and the homosexual Symonds. Their joint work on *Sexual Inversion* took place entirely through the mail, like that occurring later between Shaw and Lord Alfred Douglas. The collaborative act was one that Shaw found particularly congenial, and his attempts to combine identities ranged from the intensive and extended to the sketchy and tentative. There were political collaborations where Shaw joined forces with Fabian men like Sidney Webb, Sydney Olivier, and Graham Wallas, men he credited with knocking a lot of nonsense out of him. In "constant & intimate touch," they were "the Three Musketeers & D'Artagnan."[7] There were thousands and thousands of letters in which Shaw and his numerous correspondents played to one another. There were translations of his work where male translators submerged their identities into his. Not the least were theatrical collaborations.

Like Shakespeare in his sonnets addressed to Mr. W. H., their "onlie begetter," Shaw appears to have left coded messages in writings directed to his collaborators or describing collaborative efforts. In decoding these messages—windows into Shaw's interior world—I follow the example of current gay theorists in taking sexual figures of speech seriously, and as surfacing meanings the authors may not have consciously intended. However, even without subtext, the passages indicate a special kind of closeness and familiarity.[8]

Even before the ghostly writing enterprises with Lee, Shaw had enjoyed a significant collaboration with a male—that with Matt McNulty. It was "one of those romantic friendships that occur between imaginative boys." A later version of this 1901 description dropped the word romantic: they merely "struck up a friendship." In Dublin and Newry, the blood brothers had committed shared fantasies to paper and criticized one another's literary efforts. Four decades later, Shaw urged McNulty to catch up to him by conquering the world with a stunning book: "You are still a young man. You should see me!" But Shaw could not resist tallying up their careers—McNulty's three children and three books versus his five novels, sixteen plays, thousand lectures, million words of journalism.[9] Aided in part by his inaccurate tally of McNulty's work, using a masculine mode of assessing achievement, Shaw measured their works and McNulty fell far short.

If the number of words was linked to Shaw's sense of his masculinity, then the awesomely prolific output suggests a relentless effort to present a masculine identity to the world. Retreating from braggadocio, Shaw confessed that he was "still playing the game on the old Newry lines" and that McNulty knew "how small and timid a thing" was the reality behind the Great Man—the cultural measuring stick of masculinity giving a fraudulent reading in Shaw's case.[10]

Shaw used his writing output in other ways in expressing himself toward men. With Jules Magny, his words became a shared creation. The French journalist living in London joined the Fabians in 1890 after working closely with Shaw politically and acting as his first translator. From the outset, Shaw dominated as the two collaborated over his text. Still Shaw granted his collaborator a measure of parity. In 1889, a year in which he earned less than two hundred pounds, Shaw wanted Magny to have whatever money might be earned from the translation. Shaw took pleasure in correcting Magny's efforts and in telling printer George Standring that "you would hardly have known me in my French dress."[11]

On 5 September 1890, Shaw spent a "pleasant evening" with Magny (the adjective a rarity in his diary), reading his account of the Fabians for *La Revue Socialiste*. Shaw's recorded response is all the more surprising since his inability to finish an article for *The World* had left him feeling "tired and barren." A week later, flamboyantly adorning a letter with a series of exclamations written in French, he closed to Magny with "Sentiments les plus distingués!" By 25 November, Shaw addressed him as "Mon cher Magny." After Shaw managed to answer a series of questions in French for the newspaper *La Justice*, he proudly reported to Sidney Webb that Magny, who had revised Shaw's French—as Shaw had previously revised his—called his style masterly but "invariably wrong in the genders."[12]

A letter to Magny is notable for being both candid and cryptic. In it Shaw spelled out his principles. He defied entrenched morality with its fixed rules of conduct and objected to the marriage laws. More personally, he disputed the Don Juan view of him, which could be traced to his Irish gallantry. In his out-of-place gallantry and in "many other ways," Shaw confessed to being "as much a foreigner" as Magny. Under the pretext of offering biographical information to publicize his socialist writings, Shaw became extremely personal: "Like most lovers of art, I am fond of women; but I never bought one on the street for pleasure." Unnecessarily, he revealed that he had preserved his virginity until he was almost thirty. Even now, there were few "affairs of that sort."[13]

Writing "Mon cher Magny" two days later, Shaw protested against making saints of people who do not indulge in the usual pleasures because they have "no taste for them." He hated beefsteak so he did without it, but he never denied himself a Beethoven symphony. He might distance himself from the pleasures most people like, but still he called himself a voluptuary. He would leave it to Tanner to argue for the "elimination of the mere voluptuary from the evolutionary process."[14] Appreciating women aesthetically, the so-called foreigner and voluptuary scoffed at the patriarchal and masculine as they defined everything from marriage laws to casual sexual encounters. The letters are overly confessional, and it is left to Magny to determine how much to amend the biography for publication. Again Shaw granted a certain power to Magny, his senior by eleven years but his junior in the relationship of creator-translator, and one who devoted himself to spreading Shaw's reputation in Europe. From Shaw's perspective, it was an ideal relationship.

Collaborative roots also anchored the relationship with Frederick H. Evans, an eccentric London bookseller who endeared himself to Shaw by wearing an outlandish silk collar and talking his customers into buying *The Quintessence of Ibsenism*. Shaw came to regard Evans, a man of many talents, as one of the world's greatest photographers. During the summer of 1895, Evans proposed that he edit and publish Shaw's music criticisms from *The World*. Although nothing was to come of it, Shaw embraced the idea of a joint enterprise with Evans: "If only I could keep up the supply of capital by writing plays, we could go down to posterity together." Shaw's response revolves around the text as body, as he imagined the two taking turns interpolating comments. As to a title, "I always take the one that has been licked into shape by a thousand tongues. . . . So we will call it 'World Articles on Music' by Bernard Shaw . . . with your imprint as suggested. Stick in the passage from the Nordau article by all means if you hanker after it." As to money, "Don't stint yourself of the unhatched chickens," advised Shaw, playing with the familiar aphorism so that he clearly was the producer of the unhatched chickens—the eggs. Shaw added that he wanted to write an "erotic book" and ended his letter with an invitation: "my new toy is my bicycle. Do you bike?"[15]

Shaw stressed the collaborative nature of their proposed venture—"the manufacture of *our* book!!!!!" However, the sensuality of the text extended beyond their book: "I can't reprint the Nordau essay after making a present of the first bite to Tucker. Besides, I intensely enjoy making people swallow Liberty & the blank verse printing & so on." A few weeks later, Shaw invited himself over to Evans's home to look at his photographs, the teetotaler telling him not to buy whiskey or anything else for him. Having dawdled his time away, later he promised to work on their project "like a giant." In the country, notified of Evans's availability and eager to be photographed, Shaw would have cut his bicycling tour at once had he not been with the Webbs and Charlotte. He wondered about another Sunday. "I am specially beautiful now after my holiday—during which, by the way, I have worked like a nigger."[16]

The epithet, which included all people of color, was not as ugly in Europe as in the United States, and its use was uncharacteristic for Shaw. In *On the Rocks*, Sir Jafna Pandranath, a Ceylonese multimillionaire plutocrat, denounces those who use that slur as dirty-faced barbarians. Shaw valued work and would warn white South Africans that their "slaves . . . will have all the strength and knowledge and character that come from working" and that the "next great civilisation will be a negro civilisation." The latter idea was also voiced in *The Adventures of the Black Girl in Her Search for God* (1932). That fable concludes with the black girl marrying a red-haired socialist Irishman and managing both him and her "charmingly coffee-colored" children "very capably." The theme of racial intermarriage had already surfaced. In *Heartbreak House*, Captain Shotover, who was damned until marriage to a black West Indian woman redeemed him, tells Boss Mangan to marry a black woman and save himself. In *Back to Methuselah*, a black woman is the minister of health and the "real president" of the country while the Biological Society believes that "the future of the world lies with the Mulatto."[17]

In the letter to Evans, Shaw, having called himself beautiful, appears to be engaging in macho posturing. Referring to himself in such loaded terms, both racial and female, suggests the homoeroticism of Carpenter's "resplendent-limbed Negro" and "intertwining many-colored streams" in *Towards Democracy*, and resembles the ideal of many men who sought comradeship across class and ethnic barriers.[18]

Shaw continued his friendship with Evans, writing an appreciation of him for *Camera Work* in 1903. At the Camera Club in 1911, a musical evening featured the oddity of Shaw and Evans playing the pianola (manipulating the pedals and hand levers on the player piano), the two having shared that interest for years. Shaw praised Evans as an artist, his photographs and his music showing the "mastery of man over nature," a comment that could also describe his view of the appropriate relationship between inverts. Also holding a similar theory as to the relationship between the pianola and the camera was the young American photographer Alvin Langdon Coburn, who was often to be found at Shaw's home and whose career he promoted.[19] A great admirer of Carpenter, Coburn journeyed to Millthorpe to photograph him.

Shaw's only two articles on photographers were on Evans and Coburn. While the piece on Evans was essentially a biography, Shaw offered to "beat the big drum" for Coburn's exhibition at the Royal Photographic Society. Shaw, himself an avid photographer and greatly interested in all its technical and artistic aspects, explained the scarcity of good negatives by analogy: "the photographer is like the cod, which produces a million eggs in order that one may reach maturity." Shaw's analogy, reflecting, he said, his own personal experience, derived from the female's fertility and was reminiscent of the unhatched chickens he mentioned to Evans.[20]

The lure of photography and its practitioners never flagged, extending to the glittering serpent's eye of the cinema. Film producer Gabriel Pascal reported that early one summer morning in the mid-1920s, while swimming nude on the French Riviera, he bumped into an equally nude white-bearded swimmer clinging to a red buoy. The white-bearded swimmer wondered whether the handsome young Hungarian might be a gypsy because "that cannot be sun tan, not on that part." A good decade later Pascal announced himself at Shaw's London flat as "the young man with the brown buttocks." The outrageous announcement worked its magic, and Shaw ushered him into his flat and his life. The charismatic Pascal was given to publicly and effusively kissing Shaw, who labeled him a genius and surprised everyone by allowing him to produce film versions of several of his plays. Under Pascal's influence Shaw turned to screenwriting as he worked with the man who declared himself the incarnation of The Devil's Disciple.[21]

Earlier, art played a role in a male relationship of a different sort. From 1885 to 1888 unsigned reviews by Oscar Wilde, William Archer, and Shaw sometimes were credited to the wrong man. To sort things out Shaw declared either Wilde or himself the author of the distinctly Irish reviews. Meanwhile, though he preferred to get credit for his own brilliancies, Shaw apparently was not disturbed at being mistaken for Wilde, whom he thought "exceptionally finished in style and very amusing." Even though he found Wilde a terrible liar, Shaw felt that the playwright had a "touch of genius." Shaw defended that genius when reviewing *An Ideal Husband,* mocking those who laughed angrily at Wilde's epigrams and protested that the "trick" was obvious. The reviewer appeared to be the only one in London who could not write an Oscar Wilde play.[22]

In spite of his appreciation of Wilde's talent, Shaw harbored ambivalences toward the man. He thought it a "very handsome thing" that after the Haymarket Riots in Chicago in 1886, Wilde was the only person other than socialists willing to sign a petition supporting the anarchists. Shaw had denigrated Max Nordau as the "dupe of a theory" that "the world is going to the dogs," and he dredged up the second phrase and used it against Wilde. Writing Frank Harris, the self-described heartless man attributed a heartless quality to *The Importance of Being Earnest.* In his original review of the play Shaw had been amused by the "force and daintiness" of the play's wit, but he still thought that he had wasted an evening. Always defensive about his own sexuality vis-à-vis Harris, he now added, "I had no idea that Oscar was going to the dogs" or that there was a "real degeneracy produced by his debaucheries"; Shaw in effect was echoing Nordau's attack on Wilde's "buffoon mummery."[23] If Wilde's way of life produced degeneracy, Shaw's asceticism was meant to prevent it.

From the first Shaw had set his evolutionary vision against a Wilde work considered degenerate. *The Picture of Dorian Gray,* suggestively homosexual, was published in 1891, an expansion of chapters that had appeared in *Lippincott's Magazine* in 1890. Similarly, Shaw expanded his Ibsen lecture of 1890 into *The Quintessence of Ibsenism* in 1891. The differences between the works suggest the poles of homosexuality as Shaw understood them—Wilde's portrait of Lord Henry versus Shaw's evocation of Shelley, the depraved pervert versus the noble invert.

In 1893, Shaw sent *The Quintessence of Ibsenism* to Wilde just as he had sent it to women he wished to impress. Wilde found it "such a delight," so "stimulating and refreshing." They were both Celtic, and Wilde liked to think that they were friends: "for these and many other reasons Salome presents herself to you in purple raiment. Pray accept her with my best wishes."[24] Wilde was not only reciprocating Shaw's gift with his own work, he was expressing gratitude for Shaw's support. For only Shaw and Archer had defended *Salome,* Wilde's macabre 1892 tale of passion, against the censors. Among the select few receiving copies of *Salome* were Archer, former lover Richard Le Gallienne, and Oxford don Walter Pater.

When he had not received the play within a few days, Shaw wrote Wilde. An odd fragment gleaned from a sale catalogue is all that remains of that letter. "Salome is still wandering in her purple raiment in search of me," wrote Shaw as he played with Wilde's personification of his book. Then the usually circumspect Shaw assumed a surprising persona: "I expect her to arrive a perfect outcast, branded with inky stamps, bruised by flinging from hard hands into red prison vans, stuffed and contaminated . . . " The fragment breaks off tantalizingly in mid-sentence. Shaw's letter is rife with uncharacteristically blatant sexual imagery that centers on Wilde's creation—sexual imagery absent from Wilde's letter. There are double entendres in each of the four clauses composing the line—double entendres that are specifically homoerotic. *Outcast,* a term with homosexual connotations, is reinforced in that interpretation by the similar connotations of *branded.* Such connotations overwhelm the remaining imagery. The fragment resumes with Shaw hoping to send along *Widowers' Houses,* which Wilde will find "tolerably amusing," a blasé phrase that not only sounds more like Wilde than Shaw but also shows Shaw wanting to pursue the relationship.[25]

Wilde responded to the double entendres by linking Shaw's work with his own. Having received the promised copy of *Widowers' Houses,* Wilde labeled it "Op. 2 of the great Celtic School," his own highly successful *Lady Windermere's Fan* being Op. 1. Wilde admired the "flesh and blood" of Shaw's characters and looked forward to Op. 4, Shaw's next work; his own *A Woman of No Importance* was Op. 3. As for Op. 5, Wilde was "rather itching to be at it."[26]

Shaw followed Wilde's lead in classing their works together as he disdained the "typical poetically voluptuous play" drowned in an "overpowering *odor di femmina*." When William Archer accused Shaw of being "monstrously and fantastically wide of the truth" on the issue of serious drama and eroticism, Shaw protested that except for those of Wilde, Shakespeare, and himself he could hardly think of any plays that did not have love as the sole motive. Wilde's influence can be seen in the joyous farce *You Never Can Tell*, in which Shaw included correspondences to *The Importance of Being Earnest* despite his initial disparagement of Wilde's play. Like Wilde, he employed name changes, a search for a father, and repeated wordplay on *earnest*.[27]

Wilde's wordplay has been linked to a volume of Uranian poetry entitled *Love in Earnest*. Given Shaw's overlapping circles of acquaintances and his understanding of Wilde and his work, surely Shaw was aware of the homoerotic resonance of Wilde's wordplay. In *You Never Can Tell*, Gloria Clandon insists that love gives the lover earnestness and beauty. Her lover, Valentine, who earlier had declared himself in earnest, plays with gender as he wonders: "Do you really think it would make me beautiful?" Then he tells her she's "not in earnest. Love cant give any man new gifts." His own gift is lightness of heart, to which Gloria adds lightness of head and faith and "everything that makes a man," haughtily attacking his manhood.[28] Valentine is also light on names: he lacks a first name, the cultural signifier of gender. Allusions to gender ambivalence are underscored by the date on which the composition was completed: 18 May 1896, one month after Shaw's rapturous revelation to Janet Achurch.

Writing Harris about Wilde, Shaw offered that his own recognition that homosexuality "does not imply any general depravity or coarseness of character" came to him through "observation and reflection." Toned down for Harris's biography of Wilde, the passage becomes "through reading and observation," adding "not through sympathy," a change continued in *Pen Portraits and Reviews*. In all three versions, Shaw noted selfprotectively and revealingly, "I have all the normal violent repugnance to homosexuality—if it is really normal, which nowadays one is sometimes provoked to doubt."[29]

The two playwrights met perhaps only a dozen times, according to Shaw. Although he pronounced Wilde "fastidious" and not "habitually squalid in his habits," Shaw could not approve of someone who "loafed about" in cafés on the Continent until he died. Sapped of energy, Wilde could neither write an autobiography nor rehabilitate himself— literary energy and moral energy always were in concert for Shaw. Still, to Robert Ross,

Wilde's early lover and longtime friend, Shaw praised the "unquenchable spirit of the man."[30] He made a point of taking Wilde seriously, nominating him for membership in the proposed British Academy of Letters in 1897 just months after he was released from prison. For Shaw remembered that Wilde had made a similar point of recognizing him as a man of distinction.

Once he ran into Wilde outside the stage door of the Haymarket Theatre. Shaw revealed that "our queer shyness of one another made our resolutely cordial and appreciative conversation so difficult that our final laugh and shake-hands were almost a reciprocal confession." The heavily laden "queer shyness" and "reciprocal confession" sum up the relationship between the two men, so different from those Shaw had with women, in which he moved between the poles of Don Juanism and babyhood.[31]

Shaw never admitted that he sent Wilde either *The Quintessence of Ibsenism* or *Widowers' Houses,* and he attempted to dissuade Hesketh Pearson from doing a biography of Wilde, all of which Pearson interpreted as marks of jealousy and dislike. Another interpretation is more likely: that Shaw feared that Pearson, who knew Shaw well, might make certain connections between the two men, who exchanged inscribed copies of their works after Wilde's fall from grace. The secretive Shaw thought that Wilde's love of style led to his undoing: "Wise kings wear shabby clothes, and leave the gold lace to the drum major," wrote he, safely camouflaged in brown wool. Years later, when the nonagenarian Shaw was asked what famous man from the past he would most like to meet, he chose Wilde.[32]

The Man Who Lived in Fairyland

> I make no apology for lifting your copy out of
> the World, as I confined myself strictly to that
> part which is clearly made out of my own
> flesh and blood.
> —To William Archer, 1893

He is "one of the most active of my reviewing colleagues," wrote Shaw in 1889 of William Archer, whose famed career as an Ibsen translator began almost a decade earlier with *Pillars of Society*. Incorruptible and impervious to vulgar ambition, he devoted himself to the theater. It was Archer who rescued a grateful Shaw from poverty by opening the door to paying jobs. Where others saw a cold, humorless man Shaw found a man whose mahogany-hard exterior hid a sensitivity so acute that he could not read aloud moving passages of his own translation of Ibsen's *Little Eyolf,* handing the pages over to Shaw for fear of being overcome by emotion.[1] The men shared ideas, advice, and companionship from the first, always feeling free to criticize one another openly.

In such a spirit of candid friendship Shaw read the proofs of Archer's book *About the Theatre: Essays and Studies* (1886), arriving late at a Fabian meeting after arguing with Archer over the book. Shaw thought that all his points about acting were wrong and that Archer should spar more aggressively on the subject of Shakespeare. Shaw substituted for Archer in reviewing *A Doll's House* when the translator declined to review his own translation. Shaw discussed the play with him and conscientiously saw the production twice—the actors needed to speak up and not lapse into stage tricks. Having accompanied Archer, a temporary art critic out of his depth, to art exhibitions, Shaw refused to accept payment from his grateful friend for his expertise. "I re-return the cheque, and if you re-re-return it, I will re-re-re-return it again," he wrote just before stopping at Archer's for tea. Shaw graphically put Archer's scrupulousness into another context: "The idea of one man sucking another man's brains is a depraved individualist idea."[2]

One rainy day near the British Museum Shaw had been surprised to run into Archer, neatly draped in a buff-colored mackintosh and a clinging woman with a small, pretty face. He had never before seen Archer with a woman on his arm nor concerned with one "in any way." Shaw "feared the worst." Then, "sure enough," the two married and had a son, and Shaw was lucky to see more of Archer after his marriage than before. But Shaw objected to Archer putting his wife and son before literature, and, it seems, before him. However pure Shaw imagined his motives, Archer's tranquil marriage had aroused his jealousy. Under the guise of offering career advice he urged Archer to break loose from his wife. Archer was hurt and shocked at his friend's unfeeling suggestion, and with "wooden formality" he asked Shaw not to visit his house while he held such a disparaging view of Mrs. Archer. Shaw claimed to be not at all offended by Archer's ultimatum: "Indeed I never was offended by anything Archer ever said to me or wrote about me," although Archer often expressed remorse for spoken or written comments about Shaw.[3]

In explaining his thoughtless remark concerning Frances Archer, whom he *had* offended over his excessive praise of Janet Achurch, Shaw admitted that "I did not conceive it possible at that time that I should ever become a married man myself." In fact, Shaw was always surprised that his friends married. When Graham Wallas had "suddenly" become engaged to short-story writer Audrey (Ada) Radford, Shaw was stupefied at the "desertion." "Well, I'll be damned!" was all he could manage to Wallas. Archer would not have been surprised at Shaw's reaction. Shaw simply was "too utterly unlike the average sensual man to have any sympathetic comprehension of him." Maybe Archer was remembering that Shaw had challenged him to walk up and down Oxford Street and count the number of women he might care to "entertain sexually," assuring him that he would be surprised at his own "fastidiousness." Or perhaps he recalled Shaw's comment to him that the "tables of affinity" were based on convention and that conventions vary from place to place. Yet so comfortable was Shaw with Archer that, as Shaw's diary records, they "actually spent" an evening "telling smutty stories" with Henry Arthur Jones.[4]

With Archer, Shaw flaunted his critical "swordplay" that he served up in a goulash of mixed metaphors with the "Shaw sauce." He might insist on his own view, but he did not reproach Archer for not being Shaw: "The notion of two Shaws corresponding with one another is one which staggers even me." Neither the "Archerization of Shaw" nor the "Shawation of Archer" was desirable, though Shaw imagined "Mrs Archer in the background wondering which was the real Antipholus," the real twin in Shakespeare's *A Comedy of Errors*.[5] Shaw rejoiced in their differences and in imagining a deceptive doubleness that forced Frances Archer to the periphery of the triangle.

Mention of Archer's wife remained off limits until she became a disciple of Annie Payson Call, author of *Power Through Repose*, a system of nerve relaxation. Frances Archer embarked on her career teaching the Call method shortly after she and her husband took up separate bedrooms in 1888 (the latter detail most likely the reason Shaw no longer worried about his friend's domesticity). Nor would Shaw's wife feel particularly kindly toward Archer, Charlotte taking the opportunity of a critical review of *Man and Superman* to attack Archer as a "gross impostor." But of course Charlotte had "no sense of humor."[6]

When Archer became involved with Elizabeth Robins, an American actress and feminist, Shaw set out to antagonize her. He annoyed her by his advice at a dress rehearsal for *Hedda Gabler*. Then, after she triumphantly opened as Hedda, he enraged her by accompanying his compliments with a list of complaints about her performance. Jealously, he accused "William the Anchorite" of having tête-à-têtes with Elizabeth, expressing "moral revulsion" at Archer's pose of being "incorruptible" and warning him that ambitious actresses were after him. Then, by design or accident, Shaw put the incriminating letter into the wrong envelope and mailed it, "horror on horror's head," to Frank Harris, then editor of the *Fortnightly Review*. [7]

When Shaw stopped by her rooms to interview her for *The World*, Elizabeth became alarmed that he might print his insinuations about her relationship with Archer. Like Hedda, the Ibsen heroine at ease with revolvers, Elizabeth gestured sensationally toward her own weapon. In a letter to her the next day Shaw made light of her "noble" gesture. But in his diary he recorded that she "swore she would shoot me if I said anything she did not approve of." Whether or not her threat was purely histrionic, Shaw took it seriously; the interview never appeared. He would come to respect her as a writer with a "golden gift," offering her advice on novel writing and help in getting her play, *Votes for Women!* produced at the Royal Court Theatre in 1907. But by then she was no threat to him, as she devoted herself to art, not passion, and his attention was elsewhere.[8]

It was through Archer's translations that Shaw was introduced to Ibsen—a mighty Archerization of Shaw—although he carefully distinguished between his own agreement with Ibsen's sociological views and Archer's admiration of Ibsen's imagination. When *Widowers' Houses* opened in 1892, Archer, writing in *The World*, recounted his part in the play's eight-year "genesis" in the "womb of Time."[9] In the protracted gestation of *Widowers' Houses* one can detect a quasi-erotic jostling for power between Archer and Shaw over the body of the text. It is expressed in a fluid movement in which male and female sexual roles are exchanged, with the male role depicted as vital and creative, the female role as passive and sterile.

Archer's version of the collaboration had him providing Shaw with one of the many plots he kept in stock for the play they first called by the Wagnerian title *Rhinegold*. Having fathered the play, Archer observed Shaw in the British Museum Reading Room "laboriously writing" in the "most exquisitely neat shorthand." Shaw complained that he had used up all of Archer's plot, which Archer defended as a "rounded and perfect organic whole." Shaw periodically threatened to finish "'our play,'" which he kept from view, while Archer persisted in applying a "wet-blanket" to the "fire" of Shaw's "genius."[10] The play, begun just before Archer's marriage in October 1884, was abandoned soon after, making little progress for three years.

Shaw, having incorporated Archer's account into his own preface to the play, then picked up the story. His interest in the subverted play was aroused once again, and he dropped off the first two acts at Archer's. Now the "hallucinations" with which Archer had surrounded the play were "absent," but Shaw believed that the story "would bear four acts." Having removed all but the "central notion," Shaw had provided a figurative space in the body of his text where Archer could either "chuck in the remaining acts, or provide me with a skeleton for them."[11]

The two quarreled over the shape of the play. Shaw, like an English Ibsen, had "built for the north" while, ironically, Ibsen's translator had "designed for the southern hemisphere." Shaw wanted a "vital growth . . . like a flowering plant," Archer's "mechanistic" model was "exhausted and, for the moment, sterile." The model needed to be brought into "contact with life by having new ideas poured into it." As the struggle wore on, Shaw fought to assume the power of the male in the collaboration with his more successful colleague. While Archer contended that Shaw "had not even touched" his plot, Shaw boasted that he had laid "violent hands" on it. Archer argued that when Shaw read over his play "in cold blood, he would see what impossible stuff it was." Shaw trumpeted that "my genius has brought the romantic notion which possessed you, into vivid contact with real life."[12]

Shaw recorded in his diary that after tea on 6 October 1887, he went to Archer's and "read the unfinished drama. A long argument ensued, Archer having received it with great contempt." Later Shaw added that Archer then "fell into a deep slumber; and I softly put the manuscript away and let him have his sleep out." Having forced his version of their shared creation on the resisting Archer, the now dominant Shaw watched him slumber like an exhausted lover. Left with the "two abortive acts," Shaw eventually had to "fish up the tainted treasure" from the Rhine and "make it last out another act and a half." "I had to invent all by myself."[13] By fishing up the drowned embryo of the play, Shaw proved himself as a man and an artist. He was able to invent all by himself.

Though he flaunted his active role over the submissive Archer, Shaw persisted in calling himself the victim and Archer the defaulter. Only after forcing his collaborator into default and submission was Shaw free to assert himself on the stage. The spectral presences of Ibsen and Wagner notwithstanding, Shaw triumphantly proclaimed that his view practically excluded collaboration. Nevertheless, when Archer was working on *National Theatre: Scheme & Estimates* (1907, privately printed 1904), Shaw advised him, offering to contribute a section on platform accomplishments. He would allow actor and producer George Alexander to sign it, would sign it himself, or would "impose the authorship on you, as you please."[14] When Archer's book appeared, it was cosigned by Harley Granville Barker.

Decades after the failed *Rhinegold* collaboration Archer had a dream that he turned into a successful play, *The Green Goddess,* but only after he asked Shaw to finish the play for him. Shaw refused, denouncing Archer's need for a collaborator and diagnosing him as suffering from a "ghastly determinism that strangles the children of your imagination as they are born." "Let them rip," cried Shaw, who with Archer's help had learned how to achieve self-generation through art.[15]

Shaw recounted the history of *Widowers' Houses* more than once, repeating it in the tribute he wrote after Archer died. In so doing Shaw gave public sanction to the private struggle over literary and personal dominance that defined his relation to his friend. For Shaw felt a strong bond of affection toward the man who more than anyone had helped him chart his career—first by introducing him to journalism, then by tempting him into writing plays. Archer, an unworldly man who read Thoreau and called his cottage Walden, was fondly remembered as one who had lived in "fairyland" and held a fairyland conception of the stage. He was a man of whom Shaw had "not a single unpleasant recollection." The unpretentious Scotsman who thought it a great joke to be diagnosed with amblyopia—a first-class eye that does not see anything—contrasted with Shaw, who was inordinately proud of his better-than-normal vision. The Archer whose humanity made Shaw feel apologetic for his own shortcomings was a mirror of his better self. He described Archer's position exactly as he described his own: his kingdom was not of this world. Indeed, the "real Archer" was "like myself."[16]

Warm friends until the end, on 14 December 1924, Shaw wrote Archer a long personal letter in response to his "Psychology of George Bernard Shaw" in the Christmas issue of *The Bookman.* Three days later Archer informed Shaw of an imminent cancer operation, downplaying it. Yet filled with unarticulated foreboding, the stalwart friend overcame his emotional reticence to write: "I have never wavered in my admiration and affection for you, or ceased to feel that the Fates had treated me kindly in making me your contemporary and friend. I thank you from my heart for forty years of good comradeship." Shaw was en route to Madeira when Archer died ten days later. In fury and grief, Shaw lashed out against the surgeons. When he returned to an "Archerless London" he felt that it had entered a "new age in which I was lagging superfluous. I still feel that when he went he took a piece of me with him."[17]

A New Hermes

You end as an ascetic . . . because . . . you
cannot ravish the Venus de Milo or be
ravished by the Hermes of Praxiteles.
—To Frank Harris, 1930

To Harris, Shaw declared himself a devotee of the Uranian Venus. He wrote of imaginary amours with goddesses and devils that sterilize and "spoil you for real women or—if you are a woman—for real men." Revised for publication, vague amours "spoil us for women and real men." The goddesses and devils have vanished, along with the overly obvious qualification, while a plural first person gives the impression that Shaw is candidly describing a general condition. As Shaw well knew, Plato in the *Symposium* attributes the origin of homosexual love to the inspiration of the heavenly (Uranian) Aphrodite (Venus, of course, her Roman counterpart). In Greek mythology, Aphrodite sprang to life from the foam gathered about a sea impregnated by the severed genitals of Uranus. The "foam-born" Aphrodite resonates with Macduff the Unborn, who is also not of woman born, the historical mythology Shaw invoked for himself.[1]

In *Getting Married*, a play in which Shaw uses the classical unities of time and place to return to the form of ancient Greek drama, the playwright resembles not only the lovestruck St John Hotchkiss but also Lesbia Grantham, the woman who neither needs nor wants a husband. (True to her name, she will not "grant him," the general, what he wants.) Like Shaw, Lesbia is fastidious, an opponent of vaccination, hates tobacco, and sleeps with the window open. She admits she chose celibacy because real men can't compete with her imaginary adventures with heroes and archangels. Though lesbians were far less conspicuous than male homosexuals and the term itself was not widely used at the time of the play, Shaw undoubtedly was aware of the connotations of his character's name. He was familiar with Greek literature, and Ellis and Symonds use the term in *Sexual Inversion*, as did Krafft-Ebing in his earlier *Psychopathia Sexualis*. In his play Shaw did more than allude to the ancient isle of Lesbos, home of Sappho: he portrayed himself as a woman—specifically, a woman whose name indicates homosexual love. It was not the first time Shaw had played with the term. In *Caesar and Cleopatra*, the effeminate aesthetic Apollodorus calls the great soldier a "creative poet-artist," wonders who would drink Roman wine "when he could get Greek," and urges, "Try the Lesbian, Caesar."[2]

Shaw left other signs that he did not consider himself the average heterosexual male, one so blatant that he appeared to be daring the world to read it. In April 1906 he traveled to France to sit for a bust by Auguste Rodin. The sittings took place during several weeks at the artist's treasure-filled home-studio in Meudon, a brief train ride from the Hôtel Palais d'Orsay in Paris, where Shaw and Charlotte were staying.

Shaw's timing was impeccable, for with great fanfare Rodin's monumental statue *The Thinker* was inaugurated outside the Panthéon. Visiting in Paris was Sidney Cockerell, curator of the Fitzwilliam Museum and former secretary of William Morris's Kelmscott Press. Shaw invited him to lunch and to the ceremony. In awe of Rodin's artistry, he confided to Cockerell that only Morris had made such an impression of greatness on him. In such a spirit of awe would Shaw present Rodin with the Kelmscott *Chaucer*, Morris's masterpiece of the art of the printed book. He would also recall Rodin's unforgettable character when fashioning Peter Hardmouth in his 1934 playlet *The Six of Calais*—fittingly so, since the artist's monument *The Burghers of Calais* commemorated the six who offered themselves to Edward III to save their besieged city.[3]

In Shaw's opinion, any contemporary of Rodin who allowed his bust to be made by anyone else was a "stupendous nincompoop." Rodin was more than the greatest living sculptor: he was the "greatest sculptor of his epoch." Shaw, seeking immortality through art, wrote only partly tongue in cheek that the bust would ensure him a place in the biographical dictionaries a thousand years hence as "'Shaw, Bernard, subject of a bust by Rodin: otherwise unknown.'" Shaw regarded the bronze cast as an especially "cherished masterpiece," forged more intimately from the master's hand than the two others in marble and in terra-cotta. Shaw compared Rodin to Praxiteles and Michelangelo, whose nude sculptures of men Shaw never ceased admiring: anyone who wanted to put a fig leaf on the statue of Hermes was guilty of public indecency.[4]

Shaw did not sit nude for Rodin, but he did the next best thing. The morning after the unveiling of Rodin's statue Shaw suggested a startling idea to Alvin Langdon Coburn. Having invited Coburn to Paris to meet and photograph Rodin, Shaw himself wanted to be photographed—nude, after his morning bath, in the pose of *The Thinker*. The twenty-three-year-old photographer, who had already photographed Shaw "in almost every conceivable way," complied. Shaw's version differs from Coburn's, however. It has Coburn happening on him just as he left his bath and laughingly telling him to look pleasant and be still. Why Coburn would be there with his camera at such an intimate moment is not explained. Shaw's version implies that the sight of his nude body prompted Coburn to photograph it. Certainly Coburn, who was to make more than fifty portraits of Shaw, thought him "quite proud of his figure, and well he may have been, as the photograph testifies."[5] Photographic testimony reveals a lean, remarkably muscular, well-toned body—a youthful body attached to a face no longer young. Also revealed are certain discordancies between flesh and spirit, strength and vulnerability. As the right hand grasps the left knee, reversing Rodin, the fingers are folded under like a piece of statuary, the hand defenseless and feminine, in contrast to the bulging manly biceps of the crooked left arm.

Later, writing a tribute to Rodin, Shaw recalled the photograph, linking an artistic representation of his own body with the great sculptor's work. There was another link to the sculptor as Coburn included an account of photographing Rodin in the chapter titled "George Bernard Shaw," thereby giving Shaw precedence in that particular triangle. Coburn had plenty of reason to elevate Shaw, because the older man helped him find subjects by introducing him to many of his famous friends. To help Coburn get a group photograph of four playwrights, as requested by Archer, Shaw invited J. M. Barrie, John Galsworthy, and Harley Granville Barker to lunch. He also gave Coburn a letter of introduction to Mrs. Patrick Campbell in which he suggested she let Coburn photograph her nude, as he had been, a suggestion she ignored.

Shaw, always aware of audience, believed in the power of the camera and was one of the first to embrace photography as art. He touted the authority of the camera over that of the pencil and paintbrush. Wanting truthfulness, he rejected imposture and retouching. Ironically, a shocked public cried fraud when Coburn exhibited the photograph, and both photographer and subject were besieged by the press: "But though the body was my body, the face was the face of my reputation. So much so, in fact, that the critics concluded that Mr Coburn had faked his photograph and stuck my head on somebody else's shoulders"—a compliment to Shaw's body that he relished relating. Coburn thought Shaw "very amused" by the sensation and called it a private joke between them. Given permission to do what he liked with the photograph, Coburn declined to publish it during Shaw's lifetime.[6]

In assuming the pose of *The Thinker*, the one-time art critic displayed himself as an object, much as European oil painters displayed the female, their nudes painted with a male spectator in mind. In his photograph, Shaw, like some new Hermes, mimicked the pose of a statue fashioned after the Greeks, making himself into his own ideal work of art. "Here the exposure is precisely right, and the definition exquisite without the least hardness," he wrote. That is, his lighted body is presented against an indistinct background, giving it a romantic, feminine quality. Shaw, immobile in contemplation, does not face the camera. He is the spectator of himself (like women in our culture), even as he is the passive object to be viewed. Yet when photographing nudes, Shaw thought that for the camera to avoid the face "teaches people to be ashamed of their bodies," and he ridiculed Edward Steichen for allowing his nudes to look away from the camera.[7]

In an earlier (clothed) portrait by Frederick H. Evans, he had kept his eyes averted because, as he told Ellen Terry, if he looked at the spectator, the "fatal spell would operate at once." Aware of potential spectators, it was he who was held captive by a fatal spell—the gaze of his unknown voyeurs who feminized him and to whose eyes he submitted. In posing nude, Shaw claimed he wanted to eliminate the mask of clothes that forms the disguise of reputation, for "the mask cannot be penetrated by the camera. It is transparent only to the eye of a veritably god-like artist." That artist was Rodin, whose hand worked "as the Life Force works."[8]

Witnessing the interaction of the two great artists was poet Rainer Maria Rilke, Rodin's secretary, who marveled at Shaw's intense energy and was summarily fired by Rodin when the sittings ended. Shaw, whether standing, or sitting in a child's chair, joyously watching the decapitation of his bust, or expressing himself with "violence" (as Rodin put it), submitted unconditionally to the full-bearded, godlike artist, a man of near legendary sexual appetite. According to one report, "in the course of a conversation," the aging Rodin's hands "would caress and crush every breast and phallus within reach." The sensual and tactile Rodin was able to penetrate the "brilliant fiction known as G. B. S.," laying bare "what is really there, not what you think is there." In his bust of "Monsieur 'Benarre Chuv,'" he claimed to have captured a "'young Moses,'" as he wrote his delighted subject.[9]

Penetrated and possessed by the gaze of others, Shaw wanted to please and displease at the same time. The famous literary man stripped of his clothes would be expected to cause a sensation—the famous literary man who willingly posed nude, like a woman or a Greek statue. Indeed, he remains the only person of such literary celebrity ever to make a point of being photographed nude. In an essentially theatrical gesture, the Jaegerized Shaw, who flouted the dress code of patriarchy, went one logical step further, violating the image of the empowered male. Paradoxically, as he displayed himself as a woman for all the world to see, he revealed that the disguise of the bloodless, sexless intellectual did not hide the soft, limp contours of the effeminate man but the hard, muscular body of the warrior.

Several other nude photographs depict Shaw in less masculine poses. In 1904, Shaw, who was fond of self-portraits, took a nude frontal photograph. A reclining Shaw is shown reading a book that rests on his thigh, the position and curvature of body, arms, and legs, even the averted eyes, recalling those of Titian's nude painting *The Venus of Urbino*. Shaw thought sculptors might use ingenuity "to avoid the necessity of dealing with the penis at all," and here he appears to take his own advice.[10] But whether by design or accident, the camera angle from above proves the book not quite adequate as a fig leaf.

On the beach near Studland Bay, Dorset, one clear day in 1901, Shaw discarded his clothes and was photographed nude a number of times by his companion. One shot shows him with arms exuberantly outstretched to the sky. He is captured from behind as he faces away from the camera—unlike the Coburn photograph, where he is shown neutrally from the side. Another shot shows him, hand on hip, smiling and at ease. More seductively during another equally pleasant outing, he is shown reclining on the sand among the rushes, his arm shielding his face from the sun, refusing to challenge voyeurs. Again he is caught from behind, his pose reminiscent of that assumed by many female artists' models. Unselfconsciously the camera focuses on his buttocks—gluteus maximus, gluteus medius, and gluteus minimus in all their naked glory. The camera in these instances both reveals and conceals, for it seems that the new Hermes was the creator and not the created, the photographer and not the subject. His name was Harley Granville Barker.[11]

Heartbreak, Secrecy, and the "marvellous boy"

> Silence! I say, let the heart break in silence.
> —Captain Shotover, *Heartbreak House*

A number of Shaw's plays were conceived as responses to men he knew. *Man and Superman* took up drama critic Arthur Bingham Walkley's joking challenge that the allegedly bloodless Shaw write a Don Juan play. Shaw claimed to see the resulting play in a direct line with Goethe: the great German writer had anticipated him in the scene where Mephistopheles falls in love with a male angel and loses his bargain.[1] A somewhat different challenge came from Yeats, who wanted a play to support the Irish Literary Theatre. Shaw responded with *John Bull's Other Island* (1904), the only play he set in his native land. Predictably, it clashed with the neo-Gaelic spirit Yeats sought and was refused the stage at the Abbey Theatre in Dublin.

The old enmities surfaced as Yeats found Shaw's evocation of the Irish character objectionable, for, influenced by Galton, Shaw dramatized the effect of climate on culture and race. In the play, the transplanted Irishman Larry Doyle, a man with *"cold grey eyes"* and *"fine fastidious lips,"* describes the hypnotic and deleterious effect of the Irish climate: "your wits cant thicken in that soft moist air, on those white springy roads, in those misty rushes and brown bogs, on those hillsides of granite rocks and magenta heather." One day long before on the Irish hills, a dreaming George had suddenly realized that he had to escape that ennervating climate.[2]

The Irish climate Shaw described—soft, moist, boggy—is decidedly feminine, its only hardness the granite rocks themselves, reminiscent of his mother. This evocation of climate opposed the icy, hard, masculine north he otherwise claimed for himself. Invoking his descent from Macduff, he found Scotland "quite native" to him, while he insisted that he never thought of an Englishman as his countryman. He was both Irish and not Irish, willing himself to cold masculine clarity, exiling himself from the misty clutch of the dangerously feminine Irish hills that seduce men into passivity. Having been born to breathe the air of racial, national, and sexual ambiguity and ambivalence, there was no escape: "the geographic climate is eternal and irresistible." Very late in life he was still sounding the same refrain: "Eternal is the fact that the human creature born in Ireland and brought up in its air is Irish."[3]

Inspired by events rather than overt challenge, Shaw wrote *The Doctor's Dilemma* in response to Archer's outpouring at the death of Ibsen. The timing coincided with Harley Granville Barker's desire for a new play for the Royal Court Theatre. It was left to Charlotte to remind her husband that he had considered Sir Almroth Wright's dilemma dramatic. Archer praised the intellectual aspects of the resulting play but thought that the stage death should have been handled more seriously.[4]

In fashioning a playwriting dialogue with other men, Shaw responded to Barker most of all. As a director, Barker was readying offerings for the 1910 repertory season at the Duke of York's Theatre even though his own play, *The Madras House*, was unfinished and production loomed. American impresario Charles Frohman and Scottish playwright-novelist J. M. Barrie both appealed to Shaw to reason with Barker. Instead, Shaw picked up his pen and completed the act himself. Although Barker's sympathy was with the man, Shaw favored the woman. Seeing his work reversed along gender lines infuriated Barker, who quickly finished his play in his own way. If Shaw goaded the dallying Barker into action, Barker had already goaded Shaw artistically. According to Lillah McCarthy, a grinning Shaw raced home to write *Misalliance* after he heard Barker read *The Madras House*.[5]

Misalliance was first presented on 23 February 1910 as part of the repertory season directed by Barker at the Duke of York's Theatre. This was just two weeks before the debut of *The Madras House*, and the two plays abounded in correspondences that audiences would recognize—from the glass pavilion and Turkish bath of *Misalliance* to the Crystal Palace and Moorish imagery of *The Madras House*. Moreover, the latter play begins with thematic allusions to *The Doctor's Dilemma*. By this time theater audiences had become accustomed to direct or oblique cross-references between the work of the men. For example, in Barker's *The Voysey Inheritance* (1905), Alice Maitland, like Ann Whitefield, proposes, and Edward Voysey's sensitive character resonates with Adolphus Cusins in *Major Barbara*, written the same year. While Shaw played with variations on themes of energy and vitality, Barker explored themes of sterility and loss—strikingly in *Waste*, where Barker boldly deals with a young woman's death after an illegal abortion. Over the span of three decades almost a dozen plays were written by the two men in dialogue with each other, and there was a further mutual influence in character, theme, and technique that goes beyond those plays.[6]

Significantly, *Heartbreak House*, completed in 1917 and published in 1919, marked a "departure in technique and mood" for Shaw, as Eric Bentley has noted. Also in 1919, Barker began *The Secret Life* (completed in 1922), a play abounding in references and allusions to Shaw's work.[7] That the plays are related is certain, but the reason Barker responded—and responded as he did—has remained a mystery.

In the early part of the twentieth century Harley Granville Barker was the most highly regarded director in the British theater, famous for his innovative and intelligent productions and for his separate reputations as actor and playwright. It was Barker's mission to exalt the theater as he tried to forge again the bond that had linked theater and audience in ancient Greece. His vision for a naturalistic and intellectual theater of truth, such as Shaw himself urged, profoundly influenced modern theater.

To that end, and largely with Shaw's financial backing, Barker entered into a theatrical partnership with John Eugene Vedrenne to stage serious drama at the Royal Court Theatre, the kind of drama that commercial West End theaters avoided. In the three years of that partnership, 1904 to 1907, the Court became an author's theater. Its acclaimed repertory seasons were a beacon in the movement to establish a National Theatre in England, toward which Barker labored with Archer. Barker's later productions at the Savoy Theatre, staged from 1912 to 1914, proved that the champion of Shaw was also a champion of Shakespeare. His faithful attention to the original Shakespeare, staged with "unprecedented artistic splendor," seemed to Shaw nothing less than a "blessed revelation" of Shakespeare. For Barker cleared the stage of the inflated elocution and crush of decorative scenery that Shaw had criticized in the leading actor-managers— the hyperbolic "impostures" of Henry Irving and the "genteel drawing room arrangements" of Herbert Beerbohm Tree.[8]

The Court Theatre presented classic Greek dramatists (newly translated by Gilbert Murray), such continental dramatists as Ibsen and Maurice Maeterlinck (translated by Archer), and the work of young playwrights like John Masefield, Laurence Housman, and Barker himself. But most of all Shaw was produced, the popularity of his plays sustaining the venture and establishing the coterie darling as a successful playwright. Indeed, before the Court venture Shaw's drama had scarcely appeared on the commercial stage in London, despite some overseas successes. Now in collaboration with Barker, Shaw triumphantly mounted almost a dozen plays, accounting for a full 70 percent of all Royal Court performances. In full command of rehearsals, Shaw cast, directed, and staged his own plays, which nevertheless were announced as produced by Barker. "I was the producer, Granville-Barker the leading actor, and Vedrenne the business manager," Shaw informed journalist and producer C. B. Purdom (see appendix A).[9]

Actress Lillah McCarthy remembered Shaw's unselfconsciousness at rehearsals: "He could assume any role, any physical attitude, and make any inflection of his voice, whether the part was that of an old man or a young man, a budding girl or an ancient lady." As he illustrated the mood of a line, the actors watched his "amazing hands" in wonder. Shaw's close attention to detail led him to insist that Lillah adorn Ann Whitefield's mourning costume with violent ribbon.[10]

Barker's photographs record one born to be a leading man, a role he relinquished as less worthy and less esteemed than that of playwright or critic. In Shaw's eyes, this man of "fastidiously delicate taste" was by far the most cultivated person in the theater. Writing Purdom, Shaw evoked a vivid image of Barker's physical appearance. Marked by a strong strain of Italian blood, he looked as if he had stepped out of a painting by Benozzo Gozzoli. The allusion to the early Renaissance artist suggests the classicism of Barker's finely chiseled features and Shaw's association of Barker with the world of art. Gozzoli also suggested the interchangeability of gender to Shaw. In Part 2 of *Back to Methuselah—The Gospel of the Brothers Barnabas*—the "Simple-Lifer" Savvy is a *"vigorous sunburnt young lady with hazel hair cut to the level of her neck, like an Italian youth in a Gozzoli picture."*[11] Given Barker's sensitivity, aloofness, and visibility, it was perhaps inevitable that he be enveloped in myth, especially after his withdrawal from public life. Part of that myth involved Shaw, who quietly but misleadingly fostered it.

In what turned out to be his final letter to Archer, Shaw discussed Barker at length, recalling that at one of their earliest rehearsals together, Barker had bothered him by remarking, "'Oh! youre exactly the same age as my father.' (I had up to that moment regarded him as a contemporary)." The story was well rehearsed by the time of its telling to Archer, Shaw having mentioned the remark almost immediately to Charles Charrington in 1901. Shaw would repeat it yet again in a letter to the *Times Literary Supplement* after Barker's death. Born in 1877, Barker, like so many of Shaw's intimates, predeceased him: "it seemed impossible."[12]

Underscoring Barker's youth when Shaw first met him was the fact that he was extremely boyish looking. Somerset Maugham remembered the Barker of about 1902 as "very young," with "charm and gaiety and a coltish grace." But Maugham thought that an artist "needed more force, more go, more bluntness, more guts, more beef." About the same time, October 1903, Shaw marveled at Barker's youth, "he is very young—only 24." One year later, Shaw praised Barker to actress Ada Rehan as "at 24" a "very remarkable young man" who derived his artistic genius from an Italian grandfather.[13] In fact, Barker was only a few weeks short of his twenty-sixth birthday (25 November).

By pretending to have regarded Barker as his contemporary while making clear that he was not, Shaw emphasized their intellectual empathy for each other—and the difference in their ages. For it had not escaped notice that there was a close bond between the two men. After he came to know Shaw, Barker moved to 8 York Buildings, Adelphi, near Shaw at 10 Adelphi Terrace, making Barker's frequent visits very convenient. The obvious feelings of affection between the two men sparked a rumor that persists to this day: that Barker was Shaw's illegitimate son. Edith Bland asked Shaw to his face if the rumor was true, a tale he recounted well after the fact to Archer. In the midst of the Court Theatre collaboration with Barker, Shaw mocked (and fueled) the rumor by writing

Arthur Wing Pinero: "Some of them swear by Barker: others hint that he is my natural son; but most of them reject this hypothesis on the ground that I am physically incapable of parentage." After visiting Shaw, Archibald Henderson noted the crush of admiring younger men. While Alvin Langdon Coburn was treated as a nephew, Barker alone was treated like a son. On his side, Barker was Shaw's "most devoted disciple."[14]

The closeness of the relationship has led Shaw biographer Stanley Weintraub to call Barker a surrogate son to Shaw, a view that Barker biographer Eric Salmon endorses. It is of more than passing interest that Salmon uncovered no reminiscences, no letters— nothing to indicate that Barker had casual relations with women. But he did turn up two or three people who confided their beliefs that Barker had homosexual leanings. They include director Norman Marshall, whose opinion, offered the year before his death, "should be seriously regarded," because he was "on terms of personal friendliness" with Barker.[15] Salmon never considers Barker's possible homosexuality in relation to Shaw, however. Instead, he repeats the rumor that Shaw fathered Barker.

There is no doubt that a close relationship existed between the men. But the exact nature of the relationship remains unclear. To Ellen Terry, Shaw wrote, "That young man is a genius—a cold hearted Italian devil, but a noble soul all the same."[16] The code word genius, along with the noble soul and the handsome Italian (Uranians were especially fond of Italians) all show Shaw romanticizing Barker and adopting the pattern of the idealized Greek love of older man to younger man, the higher order of love appropriate to the aesthetic artist.

Barker was twenty-two and Shaw forty-three when they met. Barker's decade-long list of stage credits already included the title role in William Poel's 1899 production of Shakespeare's *Richard II* when the actor appeared in the Stage Society's production of Gerhart Hauptmann's *The Coming of Peace*. He so impressed Shaw that only three weeks after that Sunday evening performance Barker was back onstage, this time as Marchbanks for the 1 July 1900 Stage Society production of *Candida*. Barker turned out to be the "success of the piece." It was an astonishing bit of luck to find him, Shaw told Archer, ignoring the fact that both Charles Charrington and Henry Arthur Jones had suggested Barker for the part.[17]

Barker turned out to be the perfect Shavian actor. As theater critic Desmond MacCarthy put it, "It is in his representation of intellectual emotions that he excels." The "lyrical mood" and "contemplative ecstasy" that MacCarthy praised in Barker's performance was, in Shaw's view, the expression of the man more than the actor. He assured Barker that Marchbanks is a part that cannot be acted: "it is a question of being the creature or at least having him in you." To cast Marchbanks was either an "insuperable difficulty," or, in Barker's case, "no difficulty at all." The month after his acclaimed performance Barker requested an autographed photograph from Shaw, who complied but wondered, "Why the deuce doesn't Evans do a portrait of *you* and present a copy to *me*?"[18] This letter, dated 22 August 1900, was the first that Barker kept. Another important correspondence had been launched, but this one was just a shadow of the relationship, not the relationship itself. The letters are informative, frequently about theatrical matters, but their impersonal tone and lack of revelation—the reverse of Shaw's confidential letter-writing personae—are at odds with the observed closeness of the men.

Soon Shaw was advertising Barker's poetic playwriting qualities. For a "fairy scheme" of Mrs. Patrick Campbell, possibly a translation of an Edmond Rostand play, Shaw declined to meddle: "it would give it a flavour of brimstone." But he thought Barker capable of the necessary "delicate quaintness." Shaw informed Jones that Barker was "always useful when a touch of poetry and refinement is needed." The "exquisiteness" that characterized *The Marrying of Ann Leete* (1899) came from a "curious delicacy of style," its having a "sort of dainty strangeness about it," Shaw wrote Siegfried Trebitsch. To Archer, Shaw praised the play as "by far the finest bit of literature" since Robert Louis Stevenson's romantic novel *Prince Otto* and "much more original." In Barker's "restrained elegance and fine taste" Shaw found a complement to his own "ring-and-sawdust comedy."[19]

Seven months after Barker's success in *Candida* he completed work on his own play, *Agnes Colander*. Written when Barker was fresh from playing the "strange creature" Marchbanks, then called Marjoribanks, the play examines issues of celibacy, purity, and platonic friendships.[20] *Agnes Colander* also includes a character named Marjoribanks—here metamorphosed into a woman named Emmaline—the initials E. M. the same as Shaw's character.

Marchbanks opened the floodgates on Shaw parts for Barker. He was "*very* good" as the "fatheaded" Captain Kearney in the 1900 Stage Society production of *Captain Brassbound's Conversion*. Initially, Shaw told Barker that casting him in the part was a "disgraceful outrage on nature," given his "divine gifts of youth, delicacy and distinction." Shaw distinguished between those gifts and the "curious effeminacy" of Courtenay Thorpe: as a possible Captain Brassbound he would be "appalling." Barker's natural gifts were seen to greater advantage when Shaw rehearsed him as Napoleon for a performance of *The Man of Destiny*, arranged by J. T. Grein. It was then that Barker realized how old Shaw was, the self-willed young man advising the playwright that his play was based on anticlimax.[21]

Napoleon was followed by the "*pleasant, pretty, smartly dressed, cleverly good-for-nothing*" Frank Gardner in Shaw's production of *Mrs Warren's Profession* for the Stage Society in 1902. But Shaw scolded Barker, calling his Frank incorrigibly poetic instead of good for nothing. When an edition of the play was published with twelve photographs by Evans, Shaw gave "Frank the First" a copy. Barker strode the boards at the Court Theatre in *John Bull's Other Island* as the defrocked Peter Keegan, who is "not a priest" and "not a man," and as Larry Doyle. In *How He Lied to Her Husband*, Barker played the lover, a *"very beautiful youth."* He played Valentine in *You Never Can Tell* and Cusins (foundling and professor of Greek) in *Major Barbara*. As the *"pretty, though not effeminate"* Dubedat in *The Doctor's Dilemma*, he made the death ghastly: "people used to go out & faint & ask for brandy," complained Shaw.[22] He moved from General Burgoyne to Dick Dudgeon in *The Devil's Disciple*, and from Sergius to Bluntschli in *Arms and the Man*. In 1910 it was Barker as Shakespear in *The Dark Lady of the Sonnets* (see appendix B).

In the professional relationship between the two, Shaw assumed the role of instructor, urging Barker, as he had urged Alice Lockett, "to become as a little child again." Shaw seemed determined to prove to "the marvellous boy" that he was more than a "vulgar old buffer" who was "devilish clever." Shaw's habit of working closely with the acting company was fruitfully adopted by Barker as he sought expressiveness on the stage. Wearing sandals, chewing nuts, leaving notes on dressing-room mirrors, Barker exhorted and inspired—"Be Swift. Be Swift. Be not Poetical." At a rehearsal of one of Shaw's plays, he instructed the cast to "please remember that this is Italian opera."[23] Barker followed Shaw's lead in more than the theater. He shared Shaw's interest in boxing as an artistic display, and he became a Fabian in 1901, serving on the executive committee from 1907 to 1912.

Shaw and Barker saw eye to eye in their support of new talent. Barker collaborated in 1904 with Laurence Housman on *Prunella*, which was presented at the Court Theatre. Shaw made a point of helping Housman, one of the few individuals ever positively linked to the secret Order of Chaeronea. In 1908, defending himself against the charge of being a "millionaire Socialist," Shaw wrote McNulty that he would not let *Getting Married* be produced at the Haymarket Theatre unless the management staged plays by young men, specifically Housman and John Masefield—theatrical ventures that cost Shaw time and money. Masefield had gotten his start in the theater when, as a shy young deckhand, he came to Barker whistling sea chanties that he had composed on a windjammer. Having enthralled Barker, Masefield saw his sea chanties immediately incorporated into the second act of *Captain Brassbound's Conversion*.[24] The instincts of Barker and Shaw proved right concerning Masefield, who was drawn to tragic themes and experimented with weaving verse into his drama. He was named poet laureate of England in 1930.

Barker initially was considered for the role of the effete poet Octavius in the acclaimed 1905 Court production of *Man and Superman*. Instead, he played Shaw's first Tanner in full red-bearded Shavian regalia. One critic praised Barker's acting skill but thought he was "too young and pretty for the part." Playing opposite Barker was Lillah McCarthy. A decade earlier Shaw had been impressed by Lillah when as a young Lady Macbeth he found her "flashing eye" and "indomitable bearing" to be "very nearly thrilling," although she needed time to learn her craft. Then one day at Adelphi Terrace in walked a beautiful woman dressed in green who said, "'The ten years are up! I've learnt my business, as you told me,'" recounted Shaw. It reminded him of the scene in which the young Hilda Wangel came to the masterbuilder Solness. Shaw took one look at Lillah and burst out, 'There you are—Ann Whitefield!'"[25]

The masterplaywright would decide that Lillah was not only Ann, but she was also Jennifer Dubedat (opposite Barker), Raina (opposite Barker's Sergius), and Gloria Clandon. Shaw credited her with being more than an intelligent actress, for she understood how to present herself heroically, qualities he needed. Admiring her like an artwork, Shaw described her as a woman with the "figure and gait of a Diana" who was "beautiful, plastic, statuesque, most handsomely made, and seemed to have come straight from the Italian or eighteenth century stage." Most of all, Lillah had imagination, "the first natural qualification of an actress who is not a mere puppet."[26]

Years before Lillah and Barker had toured together as young actors in Ben Greet's Shakespeare and Old English Comedy Company. Now, to complete the autobiographical mimicry surrounding Shaw's autobiographical courtship play, life imitated art, for the leading man was enticed into marrying the leading lady. As the pair reenacted the roles of Shaw's fictional characters, they played those roles even more imaginatively, as if Tanner were identical with his creator. Tanner was "Shaw to the life!" exclaimed Lillah. Not long before he proposed, the Shaw impersonator gave Lillah his photograph, inscribing it "To 'Ann' in ransom from 'John Tanner.'" Portentously for the ensuing marriage, Barker closed his inscription "in comradeship."[27]

In a secret ceremony known only to Shaw and Vedrenne, Barker and Lillah married on 24 April 1906 at the West Strand Registry Office, where Shaw and Charlotte had married eight years earlier. The young couple then followed Shaw to Rodin's light-filled studio at Meudon, where they watched as Rodin worked, Lillah marveling at the enormous room, which seemed to float "like an ark upon the sea of a wonderful garden." Then they continued their Shaw-inspired honeymoon in Berlin by viewing the Max Reinhardt production of *Caesar and Cleopatra*.[28]

Having married, Barker suddenly changed his professional name from the abbreviated Granville Barker to the full Harley Granville Barker. "I really cannot stand Harley. Let's call him Grannie—Annie's Grannie," cried Shaw to Lillah, demoting Barker to the role of Roebuck Ramsden, Ann Whitefield's avuncular and ineffectual guardian. Shaw mocked the name change with B. Vulgar and Arley, offering to compromise with Barley. As a wedding present, Shaw presented the couple with a Bechstein piano with a pianola attachment, exactly the piano he himself enjoyed. Despite his good wishes for the couple, he felt "instinctively dismayed" at the marriage.[29]

The Barkers' honeymoon was short-lived. During the summer Barker spent ten days with the Webbs in Bertrand Russell's house near Oxford, mostly without Lillah, who visited for a single Sunday. Beatrice Webb thought Barker had not emancipated himself from Shaw's influence or "found his own soul," a commentary on the intimate relationship so apparent between the men. Beatrice found Barker lacking in warmth and "a better friend than a husband." Although she found Lillah attractive and "hard-working and dutiful," in a gloomy but prophetic pronouncement, she thought Barker bored by his bride.[30]

When they married, Barker was in delicate health, having neglected himself, and he submitted to the ministrations of the dutiful Lillah just as Shaw had submitted to Charlotte. The Barkers first lived at 3 Clement's Inn, with Lillah ensconced on the lower floor, Barker on the upper. Some time later Henderson described them as living apart "in the modern manner, quite independently of each other." Meeting at the Shaws', Barker would kiss his wife very, very lightly on the cheek, but otherwise they did not touch, "like friendly but distant cousins."[31]

Marriage did not interfere with the relationship between Shaw and Barker, a relationship characterized by intellectual vitality and artistic sensibility. So at home were they in the world of literature that they could amuse themselves by conversing entirely through quotation from Shakespeare and Dickens. They traveled together and they vacationed together, with and without their wives. When Charlotte sailed for Rome the men motored about for a week. Stopping to view hydro-aeroplanes at Windermere, they playfully took turns climbing onto a large scale suspended from a nail on the hangar wall. Shaw successfully weighed himself (he was 160 pounds). But when Barker lay back on the scale the nail bent, sending him crashing with an "appalling bang" and giving Shaw a "fright." When Lillah came down with a sore throat, Shaw accompanied Barker to a festival at the Academy of Eurythmics in Dresden. As Shaw put it: "I took Lillah's place."[32]

After Bessie died on 19 February 1913, following three paralytic strokes, Shaw, not wanting the "burial horrors" of a procession of mourners, kept the arrangements private except for Barker and the undertaker: "it was best with us three." They were joined by the parson at her cremation three days later at Golders Green. Because of illness, even Lucy stayed away. Shaw the romantic pyromaniac described the cremation in detail to Mrs. Patrick Campbell. The violet-draped coffin moved into the furnace feet first, and then the feet "burst miraculously into streaming ribbons of garnet colored lovely flame, smokeless and eager, like pentecostal tongues," and as the coffin sprang into flame, "my mother became that beautiful fire."[33]

It was to Barker that Shaw first confessed his infatuation with the glamorous Stella Campbell (affectionately called Mrs. Pat), for whom he created Eliza Doolittle. On 26 June 1912 he called upon the beautiful actress at her home in Kensington Square to read

Pygmalion to her. When she had played Ophelia fifteen years earlier he had immediately vowed to teach that "rapscallionly flower girl" something. Now taking Shakespeare's place, unable to separate the actress from his creative vision, he ended his visit madly in love with his own flower girl—embodying the Pygmalion legend himself. It lasted for "very nearly 36 hours," he wrote Barker four days later. He wrote virtually the same account to Ellen Terry—male and female incarnations of theatrical inspiration for him, they would understand. To Ellen he also implied that his love letters to Stella were a game.[34]

The fascination with his "Dearest liar" exceeded thirty-six hours, however, paining Charlotte as Shaw indiscreetly met with and raved about Stella. When the widowed Mrs. Pat began talking of marrying George Cornwallis-West—"the other George"—Shaw left for Dresden with Barker. Only weeks after their return to England, Barker and Shaw were together again at the Torcross Hotel in Devon, Shaw sea bathing, saving Lillah from a treacherous giant wave, and writing Stella of his feat—Stella, who a few days later would make an early-morning escape from the Guilford Hotel in Sandwich where Shaw had followed her. "Back from the land of broken promise," he raged in wounded vanity at her, the "shallow hearted thing!" "Your dear letters are not true—but they are wonders!" answered Stella. The storm subsided in a few days as he made excuses for her. He consoled himself that the "order of nature" was restored to his imagination: "It is I who cared, you who didn't." Then he wondered of himself, "Did you ever meet so feminine a creature?"[35]

Shaw dramatized his version of the romance with Stella in the Interlude separating the two acts of *The Apple Cart* (1928). There the "strangely innocent relations" between King Magnus and Orinthia, his mistress, are meant to refute any suggestion that the real-life version was sexual. For Orinthia was so widely recognized as being fashioned after Stella that even before production London buzzed with talk that Edith Evans had the role. An incensed Stella was further horrified at what she considered Shaw's unflattering portrait of her. He admitted to her that its "scandalous climax" was a "reminiscence" of "bits and scraps" of Kensington Square.[36]

The Interlude is set in Orinthia's boudoir, and she speaks her mind. The king's wife makes him look ridiculous. No one "can imagine what you do with her." His lack of manhood is a recurring motif. Complimenting him, Orinthia says he has "almost the makings of a first rate woman." Annoyed with him, she calls him a "mollycoddle," not a "real man." When she holds onto him and refuses to let go, Magnus tackles her and the two roll over each other on the floor. Once Shaw had startled Charlotte by rolling her around and "pummeling her from head to foot," a remedy to shake illness out of her that he recommended to a bed-ridden Stella.[37] But then he dared not pummel the ill actress because she was already too sore. In *The Apple Cart,* the relation of the Interlude to the rest of the play is oblique—Magnus, impotent as king and as lover, flaunts his playfulness as a badge of superiority.

Shaw's advertised indiscretion with Stella resurrected the image of a Don Juan unable to resist the charms of a beautiful woman, the scandal meant to drown out any whispers about his masculinity. For one reason that he recovered so quickly from the disappointment of having his "queen of heaven" slip away that morning at the Guilford Hotel was that Barker needed him. He was "already in hysterics" over *Androcles and the Lion* (1912), which he was readying for its London premiere.[38]

As much as Shaw could help Barker in the theater, he proved impotent to help him in his marriage. The fairy-tale marriage of the beautiful Lillah and the handsome Harley was based on their shared love of theater, but the romantic imagination that vitalized their stage life led them astray in real life. For the time came when Barker confessed to her that he did her a great wrong in asking her to marry him—even though he had explained then how mixed his feelings were. He had never loved her as he ought to love a woman to be married to her. Cryptically, Barker also wrote her that he could not lie about it, but as she would not believe what he did tell her, it became difficult to tell her more. It had seemed to him wiser "to let the thing itself have its test." It was no comfort to hear Shaw's opinion two weeks later: "I gravely doubt whether Harley is fit for married life at all."[39]

Barker, in New York for the 1915 repertory season, was swept off his feet by Helen Huntington, the wife of the American millionaire Archer M. Huntington. Helen Huntington was ten years older than Barker, apparently the ideal age difference for him to put her on a pedestal and worship her for all he was worth. One story has Barker adoringly standing watch outside Helen's house on East 57th Street, blowing kisses as she turned off her bedroom light for the night.[40] The former Tanner behaved like Freddy in the film version of *Pygmalion*.

Shaw, who never believed the marriage would last, tried to arrange the divorce. In August 1917 he assured Lillah that there was no humiliation involved in Harley's desertion, but he shared her sense of a knockdown blow: "it knocked the stage from under you in a sense: indeed it did the same to me." He took it hard: they were both being jilted for Helen. "We have seen lots of Harley," he reported two weeks later. Barker was spending weekends at the Shaws' country house at Ayot St. Lawrence in Hertfordshire, where he kept a spare suit of clothes in what was virtually a second home to him. In happier times, Barker had chased women away from Shaw, supposedly at Charlotte's request, even threatening to shoot one who persisted in showing up at Ayot St. Lawrence.[41]

Shaw advised Lillah that she could do nothing for Harley but set him and herself free, advice he could never quite follow himself. Tenderly, he comforted her: "Look up, dear, look up to the heavens. There is more in life than this. There is much more." After a painful parting from Lillah, Barker married Helen in 1918. Once again Barker signaled his change of marital status by changing his name like a woman, this time by adding a hyphen between Granville and Barker. Like Shaw, he married into money, and without any expectation of fathering children, since his wife was over fifty. Bitterly, Shaw said Barker was "completely dominated" by his second wife: "She made him throw over Socialism as well as Shaw; she made him do translations of Spanish plays, or put his name to her translations; she cut him off from all commerce with the theatre."[42]

Shaw described Helen Huntington, who had been married to a capitalist, as "one of those people whose face I can never remember, her appearance being entirely negative." This description obliquely echoes the one Shaw gives the thieving capitalist Boss Mangan in *Heartbreak House:* his features are *"so entirely commonplace that it is impossible to describe them."* Shaw's strong antipathy to the woman was evidenced in a strange incident. In 1925 at King's College, where Barker had lectured movingly on Shakespeare, Shaw rose, as agreed, to second the vote of thanks to him. But in a breach of decorum Shaw lengthily added that Barker's retirement from the theater was a public scandal. Then something "most extraordinary" happened, remembered Shaw. Leaving the platform, he was struck by excruciating pain from his skull to the base of his spine. For several weeks he was bedridden and helpless, confounding the doctors. Then one month to the hour since he had been stricken, the pain "instantly and miraculously" left him. Shaw's physical pain and paralysis appear to be outer manifestations of the emotional pain and paralysis he suffered over losing Barker. Yet he blamed Helen for his mysterious disablement, for Lady Colefax reported watching Helen, seated just behind Shaw as he spoke, fixing her eyes on him with hate. Shaw believed that Helen had the power of the evil eye, so he had "not the slightest doubt" that she had bewitched him.[43]

Shaw told the same story of bewitchment to Hesketh Pearson and to Molly Tompkins, an impetuous young American actress who had crossed the Atlantic in 1921 with husband and baby in tow for the express purpose of founding a Shavian theater. A decade later, Shaw warned Molly not to mention his name in Helen's presence for fear Molly might draw upon herself some of Helen's "lethal malignity." Most certainly she would lose the acquaintance of "G. B.," wrote he, who was G. B. S. to his "particular friends." In a tone of real regret, Shaw gave Barker the highest possible praise: "He was a playwright in the running with myself," but now he was almost forgotten. If he had stayed with Fabian politics, Shaw thought that the Labor Party would have made him a peer. Though cut off from Barker, Shaw was still trying to get him produced at the Malvern Festival. He even tried to have him knighted "to please *her,*" desperately hoping that Helen would allow the men to resume their friendship. Having warned Molly to be careful, he asked for any news of Barker: "He has an Italian strain in him and was meant to be a man of genius."[44]

Molly Tompkins, more than forty years Shaw's junior, had entered the playwright's life at the right moment, taking Barker's place as the darling of the hour. Only months after Shaw's ill-fated speech at King's College, he wrote of romance to Molly by invoking the familiar polarity of the elysian fields and "this solid earth." Their May-September relationship had to survive the intimacies of two summer idylls in Italy that were incompletely chaperoned by their spouses. Of Molly's memory of one golden day by a river, Shaw had nothing to say. Like Ellen Terry and Janet Achurch and Florence Farr and Stella Campbell and Barker, the enchanting and lovely "Mollikins" was a theatrical performer whom he could romanticize and teach. Whether a man is "fastidious about women" depends a "good deal" on his mother, he instructed her. As fastidious as ever, he refused to be made a "hog of" by a "Vamp fiend."[45] On that note, he continued a warm friendship with a Benedictine nun, Sister Laurentia McLachlan, to whom in 1924 he had given a copy of *Saint Joan* inscribed from Brother Bernard.

Communication between Shaw and Barker had halted. Barker, however, was among those who signed a letter of protest drawn up by Shaw and Desmond MacCarthy after Scotland Yard burned Radclyffe Hall's lesbian novel *The Well of Loneliness* in 1928. A few years later Barker's legal adviser sent him a prepublication copy of the preface Shaw had written for Lillah's memoirs. Angry over Shaw's detailed comments on the breakup of his marriage to Lillah, Barker suddenly burst in one day "as if he had only been away a few hours." Despite Barker's agitation, there were glimpses of the old friendliness and the old feelings during the visit. Twenty minutes after driving away, Barker, brimming with emotion, returned to bid Charlotte one more farewell. Barker's reluctance at having his love life publicized had an unexpected result. Subsequently, with the help of her new husband, the botanist Sir Frederick Keeble, Lillah saw to it that all reference to Barker was excised from her book.[46] At some point Shaw managed to tell Barker his story of bewitchment, but Helen's total domination of her husband remained to the end as far as Shaw knew.

Shaw and Helen faced off like great antagonists, their feelings fed by mutual suspicion and jealousy. For once Shaw's pain was real as he vainly tried to act the familiar role of knight in shining armor, determined to save Barker from Helen for the sake of art and himself. "Harley must be rescued at all costs," he vowed in 1924 to Florence Emily Hardy, the second wife of novelist Thomas Hardy. Shaw refused to believe that Barker was an "extinct volcano," but he thought that Helen was "sitting on the crater." By December, Shaw announced Barker's "extinction" as "an amazing and disconcerting phenomenon."[47]

Among those Shaw stirred into action on an "imaginary Barker Relief Expedition" was none other than Lawrence of Arabia, the famed war hero who became a legend in his own time. T. E. Lawrence was friendly with Barker, visiting at his home, Netherton Hall—or, as Shaw called it, "Nethermost Hell," a label he attributed to certain "fashionable ladies." Shaw and Lawrence had met somewhat accidentally at Adelphi Terrace in

March 1922, when Lawrence accompanied Sidney Cockerell there. That August, Lawrence asked Shaw to read *Seven Pillars of Wisdom*, the enormous manuscript he had written about his experiences during World War I. Shaw agreed, but he procrastinated so long that Charlotte plowed through it first. In 1923 the hero-worshipping Lawrence enlisted in the army as Private T. E. Shaw, a name he legally adopted in 1927, prompting rumors that *he* was Shaw's illegitimate son. The rumor was publicly and immediately acknowledged by Shaw, who wrote that Lawrence's new name "caused him to be taken for my son one day by a clergyman at the house of Thomas Hardy."[48]

The Shaws took to Lawrence, who visited them regularly and invited them to visit his tiny cottage, Clouds Hill. Charlotte was especially open to him, and an intimate, even puzzling correspondence ensued. Was Charlotte a surrogate for her husband as Lawrence confessed to a desire for outward degradation and filth to match his inner feelings, and of a fear of seeming a novice in a brothel? After finally reading *Seven Pillars of Wisdom*, Shaw called it a masterpiece, "one of the few best of its kind in the world." Scrupulously emending, revising, and deleting, Shaw also rewrote Lawrence's descriptions of homosexuality among the Arab troops. Punctuation aside, Shaw warned Lawrence that his corrections were so important he had better "swallow them literally." Shaw the silent collaborator altered for public view the life story of the man who adopted his name, laboring over what Lawrence called his "sludge" just as if it were the "real tissue." As he was revising *Seven Pillars of Wisdom*, Shaw was writing *Saint Joan*. He gave Lawrence copies of his play inscribed "to Shaw from Shaw."[49] It was a gift from one genius to another about a third. Once again the essential characteristics of genius were genderless. There was something else as well: a cry of the misunderstood genius galvanized by loss—Shaw's response to Barker's personal and artistic defection.

Lawrence brought a strange twist to the Barker-Shaw story. Barker addressed Lawrence as "My dear Shaw," telling him that he had a "'Daimon,'" like everyone with a surplus of vitality. As a patently bogus Shaw, Lawrence asked Barker to read *Seven Pillars of Wisdom*. Meanwhile, Lawrence read Barker's *The Secret Life*, reporting back that "Shaw (the real one)" deplored Barker's "introduction of stuff which would have made eight plays if beaten out thin." Shaw's criticism of Barker sounds like Archer's criticism of Shaw over *Rhinegold*. Lawrence himself was most interested in the character Evan Strowde. "Your women passed me by, (revenge perhaps, for I usually pass them, in the flesh)." Lawrence thought that Barker had hidden the carnal out of shame or fear, or "like Shaw, in revenge." The picture of "an author and a would-be (would have been?), exchanging books, & tasting each other meditatively" was one Lawrence relished.[50] With Lawrence the pseudo-Shaw acting as intermediary, the members of the tentative male ménage à trois tasted one another meditatively while the lethal ménage à trois of Helen/Harley/Shaw consumed one another from a distance.

But it was no use. By now Barker was a "lost soul," a "damned soul," Shaw's verdict like an echo of doom from *Heartbreak House.* "We do not live in this house: we haunt it," cries Hector Hushabye, who is dashing, intelligent, sensitive, and useless. Acting in his own private drama, he masquerades as the suavely melodramatic Marcus Darnley and parades in Arab costume. Married to Hesione, who exercises supernatural powers over men, he rages impotently against "vampire women, demon women," crying out: "Is there any slavery on earth viler than this slavery of men to women?"[51] All of this sounds like Shaw's view of the Helen/Harley relationship, and it may not be accidental that both Hesione Hushabye and Helen Huntington have the same initials.

Heartbreak House is set in an English country house built to resemble a sailing ship. On this metaphorical voyage, two radically different ship metaphors are fused. The submerged metaphor—the ship of fools—suggests the medieval Europe of Sebastian Brant's *Narrenschiff* (1494), the most famous literary work of its time, with Brant's catalogue of folly reading like a satiric gloss of *Heartbreak House.* More overtly, the world of ancient Greece is intimated via Plato's allegory of the ship of state and the characters' mythological names, remnants of a heroic past. In this dramatic fable Shaw artfully presents his thesis: England, representative of Western civilization, is drifting toward disaster because of moral apathy. There is no essential difference between the ship of state and the ship of fools, a bitterly ironic vision.[52]

Like the inhabitants of *Heartbreak House,* Barker was a fool seduced by money into marrying Helen. "Harley always loved luxury," Shaw told St. John Ervine. The cultivated Barker was associated with Greek culture through Gilbert Murray, the translator of Greek plays; through the productions of Greek plays at the Court Theatre; and through Greek love. Like Shaw, he was a member of the homosexual-dominated British Society for the Study of Sex Psychology. In *The Secret Life,* Oliver Gauntlett may be a member of a secret society: "The men with the secrets that count will know each other when the time comes, won't they?"[53] In his play, Barker makes Oliver the unacknowledged son of Evan Strowde, perhaps craftily alluding to the rumor that Shaw was *his* father—the protective rumor that concealed the nature of their relationship.

Through Hector, who calls himself a warrior, Shaw evokes parodic echoes of the Trojan War hero. Similarly, Barker's name, which means to advertise by persistent outcry, becomes transformed into a parodic opposite—Hushabye. And to hector means to intimidate by bluster or personal pressure, similar to the verbal act a barker performs. Hector's character also has an explicit autobiographical parallel to Shaw. In the play's final scene, as the drone of the bomb-carrying zeppelins grows louder, Hector turns on the lights and tears down the curtains, living courageously for a single moment as the ship of fools moves toward judgment.

Shaw's neighbors in Ayot St. Lawrence gossiped that he must be a German spy because he kept a light on in a high window. Meanwhile, he boasted that no place in London was more brightly lighted than Adelphi Terrace. To neighbor T. Fisher Unwin, Shaw contended that the lighting partly checked the "tendency to treat the Terrace as a public urinal at night." Seemingly impervious to the threat of zeppelins, Shaw cited a "mulish objection" to having the risk interfere with his normal activities "in the smallest degree." He supposed the Germans would begin to use parachuted flares to light up targets, and then "we may as well turn up all our lights and tear down all our blinds." The date of this letter is 15 February 1916.[54]

In early February, Barker and Lillah met at Shaw's London flat to talk, but despite his wife's pleas, Barker refused to leave Helen. After spending a weekend in Ayot St. Lawrence, Barker left for France to do public relations work for the Red Cross. On 4 March 1916, Shaw began *Heartbreak House*, writing, he confessed to Stella Campbell, "to prevent myself crying." He had never felt so morose in his life: "I feel suicidal." In May, with Barker in America and liable for military service, "everything has gone to the devil."[55]

By fall, Shaw's fears seemed justified. Back in England to serve in the army, a khaki-clad Harley announced over lunch that he had given up the stage.[56] During his February visit to Adelphi Terrace, Barker undoubtedly would have noticed Shaw's penchant for bright lights, and the two were likely to have discussed such dangerous bravado. Shaw's letter to Unwin is proof that it was on his mind. Later Shaw could expect Barker to recognize the corresponding scene in his play and see the autobiographical allusion to Shaw—and to himself in the character of Hector. The dual shifting identification suggests a privately acknowledged intimacy.

In his great political allegory addressed to the leisure classes, Shaw hid an impassioned personal plea. Captain Shotover's ominous decree, "Navigation. Learn it and live; or leave it and be damned," was also an urgent warning to the drifting, leisured Barker—who is mentioned by name twice in the Preface—that he must act to save himself. The falling bombs that end *Heartbreak House* explode in a moonless, tranquil garden, creating a domesticated version of the Wagnerian *Götterdämmerung*. Shaw himself compared his play to Wagner, writing that he had created a "palace of enchantment, as in the second act of *Parsifal*."[57] Barker not only understood Shaw's coded message, he replied with his own coded message—a message that goes beyond thematic and dramaturgical parallels between the plays.

The Secret Life opens to the strains of *Tristan und Isolde*. The setting is one evening at summer's end in a country house facing the sea. On a loggia offstage are three men, close friends. One man accompanies himself on the piano and sings Isolde's final aria, her Liebestod over the death of Tristan. Listening is Joan Westbury, who stayed with her husband despite her love for Evan Strowde. Then she speaks to Strowde under a moon that "might be a ship on fire." The two, who have not so much as kissed, have been in love for eighteen years. Joan is certain that she could not have lived her love: it would have killed her. And so she kept her love for Strowde (a man who serves barley-water) a "secret from my everyday self."

In this haunting, mysterious drama of subtexts tracing the wintertime of souls and flickering with themes of love, self, and spirit, Barker weaves variations on the meaning of Wagner's opera and Shaw's play. He also sent Shaw a signal. For it was some eighteen years earlier that Shaw and Barker were in the flower of their friendship, and, like Strowde and Joan, "loved the unattainable in each other." Over the years, holding onto his unconsummated love, Strowde has come to believe in "what's unattainable from life and nothing else can content me or stir me now." He would sooner trust fools, "if fools would take heart," than disillusioned men.[58]

Long before, Shaw's devotion to *Tristan und Isolde* had been the catalyst in sparking the friendship with Archer. But Bessie Shaw objected to Isolde's "erotic emotion" as "unladylike and indecent." Also unsympathetic was Charlotte, who asked for a halt to the "caterwauling" whenever Shaw sang the score for her. His mother and wife aside, Shaw took pleasure in the "seas of sentiment" drowning Isolde. Indeed, *Tristan und Isolde* is another of the Wagnerian operas that have fascinated gay men. Isolde's Liebestod is built on beliefs woven into opera and homosexual culture: among them, that gender dissolves in an unsanctioned love affair and that gay love "grows social, sublimated, and audible by passing through the soprano voice," as contemporary gay critic Wayne Koestenbaum puts it. But in *The Secret Life* there is no soprano voice during the Liebestod. Full of intense love-longing, men become women at the outset of Barker's play. The men themselves express Isolde's transfiguration as she expires in rapture upon Tristan's lifeless body. Later Strowde says of irrevocable loss, "The breaking of a last link brings relief with it too."[59]

"Do you ever see Granville-Barker now?" asked Shaw plaintively of Gilbert Murray in 1940. Barker was forbidden to communicate with him, as the evil-eyed Helen "sticks pins into wax images of me; but we are—on my side certainly, as I suspect on his also—as good friends as ever." Two years later, to O. B. Clarence, who had acted in a "'silly ass'" part alongside Barker, he recalled the "young genius" as one of the first acting successes in London productions of his plays. How often Shaw's memory was jogged by fondly kept photographs no one can say. One prized photograph was taken by Shaw in 1901 and submitted to the *Times Literary Supplement* on Barker's death. Shaw so valued a 1900 crayon drawing of Barker by John Singer Sargent that he bequeathed it to the National Gallery, London.[60] Both photograph and drawing show a stunningly handsome young man with a cleft chin and capture a quality that is more darkly inscrutable than insouciant, the young Harley who so fascinated Shaw.

Hesketh Pearson thought that the estrangement from Barker was Shaw's most deeply felt loss until Charlotte's death, for it was the "only important matter about which he asked me to be reticent." Yet Shaw insisted that the separation "was not an estrangement," citing Barker's reply "on our old terms" after he notified him of Charlotte's death. One day when he was out walking with St. John Ervine, the latter mentioned that they were near Barker's house—whose threshold Shaw had never crossed. At Ervine's comment, Shaw exclaimed, "Oh, Harley!" in a tone Ervine had never heard him use.[61]

For Barker, the separation from Shaw virtually brought to a close an extraordinarily productive theatrical life. For Shaw there was a mighty artistic outpouring in the years immediately following that separation—*Heartbreak House, Back to Methuselah,* and *Saint Joan*—immense cautionary tales of human fallibility and possibility. And then a withering—although his vitality still was so great that only by comparison with the work of his younger self can it be called a withering at all. In 1928, Barker published his last play, *His Majesty.* Shaw immediately responded with his first play in five years, *The Apple Cart,* which drew attention to his amorous indiscretion of years past. Where Barker's king is forced into abdication, Shaw's impotent King Magnus only threatens abdication. What Shaw called the tragedy of Barker's life was his tragedy as well.[62] Without Barker, Shaw lost a vital earthly contact, the ballast that had kept him from tarrying too long in a fanciful ethereal realm. So too in the art, beginning with *Heartbreak House,* his later plays were predominantly allegorical, as wishfulness, longing, and didacticism merged.

On his deathbed, longing for earthly release, Shaw talked of Barker, whom he had last seen eighteen years before at the painfully effusive parting of 1932. The actor and producer Esmé Percy, a self-aware gay man, listened as Shaw accused Barker of not really understanding his plays, Percy finding Shaw's accusation "bewildering." The outpouring of feeling from the dying man had been foreshadowed four years earlier. On learning of Barker's death, he had written for publication: "The shock the news gave me made me realize how I had still cherished a hope that our old intimate relation might revive."

Algernon Charles Swinburne, the Pre-Raphaelite, Greek-infatuated poet, cries out in *Dolores* that "love is more cruel than lust." Picking up and embellishing the poem addressed to a woman, Shaw grieved:

> Marriage and death and division
> Make barren our lives
> and the elderly Professor could have
> little use for the nonagenarian ex-playwright.[63]

In a posture of submission and brimming with sorrow laced with regret, the world-famous playwright publicly mourned his young genius, the marvelous boy of long-gone glory days.

Finale

Denunciations of homosexuality as depraving
and detestable may have an unsuspected and
deeply wounding effect on one's most justly
valued friends. The wisest and best inverts
never tell.

—To the Very Reverend Albert Victor Baillie,
1928

In charting the themes of Shaw's life I have found his last half-century essentially identical to his first. He remained a wool-wearer, a vegetarian, a eugenicist, an anti-vivisectionist, an antivaccinationist, and a Fabian, establishing for himself the continuity his psyche demanded. By his seventieth birthday he had achieved an unprecedented international celebrity, unsurpassed even by the great religious and political leaders. His every word was recorded, his every movement publicized. That year, 1926, the Swedish Academy awarded him the Nobel Prize for Literature (for 1925). Wanting neither the honor nor the money, he finally agreed to accept both, immediately transferring the funds to the newly created Anglo-Swedish Literary Foundation headed by the Crown Prince of Sweden. In the same spirit, he declined to be knighted. In 1938, after his screenplay of *Pygmalion* earned him an Academy Award, he became the only Nobel laureate also to win an Oscar.

Shaw would live until 1950, only partly shaded from the glare of the spotlight at Shaw's Corner, Ayot St. Lawrence. During his lifetime and afterward, the famous and the anonymous, the young and the old would come in pilgrimage to the former village rectory. There was the eighty-eight-year-old G. B. S. in the garden chopping wood, the ninety-year-old walking briskly about, the ninety-two-year-old greeting Ingrid Bergman at the gate (having wooed her with a copy of *Saint Joan* inscribed "with great respect"). To celebrate his ninety-fourth birthday he wrote a little play, *Why She Would Not*, godlike, in seven days. Like the Dublin Sonny who spent his days perched on a clerk's stool, the ancient Shaw sat before his writing table in the tiny wooden hut built on the example of Thoreau and Carpenter. But it was not for bird watching or flower hunting, he was quick to point out. *His* days were spent writing, thinking, and imagining, his way of telling himself stories, just as he had when he was a boy, just as the grown man did to lull himself to sleep at night.[1] His mind remained unclouded, his wits undimmed, his curiosity unslaked to the very end.

When Matthew Edward McNulty died in May 1943, Shaw asked whether he might see a photograph of his old friend in his later years: "I will return it." After Charlotte died on 12 September 1943, he wrote Lord Alfred Douglas that her end was "touchingly happy, making grief and sorrow impossible," leaving him "exaltedly serene and vigorous." He personally notified Sidney Webb, to whom Charlotte had left a legacy, and of course Lillah, as well as Harley. He missed Charlotte more than he wanted to admit. On 10 September 1950, while tending the garden he loved, he tried to prune a tree, slipped, and fell. Unable to rise, he blew the whistle he wore around his neck for emergencies, like his own Captain Shotover. Rescued by servants, he did not recover from a fractured thigh. He lingered until 2 November, during his last days longing for his "damned vitality" to release him to the peace of death.[2]

He was cremated at Golders Green, following Charlotte there, his coffin strewn with rose petals and laurel leaves and bearing a spray of rosemary "for remembrance" from Ellen Terry's garden, no eulogy but the final words of Mr. Valiant-for-truth from *Pilgrim's Progress*. His body was reduced to the carbon and potash that were its constituent elements and that he imagined would reenter the life force; the ashes of husband and wife were mixed together. Desexualized, disembodied, purified by violet flame, they were joined in death as they had never been in life. Once as a child he had dreamed that God was in the sky over his garden.[3] Now he became his garden as the commingled ashes were sprinkled around the grounds of his Ayot St. Lawrence home—around the paths, the rose beds, the lawn-covered bank that held a bronze statue of Saint Joan, the earthly space in which the playwright had tilled the fertile garden of his imagination for half his long life.

Over the years Shaw sometimes took stands that grieved his devoted admirers—longing for a superman, he was blind for too long to the terrible evil of dictators in his own time. But if he was not the prophet his adulators claimed, neither was he the buffoon his detractors dismissed. Like twentieth-century feminists, for Shaw, missionary and artist, the personal was the political as he labored unceasingly in the service of a higher cause, always without malice. Finally, in spite of his complex psychic landscape, he proved himself a friend to women. While Shaw the artist worshipped their beauty, Shaw the man identified with them—with women's plight and status and with their risky relationship to men. From the perspective of his own peculiar nature—part saint, part Mephistopheles—he envisioned a genderless world presided over by a female Life Force.

Shaw's constant lament that the genius, the saint, and the poet were all born before their time reflected his uneasy sojourn in a world where he felt the lacerations of shame and difference, even as he constructed elaborate fortifications to conceal crucial parts of his self-identity from the world. "I am; therefore I think," asserts Don Juan, overturning Descartes. Submerged was another reading for the playwright: I am an artist / genius / homosexual; therefore I think according to my special nature. Shaw wanted to be another Michelangelo, but could not draw; a musician, but could not play; a singer, but had no voice. And so Shaw lived by his own dictum: "it's not what a man would like to do, but what he *can* do, that he must work at in this world." Paradoxically, even as he believed that heredity and early childhood had ineradicably marked him, like his own Joan he struggled to save himself by transcending flesh, sacrificing himself on the altar of human evolution. In his own voice he proclaimed: "This is the true joy in life, the being used for a purpose recognized by yourself as a mighty one."[4]

Shaw was born before his time, and all his modes of being reflected this perspective. In the social world, he was the artist-genius as outsider, preaching eugenics, searching for signs of the superman; in the biological world, he was the ascetic celibate; in his private world, he was the self-branded one, seeking spiritual salvation in an elusive bodiless realm. And yet wittily, brilliantly, jubilantly he played his many parts on the great stage of the world.

If life shaped art, so too art shaped life, sustaining and transforming, offering a restorative pathway back into life. The art, like the life, traced a flaming trajectory toward the luminous ethereal realm of the imagination, a trajectory that had beckoned thrillingly and seductively long before on Dalkey's furze-covered hill. Paradoxically wanting to be in the world and to retreat from it, to be himself and not to be himself, he plucked shimmering skeins of moral fancy from his life, weaving parables for humanity. His quest was the heroic one of the romantic and the mystic alike—a grail-like quest for a serene perfection not given to human beings. Yet wonderfully, that pristine ideal was rooted in a forgiving precept: "all truly sacred truths are rich in comedy."[5]

Bernard Shaw accepted responsibility for the genius and homosexuality that he believed to be his twin inheritance, creating his own system of values, giving meaning to his life. As he strove to materialize an exalted realm of art and passion, intellect and morality, possible only in a visionary future, he made himself into what he celebrated: "a pioneer in the forward march of the human spirit."[6] Armed with artistic and intellectual courage, braced by a resilient comic vision and godlike energy, the fantastic sojourner threaded his way through an intricate spiritual and psychic labyrinth, forging his own destiny—crowning himself superman ascendant.

Appendix A

Shaw Plays Produced at the Royal Court Theatre Under the Management of Harley Granville Barker and John Eugene Vedrenne (with date of first performance)

All programs for the Royal Court Theatre are reproduced in MacCarthy, *The Court Theatre*, 125–169.

1904	26 April, *Candida*
	1 November, *John Bull's Other Island*
1905	28 February, *How He Lied to Her Husband*
	2 May, *You Never Can Tell*
	23 May, *Man and Superman* (without the third act)
	28 November, *Major Barbara*
1906	20 March, *Captain Brassbound's Conversion*
	20 November, *The Doctor's Dilemma*
1907	5 February, *The Philanderer*
	4 June, *Don Juan in Hell* (third act of *Man and Superman*)
	4 June, *The Man of Destiny*

In addition to working with Shaw on his productions, Barker is credited with directing the first performances of the following plays:

1903	7 June, *The Admirable Bashville*, Imperial Theatre
1907	16 September, *You Never Can Tell*, Savoy Theatre
	14 October, *The Devil's Disciple*, Savoy Theatre
1913	1 September, *Androcles and the Lion*, St. James's Theatre

New productions in the United States:

1915	27 January, *Androcles and the Lion*, Wallack's Theatre
	25 February, *The Doctor's Dilemma*, Wallack's Theatre

Appendix B

First Appearance of Harley Granville Barker
in Shaw Roles

For information on the roles Barker played, his productions, and his writings, see
Purdom, *Harley Granville Barker,* 288–309.

1900	1 July, Marchbanks, *Candida*
	16 December, Captain Kearney, *Captain Brassbound's Conversion*
1901	29 March, Napoleon, *The Man of Destiny*
1902	5 January, Frank Gardner, *Mrs Warren's Profession*
1904	1 November, Peter Keegan, *John Bull's Other Island*
1905	7 February, Her Lover, *How He Lied to Her Husband*
	2 May, Valentine, *You Never Can Tell*
	23 May, John Tanner, *Man and Superman*
	28 November, Adolphus Cusins, *Major Barbara*
1906	20 November, Louis Dubedat, *The Doctor's Dilemma*
1907	14 October, General Burgoyne, *The Devil's Disciple*
	23 November, Dick Dudgeon, *The Devil's Disciple*
	30 December, Sergius, *Arms and the Man* (later, on tour, Captain Bluntschli)
1910	24 November, William Shakespear, *The Dark Lady of the Sonnets*
1911	30 June, Larry Doyle, *John Bull's Other Island*

Notes

Abbreviations

The following abbreviations appear in the notes.

CL 1–4: Bernard Shaw: Collected Letters, vol. 1 (1874–97),
  vol. 2 (1898–1910), vol. 3 (1911–25), vol. 4 (1926–50).
  Laurence brackets estimated dates; I use those dates without
  brackets.
CP Collected Plays
CW Collected Works. Individual volumes will be identifed on first appearance in the notes.
MCE Major Critical Essays, vol. 19 in *Collected Works*
OTN Our Theatres in the Nineties, 3 vols. (vols. 1–3 appear as 23–25 in *Collected Works*).
SSS Sixteen Self Sketches

Preface

　1. SSS, 6.
　2. On "world design" see, e.g., Binswanger, *Being-in-the-World*.
　3. Bentley, "Shaw Dead," 406.

Chapter 1: Casting a Downstart

　1. On family background see letter to Thomas Demetrius O'Bolger, February 1916, *CL* 3: 361–363. A revised version of a portion of this letter appears in *SSS* as "My Mother and Her Relatives"; there Bessie "innocently" lets out the secret of her father's plan to remarry, 11. See also letter to F. Harris, 5 June 1930, *The Playwright and the Pirate: Bernard Shaw and Frank Harris: A Correspondence* (hereafter *Shaw / Harris*), 223–226.

　2. *CL* 3: 362; to Archibald Henderson, in Henderson, *Man of the Century*, 15 (hereafter *Man*).

　3. Preface to *Immaturity, CW* 1: x (hereafter cited as PI).

　4. PI, xi–xii.

　5. *CL* 3:363; on christening see "In the Days of My Youth," first published 17 September 1898 in the magazine *Mainly About People*, revised version in *SSS*, 45.

6. Rattray, *Bernard Shaw: A Chronicle*, 12. On Macduff, to St. John Ervine, 28 April 1936, *CL* 4: 430. The details of Shaw's birth have just come to light. Dr. Ringland, Master of the Coombe Lying-In Hospital from 1841 to 1876, kept a diary known as "The Ringland Chronicle." In it he recorded being in attendance at Shaw's birth. Although the diary burned during World War II, one of Ringland's successors at the hospital had taken notes. Recently, Dr. Michael Turner, the current Master of what is now known as Coombe Women's Hospital, discovered the surviving information, some of which is reported in the 1994 pamphlet *The Saving of Shaw's Birthplace*. Further information was relayed to me by Turner in a letter of 21 February 1995.

7. Shaw's Postscript to Harris, *Bernard Shaw*, 428.

8. *SSS*, 2–4.

9. To Peter and Iona Opie, 8 June 1950, *CL* 4: 866.

10. To Ellen Terry, 11 June 1897, *CL* 1: 773; and *Ellen Terry and Bernard Shaw: A Correspondence* (hereafter *Terry / Shaw*), 196. Many of Shaw's letters are collected in separate volumes to individuals, but hereafter such volumes will be cited only when the correspondence does not appear in *Collected Letters*.

11. PI, xiii; to E. Terry, *CL* 1: 773; *SSS*, 12.

12. Preceding two paragraphs, to E. Terry, *CL* 1: 773. See also *SSS*, 12.

13. *SSS*, 12; to T. D. O'Bolger, February 1916, *CL* 3: 366. To explain the disillusion that Shaw cites, Pearson quotes Shaw in *George Bernard Shaw*, 19; for Henderson, "the shock went very deep" (*Man*, 12); for Ervine, the "disillusionment of a child is a bitter experience" (*Bernard Shaw*, 21); for Holroyd, "the mark it left on him was one of incredulous disillusion" (*Bernard Shaw* 1: 16).

14. The loss of continuity put him at the "mercy of the world," as Martin Heidegger might say, and it was a "mundanization" of existence, to use Ludwig Binswanger's term; see Binswanger, *Being-in-the-World*, 295. Nonpsychological corroboration of this point comes from Richard M. Ohmann's stylistic analysis, which shows the importance of discontinuity in Shaw's nondramatic prose; see Ohmann, *Shaw: The Style and the Man*, 40–72.

15. Ada Tyrrell (1854–1955) quoted in Harris, *Contemporary Portraits* 2: 42. She appeared on a BBC program in 1954 with her daughter Lady Constantine Geraldine Hanson, who repeated the comment about the piano. Originally published as "George Bernard Shaw" in *Irish Literary Portraits*, ed. W. R. Rodgers (London: BBC, 1972). A. M. Gibbs has collected reminiscences about Shaw in *Interviews and Recollections* (hereafter *Interviews*); and quotes Lady Hanson on p. 6; on Shaw's memory, replies to a questionnaire by Frank Harris and originally published as "Who I Am, and What I Think," in two installments in *The Candid Friend*, 11 and 18 May 1901, revised and abridged for *Shaw Gives Himself Away* (1939) and again for *SSS*, 48–55, quotation from *SSS*, 51; original 11 and 18 May pieces are reprinted in Laurence, *Selected Non-Dramatic Writings of Bernard Shaw;* to A. Tyrell, 14 July 1949, *CL* 4: 852; on Bessie see PI, xxiv.

16. PI, xxvi–xxvii. Erikson's interest is in the general applicability of his own theory (*Identity: Youth and Crisis*, 142–150). H. Pearson merely quotes Shaw (*George Bernard Shaw*, 19–29); Henderson paraphrases Shaw (*Man*, 12); Dervin discusses the alcoholic's oral dependence (*Bernard Shaw*, 114–117); Holroyd does not probe the meaning of the incident, citing the "hilarious Shavian gloss" on George Carr Shaw's alcoholism (*Bernard Shaw* 1: 31).

17. PI, xxvi; to F. Harris, 7 August 1916, *Shaw / Harris*, 36. A slightly different version appears in Harris, *Oscar Wilde*, 396, and as "Oscar Wilde" in *Pen Portraits and Reviews* (hereafter *Pen Portraits*), *CW* 29, 306.

18. PI, xxvi, xxvii.

19. To F. Harris, 24 June 1930, *CL* 4: 191.

20. To St. John Ervine, 31 October 1942, *CL* 4: 646.

21. *CP* 2: 783, 784; Preface to *Shaw's Music*, originally written in 1935 (published 1937) as a Preface to *London Music in 1888–89 as Heard by Corno di Bassetto* (hereafter *Music*), 1: 40.

22. Preface to *Music* 1: 39–41; to St. John Ervine, 26 July 1949, *CL* 4: 853; *SSS*, 20.

23. Ada Tyrrell thought Sonny "very dignified," and a Mr. Fry (probably Joseph Foy) described him as "very correct." On memories of childhood friends see *Interviews*, 7, 10, 11. On watercolors see "Pictures: A Shavian Preface," *Bernard Shaw on the London Art Scene, 1885–1950* (hereafter *London Art*), 47.

24. Rosset, *Shaw of Dublin*, 178; *SSS*, 23; Preface to *Misalliance*, *CP* 4: 39–40. The house on Sandy Cove Road is now an inn where I spent a pleasant interlude among Shavian ghosts one August.

25. "Biographers' Blunders Corrected," *SSS*, 109; "A Secret Kept for 80 Years," *SSS*, 20.

26. *SSS*, 22, 24; Rosset lists Sonny's classmates by religion and by father's occupation (*Shaw of Dublin*, 185–186).

27. To St. John Ervine, 31 October 1942, *CL* 4: 645. Holroyd, like Rosset and O'Donovan, sees Shaw's feelings at school as related to Lee (Holroyd, *Bernard Shaw* 1: 36; Rosset, *Shaw of Dublin*, 189; O'Donovan, *Shaw and the Charlatan Genius*). O'Donovan traces Shaw's Dublin life and Lee's origins, his book appearing one year after *Shaw of Dublin*. Rosset's findings do not support his conviction that Shaw was a bastard, but all Shaw biographers since 1964 are indebted to his industry, as well as to O'Donovan's more balanced research. Virtually no new information has surfaced since then. Holroyd's work follows Rosset and O'Donovan and the Freudian interpretation of those findings in Silver, *Bernard Shaw*.

28. *SSS*, 25, 24, 22.

29. *SSS*, 23, 28; to Grace Goodliffe, 25 October 1949, *CL* 4: 857.

Chapter 2: Ménage à trois and Ecstasy

1. To A. Henderson, 3 January 1905, *CL* 2: 499; to T. D. O'Bolger, February 1916, *CL* 3: 360. On Lee's origins see Rosset, *Shaw of Dublin*, 30–53.

2. On Lee's Dublin genius see O'Donovan, *Shaw and the Charlatan Genius*, 62–78; to T. D. O'Bolger, February, *CL* 3: 358. When actor Robert Loraine suffered a leg injury in World War I, Shaw wrote him that "there is not the least reason why Higgins should not be lame, or Tanner lame, or any of the rest of my heroes. So long as you have a mouth left and one lung to keep it going, you will still be better than the next best: my pieces are not leg pieces" (Loraine, *Robert Loraine*, 247).

3. "The Chesterbelloc," *Pen Portraits*, 77.

4. On Lee's residences see O'Donovan, *Shaw and the Charlatan Genius*, 53; Rosset, *Shaw of Dublin*, 118–119; "Am I an Educated Person," *SSS*, 72.

5. To Patricia Devine, 3 May 1944, *CL* 4: 707.

6. On sojourner see PI, xlvii; to G. Goodliffe, 25 October 1949, *CL* 4: 857–858; to A. Tyrrell, 8 June 1950, *CL* 4: 867.

7. *SSS*, 72; Shaw incorrectly writes that Lee purchased Torca Cottage, but Rossett located the record of the lease (see Preface to *Music* 1:37, Rossett, *Shaw and the Charlatan Genius*, 223–226).

8. PI, xxi–xxii; to T. D. O'Bolger, February 1916, *CL* 3: 373.

9. McNulty, "Memoirs of G. B. S.," *The Annual of Bernard Shaw Studies* (hereafter *SHAW*) 12: 18; PI, xxii; *SSS*, 114.

10. To John G. Fitzgerald, 12 April 1947, *CL* 4: 794; to Edith Livia Beatty, 20 September 1907, *CL* 2: 714.

11. *Man and Superman*, *CP* 2: 571–572. See also letter to H. Pearson, 15 March 1939, *CL* 4: 527.

12. *Back to Methuselah*, part 1, *CP* 5: 345.

13. Preface to *Music* 1:37; to F. Harris, 20 June 1930, *CL* 4: 189; to T. D. O'Bolger, 24 February 1916, *CL* 3: 375.

14. *CL* 3: 375.

15. To A. Henderson, 3 January 1905, *CL* 2: 499; to T. D. O'Bolger, February 1916, *CL* 3: 356. O'Donovan notes the thirty-year interval (*Shaw and the Charlatan Genius*, 27).

16. *SSS*, 46; to T. D. O'Bolger, February 1916, *CL* 3: 368–369; to G. Goodliffe, 3 December 1942, *CL* 4: 651.

17. Preface to *Music* 1: 41; to T. D. O'Bolger, February 1916, *CL* 3: 371.

18. Preface to *Music* 1:41–42.

19. To T. D. O'Bolger, February 1916, *CL* 3: 372; *Back to Methuselah*, part 5, *CP* 5: 630; Galton, *Hereditary Genius*, 329, 237; Galton, *Inquiries into Human Faculty*, 19.

20. To T. D. O'Bolger, February 1916, *CL* 3: 372; to T. D. O'Bolger, 7 August 1919, *CL* 3: 628; undated entry, *The Diaries, 1885–1897* (hereafter *Diaries*) 1: 28–29.

21. PI, xxix, xxiv, xxviii; to G. Goodliffe, 3 December 1942, *CL* 4: 652.

22. To T. D. O'Bolger, February 1916, *CL* 3: 366–367, 371. See also *SSS*, 15–16.

23. *SSS*, 14; Harris, *Bernard Shaw*, 70–71.

24. Preface to *Misalliance*, *CP* 4: 114.

Chapter 3: The Worst Mother Conceivable

1. *bitch*: *SSS*, 107; Mrs. Musters' comment recorded in Laurence's footnote, McNulty, "Memoirs of G.B.S.," *SHAW* 12: 26; to T. D. O'Bolger, February 1916, *CL* 3: 365.

2. Letter of Bessie Shaw to A. Henderson, 21 May 1908, *Man*, xxvi.

3. *nullity*: to Charles MacMahon Shaw, 17 November 1937, *CL* 4: 479; see also *SSS*, 93. "How to Become a Model Parent," in *The Shavian* (Dublin), no. 1 (Spring 1946): 1; see also Allan Chappelow, *Shaw: "The Chucker-Out"* (New York: AMS Press, 1969), 35. Chappelow reprints many miscellaneous Shaw writings. On Bessie, to T. D. O'Bolger, February 1916, *CL* 3: 364; see also *SSS*, 13.

4. Preface to *Music* 1: 38–39; to T. D. O'Bolger, February 1916, *CL* 3: 362, 365.

5. Preface to *Music* 1: 38, 32; *SSS*, 14.

6. Preface to *Music* 1: 32; to St. John Ervine, 28 April 1936, *CL* 4: 429; *worst:* Preface to *Music* 1: 31.

7. Preface to *Music* 1: 39.

8. On tricking McNulty see the latter's memoir, *SHAW* 12: 7–9. In the margin of a copy of McNulty's account, Shaw wrote that the broken window was a legend at the Dublin English Scientific and Commercial Day School before he arrived there. on being tired, to A. Henderson, *Man*, 19; *power:* PI, xxix.

9. *SSS*, 9; Preface to *Music* 1: 39.

10. To T. D. O'Bolger, February 1916, *CL* 3: 361, 365.

11. To Mrs. P. Campbell, 22 April 1913, *CL* 3: 167; *Misalliance, CP* 4: 166.

12. *CL* 3: 360; Preface to *Music* 1:41; on learning about the four elements see Henderson, *Man*, 28.

13. *sprite:* Shaw quoting Beatrice Webb to E. Terry, 8 September 1897, *CL* 1: 801; *gravitation:* to T. D. O'Bolger, 9 October 1919, *CL* 3: 637; *brimstone:* to E. D. Girdlestone, 26 September 1890, *CL* 1: 266; *miraculously:* to Mrs. P. Campbell, 22 February 1913, *CL* 3: 152; *phenomenon:* Preface to *Music* 1: 34, 41.

14. To Frederick Jackson, 18 September 1910, *CL* 2: 941–942.

15. *CL* 2: 941–942.

16. *CL* 2: 943; "Shaw Speaks to His Native City," in *The Matter with Ireland*, 291.

Chapter 4: Stopgap and Impostor

1. *Nine Answers by G. Bernard Shaw* (privately printed [sixty-two copies] for Jerome Kern, 1923); Shaw protested the piracy but took no legal action since no copies were sold to the public; see Laurence, *A Bibliography* 1: 153–54, and *Interviews*, 23; to Manning D. Robertson, 3 February 1943, *CL* 4: 663; *SSS*, 47; Preface to *Music* 1: 44; Henderson, *Man*, 32.

2. Epistle Dedicatory to *Man and Superman, CP* 2: 519; conversation with A. Henderson recorded in *George Bernard Shaw: His Life and Works* (hereafter *Life*), 240.

3. Preface to *Terry / Shaw*, ix, xiv.

4. Preface to *Music* 1:45. On Bessie's singing roles see the letter to A. Henderson, 3 January 1905, *CL* 2: 499.

5. "Some Instruments and How to Play Them," *The Star*, 8 March 1889, *Music* 1: 574.

6. McNulty, "Memoirs of G. B. S.," *SHAW* 12: 6–7, 12. McNulty included this episode in a much briefer account of his friendship with Shaw published early in the century (see "George Bernard Shaw as a Boy," *The Candid Friend*, London, 6 July 1901). Shaw's marginal notes are reproduced alongside the article in *Interviews*, 17–21.

7. For further details on McNulty see Laurence's introduction to McNulty, "Memoirs of G. B. S." (*SHAW* 12: 1–2; quotations from McNulty on 12, 9, 11).

8. *soul histories:* to A. Henderson, 3 January 1905, *CL* 2: 504. One version of this account appears as "My Office-Boyhood," *SSS*, 33; another is included in the Preface to *Immaturity*. McNulty, "Memoirs of G. B. S.," *SHAW* 12: 14–15.

9. Shaw's note, *SHAW* 12: 12; M. E. McNulty to Shaw, 12 September 1941, McNulty, "Memoirs of G. B. S.," *SHAW* 12: 45.

10. To E. Terry, 16 September 1896, *CL* 1: 656; *pillarable: SSS,* 32; *The Irrational Knot, CW* 2: 282.

11. To A. Henderson, 3 January 1905, *CL* 2: 504, 503.

12. *SSS,* 31, and PI, xxxiv–xxxv; *Immaturity, CW* 1: 56; to A. Henderson, 3 January 1905, *CL* 2: 502.

13. PI, xxxvii, and to A. Henderson, 3 January 1905, *CL* 2: 503–504; on Smyth, to T. D. O'Bolger, 7 August 1919, *CL* 3: 630.

14. Shaw, *The Intelligent Woman's Guide to Socialism and Capitalism,* 339.

15. PI, xxxvi; *SSS,* 36–37.

16. *SSS,* 38. Shaw's last visit to Ireland was in 1923. For an account of Shaw's visits see Nicholas Grene, "Shaw in Ireland: Visitor or Returning Exile?" *SHAW* 5: 45–62.

17. PI, xxxvi.

18. To Mrs. P. Campbell, 3 April 1913, *Bernard Shaw and Mrs. Patrick Campbell: Their Correspondence* (hereafter *Shaw / Campbell*), 115.

19. *Immaturity,* 11, 52.

Chapter 5: Unmaskings and Dublin Curtain

1. See O'Donovan, *Shaw and the Charlatan Genius,* 72–78.

2. To T. D. O'Bolger, February 1916, *CL* 3: 369; Preface to *Music* 1: 52, 43; Holroyd, stating that "it is now possible to put some of these facts back in their original places," relies on McNulty's unsubstantiated report that after the Shaws mutually agreed to separate, George Carr Shaw initiated divorce proceedings, naming Lee. It appears, however, that McNulty took wishful talk for fact. More recently than Holroyd, Dan H. Laurence, editor of the McNulty papers, finds the decision to separate unilateral on Bessie's part: "No evidence exists to indicate that George Carr Shaw accepted the situation other than with his usual diffidence, passivity, and good nature." See Holroyd, *Bernard Shaw* 1: 50, and *SHAW* 12: 20.

3. *SSS,* 92, and to C. M. Shaw, 17 November 1937, *CL* 4: 479; "How To Become a Model Parent," *The Shavian* 1; see also Chappelow, *Chucker-Out,* 35.

4. To Lucy Shaw, 24 February 1875, *CL* 1: 9.

5. To Bessie Shaw, 24 February 1875, *CL* 1: 11–12; *CL* 1: 10.

6. On Lee's ambition see letter to A. Henderson, 3 January 1905, *CL* 2: 500; on Shaw's lack of ambition see letter to T. D. O'Bolger, *CL* 3: 630.

7. Preface to *Music* 1: 35.

8. Preface to *Music* 1:43; to A. Tyrrell, 28 January 1928, *CL* 4: 87.

9. *Hermit:* 1872 entry, *Diaries* 1: 20; see also M. E. McNulty to Shaw, 12 September 1941, *SHAW* 12: 45; on Bell, to A. Henderson, 3 January 1905, *CL* 2: 504–505.

10. Preface to *Music* 1:55.

11. *Evening Post,* Bristol, 3 December 1946, rpt. in *The Matter with Ireland,* 11–13.

12. Preface to *Terry / Shaw,* xxi, on Irving, xxiv, xxxii. On the Dublin stage productions that Shaw attended see *Terry / Shaw,* xviii–xxiv, and PI, xlvii. For a full account of the Dublin theater see Meisel, *Shaw and the Nineteenth-Century Theatre.*

13. *CL* 1: 11; "The New Magdalen and the Old," 2 November 1895, *Drama Observed* 2: 434. Dukore's emendations clarify a confusing line; see *OTN* 1: 243. Dukore's recent work

supersedes *OTN,* but for the convenience of scholars I will note the corresponding *OTN* pages as well.

14. To C. Uniacke Townshend, 29 February 1876, *CL* 1: 14.

15. *Diaries* 1: 27; PI, xxxv.

16. *SSS,* 38 (facing); to C. Uniacke Townshend, 23 March 1875, *CL* 1: 13; Laurence cites Shaw's frugality, *CL* 1: headnote, 14.

17. Foreword, *An Unsocial Socialist, CW* 5: ix.

18. Shaw called himself an "incorrigible histrionic mountebank," *SSS,* 66; on Trefusis as mountebank, *An Unsocial Socialist,* 110; on Henrietta, *An Unsocial Socialist,* 12, 10.

19. PI, xxxvii, xxxvi, xxxviii.

Chapter 6: The Complete Outsider

1. The funeral was on 30 March. Laurence writes that Holroyd "added to the confusion by reporting that Shaw, on his arrival in London, had traveled with his mother and Lucy to Ventnor to attend the funeral." Laurence states that Shaw "did not leave Dublin until two days after the funeral, and did not reach Ventnor until 3 April at earliest" (McNulty, "Memoirs of G. B. S.," *SHAW* 12: 23, footnote 32; Holroyd, *Bernard Shaw* 1: 60).

2. On 13 Victoria Road, PI, vii; to M. E. McNulty, 3 June 1876, *CL* 1: 19.

3. To M. E. McNulty, 3 June 1876, *CL* 1: 19; Preface to *Irrational Knot,* xviii.

4. May 1876, *Diaries* 1: 30.

5. PI, xlviii.

6. *Immaturity,* 95; PI, xxxix.

7. PI, xxxviii; Preface to *Music* 1: 49; to T. D. O'Bolger, February 1916, *CL* 3: 357.

8. Farmer, *Bernard Shaw's Sister and Her Friends,* 31.

9. Introduction, *Music* 1: 13–14; PI, xxxix. Holroyd attributes Shaw's shame to the "deception of ghostwriting," which was "like a step back into cowardice" (*Bernard Shaw* 1: 63).

10. Letter to M. H. Mushlin, 14 December 1947, Henderson, *Man,* 946.

11. To F. Harris, 7 August 1916, *Shaw/Harris,* 36; to Arnold White, 5 October 1879, *CL* 1: 23.

12. *The Hornet* reviews: "Pauline," 29 November 1876, *Music* 1: 62; "English Opera," 6 December 1876, *Music* 1: 67; "Liszt the Charlatan," 20 December 1876, *Music* 1: 73; "Amateur Opera," 2 May 1887, *Music* 1: 120; "The Quicksands of Honest Criticism," 7 March 1877, *Music* 1: 95.

13. "How to Become a Musical Critic," December 1894, *Music* 3: 343–344.

14. Introduction, *Music* 1: 13; "A Typical Popular Vocalist," *The Hornet,* 26 September 1877, *Music* 1: 189; Donald Shaw to Lee, 11 May 1877, British Library, quoted from Holroyd, *Bernard Shaw* 1: 63.

15. Preface to *Music* 1: 49–50.

16. To T. D. O'Bolger, February 1916, *CL* 3: 359, 358.

17. To T. D. O'Bolger, February 1916, *CL* 3: 360

18. To M. H. Mushlin, 14 December 1947, Henderson, *Man,* 946; *scamp:* Preface to *Music* 1: 43; O'Donovan discusses *The Voice* and its author in *Shaw and the Charlatan Genius,* 66, 89,

142–148. *The Voice*, original version, quoted in St. John Ervine, *Bernard Shaw*, 38; Shaw's revision published in Henderson, *Man*, 947–948.

19. *Man*, 948.

20. PI, xxxviii, xlviii.

Chapter 7: Passion's Progress

1. December 1877, *Diaries* 1: 30; PI, xlviii.

2. On homosexuals see Croft-Cooke, *Feasting with Panthers*, 265; *Immaturity*, Shaw's footnote (1930), 73.

3. PI, xxiii, xxvi.

4. *Passion Play, CP* 7: 493, 499, 500.

5. *Passion Play, CP* 7: 502, 498, 494, 491, 497.

6. To Henry Arthur Jones, 11 June 1894, *CL* 1: 444; Rodin to Anthony M. Ludovici, *Personal Reminiscences of Auguste Rodin*, 120–121; from an unpublished memoir of Geraldine Spooner quoted by Weintraub, *Diaries* 1: 366.

7. Barbara Bellow Watson notes that Shaw, through Dorothy, approached society "through the being who stood at the bottom of a hierarchy of dominations" (Watson, *A Shavian Guide to the Intelligent Woman*, 41).

8. *My Dear Dorothea*, footnote, 52.

9. PI, xlii.

Chapter 8: Life Among the Artists

1. To George Bentley, 25 December 1879, *CL* 1: 25; Dan H. Laurence reports that "The Brand of Cain," which disappeared in the mails, concerned a mark on the forehead of a woman murderer. Given Shaw's sense of being indelibly marked, the gender change is of interest. (Holroyd misses the gender change because he transcribes the title as "The Burial of Cain," Holroyd, *Bernard Shaw* 1: 80.) To Richard Bentley & Son, 15 January 1880, *CL* 1: 26.

2. Preface to *Music* 1:29; PI, xlii; to Macmillan & Co., 1 February 1880, *CL* 1: 27.

3. *Immaturity*, 130.

4. *Immaturity*, 99–100.

5. *Immaturity*, 82.

6. To A. White, 5 October 1879, *CL* 1: 23–24; additional paragraph of that letter printed in Ervine, *Bernard Shaw*, 65.

7. *distasteful:* Edison Telephone Co. entry, *Diaries* 1: 22; *worried*, PI, xxxix; to Mr. Dauglish, 31 December 1879, *CL* 1: 25–26.

8. Preface to *Irrational Knot*, ix; Edison Telephone Co. entry, *Diaries* 1: 23; 5 June 1880, *Diaries* 1: 31.

9. September 1881, *Diaries* 1: 32; Preface to *Irrational Knot*, xviii; to Hubert Bland, 18 November 1889, *CL* 1: 228–229.

10. Preface to *Irrational Knot*, xxii.

11. *Irrational Knot*, 349; Lucy as Primrose, December 1879, *Diaries* 1: 31. For more on Lucy's acting career see Farmer.

12. PI, xlv.

13. Edel, *Henry James*, 329, 284, 275; letter to Grace Norton, 7 July 1878, quoted in Edel, 279; Charles MacMahon Shaw, *Bernard's Brethren*, 110 (facing).

14. To A. Henderson, 3 January 1905, *CL* 2: 505; on Aileen Bell see April 7 entry and Weintraub's note, *Diaries* 1: 75. For the decade 1875–1885, Shaw's "diary" consists of sketchy sporadic notes.

15. March 1879, *Diaries* 1: 30; *Temperament:* to A. Henderson, 3 January 1905, *CL* 2: 484; on Deck see *SSS*, 64; first entry, 1880, *Diaries* 1: 31; Preface to *Pygmalion, CP* 4: 659–663.

16. On Lady Wilde and her receptions see H. Pearson, *Oscar Wilde, 93–94;* November 1879, *Diaries* 1: 31.

17. Prince of Wales quoted in Ellmann, *Oscar Wilde,* 128; to F. Harris, 7 August 1916, *Shaw / Harris,* 30.

18. *Shaw / Harris,* 35; on aesthete as euphemism see Ellmann, *Oscar Wilde,* 84.

19. On didactic art, see, e.g., Preface to *Pygmalion, CP* 4: 663; *Shaw / Harris,* 30; to Max Beerbohm, 15 September 1903, *CL* 2: 374.

20. *Shaw / Harris,* 34.

21. To Elizabeth Lawson, 16 January 1880, *CL* 1: 29.

22. James, *A Portrait of a Lady,* chap. 43. On the cultural and personal meaning of the waltz see my articles "From Eroticism to Transcendence" and "The Elegant Passion."

23. *Immaturity,* 136, 267. Because Holroyd misreads Hawkshaw as "Hawksmith, (a sort of Smith gone wrong)," he loses the autobiographical echo (Holroyd, *Bernard Shaw* 1: 75). For a critical analysis of the novels see Dietrich, *Portrait of the Artist as a Young Superman.*

24. Preface to *Irrational Knot,* xviii; lecture of 22 May 1884, "Our Lost Honesty," in *The Road to Equality,* 5.

25. Epistle Dedicatory, *Man and Superman, CP* 2: 519–520.

26. On joining Zetetical Society, 28 October 1880, *Diaries* 1: 31, letters to J. M. Fells of 24 and 25 October 1880, *CL* 1: 34–35; on Shaw's nervousness see "How I Became a Public Speaker," *SSS,* 56–57; see also Henderson's corroboration from a witness (apparently Fells), *Man,* 138.

Chapter 9: Marked by Mortality

1. December 1880, January 1881, and May 1881, *Diaries* 1: 31.

2. See letters to Richard Bentley & Son, 14 July 1881, to Smith, Elder & Co., 14 July 1881, to J. M. Fells, 23 August 1881, to Lee, 24 August 1881, to Pattie Moye, 25 September 1881, *CL* 1: 38–41; May and October 1881, *Diaries* 1: 31–32.

3. To J. M. Fells, *CL* 1: 40.

4. Winsten, *Salt and His Circle,* 217.

5. 5 October 1926, *Doctors' Delusions, CW* 22 (hereafter *DD):* 106.

6. Henderson notes the location of the pockmarks, *Man,* 81; on the Mayas see Manning and Fabrega, "Experience of Self and Body," 264–265.

7. Quoted in Henderson, *Playboy and Prophet,* 660.

8. February, *Diaries* 1: 32; to J. M. Fells, 30 January 1882, *CL* 1: 47.

9. *Love Among the Artists, CW* 3: 99.

10. Preface to *Music* 1: 42.

11. No study examines the personal meaning of Shaw's feelings about medicine. The single study on Shaw and the medical profession puts Shaw's ideas in the context of the humanist tradition of medical history (see Boxill, *Shaw and the Doctors*). Some typical comments: Bertrand Russell finds that Shaw's "whole attitude in biological matters was antiscientific" ("George Bernard Shaw," 4); William Irvine charges Shaw with "prejudice and eccentricity" (*Universe of G. B. S.*, 274); Holroyd states that "Shaw's campaign against vaccination formed part of his objection to the rising superstition of science" (Holroyd, *Bernard Shaw* 1: 92).

12. *CP* 6: 437.

13. Review of Edmund Gurney's *Tertium Quid*, "Tertium Quiddities," *Pall Mall Gazette*, 2 December 1887, collected in *Bernard Shaw's Book Reviews* (hereafter *Book Reviews*), 370–371.

14. Preface to *DD*, xiv; *Everybody's Political What's What* (hereafter *Everybody's*), 247. See also "The Revolutionist's Handbook," *CP* 2: 795. On the Victorian concept of health see Haley, *Healthy Body*.

15. To C. Payne-Townshend, 8 April 1898, *CL* 2: 29.

16. Quoted in Haley, *Healthy Body*, 117.

17. *DD*, 84, 71; *murder:* stock letter reply, Chappelow, *Chucker-Out*, 24; on baby see *DD*, 10.

18. *DD*, 106; on decline in typhoid deaths see *DD*, 131; *DD*, 72; on grandfather see *DD*, 75.

19. Eric Bentley writes that Shaw deals in half-truths—"a side of the truth which deserves special notice"—and calls the "Preface on Doctors" introducing *Doctor's Dilemma* the "outstanding account" of the "social pathology" of doctors (*Bernard Shaw*, 73, 83). *DD*, 122, 9–10.

20. Lecture at the Queen's Large Hall, London, 22 May 1900, published in *Shaw on Vivisection*, 16; on being typified and objectified see *DD*, 63–65.

21. *saviors: DD*, 85; *DD*, 51; *instep: Everybody's*, 241–242; see also "G. B. S. Vivisected," 14 May 1898, *Drama Observed* 3: 1056–1059, and *OTN* 3: 401–405; on carbolic acid see "Preface on Doctors," *CP* 3: 250; on croup, to Leo Tolstoy, 14 February 1910, *CL* 2: 902; see also *The Shewing-Up of Blanco Posnet; phagocytes: Everybody's*, 244.

22. On Shaw's disgust at tobacco smoke see *SSS*, 97–98; *stank: Everybody's*, 242; *drenched: DD*, 83; *darkness: Everybody's*, 242.

23. *DD*, 106; *Everybody's*, 247.

24. *DD*, 8–9.

25. *DD*, 77. On the role of myth in the structure of *Man and Superman* see my article "Ann and Superman."

26. Henderson, *Playboy*, 659; Nichols, *All I Could Never Be*, 145–146. Nichols, who was more than forty years younger than Shaw, recalled Edward Bootle-Wilbraham, fifth Earl of Lathom, being sprayed with the fragrance New Mown Hay while arrogantly praising the inspired odor of "Suivez moi, jeune homme" ("Follow me, young man"), and remembered that Ned Lathom found "plenty of young men eager enough to follow him" (43).

Chapter 10: Yearning for Fragility

1. Quoted in Elliot, *Dear Mr Shaw*, 149.

2. Shaw wrote E. D. Girdlestone that he did not drink coffee, 10 September 1890, *CL* 1: 262. His diary, however, which provides a wealth of detail on his eating places and habits, shows him indulging on rare occasions; see, e.g., 24 November 1886 and 31 January 1887, *Diaries* 1: 215, 238.

3. 1931 comment quoted in Elliot, *Dear Mr Shaw*, 157; *SSS*, 58; to Denis Wennling, 16 November 1928, *CL* 4: 117; from Doris Arthur Jones, *Taking the Curtain Call*, 187.

4. Holroyd, like Henderson, agrees with Shaw's self-analysis that he was a different man after becoming a vegetarian. In contrast, H. Pearson notes that Shaw "had plenty of energy before he became a vegetarian." (Holroyd, *Bernard Shaw* 1: 90; Henderson, *Man*, 782; H. Pearson, *George Bernard Shaw*, 67.) Dervin calls Shaw's vegetarianism the remains of an infantile "jungle of orality" *(Bernard Shaw*, 44); for Holland, Shaw was "a man much concerned with his mouth, but less with taking in . . . more with keeping things out of it" (*The I*, 61).

5. To Sylvia Beach, 13 November 1949, *CL* 4: 858; see also letter to Cliff Keane, 12 January 1914, *CL* 3: 216; Elliot, *Dear Mr Shaw*, 149.

6. To A. Henderson, Henderson, *Man*, 777.

7. From the manuscript of *The Voice*, published in Henderson, *Man*, 947.

8. To C. Keane, 12 January 1914, *CL* 3: 216; "Morris as I Knew Him," introduction to Morris, *William Morris: Artist, Writer, Socialist*, 2: xxiv; "Herbert Ward's Africa," *The World*, 24 July 1889, collected in *London Art*, 291; *SSS*, 53. In the Preface to *Farfetched Fables*, Shaw calls transubstantiation the "heathen rite of eating the god" (*CP* 7: 398).

9. Stock reply, printed postcard, Laurence, *A Bibliography* 2: 844; *CP* 2: 686; *CP* 5: 597, 623.

10. Quoted from Henderson, *Man*, 781; on Pepys, see Raymond Blathwayt "What Vegetarianism Really Means: A Talk with Mr Bernard Shaw," *Vegetarian*, 15 January 1898, 41; see also *Interviews*, 402; *CP* 7: 448; to S. Trebitsch, 23 August 1950, *Bernard Shaw's Letters to Siegfried Trebitsch* (hereafter *Shaw / Trebitsch*), 468.

11. To Mrs. H. Ward, 1 December 1897, *CL* 1: 824; to C. Payne-Townshend, 4 April 1898, *CL* 2: 27.

12. *Diaries* 1: 31; to T. D. O'Bolger, 16 March 1920, *CL* 3: 672; to J. Achurch, 8 July 1895, *CL* 1: 539; to E. D. Girdlestone, 18 September 1890, *CL* 1: 263.

13. To Mrs. T. P. O'Connor, 17 May 1888, *CL* 1: 189; to E. D. Girdlestone, 10 September 1890, *CL* 1: 262; to E. D. Girdlestone, 18 September 1890, *CL* 1: 263; on boiling, to C. Keane, 12 January 1914, *CL* 3: 216; *anorexia:* to H. S. Salt, 29 August 1938, *CL* 4: 507.

14. "The Conflict Between Science and Common Sense," *Humane Review*, April 1900, quoted from Henderson, *Man*, 783; "Life Without Meat," *Daily Chronicle*, 1 March 1918, *DD*, 157–158, 161; to E. Terry, 3 March 1897, *CL* 1: 729; *stoked up: DD*, 161.

15. To H. S. Salt, 29 August 1938, *CL* 4: 506; *Back to Methuselah, CP* 5: 630; H. Pearson, *George Bernard Shaw*, 330.

16. *Back to Methuselah, CP* 5: 623; *Shaw on Vivisection*, 16.

17. On dissection see letter to A. Henderson, 17 January 1905, Henderson, *Man*, 37; on Bessie and *The Voice* see letter to M. H. Mushlin, 14 December 1947, Henderson, *Man*, 946–947; on castrati see "Singing, Past and Present," *Music* 1: 326–327. For a medical perspective on the castrati see Peschel and Peschel, "Medical Insights into the Castrati in Opera."

18. "Looking Backward," in *Shaw on Vivisection*, 56.

19. *Man and Superman*, CP 2: 557.

20. To E. Terry, 5 August 1897, CL 1: 792; *Back to Methuselah*, CP 5: 623.

Chapter 11: The Noble Art

1. See April 1882 summary entry, *Diaries* 1: 32; for a sketch of Beatty see Laurence's headnote, CL 1: 19–20.

2. Badcock includes pieces by Egan in a two-volume work published in 1826. See *Selections from the Fancy: or True Sportsman's Guide*, by An Operator [Badcock], with a foreword by George Plimpton (Barre, Mass.: Imprint Society, 1972). See also Pierce Egan, *Boxiana: Sketches of Ancient and Modern Pugilism* (London: G. Smeeton, 1812).

3. Shaw said the model for Byron was the boxer Jack Burke, a remark causing much confusion. It has not been previously recognized by scholars tracking Byron's model that there were *two* Jack Burkes (not to mention the English champion James "Deaf" Burke earlier in the century), and the wrong Burke has been cited. Shaw's Burke was the "Irish Lad" (1861–1897), a scientific English pugilist (weight range 154 to 170 pounds) who engaged in brief contests (a number of them in Australia and South Africa) and whose opponents included American heavyweight champion John L. Sullivan. There was also the 130-pound Texan "Young Jack Burke" (ca. 1863–1913), who in 1893 fought Andy Bowen to a draw in New Orleans in the longest recorded glove fight in boxing annals—110 rounds, lasting seven hours and nineteen minutes—one of the feats regularly attributed to Shaw's Burke.

4. *romantic coward: Sunday News*, 10 July 1927, rpt. in *Shaw's Champions* (hereafter *Champions*), 159; Green usefully reprints a number of Shaw letters and articles on boxing; *imaginary reputation:* "64 Years Later," typescript Preface added March–April 1946 to the manuscript of *Cashel Byron's Profession*, first published in *Shaw: An Autobiography 1856–1898* 1: 98; Stanley Weintraub traces Shaw's interest in the sport in "G. B. S., Pugilist and Playwright," *The Unexpected Shaw: Biographical Approaches to G. B. S. and His Work* (New York: Frederick Ungar, 1982), 37–45; *boxing . . . pardonable:* "Bernard Shaw on the Defeat of Carpentier," *Sunday Chronicle*, 1 October 1922, rpt. in *Champions*, 128. In 1884 anthropometric devices weighed the fully dressed Shaw at 142 pounds (Henderson, *Life*, 493).

5. To G. Tunney, 9 June 1948, CL 4: 821.

6. See 23 and 31 March 1885, *Diaries* 1: 72, 74; 11, 13, and 14 April 1885, *Diaries* 1: 76–77; 18 May 1885, *Diaries* 1: 85; 9 November 1885, *Diaries* 1: 124.

7. *noble:* Preface to *Cashel Byron's Profession*, CW 4: xii, and letter to P. Beatty, 6 April 1901, CL 2: 225; 13 April 1885, *Diaries* 1: 77.

8. *Cashel Byron's Profession*, 65; to Norman Clark, 15 December 1919, CL 3: 649.

9. Preface to *The Admirable Bashville*, CP 2: 433.

10. For full details of parallels between Shaw's hero and Corbett and Tunney, see Green,

Champions. On Tunney as Cashel, Shaw is quoted in Henderson, *Man*, 102, note 14; on Brioni see letters to Tunney, 31 August 1928, 24 April 1929, and Tunney's account in Green, *Champions*, 176–177. Tunney wrote about his career and on boxing science. He called the straight left-hand jab to the face (Shaw's best punch) "the most useful punch in the boxer's list"; see Tunney, *Boxing and Training* (New York: A. G. Spalding and Bros., 1928), 5. Henderson, like Tunney, lectured at Yale University, but on Shaw, not Shakespeare, and requested a manuscript on behalf of the university. Shaw replied: "I cannot understand this Yale business. What is Yale? They make locks, don't they?" 4 May 1922, Beinecke Rare Book and Manuscript Library; see also Henderson, *Playboy*, 21.

11. On Tunney to N. Clark, 21 February 1929, *CL* 4: 130; *seamy:* "The Great Fight, By the Author of 'Cashel Byron's Profession,'" *The Nation*, 13 December 1919; *no sports:* "64 Years Later," *Shaw: An Autobiography* 1: 98; *instantaneous:* Preface to *Cashel Byron's Profession*, xvii. Shaw's formulation resembles Jean-Paul Sartre's "the body is *lived* and not *known*"; see *Being and Nothingness*, 324. Sartre further emphasizes the primacy of such body knowledge in the formulation: "J'existe mon corps: telle est sa première dimension d'etre," using *existe* as a transitive verb; see Jean-Paul Sartre, *L'être et le néant* (Paris: Librairie Gallimard, 1943), 418.

12. Preface to *Cashel Byron's Profession*, x–xi.

13. *Cashel Byron's Profession*, 89, 140, 25.

14. To A. Tyrrell, 8 June 1937, *CL* 4: 469; to Lewis Wynne, 26 November 1928, *CL* 4: 121; *Cashel Byron's Profession*, 91; "64 Years Later," *Shaw: An Autobiography* 1: 98.

15. *CP* 2: 475.

16. *Cashel Byron's Profession*, 36–38.

17. Lawrence, *Lady Chatterley's Lover*, 66; "A Propos of *Lady Chatterley's Lover*," 318–319.

18. Preceding several paragraphs, "The Great Fight," *The Nation*, 13 December 1919, rpt. in *Champions*, 102–105.

19. To N. Clark, 15 December 1919, *CL* 3: 649; "The Great Fight," *The Nation*, 13 December 1919, rpt. in *Champions*, 106.

20. On ancient Greek boxing matches see J. A. Symonds, "A Problem in Greek Ethics," in Ellis and Symonds, *Sexual Inversion*, 208; "The Great Fight," *The Nation*, 13 December 1919, rpt. in *Champions*, 107; *Cashel Byron's Profession*, 145.

21. To Lawrence Langner, 3 April 1940, *CL* 4: 551; *The Millionairess*, *CP* 6: 892.

22. "George Bernard Shaw Finds Prize Fighting Not So Sanguinary," *Evening World*, 9 July 1927, p. 12, col. 1; *CP* 2: 465.

23. Ernest Hemingway, *Death in the Afternoon* (New York: Charles Scribner's Sons, 1932), 247, and on the old lady see esp. 70–71, 82, 95; "Carpentier-Siki Scandal," *Sunday Chronicle*, 10 December 1922, rpt. in *Champions*, 130–134.

24. To S. Winsten, in *Shaw's Corner*, 195.

25. To G. S. Viereck, 24 February 1926, *CL* 4: 14; "Carpentier-Siki Scandal," *Sunday Chronicle*, 10 December 1922, rpt. in *Champions*, 131.

26. In the 1899 edition of *Who's Who*, under "Exercises" Shaw wrote "anything except sport"; to Kathleen Hilton Young, 20 May 1926, *CL* 4: 23; McCarthy, *Myself and My Friends*, 88.

27. *Heartbreak House*, *CP* 5: 176.

Chapter 12: Socialism and Salvation

1. PI, xviii–xix, xxxvi.

2. To H. Garland, 29 December 1904, *CL* 2: 476; "Who I Am, and What I Think," *The Candid Friend*, 11 May 1901. The passage quoted here is not in *SSS;* see Laurence, *Selected Non-Dramatic Writings of Bernard Shaw*, 448. Holroyd writes that "George's book enabled Shaw to come to terms with his own past." However, Shaw never came to terms with his past, and George had an entirely different meaning for the life history (see Holroyd, *Bernard Shaw* 1: 128).

3. Preface to *Saint Joan, CP* 6: 33.

4. *CP* 6: 20; *SSS,* 66.

5. *SSS,* 66–67.

6. Shaw's Preface to Winsten, *Salt and His Circle,* 13; "How William Archer impressed Bernard Shaw," *Pen Portraits,* 3.

7. Preface to *Irrational Knot,* viii; "The New Politics," in *The Road to Equality* (hereafter *Road*), 84; *SSS,* 58, 50.

8. To A. Henderson, 3 January 1905, *CL* 2: 486; "Special Report" of Fabian Conference, 11 June 1886, British Library of Political and Economic Science, quoted in Willard Wolfe, *From Radicalism to Socialism,* 123; H. Pearson, *George Bernard Shaw,* 68.

9. *SSS,* 49.

10. *SSS,* 59.

11. *SSS,* 50; "The New Politics," *Road,* 85.

12. PI, xix; *An Unsocial Socialist,* 110; on the capitalist as highwayman see "Our Lost Honesty," *Road,* 4–11. See also "The Economic Basis of Socialism," in *Essays in Fabian Socialism, CW* 30: 3–30, and "Socialism and Human Nature," *Road,* 100.

13. *SSS,* 109.

14. W. L. Phillips, *Why Are the Many Poor?* Tract no. 1, Fabian Society, London, 1884; Shaw, *The Fabian Society: What It Has Done and How It Has Done It,* Tract no. 41, Fabian Society (1892), in *Essays in Fabian Socialism;* on Hyndman's Federation see "The New Politics," *Road,* 87; on Marx and Engels see Weeks, *Coming Out,* 144–145.

15. Shaw, *A Manifesto,* Fabian Tract no. 2, Fabian Society, London, 1884. Pease reprints the tract in *The History of the Fabian Society,* 41–43.

16. *SSS,* 65.

17. To Ada Breakell ca. February 1884, in Doris Langley Moore, *E. Nesbit,* 76; Harris, *Bernard Shaw,* 80; minutes, Fabian Papers, Oxford, quoted in *The Fabians,* 71; Winsten, *Salt and His Circle,* 207.

18. On fatalism see "Our Lost Honesty," *Road,* 17; on will, from the manuscript Shaw showed to Henderson (*Life,* 488).

19. "University Economics," *Pall Mall Gazette,* 26 December 1888, *Book Reviews,* 461; Shaw, "What Socialism Will Be Like," lecture of 12 July 1896, *Platform and Pulpit,* 31. For a lucid discussion of collectivism and an account of Shaw's fling with anarchism see Wolfe, *From Radicalism to Socialism,* 251–291.

20. On C. Wilson and reading circle see 1884 and 1885 summary notes, *Diaries* 1: 33, 54; "The Fabian Society," *Essays in Fabian Socialism,* 129–130; 19 September 1890, *Diaries* 1: 650; "Socialism and Human Nature," *Road,* 101.

21. "The Fabian Society," *Essays in Fabian Socialism,* 138; Annie Besant, *An Autobiography,* 325; see also *Pall Mall Gazette,* 15 November 1887.

22. *Pall Mall Gazette,* 14 November 1887; 13 November 1887, *Diaries* 1: 314–315; *skedaddled:* to W. Morris, 22 November 1887, *CL* 1:177; on Annie as heroine see "The Fabian Society," *Essays in Fabian Socialism,* 139.

23. Eleanor Marx to Laura Lafargue, 16 November 1887, in Kapp, *Eleanor Marx* 2: 229; to W. Morris, 22 November 1887, *CL* 1: 177; H. Pearson, *George Bernard Shaw,* 83.

24. "Fabian Essays Twenty Years Later," Preface to the 1908 Reprint of *Essays in Fabian Socialism,* 304; "Fabian Essays Forty Years Later: What They Overlooked," Preface to the 1931 Reprint of *Essays in Fabian Socialism,* 320. Holroyd misreads the passage as "Morris was not right," thereby reversing Shaw's meaning (*Bernard Shaw* 1: 190).

25. Napoleon quoted in Spengler, *Decline of the West* 1: 144; from the manuscript Shaw showed to Henderson (*Life,* 487).

26. "The New Radicalism," *Road,* 31, 35.

27. "The Economic Basis of Socialism," *Essays in Fabian Socialism,* 30; "Socialism and Human Nature," *Road,* 96, 100.

28. To C. Charrington, 28 January 1890, *CL* 1: 238.

29. On Shaw and Stalinism see Bentley, "Shaw in 1978," in *Thinking about the Playwright,* 86–97. Through the Fabians, Shaw achieved political influence. Fabians infiltrated the ranks of civil servants, trade-union officials, and politicians and helped organize the Labour Party (in 1906), with which they still have close ties.

Chapter 13: The Jaegerized Butterfly

1. On Shaw's "rurophobia" see "A Sunday on the Surrey Hills," *Pall Mall Gazette,* 25 April 1888, rpt. in *Short Stories, Scraps and Shavings,* 217–221; *Noble Savage:* Shaw's Preface to Winsten, *Salt and His Circle,* 12.

2. On Victorian water cures see Haley, *The Healthy Body and Victorian Culture,* 16–17.

3. Shaw's "history of quack medicine" remains unlocated; Laurence describes it in *A Bibliography* 2: 881–882.

4. On little girl, 7 September 1887, *Diaries* 1: 297; on spectacles, 28 September 1887, *Diaries* 1: 301. Exceedingly spare, written with clipped phrases and abbreviations, Shaw's diary richly reflects his quotidian reality and is more instructive than the notes of 1875–1885. But it is not a journal of ideas or meditations, nor of secret thoughts and feelings.

5. 1885 summary entries, *Diaries* 1: 53–54.

6. 11 January 1885, *Diaries* 1: 55; 28 March 1887, *Diaries* 1: 73.

7. On multiple activities, 21 March 1885, *Diaries* 1: 71; 6 April 1885, *Diaries* 1: 75; 30 January 1885, *Diaries* 1: 56–57.

8. 25 March 1885, *Diaries* 1: 72.

9. To J. Kingston Barton, 19 April 1885, *CL* 1: 132; on holiday, to St. John Ervine, 11 May 1936, *CL* 4: 431. Holroyd writes "brave" instead of "Grave," thereby missing the pun—and Shaw's state of mind (*Bernard Shaw* 1: 122).

10. To R. Frederick Shaw, 23 April 1885, *CL* 1: 134; see also Laurence's headnote on the financial affairs of the family, 133.

11. To Mrs. W. Archer, 18 March 1885, *CL* 1: 127; to J. L. Mahon, 13 April 1885, *CL* 1: 131–132.

12. 20–24 April 1885, *Diaries* 1: 78–79.

13. On putting papers in order and boxing see 18 and 19 May 1885, *Diaries* 1: 85; 1 June 1885, *Diaries* 1: 88; Shaw's note is unclear, but because he does not list the expense, the braces appear to be for Archer; 10 August 1885, *Diaries* 1: 103.

14. 19 June 1885, *Diaries* 1:91.

15. To T. D. O'Bolger, 7 August 1919, *CL* 3: 630.

16. Harris, *Bernard Shaw*, 102; of Shaw's Jaeger clothes Holroyd concludes that "the woollen Shaw look[ed] at women more confidently" (*Bernard Shaw* 1: 161).

17. 11 August 1885, *Diaries* 1: 103.

18. Harris, *Bernard Shaw*, 103. The self-interview is reprinted as "The Playwright on His First Play," in *CP* 1: 122–132. On *You Never Can Tell*, rpt. from chap. 16 of Cyril Maude's *The Haymarket Theatre*, written by Shaw, *CP* 1: 802.

19. On underwear see "Shaw's Portrait by Shaw, or How Frank Ought to Have Done It," in Harris, *Contemporary Portraits*, 328; see also *SSS*, 126. There are numerous entries in the diary noting trips to Jaeger's: e.g., coat, 14 April 1886; hat, 6 May 1886; boots, shirts, pants, 15 January 1887, *Diaries* 1: 161, 167, 234; on gloves see Maud Churton Braby, "Dress and the Writer: A Talk with Mr George Bernard Shaw," *World of Dress*, March 1905, rpt. in *Interviews*, 403. On clothing reform see Newton, *Health, Art and Reason*. Knee breeches were also worn in court and by athletes and aesthetes. Earlier, Oscar Wilde had favored knee breeches.

20. For the stories in greater detail see Henderson, *Life*, 491–492; Harris, *Bernard Shaw*, 104–106.

21. To I. Beatty, 4 September 1885, *CL* 1: 138; to C. Charrington, 8 November 1895, *CL* 1: 569.

22. *Punch*, 31 March 1883.

23. To E. Terry, 5 October 1896, *CL* 1: 673. J. C. Flugel calls the development of austerity in male dress "The Great Masculine Renunciation" (see Flugel, *Psychology of Clothes*, 110–113 and chap. titled "Protection," 68–84).

24. To E. Terry, 31 December 1897, *CL* 1: 839–840.

Chapter 14: Overfed on Honeydew

1. *CP* 2: 665.

2. *Diaries* 1: 26, 30. On verses see McNulty, "Memoirs of G. B. S."; on the identity of Calypso see Laurence's footnote same page, *SHAW* 12: 27.

3. 1876 entry, *Diaries* 1: 30; *Immaturity*, 76.

4. 15 January 1888, *Diaries* 1: 339; to the Rev. Stewart Headlam, 26 December 1922, *CL* 3: 802.

5. 1877, 1888, and 1879 summary entries, *Diaries* 1: 30. On "La Carbonaja," both Weintraub and Laurence note the pun; see *Diaries* 1: footnote 1, 34, and headnotes in *CL* 1: 593 and *CL* 3: 801.

6. Verse quoted from headnote, *CL* 1: 63.

7. *grown up:* to Alice Lockett, 11 September 1883, *CL* 1: 65; *vilest:* to A. Lockett, 9 July 1884, *CL* 1: 91; J. Lockett to Shaw, quoted in headnote, *CL* 1: 96; *dual:* to A. Lockett, 6 November, *CL* 1: 72; *An Unsocial Socialist*, 198, 199.

8. *An Unsocial Socialist*, 178; to V. O. Plenazár, 15 July 1929, *CL* 4: 154.

9. On chains, to A. Lockett, 9 September 1883, *CL* 1: 64; *rescue:* 11 September 1883, *CL* 1: 65; *wretch:* 29 November 1883, *CL* 1: 75; *devil:* 19 November 1883, *CL* 1: 73.

10. Epistle Dedicatory to *Man and Superman*, *CP* 2: 498–499; 1884 summary entry, *Diaries* 1: 33; on old flame, to C. Payne-Townshend, 7 November 1897, *CL* 1: 822.

11. E. Huddart to Shaw, 4 January 1881, in Hugo, "Very Innocent Epistles," *SHAW* 10: 5, Shaw's relationship with Huddart outlined 1–11; to A. Lockett, 16 October 1884, *CL* 1: 100.

12. To A. Lockett, 5 November 1883, *CL* 1: 70; 19 August 1886, *CL* 1: 158; on Bessie, 13 October 1884, *CL* 1: 98; A. Lockett to Shaw, 15 October 1884, *CL* 1: 98.

13. To A. Lockett, 16 October 1884, *CL* 1: 99; A. Lockett to Shaw, 7 October 1883, *CL* 1: 67.

14. *dual self:* to A. Lockett, 11 September 1883, *CL* 1: 66, and 19 August 1886, *CL* 1: 158; 7 July 1884, *CL* 1: 90.

15. To A. Lockett, 19 August 1886, *CL* 1: 158.

16. To A. Lockett, 19 August 1884, *CL* 1: 95; to M. E. McNulty, 3 June 1876, *CL* 1: 19.

17. M. E. McNulty to Shaw, 17 February 1883, McNulty, "Memoirs of G. B. S.," *SHAW* 12: 31. McNulty puts Shaw's request to destroy their letters as coming "some years" after Shaw arrived in London. Much later Shaw alludes to the destroyed letters but places the action within the time frame of his Dublin years (*SHAW* 12: 27; *SSS*, 33); on Lucy and McNulty, November 1876, *Diaries* 1: 30.

18. To A. Lockett, 9 September 1883, *CL* 1: 64.

19. Letters to each other, 11 September 1883, *CL* 1: 65; letters to each other, 6 November 1883, *CL* 1: 71.

20. To A. Lockett, 19 August 1884 *CL* 1: 95; to A. Lockett, 8 October 1883, *CL* 1: 68.

21. To A. Lockett, 8 October 1885, *CL* 1: 142–143; *children:* to A. Lockett, 6 November 1883, *CL* 1: 72.

Chapter 15: Seduced and Betrayed

1. To F. Harris, 24 June 1930, *CL* 4: 191.

2. On properties, to Dorothy Massingham, 13 January 1925, *CL* 3: 900; *virgin:* to F. Harris, *CL* 4: 191; 4, 10, and 13 July 1885, *Diaries* 1: 95–96.

3. 17 and 18 July 1885, *Diaries* 1: 97.

4. 19 to 24 July 1885, *Diaries* 1: 98–99.

5. 25 July 1885, *Diaries* 1: 99; summary entry, *Diaries* 1: 55.

6. Byron, *Don Juan*, canto 1, stanza 117; to D. Massingham, *CL* 3: 899–900; Epistle Dedicatory to *Man and Superman*, *CP* 2: 507.

7. To F. Harris, 20 June 1930, *CL* 4: 189; to F. Harris, 24 June 1930, *CL* 4: 191; *Back to Methuselah*, *CP* 5: 348; to F. Harris, 24 June 1930, *CL* 4: 192.

8. 26, 28, and 29 July 1885, *Diaries* 1: 99–100.

9. 30 July to 3 August 1885, *Diaries* 1: 100–101.

10. 3 August to 5 August 1885, *Diaries* 1: 101–102.

11. 25 July 1885, *Diaries* 1: 99.

12. 1885 summary entry, *Diaries* 1: 55.

13. See, e.g., 29 December 1885 and 15 August 1886, *Diaries* 1: 128, 191. Amazingly, given the number of readers of the diaries, this juxtaposition of "Mother" has escaped notice. Weintraub writes that the code "apparently included failed opportunities (o)" (note for 2 August 1885, *Diaries* 1: 101); to G. Murray, 14 March 1911, *CL* 3:17.

14. To F. Harris, 24 June 1930, *CL* 4: 192.

15. 7, 10, 14, 15, and 16 September 1885, *Diaries* 1: 110–111; "Historical Instruments," 19 September 1885, *Music* 1: 360.

16. 21 September 1885, *Diaries* 1: 113; to I. Beatty, 22 September 1885, *CL* 1: 140. See also 22 and 27 September 1885, *Diaries* 1: 113–114; *SSS*, 59.

17. J. Patterson to Shaw on 28 May 1886 quotes his letter to her of 22 September 1885, British Library (hereafter BL) (quoted from M. Peters, *Bernard Shaw and the Actresses*, 31). Peters richly and sensitively details Shaw's day-to-day interactions with women and has not been supplanted in this area by more recent biographical forays. We agree that Shaw harbored ambivalent feelings toward women. But we treat those phenomena differently and come to quite different conclusions about their meaning, Peters attributing Shaw's behavior to "puritanism," a split between intellect and passion (see 46–47).

18. 10 February 1886, *Diaries* 1: 145.

19. *insatiable:* to F. Harris, 24 June 1930, *CL* 4: 192; on advertising prospectus see Preface to *Music* 1: 50, and 6 January 1886, *Diaries* 1: 137; 9 and 12 January 1886, *Diaries* 1: 138; on his rivals, 22 July 1889, *Diaries* 1: 524.

20. 9 and 13 May 1886, *Diaries* 1: 168–169; 26 June 1886, *Diaries* 1: 179; also 1885 summary entry, *Diaries* 1: 34. On 28 June, Shaw repaid the florin, *Diaries* 1: 180.

21. Moore, *E. Nesbit*, 76, 84; see E. Bland's letter to Olive Schreiner (n.d.) and Schreiner's letter to Havelock Ellis (October 1888), quoted in Moore, 110. Schreiner's *Story of an African Farm* was published in 1883 under the pseudonym Ralph Iron.

22. 1885 summary entry and 11 May 1887, *Diaries* 1: 34, 268; Shaw quotes E. Bland to Molly Tompkins, 22 February 1925, *CL* 3: 904–905; Moore, *E. Nesbit*, 84. Apparently 29 Fitzroy Square was conducive to the writing life. Virginia Woolf would later live at that address, which is on the west side of the square.

23. Jenny's letter of 11 May 1886 quoted in *CL* 1: 151; to I. Beatty, 10 March *CL* 1: 150–151; to J. Patterson, 10 March, *CL* 1: 152.

24. 31 December 1885, *Diaries* 1: 134.

25. 23 September 1888, *Diaries* 1: 415; to E. Terry, 8 September 1897, *CL* 1: 801–802.

26. 16 October 1891, *Diaries* 2: 760; letters to *The Star* of 17 July 1893 and 25 July 1893, reprinted in Laurence and Rambeau, *Agitations: Letters to the Press, 1875–1950*, 25–30.

27. *The Quintessence of Ibsenism, MCE*, 38; M. Peters notes Jenny's influence behind this passage (*Bernard Shaw and the Actresses*, 87–88). For the relation of *Quintessence* to the drama see Turco, *Shaw's Moral Vision*, and Wisenthal, *Marriage of Contraries*.

28. *Quintessence, MCE*, 44.

29. On taking the letters see 24 December 1887, *Diaries* 1: 326; Jenny's note of 25 Decem-

ber 1887 quotes Shaw's letter to Annie, BL, in M. Peters, *Bernard Shaw and the Actresses*, 44; J. Patterson to Shaw, 23 August 1887, BL, in Holroyd, *Bernard Shaw* 1: 250; on Jenny pleading, quoted in M. Peters, *Bernard Shaw and the Actresses*, 31–32; 47; J. Patterson to Shaw, 20 October 1888, BL, in M. Peters, *Bernard Shaw and the Actresses*, 47.

30. To T. D. O'Bolger, February 1916, *CL* 3: 364.

31. *CP* 3: 583, 627, 622.

32. *CP* 4: 317.

33. To Lady Rhondda, 20 April, 1930, *CL* 4: 183; to Herbert Brewer, January 1937, *CL* 4: 460.

34. Preface to *Music* 1: 50; 30 November, 1 December, *Diaries* 1: 217–218; to A. Henderson, 3 January 1905, *CL* 2: 500; McNulty, "Memoirs of G. B. S.," *SHAW* 12: 19; to T. D. O'Bolger, *CL* 3: 360.

35. To T. D. O'Bolger, 3 November 1921, *CL* 3: 746, 747, and 14 June 1922, *CL* 3: 774, 775; to Ignatius MacHugh, 24 August 1923, *CL* 3: 844–845.

36. To Viola Tree, 17 December 1911, *CL* 3: 66; to M. H. Mushlin, 14 December 1947, Henderson, *Man*, 946.

37. Preface to *Music* 1:44–50; on beauty of birds see *Man and Superman*, *CP* 2: 662. On referring to himself as Svengali see Shaw's self-interview, *CP* 1: 799, 800, 802.

38. Shaw mentions Emma Seiler's laryngoscopic investigations in a review of Morell Mackenzie, *Hygiene of the Vocal Organs*, 26 July 1886, *Music* 1: 470. On laryngoscope see *Music* 1: 100; on pharynx, *fecundity*, see Preface to *Music* 1: 45, 50; to M. H. Mushlin, 14 December 1947, Henderson, *Man*, 946.

Chapter 16: Don Juan's Revenge

1. To E. Terry, 8 September 1897, *CL* 1: 801.

2. On Mary De Morgan see "Morris as I Knew Him," xxv–xxvi.

3. To E. Terry, 8 September 1897, *CL* 1: 801; 14 April 1888, 8 May 1888, *Diaries* 1: 366, 374; 21 April 1890, *Diaries* 1: 609.

4. 23 February 1885, *Diaries* 1: 63–64; G. Black's letter of 31 March 1889, quoted in note to the diary entry, 64.

5. 12 and 24 April 1888, *Diaries* 1: 365, 369; on meeting see 11 March 1885, *Diaries* 1: 68; on singing see 4 June 1887, *Diaries* 1: 274; on escorting see 16 December 1887, *Diaries* 1: 323; on poem see 8 February 1888, *Diaries* 1: 347; G. Gilchrist to Shaw, 26 March 1888, quoted in *CL* 1: 105.

6. *abuse:* 1 April 1888, *Diaries* 1: 362; *gossip:* 23 April 1888, *Diaries* 1: 369; on Hampstead Heath see 27 January 1889, *Diaries* 1: 462; *astonished:* 20 June 1890, *Diaries* 1: 627.

7. Hyndman, *Record of an Adventurous Life*, 318; "The New Politics," *Road*, 85.

8. On *Alone*, 1885 summary entry and 30 January 1885, *Diaries* 1: 54, *Diaries* 1: 57; facsimile program and letter to Mary Grace Walker, 23 January 1885, *CL* 1: 114–115; on Krogstad, 5 May 1885, *Diaries* 1: 81, and Preface to *Irrational Knot*, xxi–xxii. The title of the Ibsen play is now usually translated *A Doll House*, without the possessive. But since Shaw always used the possessive, I will follow his custom.

9. *SSS*, 103–104; Olive Schreiner to Havelock Ellis, 2 August 1884, *The Letters of Olive Schreiner, 1876–1920*, 36; Preface to *Salt*, 13.

10. 28 February 1885, *Diaries* 1: 65; to Lady Rhondda, 20 April 1930, *CL* 4: 184.

11. 2 April 1889, *Diaries* 1: 486.

12. To C. Payne-Townshend, 4 April 1898, *CL* 2: 26; to A. Henderson, 15 July 1905, *CL* 2: 538.

13. Besant, *An Autobiography*, 99–100.

14. To Lady Rhondda, 9 February 1927, *CL* 4: 48.

15. Besant quoted in Nethercot, *The First Five Lives of Annie Besant*, 213, 216, Shaw quoted on 221; 21 and 31 January 1885, *Diaries* 1: 56, 57.

16. *personal:* 1886 summary entry (entered 26 December 1887), *Diaries* 1: 326; *intrigue:* 1887 summary entries, *Diaries* 1: 230, 34; 24 December 1887, *Diaries* 1: 326; on contract see H. Pearson, *George Bernard Shaw*, 112.

17. 1887 summary entry, *Diaries* 1: 230.

18. On sparring with Robertson, 19 February 1886, *Diaries* 1: 147; on hair see H. Pearson, *George Bernard Shaw*, 112.

19. Taylor disputes Shaw's effect on Annie (*Annie Besant*, 185–187); on receiving *The Secret Doctrine* and sending it to Annie see 1889 summary entry, *Diaries* 1: 574. This contradicts editor W. T. Stead's memory of sending it directly to Annie (Taylor, *Annie Besant*, 239–240).

20. Quoted from H. Pearson, *George Bernard Shaw*, 113; to E. Robins, 28 November 1936, *CL* 4: 449; to Georgina Musters, 4 July 1948, *CL* 4: 824.

21. Quoted in Ervine, *Bernard Shaw*, 157; to B. Newcombe, 31 March 1896, *CL* 1: 620; *CP* 2: 557.

22. Lucy quoted in Farmer, *Bernard Shaw's Sister and Her Friends*, 84, 53, 218; "The 789th Performance of Dorothy," *The Star*, 13 September 1889, *Music* 1: 781, 780.

Chapter 17: Tailoring the New Woman

1. 7 November 1889, *Diaries* 1: 556; 19, 21, and 22 June 1891, *Diaries* 2: 732; on trip to Continent, 17, 20, and 23 April 1889, *Diaries* 1: 490–492.

2. Archer, quoted in "The Author's Preface" to 1893 edition of *Widowers' Houses, CP* 1: 38; "Sardoodledom," *Saturday Review*, 1 June 1895, *Drama Observed* 2: 353–359, and *OTN* 1: 140–147; Jones quoted, *SSS*, 40.

3. To R. G. Bright, 10 June 1896, *CL* 1: 632; *Pinerotic:* to W. Archer, 18 March 1895, *CL* 1: 501.

4. *SSS*, 10; *fastidious:* to J. Magny, 16 December 1890, *CL* 1: 279.

5. See Rank, *Don Juan Legend*, for a full spelling-out of the theme.

6. "The Author's Preface" to 1893 edition of *Widowers' Houses, CP* 1: 44.

7. "Mainly about Myself," Preface to *Plays Unpleasant, CP* 1: 25.

8. "The Author to His Dramatic Critics," *Prefaces*, 673–674; the comment of R. L. Stevenson to W. Archer was published in *Letters of Robert Louis Stevenson*, ed. Sidney Colvin (New York, 1899; London, Methuen, 1900), 2: 107; and in Henderson, *Man*, 128. Shaw

included a suppressed, unflattering portion of Stevenson's letter in his 1901 Preface (rpt. 1930) to *Cashel Byron's Profession,* xix–xx. Archer's review, 14 December 1892, *The World,* in *Shaw: The Critical Heritage,* 53; to W. Archer, 14 December 1892, *CL* 1: 373.

9. *Prefaces,* 675–676.

10. "An Aside," in McCarthy, *Myself and My Friends,* 8.

11. "An Explanatory Word from Shaw," in *Florence Farr, Bernard Shaw, W. B. Yeats: Letters* (hereafter *Farr / Shaw / Yeats*), ix; Yeats, *Autobiographies,* 121.

12. 7 May 1890, *Diaries* 1: 614; "A Critics' Trade Union," *The Star,* 9 May 1890, *Music* 2: 64. Shaw gives three versions of his first meeting with Florence: *Farr / Shaw / Yeats,* x; H. Pearson, *George Bernard Shaw,* 118; and letter to J. Achurch, 6 January 1891, in M. Peters, *Bernard Shaw and the Actresses,* 68. On talk and concert, 4 and 11 October 1890, *Diaries* 1: 655, 657; *amiable:* to E. Terry, 25 September 1896, *CL* 1: 668; on the walls see Yeats, *Autobiographies,* 123.

13. On brandy, 5 March 1892, *Diaries* 2: 802; on dresses and the role, 11 February 1891, *Diaries* 2: 696; to C. Charrington, 30 March 1891, *CL* 1: 287.

14. To C. Charrington, 30 March 1891, *CL* 1: 288; *suddenly:* to J. Achurch, 17 June 1889, *CL* 1: 216; 23 June 1889, *Diaries* 1: 514; *terrified:* to C. Charrington, 28 January 1890, *CL* 1: 239.

15. 4 May 1891, *Diaries* 2: 718; to F. Farr, 4 May 1891, *CL* 1: 298.

16. To F. Farr, 1 May 1891, *CL* 1: 296; 2 and 3 June 1891, *Diaries* 2: 727.

17. 24 August 1891, *Diaries* 2: 749; 4 and 5 February 1893, *Diaries* 2: 902–903.

18. *SSS,* 100; to D. Massingham, 13 January 1925, *CL* 3: 899; to E. Terry, 28 August 1896, *CL* 1: 644.

19. *The Philanderer, CP* 1: 185; to M. Tompkins, 22 February 1925, *CL* 3: 904. The most thorough analysis of the play is Alfred Turco, Jr., "*The Philanderer:* Shaw's Poignant Romp," *SHAW* 7: 47–62.

20. To T. D. O'Bolger, February 1916, *CL* 3: 374; to J. Magny, 16 December 1890, *CL* 1: 278.

21. "Mr Shaw's Method and Secret," a letter to the editor of *The Daily Chronicle,* 28 April 1898, in *CP* 1: 270; 27 August and 2 September 1893, *Diaries* 2: 964, 966; on blended, to W. Archer, 30 August 1893, *CL* 1: 403; *lady: CP* 1: 270; later to W. Archer, Shaw substituted "modern girl" for "modern lady," 22 June 1923, *CL* 3: 838.

22. *Mrs Warren's Profession, CP* 1: 314.

23. *CP* 1: 271; Archer, *Morning Leader,* 21 June 1902, quoted in *CL* 2: 276; Dan H. Laurence notes that Shaw apparently received an advance proof. Shaw's response to W. Archer, 20 June 1902, *CL* 2: 277.

24. To W. Archer, 15 November 1905, *CL* 2: 577; to W. Archer, 7 November 1905, *CL* 2: 574; to W. Archer, 15 November 1905, *CL* 2: 576, 579.

25. 26 November 1893, *Diaries* 2: 989; to F. Farr, 7 October 1891, *CL* 1: 313.

26. To A. Murray, 30 March 1894, *CL* 1: 422; to W. Archer, Shaw later claimed that Raina was based on Annie Besant (21 April 1898, *CL* 2: 34).

27. *The Chocolate Soldier* opened in Vienna in 1908 as *Der Tapfere Soldat;* the English-language version opened on Broadway in 1909.

28. To F. Farr, 28 January 1892, *CL* 1: 332; to E. Robins, 24 October 1898, *CL* 1: 686.

29. *Leporello list: Farr / Shaw / Yeats*, x; on her approach to admirers see "How William Archer impressed Bernard Shaw," *Pen Portraits*, 21.

30. Farr quoted in J. Johnson, *Florence Farr*, 36; H. Pearson, *George Bernard Shaw*, 120; "Man," in *New Age* (London, 19 September 1907), discussed in J. Johnson, "Making of a Feminist," in *Fabian Feminist*, 198–199.

31. *secret:* see Preface to *Overruled*, *CP* 4: 829; to F. Harris, 18 September 1930, *Shaw / Harris*, 239. For the Harris biography Shaw substituted the more decorous "you may count the women who have left me nothing to desire" (*Bernard Shaw*, 224); "The Womanly Woman," *Quintessence of Ibsenism*, *MCE*, 40.

32. To J. Achurch, 23 March 1895, *CL* 1: 504; to J. Achurch, 3 May 1895, *CL* 1: 532.

33. Farr, "Note by Florence Farr Upon Her Settings," in Yeats, *Essays and Introductions*, 21; to F. Farr, 6 June 1902, *CL* 2: 274–275.

34. "G. B. S. and New York," *New Age* (London, 23 May 1907), a large portion reprinted in J. Johnson, "The Making of a Feminist," 196–197; to Henrietta Paget, 29 June 1917, *CL* 3: 478; H. Paget's letter quoted in headnote.

35. To Georgina Gillmore, 6 February 1912, *CL* 3:75. Shaw's will quoted in headnote.

Chapter 18: The Imaginary Lover

1. To J. Achurch, 23 March 1895, *CL* 1: 506, 505.

2. "Morris as I Knew Him" (hereafter "Morris"), x, xx.

3. Shaw to H. Pearson, *George Bernard Shaw*, 94.

4. "Morris," xxxix, xxiv.

5. To M. G. Walker, 23 January 1885, *CL* 1: 115; to I. Beatty, 22 September 1885, *CL* 1: 140; "Morris," xxvi–xxvii.

6. "Morris," xxvii–xxviii.

7. "Morris," xxix, xxx; H. Jackson to H. Pearson, *George Bernard Shaw*, 97; Lucy to Mabel Johnston, later Mabel Dolmetsch, reported in letter of 27 November 1947 to H. G. Farmer, 88.

8. 4 and 8 April 1886, *Diaries* 1: 158–159; 1 November 1892, *Diaries* 2: 867; *The World*, 3 October 1888, reprinted in *London Art*, 239; 14 December 1892, *Diaries* 2: 881.

9. "Morris," xxx, xxxi.

10. To E. Terry, 5 October 1896, *CL* 1: 673; to W. Archer, 6 October 1896, *CL* 1: 673; "William Morris as Actor and Dramatist," *Saturday Review*, 10 October 1896, *Drama Observed* 2: 672, 677, and *OTN* 2: 221, 227.

11. Preface to *Terry / Shaw*, xxxiv. The closest attention to the correspondence interweaves it with Shaw's daily life; see M. Peters, *Bernard Shaw and the Actresses*. To H. Pearson, the correspondence was "friendship" (*George Bernard Shaw*, 152). St. John Ervine thought the correspondence "purely for pleasure" (*Bernard Shaw*, 259). Irvine wondered about the "profit motive" (*Universe of G. B. S.*, 82). Henderson thought Shaw desired Ellen "not amorously, but ambitiously" (*Man*, 811). To Holroyd, much of the correspondence is evidence of "an attempt to undermine Ellen's faith in Irving" (*Bernard Shaw* 1: 356).

12. *Property spoon:* Preface to *Terry / Shaw*, xvi; on E. Terry as wise and witty see "Henry Irving and Ellen Terry," *Pen Portraits*, 174; Preface to *Terry / Shaw*, xxv, xxxv.

13. *dolls, actors: Terry / Shaw*, 14; *destined:* Preface to *Terry / Shaw*, xxiv; *temple:* Preface to *Three Plays for Puritans, CP* 2, 19.

14. *Bardicide:* Preface to *Terry / Shaw*, xxx; "Blaming the Bard," *Saturday Review*, 26 September 1896, *Drama Observed* 2: 663, *OTN* 2: 208.

15. *sterilized:* Preface to *Terry / Shaw*, xxxi; *battering ram:* to E. Terry, 27 January 1897, *CL* 1: 722.

16. E. Terry to Shaw, 10 March 1895, *Terry / Shaw*, 15; to E. Terry, 1 November 1895, *CL* 1: 565.

17. *Terry / Shaw*, 12; to E. Terry, 1 November 1895, *CL* 1: 565; *Napoleonad:* to E. Terry, 5 July 1896, *CL* 1: 634. For Shaw's review of *Madame Sans Géne* see *Drama Observed* 3: 827–831, and *OTN* 3: 110–116.

18. *Terry / Shaw*, headnote, 18; to E. Terry, 9 March 1896, *CL* 1: 610; *Man of Destiny, CP* 1: 622. Nina Auerbach writes that Ellen Terry hid her large hands because they revealed a "power forbidden in women" (*Ellen Terry*, 20). Auerbach, who shows the actress both acquiescing to and defying cultural roles all her life, believes that in the correspondence Ellen Terry created a more innocent self to seduce Shaw. I am indebted to Auerbach's beautifully written portrait for some details of Terry's life. The most thorough analysis of the play is Charles A. Berst, "*The Man of Destiny:* Shaw, Napoleon, and the Theater of Life," *SHAW* 7: 85–118.

19. To B. Newcombe, 31 March 1896, *CL* 1: 620, 618.

20. To E. Terry, 26 March 1896, *CL* 1: 617; *Yahoo: Terry / Shaw*, 13.

21. E. Terry to Shaw, 1 October 1897, *Terry / Shaw*, 237; *Notebooks of Henry James*, 186.

22. To E. Terry, 13 May 1897, *CL* 1: 762.

23. 12 June 1886, *Diaries* 1: 176; to E. Terry, 5 November 1896, *CL* 1: 695.

24. *fairyland, paradise:* Preface to *Terry / Shaw*, ix; *ogre:* Preface to *Terry / Shaw*, xxxi, and to E. Terry, 28 October 1900, *CL* 2: 188; *world apart:* Preface to *Terry / Shaw*, xiii; *disagreeably:* to E. Terry, 6 April 1896, *CL* 1: 623; to E. Terry, 3 November 1900, *CL* 2: 192. On the look of love see J. H. Van Den Berg, "Human Body," in Ruitenbeek, *Psychoanalysis and Existential Philosophy*, 115.

25. To E. Terry, 2 July 1897, *CL* 1: 777; *Wandering Jew:* to E. Terry, 12 October 1896, *CL* 1: 676.

26. To Mrs. P. Campbell, 11 August 1937, *CL* 4: 470.

27. *liar, slave:* to E. Terry, 21 September 1896, *CL* 1: 659; *ulterior motives:* Preface to *Terry / Shaw*, xii; *god:* to E. Terry, 5 July 1892, *CL* 1: 349.

28. To E. Terry, 6 April, 1896, *CL* 1: 622; to A. Lockett, 19 November 1883, *CL* 1: 73.

29. Preface to *Terry / Shaw*, xv, xiv; *wisdom:* to E. Terry, 6 April, 1896, *CL* 1: 623.

30. To E. Terry, 12 October 1896, *CL* 1: 677; *dead matter:* to E. Terry 5 July 1896, *CL* 1: 635; *light green eyes:* to E. Terry, 12 October 1896, *CL* 1: 676; on the photograph, to E. Terry, 5 November 1896, *CL* 1: 695; *original:* to E. Terry, 12 October 1896, *CL* 1: 677.

31. E. *Terry to Shaw*, 26 November 1896, *Terry / Shaw*, 116–117; to E. Terry, 30 November 1896, *CL* 1: 706.

32. E. Terry to Shaw: *bountiful:* 4 November 1897, *Terry / Shaw*, 245; *Sweetiken:* 15

December 1897, *Terry/Shaw*, 248; *charming darling:* 12 April 1897, *Terry/Shaw*, 164; *Dearest silly-billy:* 17 May 1898, *Terry/Shaw*, 286; *flirting:* 10 November 1896, *Terry/Shaw*, 112. Shaw to E. Terry: *Dearest &:* 3 March 1897, *CL* 1: 730; *Dearest and Everest:* 25 March 1897, *CL* 1: 737; *my Ellenest:* 5 March 1897, *CL* 1: 731; *inhuman:* 12 July 1897, *CL* 1: 782; *fickle:* 9 April 1897, *CL* 1: 741; *jealous:* 16 November 1896, *CL* 1: 701; *I love:* 8 December 1896, *CL* 1: 712.

33. *planes:* to E. Terry, 5 November 1896, *CL* 1: 695; *love me:* 11 June 1897, *CL* 1: 774; *soul:* 2 July 1897, *CL* 1: 776; *if only:* 16 April 1897, *CL* 1: 746; *You may:* 9 April 1897, *CL* 1: 741; *Now I:* 30 November 1896, *CL* 1: 706; *Lilith:* 14–15 June 1897, *CL* 1: 774.

34. E. Terry to Shaw, 24 September 1896, *Terry/Shaw*, 74; E. Terry to Shaw, 22 September 1896, *Terry/Shaw*, 67; Shaw to E. Terry, 22 September 1896, *CL* 1: 662.

35. *as warm:* to E. Terry, 30 November 1896, *CL* 1: 706; to Shaw, 1 December 1896, *Terry/Shaw*, 121; *I was:* to E. Terry, 3 October 1899, *Terry/Shaw*, 329; *I am:* to E. Terry, 30 November 1896, *CL* 1: 706; *You cannot:* to E. Terry, 8 September 1897, *CL* 1: 801; *A Sprite:* to Shaw, 24 September 1897, *Terry/Shaw*, 235; *spritelike: SSS*, 52.

36. *treacherous:* to E. Terry, 4 November 1896, *CL* 1: 693; *soft side:* Preface to *Terry/Shaw*, xv; *knit into:* 14–15 June 1897, *CL* 1: 774–775.

37. E. Terry to Shaw, 11 November 1896, published in M. Peters, *Bernard Shaw and the Actresses*, 192; To E. Terry, 28 August 1896, *CL* 1: 645. M. Peters sees Ellen as the "mother-lover with whom [Shaw] wished to lie" (222); Dervin writes of incest and "grandiose fantasy" (*Bernard Shaw*, 326–327; Holroyd sees Shaw's "escape from incest into fantasy" (*Bernard Shaw*, 1: 368).

38. Preface to *Terry/Shaw*, xii.

39. *Man and Superman, CP* 2: 652.

40. To E. Terry, 14–15 June 1897, *CL* 1: 775; *huntress:* Preface to *Terry/Shaw*, xxxv.

41. *One does:* to E. Terry, 6 April 1896, *CL* 1: 623; *THE:* ca. 20–26 August 1896, *CL* 1: 641; *Candida, CP* 1: 593.

42. To E. Terry, 13 September 1899, *CL* 2: 101–102; *Captain Brassbound's Conversion, CP* 2: 331; to E. Terry, 8 August 1899, *CL* 2: 97, 99; *melodramatic:* "Notes to *Captain Brassbound's Conversion*," *CP* 2: 429; on Lady Cicely see *CP* 2: 417, 416.

43. To Edward Rose, 25 September 1899, *CL* 2: 103; Terry, *The Story of My Life*, 347; E. Terry to Shaw, 10 December 1902, *Terry/Shaw*, 367.

44. To E. Terry, 28 October 1900, *CL* 2: 188; Max Beerbohm, "'A Great Dear,'" 26 March 1906, *Last Theatres: 1904–1910*, 243, 245.

45. *awstruck:* Preface to *Terry/Shaw*, xxxv; *fine part:* E. Terry to Shaw, 18 March 1911, *Terry/Shaw*, 408; *most wonderful:* to E. Terry, 20 August 1912, *CL* 3: 112; *nobody:* to E. Terry, 7 January 1918, *CL* 3: 524; E. Terry to Shaw, 16 September 1912, *Terry/Shaw*, 412. Her vitality in marrying Carew supports the view that it was Shaw, not Ellen, who prevented the pair from meeting a decade earlier. Similarly, M. Peters has found the desire to meet the "most insistent theme" for Ellen (*Bernard Shaw and the Actresses*, 181). In contrast, Holroyd and Henderson attribute their not meeting to her worry about aging; both quote the letter of 23 September 1896: "I think I'd rather never meet you—in the flesh" (Holroyd, *Bernard Shaw* 1: 355; *Man*, 812). But that letter was written after a depressing second performance as Imogen:

"it was pretty bad again. . . . I'm beat." In a letter to Shaw of 2 October 1896, Ellen describes listening outside the Lyceum door: "Intended coming straight into the office, but got no further than the doormat. Heard your voice and then skedaddled home again full tilt, and, oh I was laughing. I *couldnt* come in" because "I *might* have thrown my arms around your neck and hugged you!" *Terry / Shaw*, 70, 78.

46. *inevitable:* to E. G. Craig, 15 September 1929, *CL* 4: 161; *Teddy:* to E. G. Craig, 7 September 1929, *CL* 4: 159–161; E. G. Craig, Annex to *Ellen Terry and Her Secret Self,* 15; "Gordon Craig and the Shaw-Terry Letters," *Shaw on Theatre,* 207.

47. Preface to *Terry / Shaw*, xxxvi; to E. Terry, 1 March 1920, *CL* 3: 670.

48. H. Pearson, *George Bernard Shaw,* 110; on their meeting, to F. Harris, 18 September 1930, *Shaw / Harris,* 238; *Let those:* Preface to *Terry / Shaw*, xxxvi.

Chapter 19: Triangulating Desire

1. To J. Achurch, 22 December 1894, *CL* 1: 471–472.

2. *CP* 2: 665.

3. Preface to *Plays Pleasant, CP* 1: 372; "Shaw Reveals Who Was Candida," *CP* 1: 603.

4. *CP* 1: 580, 576–577.

5. To J. Achurch, 25 January 1895, *CL* 1: 478; secret is most succinctly stated in *SSS,* 101; to S. Trebitsch, 7 January 1903, *Shaw / Trebitsch,* 32; "An Extraordinary Ordinary Play," *CP* 1: 597.

6. *CP* 1: 587, 582, 537, 535; Queensberry to Alfred Montgomery, 1 November 1894, Ellmann, *Oscar Wilde,* 426. On "marjorie" see Weeks, *Sex, Politics, and Society* (hereafter *Sex*), 111.

7. 15–16 October 1894, *Diaries* 2: 1045; see also "Bayreuth's Indifference to Beauty," *Music* 3: 301–307 and "The Bayreuth Festival," *Music* 3: 307–321; to R. Mansfield, 16 March 1895, *CL* 1: 499; to James Huneker, 6 April 1904, *CL* 2: 415. Louis Crompton calls Marchbanks a "latter-day Siegfried" and puts him in the tradition of aesthetic revolt and sexual freedom (*Shaw the Dramatist,* 39).

8. Wagner quoted in Gutman, *Richard Wagner,* 436–437; Shaw on kiss, "The Second Parsifal," 7 August 1889, *Music* 1: 731. In 1890, Shaw heard Ellis address the Wagner Society on the correspondence; see "Bassetto's Destructive Force," 7 March 1890, *Music* 1: 947; Shaw also quotes from the Wagner correspondence in *The Perfect Wagnerite, Music* 3: 509–514, note on 495. Shaw wrote that English Wagnerians "already owe more" to Ellis "than to any other man," 3 August 1892, *Music* 2: 689. Shaw mentioned Archer's work on Wagner to R. G. Bright, 2 December 1894, *CL* 1: 465. A 1949 Sotheby's catalogue listing Shaw's books for auction included the vocal score of *Parsifal,* "neatly bound in half vellum."

9. "Salt on Shaw," in Winsten, *Salt and His Circle,* 215; *Tristan's holy night:* To J. Huneker, 6 April 1904, *CL* 2: 415.

10. "Shaw Reveals Who Was Candida," 28 November 1944, *CP* 1: 601–603; to W. Archer, 21 April 1898, *CL* 2: 34.

11. To J. Achurch, 14 April 1896, *CL* 1: 625. On *molly* see Ellis, *Studies in the Psychology of Sex,* vol. 1, part 4, 45.

12. *Too True to Be Good, CP* 6: 477.

13. "Morris," xxxvii; 3 November 1888, *Diaries* 1: 429; to Mrs. A. Lyttelton, 22 December 1912, *CL* 3: 140.

14. *SSS*, 14–15; "Shaw 40 Years Later: Eric Bentley Speaks His Mind on Eleven Neglected Plays," *SHAW* 7: 9; "Woman-Man in Petticoats," *New York Times Magazine*, 19 June 1927, rpt. in *Platform and Pulpit*, 174.

15. 19–20 August 1891, *Diaries* 2: 748.

16. "Salt on Shaw," in Winsten, *Salt and His Circle*, 209, 212; to J. Achurch, 24 March 1896, *CL* 1: 615; on practicing see, e.g., 1889 summary entry, *Diaries* 1: 453.

17. To Nancy Astor, 15 April 1932, *CL* 4: 285; see also Shaw's Preface to *Salt and His Circle*, 9–10.

18. Carpenter, *Intermediate Sex*, 70; to N. Astor, 15 April 1932, *CL* 4: 285.

19. To E. Carpenter, 29 July 1896, *CL* 1: 637; Carpenter quoted in Weeks, *Coming Out*, 71; on Fabian meeting, 4 and 5 January 1889, *Diaries* 1: 455; see also Chushichi Tsuzuki, *Edward Carpenter 1844–1929: Prophet of Human Fellowship* (Cambridge: Cambridge University Press, 1980), 80.

20. To A. Henderson, 3 January 1905, *CL* 2: 490; to N. Astor, 15 April 1932, *CL* 4: 284–285; to H. S. Salt, 19 August 1903, *CL* 2: 348. On the morals of socialism see Weeks, *Sex*, 167–175.

21. To C. Payne-Townshend, 31 October 1897, *CL* 1: 818; on teaching mending see "Educational Confessions," *The Schoolmistress*, 17 November 1927, rpt. in *Interviews*, 14.

22. To N. Astor, 15 April 1932, *CL* 4: 285; to C. Payne-Townshend, 18 March 1898, *CL* 2: 17; to C. Payne-Townshend, 16 March 1898, *CL* 2: 16.

23. To C. Salt, 8 May 1939, *CL* 4: 529; Shaw's Preface to Winsten, *Salt and His Circle*, 9–10; to S. Webb, 11 April 1898, *CL* 2: 30; 8 June 1893, *Diaries* 2: 943.

24. 8 September 1885, *Diaries* 1: 110; 8 May 1897, *Diary of Beatrice Webb* 2: 114; 17 September 1893, *Diary of Beatrice Webb* 2: 37.

25. See, e.g., Jacques, 5 January 1891, *Diaries* 2: 685–686; Scheu, 24 December 1886, 3 April 1885, *Diaries* 1: 223, 74.

26. "Morris," xxx; to J. Achurch, 23 March 1895, *CL* 1: 506.

27. E. Huddart to Shaw, 19 May 1881, Hugo, "'The Very Innocent Epistles,'" *SHAW* 10: 7.

28. In her discussion of Restoration drama, Eve Kosofsky Sedgwick suggests that the man who cuckolds another has performed a sexual act on him; see *Between Men*, 49–66.

29. *SSS*, 128; *CP* 5: 358–359.

30. To St. John Ervine, *Bernard Shaw*, 383–384; to F. Harris, 24 June 1930, *CL* 4: 192, 190.

31. Ervine, *Bernard Shaw*, 384.

32. H. Pearson, *George Bernard Shaw*, 109.

33. To Hugo Vallentin, 8 November 1907, *CL* 2: 721.

34. Preface to *Getting Married, CP* 3: 508; Epistle Dedicatory, *Man and Superman, CP* 2: 496; Preface to *Overruled, CP* 4: 844–845. In linking sex with dirt, secrecy, and unspeakable disease, Shaw's associations resemble Guy Hocquenghem's view that venereal diseases play the "leading role in the paranoiac ideology concerning homosexuality" (*Homosexual Desire*, 70). Freud believed that a conflict over homosexual tendencies is associated with contamina-

tion so that the so-called "latent homosexual" experiences increased fear of contamination by disease. Based on what they saw as hostility to women, Lisbeth I. Sachs and Bernard H. Stern labeled Shaw a latent homosexual in their brief article "Bernard Shaw and His Women," *British Journal of Medical Psychology* 37 (1964): 343–350.

Chapter 20: *Scandals and* Siegfried

1. 22 August 1885, *Diaries* 1: 106.

2. On Stead as idealist, to J. Magny, 18 December 1890, *CL* 1: 279. In a special morning edition the same day as the demonstration, Stead wrote that he had "only struck the match" firing public enthusiasm (*Pall Mall Gazette*, 22 August 1885).

3. W. T. Stead to E. Carpenter, 1–2 June 1895, Edward Carpenter collection, Sheffield City Library, quoted in Weeks, *Sex*, 109.

4. On nineteenth-century middle-class sexuality see Peter Gay, *The Bourgeois Experience*, 2 vols. (New York: Oxford University Press, 1984, 1986); to F. Harris, 24 June 1930, *CL* 4: 192.

5. *Man and Superman*, *CP* 2: 647–648.

6. 26 November 1889, *Diaries* 1: 562. For a full account of the scandal and trials see Hyde, *Cleveland Street Scandal*.

7. To the Editor of *Truth*, 26 November 1889, *CL* 1: 230–232; Queen Victoria quoted in Ellman, *Oscar Wilde*, note, 409.

8. Given Shaw's feeling of being used sexually by women, a recent description of Greek practice is instructive: "the partner whose pleasure is promoted is considered 'active,' while the partner who puts his or her body *at the service* of another's pleasure is deemed 'passive'— read 'penetrated,' in the culture's unselfconscious shorthand" (Halperin, *One Hundred Years of Homosexuality*, 31; on dominant/submissive, 33).

9. To the editor of *Truth*, 26 November 1889, *CL* 1: 231; 8–9 October 1889, *Diaries* 1: 546–547.

10. 9 October 1889, *Diaries* 1: 547; 23 July, 2 August 1894, *Music* 3: 293, 308.

11. 13 and 16 October 1889, *Diaries* 1: 548, 549; 5 and 7 November 1889, *Diaries* 1: 555–556.

12. 28 October, 11 and 12 November 1889, *Diaries* 1: 553, 557–558.

13. 13 November, 22 November 1889, *Diaries* 1: 558, 561; *Music* 3: 481, 457–458.

14. 24–28 November 1889, *Diaries* 1: 562–563; *The Star*, 29 November 1889, quoted by Weintraub, *Diaries* 1: 563.

15. 1889 summary entry on health, *Diaries* 1: 454, 453; on hand, 1 December 1888, *Diaries* 1: 440; Ellis, *Sexual Inversion*, 144; Carpenter, *Intermediate Sex*, 58.

16. 14 October 1889, *Diaries* 1: 549.

17. To H. Seymour, August 1898, *CL* 2: 57; to W. T. Stead, 8 June 1887, *CL* 1: 173.

Chapter 21: *The Curious Reversal*

1. *SSS*, 15; Preface to *Misalliance*, *CP* 4: 40.

2. On *My Secret Life* see Marcus, *The Other Victorians*, 82; "The Root of the White Slave Traffic," *The Awakener*, 16 November 1912, rpt. in *Fabian Feminist*, 258; "Flagellomania," *Humanity*, May 1899, in *Crude Criminology*, *CW* 22: 292.

3. Unnamed German informant to Ulrichs, 12 January 1868, *Riddle of "Man-Manly" Love*, 2: 393; *Kertbeny* was a coinage, reversing the name Benkert, Ellis, *Studies in the Psychology of Sex*, vol. 1, part 4, footnote, 2. See also Jonathan Ned Katz, "Invention of Heterosexuality," *Socialist Review* 20, no. 1 (February 1990): 7–34.

4. On Jaeger and odor see Ellis, *Studies in the Psychology of Sex*, vol. 1, part 3, 72, 77; Krafft-Ebing, *Psychopathia Sexualis*, 27. Halperin writes that Jaeger popularized the use of the term *homosexual* as he sketches the history of the term in *One Hundred Years of Homosexuality*, note 2, 155. In the twentieth century the self-definition of being gay as a political movement arose in the late sixties; see Weeks, *Sexuality and Its Discontents*, 50.

5. Carpenter, *The Intermediate Sex*, footnote, 40; Jaeger quoted in Carpenter, *The Intermediate Sex*, 171.

6. 25 March 1890, *Diaries* 1: 602; on Schreiner and Ellis's *Studies* see Grosskurth, *Havelock Ellis*, 81; on Lees and *Sexual Inversion* see Grosskurth, *Havelock Ellis*, 145; Preface to *Getting Married*, *CP* 3: 527; Goldberg, *Havelock Ellis*, 14.

7. To Louis Wilkinson, 20 December 1909, *CL* 2: 890.

8. On Ellis's article see Weeks, *Coming Out*, 116; on *New Age*, to C. H. Norman, 24 September 1908, *CL* 2: 810.

9. To N. Astor, 15 April 1932, *CL* 4: 284; Ellis is quoted by Carpenter himself, *Intermediate Sex*, 169.

10. *CL* 4: 284; Notes to *Caesar and Cleopatra*, *CP* 2: 300.

11. d'Arch Smith, *Love in Earnest*, 31.

12. *Caesar and Cleopatra*, *CP* 2: 182.

13. On Raffalovich's mother see Ellmann, *Wilde*, 282. Shaw derided Wilde's lofty attitude toward Gray and other "more abject disciples"; see letter of 7 August 1916, *Shaw / Harris*, 32. Marc-André Raffalovich, *Uranisme et Unisexualité*, quoted in Carpenter, *Intermediate Sex*, 133–134; 26 January 1893, *Diaries* 2: 898. Ellis quoted in Weeks, *Coming Out*, 68.

14. Wilde on Le Gallienne, Ellmann, *Wilde*, 283; Le Gallienne quoted in Croft-Cooke, *Feasting with Panthers*, 5; collaboration with Leather, Koestenbaum, *Double Talk*, 163; Le Gallienne quoted by Moore, who puts the date of the romance at 1889, *E. Nesbit*, 116, xvi. On the exchange over the poems see Shaw to P. Beatty, 4 January 1893, *CL* 1: 375, including headnote, 374; 5 October 1892, *Diaries* 2: 858, including note.

15. Douglas, "For Shame, Mr Shaw!" quoted in *Bernard Shaw and Alfred Douglas* (hereafter *Shaw / Douglas*), 207; Douglas to Shaw, 25 May 1908, *Shaw / Douglas*, 208–209; Douglas to Shaw, 6 May 1938, *Shaw / Douglas*, 46–48; Shaw to Douglas, 8 May 1938, *Shaw / Douglas*, 48.

16. *pedestals:* Douglas to Shaw, 10 May 1938, *Shaw / Douglas*, 49; *Read:* to Douglas, 16 April 1931, *Shaw / Douglas*, 3; on agreed, to Douglas, 18 April 1938, *Shaw / Douglas*, 33; *malignant:* Douglas to Shaw, 18 July 1938, *Shaw / Douglas*, 69; on withdrawal of pages, to Douglas, 20 July 1938, *Shaw / Douglas*, 74–75; Douglas to Shaw, 21 July 1938, *Shaw / Douglas*, 75.

17. Shaw's introductory note to 1895, *Diaries* 2: 1060; *old-maidish:* Ervine, "Bernard Shaw," *Spectator*, 10 November 1950, rpt. in *Interviews*, 506; letter to F. Douglas, 2 February 1949, *Shaw / Douglas*, xiii–xiv.

18. To Douglas, 16 April 1931, *Shaw/Douglas*, 3; to Almroth Wright, 5 July 1938, *CL* 4: 504; Wilde quoted in Ellmann, *Wilde*, 463.

19. To Douglas, 16 April 1931, *Shaw/Douglas*, 4; to Douglas [June 1933], *Shaw/Douglas*, 15.

20. To Max Beerbohm, 15 September 1903, *CL* 2: 374.

21. Laurence notes Lucy Shaw's authorship as a possibility for the Berlioz piece, *CL* 1: 38. Lucy later published two small books, letters of advice to a young girl: *Five Letters of the House of Kildonnel* (1905) and *The Last of the Kildonnel Letters* (1908) (see Ervine, *Bernard Shaw*, 199; Farmer, *Bernard Shaw's Sister and Her Friends*, 146, 149). The books impressed McNulty, but Shaw thought they were "terrible—like the grinding of teeth in hell." See Laurence's headnote and Shaw's letter to McNulty, 13 August 1913, *CL* 3: 196–197; see also "The Taming of the Shrew," *Pall Mall Gazette*, 8 June 1888, rpt. in *Drama Observed* 1: 88–89; "In Praise of 'The Silly Season,'" *Pall Mall Gazette*, 31 August 1888, rpt. in *Agitations*, 9; Ulrichs, *Riddle of "Man-Manly" Love*, 1: 60–61, 94, and passim.

22. J. C. to the editor of *The Star*, 19 September 1888, *CL* 1: 197; Shendar Brwa to the editor of *The Star*, 20 September 1888, *CL* 1: 197; Jem Nicholls to the editor of *The Star*, 20 September 1888, *CL* 1: 199–201; 20 September 1888, *Diaries* 1: 414.

23. "Blood Money to Whitechapel," *The Star*, 24 September, rpt. in Laurence and Rambeau, *Agitations*, 10–11.

24. Preface to *Three Plays by Brieux*, *Prefaces*, 197; on writing articles, to T. Hopkins, 31 August 1889, *CL* 1: 222, 224.

25. *Cashel Byron's Profession*, 140.

26. For details of the murders see Knight, *Jack the Ripper*.

27. 23 December 1888, *Diaries* 1: 447.

Chapter 22: Pluck or Cunning?

1. Blacker, *Eugenics, Galton and After*, 38–39; Henderson, *Life*, 493.

2. Galton coined the term in *Inquiries into Human Faculty* (1883). *Cashel Byron's Profession* was completed in February 1883. Its first version had "heredity doctrine," which was changed to eugenics for its 1886 publication by Modern Press (see *Cashel Byron's Profession*, *CW*, 233, and the collations in the edition by S. Weintraub, 236). *CP* 7: 444, 453.

3. Carpenter quotes Ellis in *Intermediate Sex*, 138; Carpenter, *Intermediate Sex*, 109.

4. "The Author to the Dramatic Critics," *Prefaces*, 672; Preface to *Saint Joan*, *CP* 6: 33; 12 November 1886, *Music* 1: 475, and *Book Reviews*, 209; Galton, *Inquiries*, 58.

5. Galton, *Inquiries*, 69; to E. Terry, 27 January 1897, *CL* 1: 722; Preface to *The Sanity of Art*, *MCE*, 296.

6. Galton, *Inquiries*, 69, 59; Shaw, "Sir Almroth Wright's Polemic," *New Statesman*, 18 October 1913, rpt. as "Sir Almroth Wright's Case Against Woman Suffrage" in *Fabian Feminist*, 244–245.

7. Galton, *Hereditary Genius*, 2–3; *virile creed* quoted in Weeks, *Sex*, 129; Galton, *Inquiries*, Galton's note, 17. Shaw would live to see Galton's positive eugenics—breeding a

better race—overshadowed by the horrors accompanying the negative eugenics of Nazi Germany, the genocidal drive to eliminate the "unfit."

8. *smile:* Preface to *Farfetched Fables, CP* 7: 423; on Ibsen paper, 17 December 1890, *Diaries* 1: 678; on *The Philanderer,* 19–20 June 1893, *Diaries* 2: 947–948; *concept:* "Preface on Doctors," *CP* 3: 294; K. Pearson, "On the Inheritance of the Mental and Moral Characters in Man," 206.

9. The following citations are on Galton's lecture: 19 November 1887, *Diaries* 1: 317; 26 November 1887, *Diaries* 1: 318; 10 December 1887, *Diaries* 1: 322. The following citations are on *Luck or Cunning?:* 25 January 1887, *Diaries* 1: 236; 17 February 1887, *Diaries* 1: 243; 28 February 1887, *Diaries* 1: 246; 5, 7, and 8 March 1887, *Diaries* 1: 248; on meeting Butler, 15 November 1889, *Diaries* 1: 559; Butler on Shaw, 2 January 1897, *Samuel Butler's Notebooks,* 45; to C. Ricketts, 8 July 1907, *CL* 2: 699.

10. *The Perfect Wagnerite, Music* 3: 479; "On the Subject of Fiddling," *The Star,* 28 February 1890, *Music* 1: 935; *Samuel Butler's Notebooks,* 45–46, 263.

11. Winsten, *Salt and His Circle,* 216; letters to Butler, 24 March 1901, *CL* 2: 224, and to G. Richards, 28 March 1901, *CL* 2: 225; to H. S. Salt, 2 August 1903, *CL* 2: 341.

12. Shaw quotes Butler in *Quintessence, MCE,* 55; Carpenter, *Civilisation,* 133, 135, 141; Winsten, *Salt and His Circle,* 111.

13. To A. Douglas, 14 November 1940, *CL* 4: 587.

14. Nordau, *Degeneration,* 537–538.

15. Nordau, *Degeneration,* 22. Lombroso inspired Ellis's *The Criminal* (1890) and influenced his belief that the genius and the criminal were complementary forms of degeneration.

16. *Degenerate's View,* rpt. in *London Art,* 381, 382, and *The Sanity of Art, MCE,* 326, 328.

17. *Degenerate's View,* 383, and *Sanity,* 329; Preface to *Sanity,* 300. In examining the intellectual ideas Bentley has called the superman "perhaps the main link between Shaw's politics and his religion" (*Bernard Shaw,* 56).

18. Preface to *Sanity, MCE,* 299; Preface to *Farfetched Fables, CP* 7: 384, 383, 386, 385.

19. Carpenter, *Intermediate Sex,* 58; to L. Wilkinson, 20 December 1909, *CL* 2: 890; 17 September 1885, "Physical Expression," *Book Reviews,* 44–47; 14 September 1886, *Diaries* 1: 198; 4 October 1887, *Diaries* 1: 303. S. Weintraub suggests that the reading of Shaw's palm led to Wilde's story "Lord Arthur Savile's Crime," in which Savile's palm is read; see "'The Hibernian School': Oscar Wilde and Bernard Shaw," *SHAW* 13: 27.

20. See, e.g., meeting on "Spiritualism," 3 May 1886, *Diaries* 1: 166; on hypnosis, 23 April 1887, *Diaries* 1: 262; 23 January 1886, "A Scotland Yard for Spectres," *Book Reviews,* 100–103; *nightmare:* 29 October 1885, *Diaries* 1: 121; 6 September 1887, "Spiritualism Extraordinary!" *Book Reviews,* 325–328; on Interplanetary Society see headnote, letters to A. Clarke, 25 and 31 January 1947, *CL* 4: 792–793.

21. On Molloy as dupe see "A Novelist Born, But Not Yet Made," 5 December 1887, *Book Reviews,* 375; on Mrs. Hill, 14 June 1895, *Diaries* 2: 1083; to J. Achurch, 31 August 1895, *CL* 1: 553; Henderson, *Life,* 494–495.

22. Photograph by Emery Walker reproduced in *CL* 1: 305; Ulrichs, *Riddle of "Man-Manly" Love,* 1: 152.

23. Galton, *English Men of Science,* 98–99.

24. To E. Terry, 16 October 1896, *CL* 1: 681; Dame Knight quoted in *London Art,* 40.

25. To R. G. Bright, 22 April 1895, *CL* 1: 525; Ellis, *Studies in the Psychology of Sex*, vol. 1, part 4, 196 (Madame Blavatsky was included among the leaders that Ellis cited as either homosexual, bisexual or of "pronounced masculine temperament" [197]); to M. Gorki, 24 May 1917, *CL* 3: 475. Bertolini sees Catherine as a "figure of Shaw himself" (see *Playwriting Self of Bernard Shaw*, 153).

26. To F. Harris, 4 January 1918, *CL* 3: 522. See also letter to Daniel Macmillan, 11 September 1943, *CL* 4: 675.

27. Morris, *William Morris*, 2: 187; 2 December 1889, *Diaries* 1: 565; 7 January 1907, *Daily Graphic*, London, rpt. as "Bumps and Brains."

28. Nordau, *Degeneration*, 17. Shaw also told John that he was "physically a coward but morally a hero" (John, *Chiaroscuro*, 97, 116); *Degenerate's View*, 384, and *Sanity, MCE*, 331.

29. *Degenerate's View*, 384, and *Sanity, MCE*, 330; on stigmata, see also Preface to *The Dark Lady*, *CP* 4:293; on photographs see Galton, *Inquiries*, 6–13; 23 September 1885, "A Handbook of Physiognomy," *Book Reviews*, 50; *CP* 1: 418; *CP* 3: 84; *CP* 7: 473. Tyson notes Shaw's "value judgments on the basis of physical appearance," citing such characters as Joan, Sartorius, Tanner, and Candida, but not those that I mention (*Book Reviews*, note, 51).

Chapter 23: Son of Shakespeare

1. E. Terry to Shaw, August 1896, *Terry / Shaw*, 35; *dead:* to E. Terry, 28 August 1896, *CL* 1: 644; *false bits:* to E. Terry, 6 September 1896, *CL* 1: 650; *mother:* to E. Terry, 16 September, 1896, *CL* 1: 655; *ass:* 6 September 1896, *CL* 1: 647; "Blaming the Bard," 26 September 1896, *Drama Observed* 2: 655, and *OTN* 2: 211; *cut:* 6 September 1896, *CL* 1: 650.

2. Foreword to *Cymbeline Refinished*, *CP* 7: 180. For an analysis of *Cymbeline Refinished* using Harold Bloom's theory of misreading see Daniel J. Leary, "Shaw Versus Shakespeare: The Refinishing of *Cymbeline*," *Educational Theatre Journal* 30 (1978): 5–25. For my detailed analysis of the three plays discussed in this chapter see "Shaw's Double Dethroned."

3. Foreword to *Cymbeline Refinished*, *CP* 7: 183; Shakespeare, *Cymbeline*, act 5, scene 1, and act 2, scene 5.

4. Postcard to A. Henderson, received 24 June 1931, *Man*, 3; *birthplace:* Preface to *Shakes Versus Shav*, *CP* 7: 470; *born: SSS*, 109; *overrated:* to V. Tchertkoff, ca. August 1905, *CL* 2: 552; *damn:* to W. Archer, 8 September 1903, *CL* 2: 366; *feeling: CP* 7: 471.

5. *CP* 7: 471; Preface to *The Dark Lady*, *CP* 4: 279, 285.

6. *CP* 7: 473, 471.

7. *CP* 7: 477.

8. "Blaming the Bard," *Drama Observed* 2: 661, and *OTN* 2: 205–206; to A. Douglas, June 1933, *Shaw / Douglas*, 15.

9. *CP* 2: 772.

10. Carpenter, *Intermediate Sex*, 33; *CP* 2: 558

11. To Clement Scott, January 1902, *CL* 2: 260–261; to Mrs. A. Lyttelton, 22 December 1912, *CL* 3: 140; Carpenter, *Intermediate Sex*, 35.

12. Rattray, *Bernard Shaw*, 12–13.

13. Preface to *The Dark Lady*, *CP* 4: 294.

Chapter 24: Ascent of the Naked Skeleton

1. To W. Archer, 17 August 1890, *CL* 1: 256–257.

2. "Shakespear and Mr Barrie," 13 November 1897, *Drama Observed* 3: 941, and *OTN* 3: 258.

3. H. C. Biard, *Wings* (London: Hurst & Blackett, 1934), excerpt in *Interviews*, 211; Loraine, *Robert Loraine*, 91; to W. Archer, 7 July 1906, *CL* 2: 635; Shaw, *Daily Mail*, 19 September 1929, excerpt in *Interviews*, 210.

4. Ellis and Symonds, *Sexual Inversion*, note, 107. In a later edition "R. S." specifically projects the "old Platonic mania" onto the Roman Catholic doctrines of trinity, incarnation, and eucharist (Ellis, *Studies in the Psychology of Sex*, vol. 1, part 4, 114–115). Carpenter's *Homogenic Love* was possibly *the* first commercially published book of its kind, according to d'Arch Smith. Though published in January 1895, the title page is dated 1894 (d'Arch Smith, *Love in Earnest*, 20, 42–43, notes 73–74).

5. To B. Newcombe, 31 March 1896, *CL* 1: 618; to J. Achurch, 4 April 1896, *CL* 1: 621; to J. Achurch, 14 April 1896, *CL* 1: 625; 13 and 14 March 1896, *Diaries* 1: 1123.

6. To J. Achurch, 14 April 1896, *CL* 1: 625. *Ec-stasis* means the stepping aside from everyday life, a dynamic emerging in which past, present, and future interpenetrate. On ecstasy see Heidegger, *Being and Time*.

7. Ervine, *Bernard Shaw*, 384.

8. To J. Achurch, 14 April 1896, *CL* 1: 625; letter to J. Achurch, 8 January 1895, published in M. Peters, *Bernard Shaw and the Actresses*, 142.

9. *Back to Methuselah*, *CP* 5: 630.

10. "The Revolutionist's Handbook," *CP* 2: Shaw's note, 753.

11. To F. Harris, 20 June 1930, *CL* 4: 190.

Chapter 25: The Accidental Bridegroom

1. 16 September 1896, *Diary of Beatrice Webb* 2: 100–101.

2. For a full account of Charlotte's social life see Dunbar, *Mrs. G. B. S.*.

3. 16 September 1896, *Diary of Beatrice Webb* 2: 100–101; 21 March 1896, *Diaries* 2: 1124; to E. Terry, 5 December 1896, *CL* 1: 709.

4. To E. Terry, 28 August 1896, *CL* 1: 645–646.

5. To E. Terry, 21 September 1896, *CL* 1: 659.

6. 16 September 1896, *Diary of Beatrice Webb* 2: 100–101; to E. Terry, 24 December 1897, *CL* 1: 831.

7. See Dunbar, *Mrs. G. B. S.*, for more detail.

8. To J. Achurch, 24 August 1895, *CL* 1: 547. Hector Hushabye makes a similar complaint in *Heartbreak House*. Bertha quoted in Laurence's headnote, *CL* 1: 546.

9. To F. Farr, 14 October 1896, *CL* 1: 679; to C. Payne-Townshend, 17 October 1896, *CL* 1: 681; to J. Achurch, 30 October 1896, *CL* 1: 687; to C. Payne-Townshend, 2 November 1896, *CL* 1: 690; 9 March 1897, *Diary of Beatrice Webb* 2: 110–111.

10. To E. Terry, 4 November 1896, *CL* 1: 693; E. Terry to Shaw, 6 November 1896,

Terry / Shaw, 110; to C. Payne-Townshend, 9 November 1896, *CL* 1: 699; to C. Payne-Townshend, 16 November 1896, *CL* 1: 700; *whirlwind:* to E. Terry, 16 November 1896, *CL* 1: 702.

11. To E. Terry, 16 November 1896, *CL* 1: 702–703.

12. "The Second Dating of Sheridan," *Saturday Review*, 27 June 1896, *Drama Observed* 2: 629, and *OTN* 2: 178. M. Peters reads the two letters as sexual consummation (*Bernard Shaw and the Actresses*, 193–194); Holroyd follows her lead (*Bernard Shaw* 1: 438). In contrast, Silver sees Charlotte as a virgin who refused sex with Shaw (*Bernard Shaw*, 135). The letter to Ellen of 16 November 1896 sounds remarkably like a 1933 diary entry made by the writer Anaïs Nin in which she describes the aftermath of a sexual encounter with René Félix Allendy, her psychiatrist. She finds him an inadequate lover and writes of his nervousness and jealousy: "How differently I sense man's ordeal and diffidence. Laugh it off, conquer it. And make the man happy. And that is all. A gift. I make a gift in return for the tribute of his love. And I am free of debts. And I walk joyously away, debtless, independent, uncaptured. A little ironic. Will I write all I thought? Oh, I was diabolical." Since the Ellen Terry correspondence was published in 1931, Nin could have read it before making her diary entry (though she need not have, since she constantly edited her diaries over the years). Nin regarded herself as the essence of femininity, a female Don Juan, a female inhabited by a male spirit. She also wrote her lovers about other men and felt an affinity to the Pygmalion-like legend of Alraune, the woman created by an alchemist. That she might have consciously or unconsciously echoed Shaw, imitating his role in a love relationship, suggests her recognition of his underlying gender uncertainty. See Anaïs Nin, *Incest: From "A Journal of Love": The Unexpurgated Diary of Anaïs Nin, 1932–1934* (New York: Harcourt Brace, 1992), 11 April 1933, 137.

13. To E. Terry, 8 March 1897, *CL* 1: 733; 1 May 1897, *Diary of Beatrice Webb* 2: 111–113; 8 May 1897, *Diary of Beatrice Webb* 2: 115; 24 May 1897, *Diary of Beatrice Webb* 2: 116.

14. To E. Terry, 5 August 1897, *CL* 1: 792–793. When the E. Terry correspondence was published the passage with Charlotte's proposal was excised see *Terry / Shaw*, 224; 27 September 1897, *Diary of Beatrice Webb* 2: 123.

15. To C. Payne-Townshend, 18 October 1897, *CL* 1: 816; to C. Payne-Townshend, 3 December 1897, *CL* 1: 826; to C. Payne-Townshend, 8 December 1897, *CL* 1: 826–827.

16. To C. Payne-Townshend, 30 March 1898, *CL* 2: 24.

17. On illnesses, to C. Payne-Townshend, 5, 7, and 8 April 1898, *CL* 2: 27–29; to S. Webb, 11 April 1898, *CL* 2: 29; "The Drama in Hoxton," 9 April 1898, *Drama Observed* 3:1036, and *OTN* 3: 375.

18. To C. Payne-Townshend, 19 April 1898, *CL* 2: 32; 21 April 1898, *CL* 2: 32–33; to B. Webb, 21 June 1898, *CL* 2: 50; to C. Payne-Townshend, 27 April 1898, *CL* 2: 37–38; 7 May 1898, "Van Amburgh Revived," *Drama Observed* 3: 1051–1052, and *OTN* 3: 394–397.

19. To J. Achurch, 11 May 1898, *CL* 2: 42; to Bram Stoker, 2 May 1898, *CL* 2: 39; *annual:* to G. Wallas, 16 November 1987, *CL* 1: 823; "On Pleasure Bent," 20 November 1897, *Drama Observed* 3: 944–945, and *OTN* 3: 262–264; "G. B. S. Vivisected," 14 May 1898, *Drama Observed* 3: 1056–1059, and *OTN* 3: 401–405; "Valedictory," 21 May 1898, *Drama Observed* 3: 1059, 1061, and *OTN* 3: 405, 407.

20. To H. A. Jones, 20 May 1898, *CL* 2: 44; H. A. Jones to Shaw, 24 May 1898, D. A. Jones,

Taking the Curtain Call, 166; Shaw to M. Hecht, 23 May 1898, *CL* 2: 44; to B. Webb, 21 June 1898, *CL* 2: 51.

21. Quoted in Ervine, *Bernard Shaw,* 304; to C. Payne-Townshend, 26 April 1898, *CL* 2: 37; to B. Webb, 21 June 1898, *CL* 2: 51; *Man and Superman, CP* 2: 611, 729; *ethereal:* to B. Webb, 21 June 1898, *CL* 2: 50.

22. To H. S. Salt, 31 May 1898, *CL* 2: 46; *violently:* to G. Wallas, 26 May 1898, *CL* 2: 46; to W. Archer, 6 June 1898, *CL* 2: 48; *Man and Superman, CP* 2: 636.

23. To G. Wallas, 26 May 1898, *CL* 2: 45–46; Shaw on Wallas quoted in Henderson, *Man,* 418.

24. "Mainly About People," 2 June 1898, *The Star,* rpt. in *CL* 2: 46–47.

25. Preface to *Getting Married, CP* 3: 501, 533; *difference:* to R. G. Bright, 22 April 1895, *CL* 1: 526. On finances and *The Devil's Disciple* see Shaw's letter to Richard Mansfield, 8 September 1897. Mansfield's reply of 27 September to Shaw, and Laurence's note, *CL* 1: 803–806. Shaw mentions both his income and Charlotte's settlement on him to T. D. O'Bolger, 28 June 1922, *CL* 3: 777.

26. M. E. McNulty to Shaw, 2 June 1898, *SHAW* 12: 33; on second operation, to H. S. Salt, 28 July 1898, *CL* 2: 56; on toe, to M. E. McNulty, ca. 12 November 1898, *CL* 2: 70; *on one leg:* to B. Webb, 21 June 1898, *CL* 2: 51; *all broken, helpless:* to H. A. Jones, 25 June 1898, D. A. Jones, *Taking the Curtain Call,* 166–167; on Bedborough see Ellis, Foreword to *Studies in the Psychology of Sex,* vol. 1: xv–xix.

27. To S. C. Cockerell, 17 October 1899, *CL* 2: 111; to E. R. Pease, 30 October 1899, *CL* 2: 115.

28. *Man and Superman, CP* 2: 592–593; *Master:* Henderson, *Man,* 21; "Vegetarian and Arboreal," 30 October 1897, *Drama Observed* 3: 928–931, and *OTN* 3: 241–45.

29. To H. G. Barker, 12 August 1904, *CL* 2: 443.

30. *Man and Superman, CP* 2: 651, 683.

31. Preface to *Getting Married, CP* 3: 462; to W. Archer, 15 November 1905, *CL* 2: 579; to T. D. O'Bolger, 12 April 1916, *CL* 3: 382; to F. Harris, 24 June 1931, *CL* 4: 192. Silver, following St. John Ervine and biographical tradition, contends that it was Charlotte's wish that the marriage not be consummated. Having been "emasculated" by Charlotte, Shaw then allegedly took out his rage in *Man and Superman,* the superman really a "sadomasochistic and homicidal fantasy, born of deprivation." Silver correctly identifies Shaw's sexual passivity but incorrectly blames Charlotte—on whom Shaw wanted to place the blame. See Silver, *Bernard Shaw,* 135–175, above quotation, 169.

32. Preface to *Getting Married, CP* 3: 527; Symonds to Carpenter, 21 January 1893, *The Letters of John Addington Symonds,* quoted in Weeks, *Coming Out,* 56.

33. To E. Terry, 5 December 1896, *CL* 1: 709; to F. Harris, 24 June 1930, *CL* 4: 193.

34. Ellis and Symonds, *Sexual Inversion,* 145–147; Ellis, *Studies in the Psychology of Sex,* vol. 1, part 4, 335; *The Simpleton of the Unexpected Isles, CP* 6: 803, 807; Ellis quotes Hirschfeld's findings that fifty percent of married inverts are impotent (*Studies in the Psychology of Sex,* vol. 1, part 4, 334).

35. Woman quoted from Elliot, *Dear Mr Shaw,* 181; *SSS,* 128; Preface to *Getting Married, CP* 3: 527–528, 511.

Chapter 26: A Woman Without Petticoats

1. "Woman—Man in Petticoats," *New York Times Magazine*, 19 June 1927, rpt. in *Platform and Pulpit*, 174.

2. On men in petticoats see Hyde, *Tangled Web*, 84–88; *Major Barbara*, *CP* 3: 184.

3. On farce and infidelity see the Preface to *Overruled*, *CP* 4: 827–845; see also the introductory note in *How He Lied to Her Husband*, *CP* 2: 1031. On adultery in the theater see Eric Bentley, *Life of the Drama* (New York: Atheneum, 1964), 238.

4. Preface to *The Shewing-up of Blanco Posnet*, *CP* 3: 698. On censorship see *CP* 3: 674–762, 800–812; see letters and self-interviews on censorship appended to *Press Cuttings*, *CP* 3: 884–895. On censorship and *Mrs Warren's Profession* see Preface to the play, *CP* 1: 231–271; see also Preface to *Plays Unpleasant*, for a discussion that includes *Widowers' Houses*, 20–23.

5. Wilde to Ives, 21 March 1898, *Letters of Oscar Wilde*, 721. On Ives and the Order see Weeks, *Coming Out*, 115–127. On the ancient Greek Sacred Band see Symonds, "A Problem in Greek Ethics" in Ellis and Symonds, *Sexual Inversion*, 231. Bentley alludes to this quotation via *Monstrous Martyrdoms*, the title of a volume of his plays that includes the biographical *Lord Alfred's Lover*, the latter intended as a diptych with his book on Shaw.

6. Ellis to Norman Haire, 16 April 1924, Grosskurth, *Havelock Ellis*, 377; *cabal:* d'Arch Smith, *Love in Earnest*, 137; on the misleading accusation see Weeks, *Coming Out*, 124; Weeks mentions members, including Shaw, *Coming Out*, 136.

7. To A. Henderson, 3 January 1905, *CL* 2: 490–491.

8. For an erotics of literary collaboration beween men see Koestenbaum, *Double Talk*, which I found provocative and useful.

9. Earlier version appears as "Who I Am, and What I Think," *The Candid Friend*, 11 May 1901, rpt. in Laurence, *Selected Non-Dramatic Writings of Bernard Shaw*, 447; later version as *SSS*, 33; to M. E. McNulty, 29 June 1908, *CL* 2: 791.

10. To M. E. McNulty, 29 June 1908, *CL* 2: 792.

11. To George Standring, ca. 4 June 1889, *CL* 1: 212; see letters to J. Magny, 4 June 1889, *CL* 1: 211–212, and 7 June 1889, *CL* 1: 213; on money earned see *Diaries* 1: 574.

12. 5 September 1890, *Diaries* 1: 647; *Sentiments:* to J. Magny, 12 September 1890, *CL* 1: 262; to J. Magny, 25 November 1890, *CL* 1: 273; *genders:* to S. Webb, 12 August 1892, *CL* 1: 359.

13. To J. Magny, 16 December 1890, *CL* 1: 277–279.

14. To J. Magny, 18 December 1890, *CL* 1: 279–280; *Man and Superman*, *CP* 2: 752–753.

15. *If only:* to F. H. Evans, 14 August 1895, *CL* 1: 544; *I always:* to F. H. Evans, 27 August 1895, *CL* 1: 550–551.

16. *manufacture, Liberty:* to F. H. Evans, 25 September 1895, *CL* 1: 561; on Shaw as teetotaler, to F. H. Evans, 15 October 1895, *CL* 1: 563; *giant:* to F. H. Evans, 5 December 1895, *CL* 1: 573; to F. H. Evans, 17 September 1896, *CL* 1: 656.

17. *On the Rocks*, *CP* 6: 712; *Cape Times*, 8 February 1932, a long excerpt in Leon Hugo, "Upset in a 'Suntrap': Shaw in South Africa," *SHAW* 5: 160–61; *The Adventures of the Black Girl*, in *Short Stories, Scraps and Shavings*, 268–269, 287; *Heartbreak House*, *CP* 5: 89; *Back to Methuselah*, *CP* 5: 477, 480. Shaw thought the "sterility" of white South Africans was from

lack of pigmentation, which could be offset by intermarriage with black Africans: "the future is to the mongrel, not to the Junker . . . and if Germany boycotts me, so much the worse for German culture," he wrote S. Trebitsch, 27 June 1935, *CL* 4: 413. Shaw's racial attitudes are also revealed in his admiring comment that black actors usually act "with much more delicacy and grace than white actors"; there was no reason they could not portray Shakespeare's white Europeans and likely would give a better performance than a white company because they would "hardly venture" without some special qualifications, unlike a white company; see letter to F. V. Connolly, 18 July 1919, *CL* 3: 623.

18. *Towards Democracy*, 14.

19. "Evans—An Appreciation, 1903," *Camera Work*, October 1903, rpt. in *Bernard Shaw on Photography* (hereafter *Photography*), 96–101; *mastery: Photography*, 28. On Coburn at Shaw's home see Henderson, *Man*, 795; see also letter to Coburn, 26 July 1904, *CL* 2: 435.

20. Coburn, *Alvin Langdon Coburn, Photographer*, 36; Shaw's statement originally appeared in "Preface, Photographs By Mr. Alvin Langdon Coburn, 1906," rpt. in *Photography*, 103–106.

21. Shaw told S. Trebitsch that he had to forbid Pascal to kiss him because it scandalized villagers at Ayot St. Lawrence, 23 May 1948, *CL* 4: 818. The Shaw-Pascal relationship is documented in several places. Pascal's widow has recorded her husband's stories about himself, and his arrival at Shaw's flat is corroborated by his secretary, Blanche Patch, which suggests that the first part of the story may also be true (see Pascal, *Disciple and His Devil*, 67–68, 76–77, 86); Patch, *Thirty Years with G. B. S.*, 143; Dukore finds much early Pascal biography unverifiable but concludes that the man was so flamboyant that the stories, "however fantastic, might be true" (see his *Collected Screenplays of Bernard Shaw*, 59). On meeting Pascal see also Costello, *Serpent's Eye*, 46–48.

22. To T. Hopkins, 31 August 1889, *CL* 1: 223; to David J. O'Donoghue, 9 May 1889, *CL* 1: 210; to R. G. Bright, 19 November 1894, *CL* 1: 461; "Two New Plays," 12 January 1895, *Drama Observed* 1: 240, and *OTN* 1: 9–10.

23. To F. Harris, 7 October 1908, *CL* 2: 813; *Degenerate's View*, 381, and *Sanity*, 326–327; to F. Harris, 7 August 1916, *Shaw/Harris*, 32; "An Old New Play and a New Old One," 23 February 1895, *Drama Observed* 1: 268–269, and *OTN* 1: 44–45; Nordau, *Degeneration*, 319.

24. O. Wilde to Shaw, 23 February 1893, *Letters of Oscar Wilde*, 332.

25. To O. Wilde, 28 February 1893, *CL* 1: 384.

26. O. Wilde to Shaw, 9 May 1893, *Letters of Oscar Wilde*, 339; H. Pearson deciphers the numbers in *George Bernard Shaw*, 446.

27. To W. Archer, 18 and 22 February 1901, *CL* 2: 218–219; Archer quoted in headnote, *CL* 2: 217; S. Weintraub draws the parallels between the two plays in "'The Hibernian School'" (*SHAW* 13: 42–45). See also Thomas R. Whitaker, "Playing in Earnest," *Omnium Gatherum*, ed. Susan Dick et al. (Gerrards Cross: Colin Smythe, 1989), 416–417.

28. d'Arch Smith, *Love in Earnest*, xix; *You Never Can Tell*, *CP* 1: 765. The editor of the volume of poetry, John Gambril Nicholson, came to know Carpenter at some point, and, of course, Shaw was acquainted with a number of Uranians.

29. To F. Harris, 7 August 1916, *Shaw/Harris*, 33; Harris, *Oscar Wilde*, 393; *Pen Portraits*, 303. S. Weintraub attributes the editing of the letter to Harris; however, Shaw's retention of the revision indicates his tacit agreement that it was indiscreet (*Shaw/Harris*, 27).

30. To S. Trebitsch, 23 June 1904, *Shaw / Trebitsch*, 71; to R. Ross, 13 March 1905, *CL* 2: 521.

31. To F. Harris, 7 August 1916, *Shaw / Harris*, 31.

32. To F. Harris, 7 August 1916, *Shaw / Harris*, 38; H. Pearson, *George Bernard Shaw*, 447.

Chapter 27: The Man Who Lived in Fairyland

1. To D. J. O'Donoghue, 9 May 1889, *CL* 1: 210; on jobs, to T. D. O'Bolger, 9 October 1919, *CL* 3: 636–637; "How William Archer impressed Bernard Shaw" (hereafter "Archer"), Shaw's Introduction to *Three Plays by Archer*, 1927, rpt. in *Pen Portraits*, 30, 4.

2. To W. Archer, 16 April 1886, *CL* 1: 153–154; 11, 16, and 18 April 1886, *Diaries* 1: 160–162; on *A Doll's House*, to W. Archer, 11 June 1889, *CL* 1: 214; 7, 8, and 11 June 1889, *Diaries* 1: 508–510; *cheque, brains:* to W. Archer, 14 December 1885, *CL* 1: 146.

3. "Archer," *Pen Portraits*, 10–12.

4. *married man:* "Archer," *Pen Portraits*, 11–12; *suddenly:* to E. Terry, 5 August 1897, *CL* 1: 792–793; to G. Wallas, 27 July 1897, *CL* 1: 790; W. Archer, 14 December 1892, *The World*, rpt. in Evans, *Critical Heritage*, 51; Shaw to W. Archer, 15 November 1905, *CL* 2: 578, 576; *smutty:* 12 October 1886, *Diaries* 1: 204.

5. To W. Archer, 13 November 1891, *CL* 1: 328.

6. On Frances Archer see Whitebrook, *William Archer*, 102, 104; Shaw to W. Archer, 2 September 1903, *CL* 2: 357.

7. On rehearsal see Whitebrook, *William Archer*, 127; to E. Robins, 20 April 1891, *CL* 1: 291–292; to W. Archer, 7 November 1891, *CL* 1: 320–321; to W. Archer, 9 November 1891, *CL* 1: 322.

8. To E. Robins, 5 February 1893, *CL* 1: 380; 4 February 1893, *Diaries* 2: 902; *gift:* to E. Robins, 13 February 1899, *CL* 2: 77. Whitebrook sees the the Archer-Robins relationship as sexual (see *William Archer*). On the basis of Robins's diaries, however, Gates believes that the relationship remained platonic (see *Elizabeth Robins, 1862–1952*, 53, 88, on Shaw's help, 160).

9. The complete Archer piece is in Evans, *Critical Heritage*, 48–53; a long excerpt appears as part of "The Author's Preface" to *Widowers' Houses*, *CP* 1: 37–39.

10. *CP* 1: 38–39.

11. To W. Archer, 4 October 1887, *CL* 1: 175–176.

12. *CP* 1: 41; "Archer," *Pen Portraits*, 23; *CP* 1: 39; *violent hands:* Preface to *Plays Unpleasant*, *CP* 1: 17; on Archer's comment see *CP* 1: 39; *my genius:* to W. Archer, 4 October 1887, *CL* 1: 176.

13. 6 October 1887, *Diaries* 1: 304; "Archer," *Pen Portraits*, 8; *CP* 1: 18, 40.

14. *CP* 1: 40; on view see "Archer," *Pen Portraits*, 23; to W. Archer, 1 and 2 March 1902, *CL* 2: 264.

15. To W. Archer, 18 October 1919, *CL* 3: 640.

16. "Archer," *Pen Portraits*, 19, 31, 2, 1.

17. To W. Archer, 14 December 1924 *CL* 3: 892–895. Shaw reprints Archer's letter in the tribute to his friend ("Archer," *Pen Portraits*, 31–32, Shaw's comment, 32).

Chapter 28: A New Hermes

1. To F. Harris, 24 June 1930, *CL* 4: 191; *SSS*, 114. Bullough notes that Aphrodite was not of woman born in Ulrichs, *Riddle of "Man-Manly" Love*, 24; see also Graves, *Greek Myths*, 39, 49.

2. *Caesar and Cleopatra, CP* 2: 270, 269.

3. To S. Cockerell, 20 April 1906, *CL* 2: 618–619; on Rodin's character see Author's Note, *The Six of Calais, CP* 6: 992.

4. "Rodin," *The Nation*, 9 November 1912, rpt. in *Pen Portraits*, 238, and *London Art*, 408; *dictionaries: London Art*, 411; *cherished:* to Hugh Lane, 5 October 1908, *CL* 2: 811; to Evacustus Phipson, Jr., 14 March 1892, *London Art*, 353–354.

5. Coburn, *Alvin Langdon Coburn, Photographer*, 40; Henderson, *Life*, 226.

6. On art photography see *The World*, 12 October 1887 and 17 October 1888, and the letter of 7 September 1900 to the editor, *The Amateur Photographer*, rpt. in *Photography*, 54–59; on posing nude see "Rodin," *Pen Portraits*, 239, and *London Art*, 409; Coburn, *Alvin Langdon Coburn, Photographer*, viii.

7. On the spectator as male see Berger, *Ways of Seeing*, 45–64. Preface to Coburn Exhibition Catalogue 5, February 1906, rpt. as "Preface, Photographs, by Mr. Alvin Langdon Coburn, 1906," in *Photography*, 105; *teaches:* "The Exhibitions," 18 October 1901, *The Amateur Photographer*, rpt. in *Photography*, 70; on Steichen see "Some Criticisms of the Exhibitions. The 'Life Study,' 'The Fuzzygraph,' and 'The Under-Exposed,' 1902," rpt. in *Photography*, 88.

8. To E. Terry, 16 October 1896, *CL* 1: 680; "Rodin," *Pen Portraits*, 238, 241, and *London Art*, 409–410.

9. On photo poses, R. M. Rilke to S. Fischer, 19 April 1906, *Letters of Rainer Maria Rilke, 1892–1910* (hereafter *Rilke Letters*), 205; R. M. Rilke to C. Rilke, postmarked 19 April 1906, *Rilke Letters*, 207; *violence*: Rodin quoted by Shaw to T. D. O'Bolger, February 1916, *CL* 3: 371; on Rodin's sensuality, quoted in Grunfeld, *Rodin*, 514; "Rodin," *Pen Portraits*, 239, and *London Art*, 409; *Benarre Chuv:* Ludovici, *Personal Reminiscences of Auguste Rodin*, 120; *Moses:* to L. McCarthy, 30 May 1906, *CL* 2: 625.

10. To E. Phipson, Jr., 14 March 1892, *London Art*, 353; self-portrait reproduced in *Photography*, following p. 50.

11. Laurence has found evidence positively identifying the Studland Bay photographs as to location, date, and photographer (Barker). Laurence also believes that Barker photographed Shaw reclining—a supposition that appears very likely, for Barker regularly accompanied Shaw on holiday (letter to me, 5 September 1994). The photograph of Shaw reclining was included in "A Private View," a 1987 exhibit of nudes by the Royal Photographic Society. Out of some 140 photographs of nudes, only about 10 were of men, a number that includes 2 photographic banners of Adam and Eve commissioned for the exhibition (to me from P. Roberts, curator, the Royal Photographic Society, 26 September 1994).

Chapter 29: Heartbreak, Secrecy, and the "marvellous boy"

1. On Walkley's challenge see Epistle Dedicatory to *Man and Superman, CP* 2: 493; on Goethe, to C. Charrington, 26 December 1903, *CL* 2: 385.

2. *John Bull's Other Island, CP* 2: 901, 909; McCarthy, "How Bernard Shaw Produces Plays," rpt. *SHAW* 3: 164.

3. On Macduff, to W. Archer, 27 August 1903, *CL* 2: 352; *CP* 2: 813, 814; "Ireland Eternal and External," *The New Statesman*, 30 October 1948, rpt. *The Matter with Ireland*, 294.

4. "Mr. G. B. Shaw's Next Play," *CP* 3: 437; on Wright, to A. B. Walkley, 18 November 1906, *CL* 2: 660; on Charlotte see Dunbar, *Mrs. G. B. S.*, 191; William Archer, "About the Theatre," *The Tribune*, 21 November 1906, rpt. in Martin Quinn, "William Archer and *The Doctor's Dilemma*," *SHAW* 4: 99.

5. Suggested act 3 ending for *The Madras House, CP* 7: 609–612; L. McCarthy on *Misalliance*, Purdom, *Harley Granville Barker*, 102–103.

6. Several links between plays noted in Morgan, *Drama of Political Man*, 3, 89. When *Waste*, Barker's 1907 tragedy (rewritten in 1926), was banned, Shaw was among those who signed a letter of protest.

7. Bentley, *Playwright as Thinker*, 119. Whitaker sees Barker wielding his negative technique directly in response to Shavian dramaturgy; see "Granville Barker's Answer to *Heartbreak*," *SHAW* 10: 86.

8. Preface to 4th ed. (1923), *The Perfect Wagnerite, Music* 3: 418; on Irving see Preface to *Terry / Shaw*, xxvii; on Tree see "Tappertit on Caesar," 29 January 1898, *Drama Observed* 3:991, and *OTN* 3: 317.

9. MacCarthy tallies eleven plays, with *Man and Superman* counted as two, acts 1, 2, and 4 being produced separately from the Don Juan in Hell scene (*The Court Theatre, 1904–1907*, 123); to C. B. Purdom, 12 January 1930, *CL* 4: 170.

10. McCarthy, *Myself and My Friends*, 59; Jane Morris wore violet to her husband's funeral, giving Shaw the idea; to L. McCarthy, 14 March 1905, *CL* 2: 522; Shaw gave similar advice on Ann's costume to Frances Dillon, 21 November 1908, *CL* 2: 818.

11. "Granville Barker: Some Particulars by Shaw," *Drama*, Winter 1946, 7; see also West, *Shaw on Theatre;* to C. B. Purdom, 12 January 1930, *CL* 4: 171; *Back to Methuselah, CP* 5: 383.

12. To W. Archer, 14 December 1924, *CL* 3: 893; to C. Charrington, 27 June 1901, *CL* 2: 227; *Times Literary Supplement*, 12 September 1946, rpt. *Granville Barker and His Correspondents* (hereafter *Barker Correspondents*), 163.

13. W. S. Maugham, *The Summing Up*, quoted in Purdom, *Harley Granville Barker*, 16; to S. Trebitsch, 22 October 1903, *Shaw / Trebitsch*, 65; to A. Rehan, 27 October 1904, *CL* 2: 458.

14. To W. Archer, 14 December, 1924, *CL* 3: 894, to A. W. Pinero, 21 March 1910, *CL* 2: 912; Henderson, *Man*, 795, 855.

15. S. Weintraub, *Private Shaw and Public Shaw*, 36; Salmon, *Granville Barker*, 5, 235–236.

16. To E. Terry, 25 November 1905, *CL* 2: 582.

17. To W. Archer, 8 July 1900, *CL* 2: 175; to C. Charrington, 6 June 1900, *CL* 2: 170; D. A. Jones writes that in 1896 her father suggested Barker as a possible Marchbanks, publishing Shaw's letter of 20 February, in which he wonders about the actor H. V. Esmond (*Taking the Curtain Call*, 172).

18. MacCarthy, *Court Theatre*, 72; to H. G. Barker, 2 September 1903, *CL* 2: 360; to H. G. Barker, 22 August 1900, *Shaw's Letters to Granville Barker* (hereafter *Shaw / Barker*), 6.

19. To. Mrs. P. Campbell, 18 September 1901, *Shaw / Campbell*, 5–6; to H. A. Jones, 20 February 1902, D. A. Jones, *Taking the Curtain Call*, 178; to S. Trebitsch 22 October 1903, *Shaw / Trebitsch*, 65; to W. Archer, 27 August 1903, *CL* 2: 352; to C. B. Purdom, 12 January 1930, *CL* 4: 171.

20. To R. Mansfield, 22 February 1895, *CL* 1: 486. *Agnes Colander* was completed in January 1901. This unpublished and unproduced play illustrates Barker's "enormous preoccupation with the connection between the spiritual and the physical in the sexual relation," as well as the "relationship between sexual energy and artistic energy" (Salmon, *Granville Barker*, 68, 72).

21. To J. Achurch, 25 December 1900, *CL* 2: 208; to H. G. Barker, 7 December 1900, *Shaw / Barker*, 7; on Thorpe, to W. Archer, 27 March 1902, *CL* 2: 271; on anticlimax see "Who I Am, and What I Think," *The Candid Friend*, 11 May 1901, rpt. in Laurence, *Selected Non-Dramatic Writings*, 446.

22. *Mrs Warren's Profession*, *CP* 1: 286; to H. G. Barker, 31 December 1901, *Shaw / Barker*, 10; *"Frank the First"*: Purdom's note, *Shaw / Barker*, 11; on Keegan see *CP* 2: 925; Cusins's model in real life was Gilbert Murray, a friend of Shaw and Barker; see Shaw's letter to Murray, 7 October 1905, *CL* 2: 566. Turco sees Cusins as Shaw's attempt to "improve upon" Wagner's Siegfried (*Shaw's Moral Vision*, note, 217); on Dubedat see *CP* 3: 363; on ghastly death, to S. Trebitsch, 20 April 1908, *Shaw / Trebitsch*, 137; on lover see *CP* 2: 1032.

23. To H. G. Barker, 6 December 1904, *CL* 2: 471; *old buffer:* to C. Charrington, 27 June 1901, *CL* 2: 227, and to H. A. Jones, 20 February 1902, D. A. Jones, *Taking the Curtain Call*, 178; Barker quoted by John Gielgud, Foreword to *Barker Correspondents*, 10; Preface to *Music* 1: 57.

24. To M. E. McNulty, 29 June 1908, *CL* 2: 792; Theodore Stier, *With Pavlova Around the World*, quoted in Purdom, *Harley Granville Barker*, 56.

25. As Octavius, to H. G. Barker, 20 August 1903, *Shaw / Barker*, 15; Purdom, *Harley Granville Barker*, 40; "A New Lady Macbeth and and a New Mrs Ebbsmith," 25 May 1895, *Drama Observed* 2: 353, and *OTN* 1: 139; "G. B. S. and a Suffragist: An Intimate Interview by Maud Churton Braby," 12 March 1906, *Tribune*, rpt. in R. Weintraub, *Fabian Feminist*, 241–242; Lillah's account has her writing Shaw first before showing up, *Myself and My Friends*, 55–56.

26. Shaw, "An Aside," in McCarthy, *Myself and My Friends*, 5.

27. McCarthy, *Myself and My Friends*, 65; Humanities Research Center, University of Texas, quoted in Salmon, *Granville Barker*, 72.

28. McCarthy, *Myself and My Friends*, 66; on *Caesar and Cleopatra* see letter to S. Trebitsch, 7 May 1906, *CL* 2: 619–620, and to H. G. Barker, 7 May 1906, *CL* 2: 621–622.

29. To L. McCarthy, 30 May 1906, *CL* 2: 624–625; *dismayed:* "Granville Barker: Some Particulars by Shaw," *Drama*, Winter 1946, 12.

30. 4 September 1906, *Diary of Beatrice Webb* 3: 48.

31. Henderson, *Man*, 678.

32. On conversing in quotations, to C. B. Purdom, 12 January 1930, *CL* 4: 171; on motoring, to C. Shaw, 28 April 1912, *CL* 3: 86; *Lillah's place:* to S. Trebitsch, postmarked 30 June 1913, *Shaw / Trebitsch*, 165.

33. To Mrs. P. Campbell, 22 February 1913, *CL* 3: 151–152.

34. To E. Terry, 8 September 1897, *CL* 1: 803; to H. G. Barker, 30 June 1912, *CL* 3: 95; to E. Terry, 20 August 1912, *CL* 3: 111.

35. To Mrs. P. Campbell, 4 January 1913, *CL* 3: 144; to Mrs. P. Campbell, 9 June 1913, *CL* 3: 184; from Dresden to Mrs. P. Campbell, 30 June, 1 July 1913, *Shaw / Campbell*, 137–142; from Devon, to Mrs. P. Campbell, 2 August 1913, *CL* 3: 193–194; *broken promise:* to Mrs. P. Campbell, 13 August 1913, *CL* 3: 197; to Shaw, 15 August 1913, *Shaw / Campbell*, 160; *order of nature:* to Mrs. P. Campbell, 11 August 1913, *Shaw / Campbell*, 156; *feminine:* to Mrs. P. Campbell, 16 August 1913, *Shaw / Campbell*, 161.

36. *CP* 6: 344; on Edith Evans, to Shaw from Mrs. P. Campbell, 7 June 1929, *Shaw / Campbell*, 327; *climax:* to Mrs. P. Campbell, 31 March 1929, *Shaw / Campbell*, 314; to Mrs. P. Campbell, 6 April 1929, *CL* 4: 133.

37. *The Apple Cart, CP* 6: 342, 344–345, 348; to Mrs. P. Campbell, 8 December 1912, *Shaw / Campbell*, 64.

38. To Mrs. P. Campbell, 11 August 1913, *Shaw / Campbell*, 156; to C. Shaw, 16 August 1913, *CL* 3: 198.

39. H. G. Barker to L. McCarthy, 3 January 1916, *Barker Correspondents*, 191–192; Shaw to L. McCarthy, 19 January 1916, *CL* 3: 352.

40. On Barker's standing watch see Salmon, *Granville Barker*, 247.

41. To L. McCarthy, 17 August 1917, *CL* 3: 501; to L. McCarthy, 2 September 1917, *CL* 3: 503. Although she is not named, the threat suggests the young Erica Cotterill; see Winsten, *Jesting Apostle*, 142–143.

42. To L. McCarthy, 2 September 1917, *CL* 3: 504; Shaw's words to Lillah quoted from Purdom, *Harley Granville Barker*, 175; H. Pearson, *George Bernard Shaw*, 461.

43. *Heartbreak House, CP* 5:86; on bewitched, H. Pearson, *George Bernard Shaw*, 461–462.

44. To M. Tompkins, 8 January 1928, *CL* 4: 83; to M. Tompkins, 17 February 1931, *CL* 4: 227–228; *particular friends:* to Stella Beech, 8 November 1943, *CL* 4: 683; to M. Tompkins, 17 February 1931, *CL* 4: 228.

45. To M. Tompkins, 27 January 1926, *CL* 4: 8; on their relationship peaking see Molly's letter to Shaw, November 1945, in M. Peters, *Bernard Shaw and the Actresses*, 408–409; *fastidious:* to M. Tompkins, 24 November 1935, P. Tompkins, *To a Young Actress*, 167; *hog, vamp:* to M. Tompkins, 31 May 1928, *CL* 4: 99–100. The fullest description of Shaw's relationship to Molly is Berst, "Passion at Lake Maggiore."

46. Letters to Stanley J. Rubenstein of 9, 23, and 29 October 1928, *CL* 4: 111–112, 115–116, 117; also to Albert V. Baillie, *CL* 4: 117–119. On Hall's trial see Vera Brittain, *Radclyffe Hall: A Case of Obscenity?* (London: Femina, 1968); on Barker's return see H. Pearson, *George Bernard Shaw*, 463. For a detailed account of the deletion of Barker's name see Salmon, *Barker Correspondents*, 171–175.

47. To F. E. Hardy, 15 June 1924, *CL* 3: 880; to W. Archer, 14 December 1924, *CL* 3: 894.

48. To W. Archer, 14 December 1924, *CL* 3: 894–895. T. E. Lawrence to Shaw, 17 August 1922, Garnett, *Letters of T. E. Lawrence*, 355–357. Shaw's comment on Lawrence's new name was made in 1927 in the Preface to "Catalogue of an Exhibition of Paintings, Pastels, Drawings and Woodcuts illustrating Col. T. E. Lawrence's book 'Seven Pillars of Wisdom,'" Laurence and Leary, *Complete Prefaces* 2: 553. A decade later Shaw wrote that Lawrence's "assumption of the name Shaw had nothing to do with me"; see letter to O. A. Forsyth-Major of 27 May

1937, *CL* 4: 465. Gene Tunney wrote, however, that Shaw had confided to him that he and Charlotte very much appreciated the compliment. Letter to D. M. Holtzmann, 14 April 1960, quoted in Weintraub, *Private Shaw and Public Shaw*, 36.

49. See, e.g., letter to Charlotte, 28 September 1925, Brown, *Letters of T. E. Lawrence*, 289–291; on masterpiece, to S. Baldwin, 31 May 1923, *CL* 3: 830; to T. E. Lawrence, 7 October 1924, *CL* 3: 885; T. E. Lawrence to S. Cockerell, 15 October 1924, Garnett, *Letters of T. E. Lawrence*, 469; see also Laurence's discussion of Shaw's editing of *Seven Pillars*, in *A Bibliography* 1: 504; S. Weintraub suggests that the portrait of Joan owes much to Lawrence's self-portrait (*Private Shaw*, 47–54).

50. H. G. Barker to T. E. Lawrence, 6 December 1923, *Barker Correspondents*, 393–394; T. E. Lawrence to H. G. Barker, 7 February 1924, *Barker Correspondents*, 395–396.

51. *lost:* to F. E. Hardy, 15 June 1924, *CL* 3: 880; *damned:* to W. Archer, 14 December 1924, *CL* 3: 894; *Heartbreak House*, *CP* 5: 171, 102, 156.

52. For an analysis of the structure of the play, which demonstrates the presence and function of the ship of fools metaphor, see my article *"Heartbreak House:* Shaw's Ship of Fools."

53. Ervine, *Shaw*, 344; Barker is identified as a member of British Society for the Study of Sex Psychology in Weeks, *Coming Out*, 136; Barker, *The Secret Life*, 67.

54. On Shaw as a German spy, Mrs. Edith Reeves, quoted in Chappelow, *Shaw the Villager and Human Being*, 165–166. Mrs. Reeves named one of her sons Bernard "after Mr Shaw, who was fond of children" (167). To T. F. Unwin, 15 February 1916, typescript copy, Beinecke Rare Book and Manuscript Library, Yale University.

55. On the Barkers' meeting, to L. McCarthy, 5 February 1916, Purdom, *Harley Granville Barker*, 177; *suicidal:* to Mrs. P. Campbell, 14 May 1916, *Shaw / Campbell*, 209.

56. 12 November 1916, *Lady Gregory's Journals* 1: 8.

57. On Shotover, *Heartbreak House*, *CP* 5: 177; Barker mentioned, Preface to *Heartbreak House, CP* 5: 15, 50; to J. C. Squire, 14 October 1919, *CL* 3: 638.

58. Preceding two paragraphs, Barker, *The Secret Life*, 6, 22, 26, 29.

59. To T. D. O'Bolger, February 1916, *CL* 3: 373; to W. J. Pickerill, 13 August 1947, *CL* 4: 798; "The Bayreuth Hush," *The World*, 17 February 1892, *Music* 2: 544; Koestenbaum, *Queen's Throat*, 239; Barker, *The Secret Life*, 30.

60. To G. Murray, 23 October 1940, *CL* 4: 585; to O. B. Clarence, ca. late 1942, *CL* 4: 655–656.

61. H. Pearson, *Hesketh Pearson by Himself*, 275; to H. Pearson, *George Bernard Shaw*, 463; "Bernard Shaw," *Spectator*, 10 November 1950, rpt. in *Interviews*, 507.

62. On tragedy, to H. Pearson, *George Bernard Shaw*, 470.

63. Esmé Percy, "Memories of Bernard Shaw," *British Peace Committee News Letter*, March–April 1956, rpt. in *Interviews*, 528; *Times Literary Supplement*, 12 September 1946, rpt. in *Barker Correspondents*, 163.

Chapter 30: Finale

1. Ingrid Bergman's copy of *Saint Joan*, some of its pages uncut, is in the Wesleyan Cinema Archives. *Why She Would Not* was originally titled *The Lady She Would Not*. F. G.

Prince-White, "Bernard Shaw Is 94 Today," *Daily Mail*, 26 July 1950, excerpt appended to *Why She Would Not, CP* 7: 680; on following Carpenter see Preface to *Salt and His Circle*, 13–14; on telling himself stories see letter to A. Tyrrell, 14 July 1949, *CL* 4: 852.

2. To Vera Gargan, 15 May 1943, *CL* 4: 670; to A. Douglas, 15 September 1943, *CL* 4: 678; see the letters to S. Webb of 27 September 1943, *CL* 4: 681; to L. Keeble and F. Keeble, 18 September 1943, *CL* 4: 678; to H. G. Barker, 14 September 1943, *Shaw / Barker*, 199–200; *vitality:* H. Pearson, *George Bernard Shaw*, 473.

3. Shaw's last days are movingly described by Laurence, *CL* 4: 879–886. See also Bentley's eulogizing summation, "Shaw Dead." On the dream, 9 November 1919, *Lady Gregory's Journals* 1: 106; excerpt in *Interviews*, 12.

4. *Man and Superman, CP* 2: 667; "Nine Answers," rpt. in *Interviews*, 23; Epistle Dedicatory, *CP* 2: 523.

5. To A. Douglas, 30 November 1944, *Shaw / Douglas*, 192.

6. *Sanity of Art, MCE*, 323.

Selected Bibliography

Works by Bernard Shaw

Bernard Shaw: Agitations: Letters to the Press, 1875–1950. Ed. Dan H. Laurence and James Rambeau. New York: Frederick Ungar, 1985.

Bernard Shaw: Collected Letters: 1874–97, 1898–1910, 1911–25, 1926–50. Ed. Dan H. Laurence. New York: Dodd, Mead, 1965, 1972; New York: Viking, 1985, 1988.

Bernard Shaw: The Diaries, 1885–1897. 2 vols. Ed. Stanley Weintraub. University Park: Pennsylvania State University Press, 1986.

Bernard Shaw: The Road to Equality: Ten Unpublished Lectures and Essays, 1884–1918. Ed. Louis Crompton with Hilayne Cavanaugh. Boston: Beacon, 1971.

Bernard Shaw and Alfred Douglas: A Correspondence. Ed. Mary Hyde. New Haven: Ticknor and Fields, 1982.

Bernard Shaw and Mrs. Patrick Campbell: Their Correspondence. Ed. Alan Dent. New York: Knopf, 1952.

Bernard Shaw on the London Art Scene 1885–1950. Ed. Stanley Weintraub. University Park: Pennsylvania State University Press, 1989.

Bernard Shaw on Photography. Ed. Bill Jay and Margaret Moore. Salt Lake City: Peregrine Smith, 1989.

Bernard Shaw's Book Reviews: Originally Published in the Pall Mall Gazette *from 1885 to 1888.* Ed. Brian Tyson. University Park: Pennsylvania State University Press, 1991.

Bernard Shaw's Letters to Granville Barker. Ed. C. B. Purdom. New York: Theatre Arts, 1957.

Bernard Shaw's Letters to Siegfried Trebitsch. Ed. Samuel A. Weiss. Stanford: Stanford University Press, 1986.

The Bodley Head Bernard Shaw: Collected Plays with Their Prefaces. 7 vols. Editorial supervisor, Dan H. Laurence. London: Max Reinhardt, 1970–74.

The Bodley Head Bernard Shaw: Shaw's Music 1876–1890. 3 vols. Ed. Dan H. Laurence. London: Max Reinhardt, 1981.

"Bumps and Brains." *Daily Graphic,* London, 7 January 1907. Reprinted in *The Independent Shavian* 31, no. 1 (1993): 10–11.

Cashel Byron's Profession. Ed. Stanley Weintraub. Carbondale: Southern Illinois University Press, 1968.

The Collected Screenplays of Bernard Shaw. Ed. Bernard F. Dukore. Athens: University of Georgia Press, 1980.

The Collected Works of Bernard Shaw. 30 vols. Ayot St. Lawrence Edition. New York: William H. Wise, 1930–32.

The Complete Prefaces. Vol. 1: 1889–1913; vol. 2: 1914–1919. Ed. Dan H. Laurence and Daniel J. Leary. London: Allen Lane, 1993, 1995.

The Drama Observed. 4 vols. Ed. Bernard F. Dukore. University Park: Pennsylvania State University Press, 1993.

Ellen Terry and Bernard Shaw: A Correspondence. Ed. Christopher St. John. New York: Theatre Arts, 1931.

Everybody's Political What's What? New York: Dodd, Mead, 1947.

Florence Farr, Bernard Shaw, W. B. Yeats: Letters. Ed. Clifford Bax. New York: Dodd, Mead, 1942.

"George Bernard Shaw Finds Prize Fighting Not So Sanguinary." *Evening World,* New York, 9 July 1927, 12: 1–2.

"Granville Barker: Some Particulars by Shaw." *Drama,* no. 3 (Winter 1946): 7–14.

"The Great Fight, by the author of 'Cashel Byron's Profession,'" *The Nation,* December 1919, 384–386.

The Intelligent Woman's Guide to Socialism and Capitalism. New York: Brentano's, 1928.

A Manifesto. Fabian Tract no. 2. London: Fabian Society, 1884.

The Matter with Ireland. Ed. Dan H. Laurence and David H. Greene. New York: Hill and Wang, 1962.

"Morris As I Knew Him." In *William Morris: Artist, Writer, Socialist,* May Morris. *Volume the Second: Morris as a Socialist,* ix–xl. 1936. Reprint, New York: Russell and Russell, 1966.

My Dear Dorothea: A Practical System of Moral Education for Females Embodied in a Letter to a Young Person of that Sex. New York: Vanguard, 1956.

Platform and Pulpit. Ed. Dan H. Laurence. New York: Hill and Wang, 1961.

The Playwright and the Pirate: Bernard Shaw and Frank Harris: A Correspondence. Ed. Stanley Weintraub. University Park: Pennsylvania State University Press, 1982.

Preface to *Salt and His Circle,* Stephen Winsten. London: Hutchinson, 1951.

Prefaces. London: Constable, 1934.

Selected Non-Dramatic Writings of Bernard Shaw. Ed. Dan H. Laurence. Boston: Houghton Mifflin, 1965.

Shaw on Theater. Ed. E. J. West. New York: Hill and Wang, 1958.

Shaw on Vivisection. Ed. G. H. Bowker. Chicago: Alethea, 1951.

Short Stories, Scraps and Shavings. New York: Dodd, Mead, 1934.

Sixteen Self Sketches. London: Constable, 1949.

To a Young Actress: The Letters of Bernard Shaw to Molly Tompkins. Ed. Peter Tompkins. London: Constable, 1960.

Other Works

Albert, Sidney P. "Reflections on Shaw and Psychoanalysis." *Modern Drama* 14, no. 2 (1971): 169–194.

Auerbach, Nina. *Ellen Terry: Player in Her Time.* New York: W. W. Norton, 1987.

Bachelard, Gaston. *The Poetics of Space.* Trans. Maria Jolas. Boston: Beacon, 1958.

Barker, Harley Granville. *Granville Barker and His Correspondents.* Ed. Eric Salmon. Detroit: Wayne State University Press, 1986.

———. *Plays.* 2 vols. London: Methuen, 1993–94.

———. *The Secret Life.* Boston: Little, Brown, 1923.

Beerbohm, Max. *Last Theatres: 1904–1910.* New York: Taplinger, 1970.

Bentley, Eric. *Bernard Shaw.* Amended edition. New York: New Directions, 1957.

———. *The Playwright as Thinker.* New York: Meridian, 1946, 1965.

———. "Shaw Dead." In *Shaw: The Critical Heritage.* Ed. T. F. Evans, 403–407. Boston: Routledge and Kegan Paul, 1976.

———. "Shaw 40 Years Later: Eric Bentley Speaks His Mind on Eleven Neglected Plays." In *SHAW: The Annual of Bernard Shaw Studies,* vol. 7: *Shaw: The Neglected Plays.* Ed. Alfred Turco, Jr., 7–29. University Park: Pennsylvania State University Press, 1977.

———. *Thinking about the Playwright.* Evanston, Ill.: Northwestern University Press, 1987.

Berger, John. *Ways of Seeing.* London: British Broadcasting Corp., 1972; New York: Penguin, 1977.

Berst, Charles A. "Passion at Lake Maggiore: Shaw, Molly Tompkins, and Italy, 1921–1950." In *SHAW: The Annual of Bernard Shaw Studies,* vol. 5: *Shaw Abroad.* Ed. Rodelle Weintraub, 81–114. University Park: Pennsylvania State University Press, 1985.

Bertolini, John. *The Playwrighting Self of Bernard Shaw.* Carbondale: Southern Illinois University Press, 1991.

Besant, Annie. *Annie Besant: An Autobiography.* 2nd ed. London: Theosophical Publishing House, 1908.

Binswanger, Ludwig. *Being-in-the-World.* Trans. Jacob Needleman. New York: Basic Books, 1963.

Blacker, C. P. *Eugenics: Galton and After.* London: Gerald Duckworth, 1952.

Boxill, Roger. *Shaw and the Doctors.* New York: Basic Books, 1969.

Butler, Samuel. *Samuel Butler's Notebooks.* Selections edited by Geoffrey Keynes and Brian Hill. London: Jonathan Cape, 1951.

Carpenter, Edward. *Civilisation: Its Cause and Cure, and Other Essays.* 3rd ed. London: Swan Sonnenschein, 1893.

———. *The Intermediate Sex: A Study of Some Transitional Types of Men and Women.* 1908. Reprint, New York: AMS, 1983.

———. *Love's Coming of Age: A Series of Papers on the Relations of the Sexes.* New York: Mitchell Kennerley, 1911.

———. *Towards Democracy.* First published 1883; complete edition in four parts. London: Allen and Unwin, 1921.

Chappelow, Allan, editor. *Shaw the Villager and Human Being: A Biographical Symposium.* London: Charles Skilton, 1961.

Chesterton, G. K. *George Bernard Shaw.* 1910. New York: Hill and Wang, 1966.

Coburn, Alvin Langdon. *Alvin Langdon Coburn, Photographer: An Autobiography With Over 70 Reproductions of His Works.* Ed. Helmut Gernsheim and Alison Gernsheim. New York: Dover, 1978.

Costello, Donald P. *The Serpent's Eye: Shaw and the Cinema.* Notre Dame: University of Notre Dame Press, 1965.

Craig, Edward Gordon. *Ellen Terry and Her Secret Self.* London: Sampson Low, Marston, 1931.

Croft-Cooke, Rupert. *Feasting with Panthers: A New Consideration of Some Late Victorian Writers.* New York: Holt, Rinehart and Winston, 1967.

Crompton, Louis. *Shaw the Dramatist.* Lincoln: University of Nebraska Press, 1969.

Dervin, Daniel. *Bernard Shaw: A Psychological Study.* Lewisburg: Bucknell University Press, 1975.

Dietrich, R. F. *Portrait of the Artist as a Young Superman: A Study of Shaw's Novels.* Gainesville: University of Florida Press, 1969.

Dukore, Bernard F. "Shaw's 'Big Three.'" In *SHAW: The Annual of Bernard Shaw Studies,* vol. 4. Ed. Stanley Weintraub, 33–67. University Park: Pennsylvania State University Press, 1984.

Dunbar, Janet. *Mrs. G. B. S.: A Portrait.* New York: Harper and Row, 1963.

Edel, Leon. *Henry James: The Conquest of London, 1870–1881.* Philadelphia: J. B. Lippincott, 1962.

Elliot, Vivian, editor. *Dear Mr Shaw: Selections from Bernard Shaw's postbag.* London: Bloomsbury, 1987.

Ellis, Havelock. *Studies in the Psychology of Sex.* 2 vols. New York: Random House, 1942.

Ellis, Havelock, and John Addington Symonds. *Sexual Inversion.* 1897. Reprint, New York: Arno Press, 1975.

Ellmann, Richard. *Oscar Wilde.* New York: Knopf, 1988.

Erikson, Erik H. *Identity: Youth and Crisis.* New York: W. W. Norton, 1968.

Ervine, St. John. *Bernard Shaw: His Life, Work and Friends.* New York: William Morrow, 1956.

Evans, T. F., editor. *Shaw: The Critical Heritage.* Boston: Routledge and Kegan Paul, 1976.

Farmer, Henry George. *Bernard Shaw's Sister and Her Friends.* Leiden: E. J. Brill, 1959.

Farr, Florence. "Note by Florence Farr Upon Her Settings." In *Essays and Introductions,* W. B. Yeats, 21–27. New York: Macmillan, 1961.

Flugel, J. C. *The Psychology of Clothes.* New York: International Universities Press, [1966].

Freud, Sigmund. *Collected Papers.* 5 vols. New York: Basic Books, 1959.

Galton, Francis. *English Men of Science: Their Nature and Nurture.* London: Macmillan, 1874.

———. *Hereditary Genius.* New York: D. Appleton, 1870.

———. *Inquiries into Human Faculty.* [3rd ed.] London: J. M. Dent, [1907].

Gates, Joanne E. *Elizabeth Robins, 1862–1952: Actress, Novelist, Feminist.* Tuscaloosa: University of Alabama Press, 1994.

Gibbs, A. M., editor. *Shaw: Interviews and Recollections.* Iowa City: University of Iowa Press, 1990.

Goldberg, Isaac. *Havelock Ellis: A Biographical and Critical Survey.* New York: Simon and Schuster, 1926.

Graves, Robert. *The Greek Myths.* 2 vols. Baltimore: Penguin, 1955.

Green, Benny. *Shaw's Champions: G. B. S. and Prizefighting from Cashel Byron to Gene Tunney.* London: Elm Tree Books, 1978.

Greenberg, David F. *The Construction of Homosexuality.* Chicago: University of Chicago Press, 1988.

Gregory, Lady Augusta. *Lady Gregory's Journals,* vol. 1. Ed. Daniel J. Murphy. New York: Oxford University Press, 1978.

Grosskurth, Phyllis. *Havelock Ellis: A Biography.* New York: Knopf, 1980.

Grunfeld, Frederic V. *Rodin: A Biography.* New York: Henry Holt, 1987.

Gutman, Robert W. *Richard Wagner: The Man, His Mind, and His Music.* New York: Harcourt, Brace and World, 1968.

Haley, Bruce. *The Healthy Body and Victorian Culture.* Cambridge: Harvard University, 1978.

Halperin, David M. *One Hundred Years of Homosexuality and Other Essays on Greek Love.* New York: Routledge, 1990.

Harris, Frank. *Bernard Shaw.* New York: Garden City, 1931.

_____. *Contemporary Portraits.* 2nd ser. New York: Published by the author, 1919.

Heidegger, Martin. *Being and Time.* New York: Harper and Row, 1964.

Henderson, Archibald. *Bernard Shaw: Playboy and Prophet.* New York: D. Appleton, 1932.

_____. *George Bernard Shaw: His Life and Works.* Cincinnati: Stewart and Kidd, 1911.

_____. *George Bernard Shaw: Man of the Century.* New York: Appleton-Century-Crofts, 1956.

Hocquenhem, Guy. *Homosexual Desire.* Trans. Daniella Dangoor. 1978; reprint, Durham, N.C.: Duke University Press, 1993.

Holland, Norman N. *The I.* New Haven: Yale University Press, 1985.

Holroyd, Michael. *Bernard Shaw.* 4 vols. New York: Random House, 1988, 1989, 1991, 1992.

Hugo, Betty. "'Very Innocent Epistles': The Letters of Elinor Huddart to Shaw." In *SHAW: The Annual of Bernard Shaw Studies,* vol. 10. Ed. Stanley Weintraub and Fred D. Crawford, 1–11. University Park: Pennsylvania State University Press, 1990.

Hyde, H. Montgomery. *The Cleveland Street Scandal.* New York: Coward, McCann and Geoghegan, 1976.

_____. *A Tangled Web: Sex Scandals in British Politics and Society.* London: Constable, 1986.

Hyndman, Henry Mayers. *The Record of an Adventurous Life.* New York: Macmillan, 1911.

Irvine, William. *The Universe of G. B. S.* New York: Whittlesey House, 1949.

James, Henry. *The Notebooks of Henry James.* Ed. F. O. Matthiessen and Kenneth B. Murdock. New York: Oxford University Press, 1961.

_____. *A Portrait of a Lady.* Boston: Houghton Mifflin, 1882.

John, Augustus. *Chiaroscuro: Fragments of Autobiography.* New York: Pellegrini and Cudahy, 1952.

Johnson, Josephine. *Florence Farr: Bernard Shaw's 'New Woman.'* Gerrards Cross: Colin Smythe, 1975.

_____. "The Making of a Feminist: Shaw and Florence Farr." In *Fabian Feminist: Bernard Shaw and Woman.* Ed. Rodelle Weintraub, 194–205. University Park: Pennsylvania State University Press, 1977.

Jones, Doris Arthur. *Taking the Curtain Call: The Life and Letters of Henry Arthur Jones.* New York: Macmillan, 1930.

Kapp, Yvonne. *Eleanor Marx.* 2 vols. New York: Pantheon, 1972, 1976.

Knight, Stephen. *Jack the Ripper: The Final Solution*. London: Panther Books, 1977.

Koestenbaum, Wayne. *Double Talk: The Erotics of Male Literary Collaboration*. New York: Routledge, 1989.

————. *The Queen's Throat: Opera, Homosexuality, and the Mystery of Desire*. New York: Poseidon, 1993.

Krafft-Ebing, Richard Freiherr von. *Psychopathia Sexualis*. 7th ed. Trans. Charles Gilbert Chaddock, M.D. Philadelphia: F. A. Davis, 1900.

Laurence, Dan H., editor. *Bernard Shaw: A Bibliography*. 2 vols. Oxford: Clarendon, 1983.

Lawrence, D. H. *Lady Chatterley's Lover: A Propos of "Lady Chatterley's Lover."* Ed. Michael Squires. New York: Cambridge University Press, 1993.

Lawrence, T. E. *The Letters of T. E. Lawrence*. Ed. Malcolm Brown. London: J. M. Dent, 1988.

————. *The Letters of T. E. Lawrence*. Ed. David Garnett. 1938. London: Spring Books, 1964.

Lombroso, Cesare. *Crime: Its Causes and Remedies*. Trans. Henry P. Horton. Boston: Little, Brown, 1912. Reprint, Montclair, N.J.: Patterson Smith, 1968.

Loraine, Winifred. *Robert Loraine: Soldier, Actor, Airman*. London: Collins, 1938.

Ludovici, Anthony M. *Personal Reminiscences of Auguste Rodin*. London: John Murray, 1926.

MacCarthy, Desmond. *The Court Theatre 1904–1907: A Commentary and Criticism*. London: A. H. Bullen, 1907.

McCarthy, Lillah. "How Bernard Shaw Produces Plays: As Told by Lillah McCarthy." *New York American*, 18 September 1927, rpt. in *SHAW: The Annual of Bernard Shaw Studies*, vol. 3: *Shaw's Plays in Performance*. Ed. Daniel Leary, 163–168. University Park: University of Pennsylvania Press, 1983.

————. *Myself and My Friends*. New York: E. P. Dutton, 1933.

McNulty, Edward. "Memoirs of G. B. S." Edited and annotated by Dan H. Laurence. In *SHAW: The Annual of Bernard Shaw Studies*, vol. 12. Ed. Fred D. Crawford, 1–46. University Park: Pennsylvania State University Press, 1992.

Manning, Peter K., and Horacio Fabrega, Jr. "The Experience of Self and Body: Health and Illness in the Chiapas Highlands." In *Phenomenological Sociology: Issues and Applications*. Ed. George Psathas, 251–301. New York: John Wiley, 1973.

Marcus, Steven. *The Other Victorians: A Study of Sexuality and Pornography in Mid-Nineteenth-Century England*. New York: Meridian, 1977.

May, Rollo, Ernest Angel, and Henri F. Ellenberger, editors. *Existence: A New Dimension in Psychiatry and Psychology*. New York: Touchstone, 1958.

Meisel, Martin. *Shaw and the Nineteenth-Century Theater*. Princeton: Princeton University Press, 1963.

Merleau-Ponty, Maurice. *Sense and Non-Sense*. Trans. Hubert L. Dreyfus and Patricia Allen Dreyfus. Evanston: Northwestern University Press, 1964.

Moore, Doris Langley. *E. Nesbit*. Philadelphia: Chilton, 1966.

Morgan, Margery M. *A Drama of Political Man: A Study in the Plays of Harley Granville Barker*. London: Sidgwick and Jackson, 1961.

————. *The Shavian Playground: An Exploration of the Art of George Bernard Shaw*. London: Methuen, 1972.

Morris, May. *William Morris: Artist, Writer, Socialist. Volume the Second: Morris as a Socialist.* 1936. Reprint, New York: Russell and Russell, 1966.

Nethercot, Arthur H. *The First Five Lives of Annie Besant.* Chicago: University of Chicago Press, 1960.

Newton, Stella Mary. *Health, Art and Reason: Dress Reformers of the Nineteenth Century.* London: J. Murray, 1974.

Nichols, Beverley. *All I Could Never Be: Some Recollections.* New York: E. P. Dutton, 1952.

Nordau, Max. *Degeneration.* Translated from 2nd ed. New York: D. Appleton, 1895.

O'Donovan, John. *Shaw and the Charlatan Genius.* Dublin: Dolmen, 1965.

Ohmann, Richard M. *Shaw: The Style and the Man.* Middletown, Conn.: Wesleyan University Press, 1962.

Pascal, Valerie. *The Disciple and His Devil.* London: Michael Joseph, 1971.

Patch, Blanche. *Thirty Years with G. B. S.* New York: Dodd, Mead, 1951.

Pearson, Hesketh. *George Bernard Shaw: His Life and Personality.* New York: Atheneum, 1963.

———. *Hesketh Pearson by Himself.* New York: Harper and Row, 1965.

———. *Oscar Wilde: His Life and Wit.* New York: Harper and Brothers, 1946.

Pearson, Karl. "On the Inheritance of the Mental and Moral Characters in Man, and its Comparison with the Inheritance of the Physical Characters." *The Journal of the Anthropological Institute of Great Britain and Ireland,* vol. 33, 179–237. London: Anthropological Institute of Great Britain and Ireland, 1903.

Pease, Edward R. *The History of the Fabian Society.* New York: International Publishers, 1926.

Peschel, Enid Rhodes, and Richard E. Peschel. "Medical Insights into the Castrati in Opera." *American Scientist* 75 (November–December 1987): 578–583.

Peters, Margot. *Bernard Shaw and the Actresses.* Garden City, N.Y.: Doubleday, 1980.

Peters, Sally. "Ann and Superman: Type and Archetype." In *Fabian Feminist: Bernard Shaw and Woman.* Ed. Rodelle Weintraub, 46–65. University Park: Pennsylvania State University Press, 1977. Reprinted in *Modern Critical Interpretations: George Bernard Shaw* and *Modern Critical Views: George Bernard Shaw.* Ed. Harold Bloom, 105–123, 215–233. Hamden: Chelsea House, 1987.

———. "The Elegant Passion." *Journal of Popular Culture* 25, no. 4 (Spring 1992): 163–171.

———. "From Eroticism to Transcendence: Ballroom Dance and the Female Body." *Michigan Quarterly Review,* Winter 1991, 24–37. Reprinted in *The Female Body: Figures, Styles, Speculations.* Ed. Laurence Goldstein, 145–158. Ann Arbor: University of Michigan Press, 1991. Also reprinted in *Feminist Cultural Studies.* Vol. 2. Ed. Terry Lovell, 314–326. Cambridge: Edward Elgar, 1995.

———. "*Heartbreak House:* Shaw's Ship of Fools." *Modern Drama* 21, no. 3 (1978): 267–286.

———. "Shaw's Double Dethroned: *The Dark Lady of the Sonnets, Cymbeline Refinished,* and *Shakes Versus Shav.*" In *Shaw: The Neglected Plays,* vol. 7: *SHAW: The Annual of Bernard Shaw Studies.* Ed. Alfred Turco, Jr., 301–316. University Park: Pennsylvania State University Press, 1977.

Purdom, C. B. *Harley Granville Barker: Man of the Theatre, Dramatist and Scholar.* Cambridge: Harvard University Press, 1956.

Quinn, Martin. "William Archer and *The Doctor's Dilemma.*" *SHAW: The Annual of Bernard*

Shaw Studies, vol. 4. Ed. Stanley Weintraub, 87–106. University Park: Pennsylvania State University Press, 1984.

Rank, Otto. *The Don Juan Legend*. Trans. and ed. David G. Winter. Princeton: Princeton University Press, 1975.

Rattray, R. F. *Bernard Shaw: A Chronicle*. London: Leagrave Press, 1951.

Rilke, Rainer Maria. *Letters of Rainer Maria Rilke: 1892–1910*. Trans. Jane Bannard Greene and M. D. Herter Norton. New York: W. W. Norton, 1945.

Rosset, B. C. *Shaw of Dublin: The Formative Years*. University Park: Pennsylvania State University, 1964.

Russell, Bertrand. "George Bernard Shaw," *The Virginia Quarterly Review* 27, no. 1 (Winter 1951): 1–7.

Salmon, Eric. *Granville Barker: A Secret Life*. London: Heinemann, 1983.

Salt, Henry. *Company I Have Kept*. London: Allen and Unwin, 1930.

Sartre, Jean-Paul. *Being and Nothingness*. Trans. Hazel Barnes. New York: Philosophical Library, 1956.

Schreiner, Olive. *The Letters of Olive Schreiner, 1876–1920*. Ed. S. C. Cronwright-Schreiner. London: T. Fisher Unwin, 1924. Reprint, Westport, Conn.: Hyperion, 1976.

Sedgwick, Eve Kosofsky. *Between Men: English Literature and Male Homosexual Desire*. New York: Columbia University Press, 1985.

Shaw, Charles MacMahon. *Bernard's Brethren*. New York: Henry Holt, [1939].

Silver, Arnold. *Bernard Shaw: The Darker Side*. Stanford: Stanford University Press, 1982.

Smith, Timothy d'Arch. *Love in Earnest*. London: Routledge and Kegan Paul, 1970.

Spengler, Oswald. *The Decline of the West*. 2 vols. Trans. Charles Francis Atkinson. New York: Knopf, 1926–28.

Taylor, Anne. *Annie Besant: A Biography*. New York: Oxford University Press, 1992.

Terry, Ellen. *The Story of My Life*. New York: Doubleday, Page, 1909.

Turco, Alfred, Jr. *Shaw's Moral Vision: The Self and Salvation*. Ithaca: Cornell University Press, 1976.

Turco, Alfred, Jr., editor. *Shaw: The Neglected Plays*. Vol. 7: *SHAW: The Annual of Bernard Shaw Studies*. University Park: Pennsylvania State University Press, 1977.

Ulrichs, Karl Heinrich. *The Riddle of "Man-Manly" Love: The Pioneering Work on Male Homosexuality* (1864–1879). 2 vols. Trans. Michael A. Lombardi-Nash. Foreword by Vern L. Bullough. Buffalo, N.Y.: Prometheus Books, 1994.

Van Den Berg. J. H. "The Human Body and the Significance of Human Movement." In *Psychoanalysis and Existential Philosophy*. Ed. Henrik M. Ruitenbeek, 90–129. New York: E. P. Dutton, 1962.

Watson, Barbara Bellow. *A Shavian Guide to the Intelligent Woman*. New York: W. W. Norton, 1972.

Webb, Beatrice. *The Diary of Beatrice Webb*. 4 vols. Ed.Norman MacKenzie and Jeanne MacKenzie. Cambridge: Harvard University Press, 1982–85.

Weeks, Jeffrey. *Coming Out: Homosexual Politics in Britain, from the Nineteenth Century to the Present*. London: Quartet Books, 1977.

———. *Sex, Politics, and Society: The Regulation of Sexuality Since 1800*. New York: Longman, 1981.

————. *Sexuality and Its Discontents: Meanings, Myths, and Modern Sexualities.* London: Routledge and Kegan Paul, 1985.

Weintraub, Rodelle, editor. *Fabian Feminist: Bernard Shaw and Woman.* University Park: Pennsylvania State University Press, 1977.

Weintraub, Stanley. "'The Hibernian School': Oscar Wilde and Bernard Shaw." In *SHAW: The Annual of Bernard Shaw Studies,* vol. 13: *Shaw and Other Playwrights.* Ed. John D. Bertolini. University Park: Pennsylvania State University Press, 1993.

————. *Private Shaw and Public Shaw: A Dual Portrait of Lawrence of Arabia and G. B. S.* New York: George Braziller, 1963.

Weintraub, Stanley, editor. *Shaw: An Autobiography: 1856–1898, 1898–1950.* 2 vols. New York: Weybright and Talley, 1969, 1970.

Whitaker, Thomas R. "Granville Barker's Answer to *Heartbreak.*" In *SHAW: The Annual of Bernard Shaw Studies,* vol. 10. Ed. Stanley Weintraub and Fred D. Crawford, 85–95. University Park: Pennsylvania State University Press, 1990.

Whitebrook, Peter. *William Archer: A Biography.* London: Methuen, 1993.

Wilde, Oscar. *The Letters of Oscar Wilde.* Ed. Rupert Hart-Davis. New York: Harcourt, Brace, and World, 1962.

Winsten, Stephen. *Jesting Apostle: The Private Life of Bernard Shaw.* New York: E. P. Dutton, 1957.

————. *Salt and His Circle.* London: Hutchinson, 1951.

————. *Shaw's Corner.* London: Hutchinson, 1952.

Wisenthal, J. L. *The Marriage of Contraries: Bernard Shaw's Middle Plays.* Cambridge: Harvard University, 1974.

Wolfe, Willard. *From Radicalism to Socialism: Men and Ideas in the Formation of Fabian Socialist Doctrines, 1881–1889.* New Haven: Yale University Press, 1975.

Yeats, W. B. *Autobiographies.* London: Macmillan, 1955.

————. *Essays and Introductions.* New York: Macmillan, 1961.

Index

Index includes critical commentary in the notes.